AGITATION WITH A SMILE

AGITATION WITH A SMILE

HOWARD ZINN'S LEGACIES AND THE FUTURE OF ACTIVISM

Edited by
Stephen Bird, Adam Silver, and
Joshua C. Yesnowitz

Paradigm Publishers
Boulder • London

Permission granted by Hal Leonard and the Woody Guthrie Archive for the use of "Ludlow Massacre," lyrics by Woody Guthrie.

Published in the United States by Paradigm Publishers, 5589 Arapahoe Avenue, Boulder, CO 80303 USA.

Paradigm Publishers is the trade name of Birkenkamp & Company, LLC,
Dean Birkenkamp, President and Publisher.

Library of Congress Cataloging-in-Publication Data

Agitation with a smile : Howard Zinn's legacies and the future of activism / Stephen Bird, Adam Silver, and Joshua C. Yesnowitz, editors.
    pages cm
  Includes bibliographical references and index.
  ISBN 978-1-61205-1826 (pbk. : alk. paper)
  1. Zinn, Howard, 1922–2010—Political and social views. 2. Zinn, Howard, 1922–2010—Criticism and interpretation. 3. Social movements. I. Bird, Stephen, 1965–
  E175.5.Z56A45 2013
  303.48'4—dc23

                                                                                    2012046511

Printed and bound in the United States of America on acid-free paper that meets the standards of the American National Standard for Permanence of Paper for Printed Library Materials.

Designed and Typeset by Straight Creek Bookmakers.

17 16 15 14 13   1 2 3 4 5

Contents

Foreword

Frances Fox Piven

Howard Zinn and I became lifelong friends when I took a job in political science at Boston University in 1973. My office on the third floor of 232 Bay State Road was adjacent to his, and across the hall was our mutual pal, the flamboyant and outrageous Murray Levin. None of the other faculty were consigned to the third floor, so that corner of the building belonged to us and to our students. We talked and laughed a lot and it was altogether a wonderful arrangement. I left BU, regretfully, ten years later. But I always stayed in close touch with Howard and his wife Roz. For much of my life, Howard has been not only a friend, but part of my very consciousness. Whatever I was thinking or doing, I wanted to run by Howard. I didn't always agree with him. Sometimes I thought he was an impossible romantic, what with his infatuation with Emma Goldman, his poetry, and such. But I always wanted to hear what he thought.

Lots happened during those years at BU. There were continuing demonstrations against the Vietnam War and against ROTC on campus, helping to trigger an unending local war with the president of the university. John Silber had been dean of the College of Arts and Sciences at the University of Texas. He was at first welcomed as president of BU because he had been fired at Texas after defending faculty rights. His tenure at BU was entirely different. He seemed to think being president gave him unilateral authority over everything—even, rumor had it, the contents of our waste baskets. Defiance by those he considered his inferiors and subordinates especially infuriated him, but defiance there certainly was, and Howard became the special target of Silber's rage. In retrospect, the Silber wars seem to me utterly crazy, driven by the arrogance of a possibly deranged personality. And in the end, Silber receded into insignificance, while Howard became a luminous figure in politics and the academy. But that took a long time.

Even so, turmoil and threats notwithstanding, those years were happy for me and, I think, for Howard. Indeed, I think Howard's life was always joyous, and that had a lot to do with his almost total immersion in his kind of politics, the politics of resistance and direct action. I know many other veterans of movement politics, but I don't know anyone who so fully imbibed the pleasures of political engagement as Howard did. I think the wonderful smile for which he is famous, the kindness and generosity, and the wry good humor are all owed to the fact that Howard had made such a good life for himself and he knew it. He knew the warmth and pleasure of working with good comrades. He knew the exhilaration of being part of an effort much larger than himself, and larger also than the usual tedium of academic efforts and rewards that preoccupy us. I think that is why Howard never posed as a hero or martyr, and never complained—never whined about the unfairness of John Silber (who froze his salary and tried to stem enrollment in his classes by assigning him smaller rooms), for example. He knew he had a good life, and he showed that in his every gesture.

Enough reminiscing. I want to say something about the main preoccupations of the essays in this book, which try to place Howard's work in a broader intellectual context. An obvious approach is to ask about Howard's political philosophy. And as these essays show, the answer is not easy—partly, I think, because Howard never completely satisfied himself about the big questions of political philosophy. And yet he was, I believe, satisfied to live and work with tentative and incomplete answers, satisfied to continue to try to figure out our political possibilities. Still, some features of his political beliefs are clear.

First, Howard's thinking about politics was grounded in moral precepts. I mean by this simply that it was the moral questions about social and political life that preoccupied him, and it was the moral tenets on which he came to rely that animated his activism and his arguments.

The central moral precept that animated his activism and writing was his commitment to social justice. For Howard, the main measure of social justice was the treatment accorded to people who were at the bottom of social hierarchies, who were degraded, denied rights, and marginalized because they were poor, because of their gender or race or ethnicity or nationality or sexual orientation, or because they had fallen into the clutches of the law-enforcement authorities.

The injustices perpetrated by the powerful called for popular resistance, and that was another of Howard's core beliefs. Resistance did not mean petitions or voting or assemblies, although it might in the course of events come to include those things. Mainly resistance meant direct action, political activism outside the channels of electoral-representative institutions, and activism that included a willingness not only to break with conventional forms of political participation, but an activism so fueled by indignation that people were ready to break some of the myriad laws that usually ensure quiescence and hopelessness, and that also shield the authorities from the anger of the people. Howard believed in direct action, in protest movements. Indeed he saw such uprisings as the main instrument of such influence as ordinary people have ever achieved or will achieve in the United States.

As readers will see in the essays that follow, still another of his firmest and unyielding moral principles was his categorical opposition to war. This was not exactly a commitment to nonviolence, although he certainly preferred nonviolent strategies, partly for practical reasons. But never dogmatic, he also saw that there were historical situations in which limited violence might be necessary and justified.

I think many if not most intellectuals would be dissatisfied with these relatively simple precepts. There is little here or elsewhere in Howard's work to delineate the institutional arrangements he or we might prefer, or precisely how we are going to achieve those arrangements. There is no blueprint for how the economy, whether capitalist or socialist or social democratic or something else, should be organized. Nor are there instructions for how government should be reformed, whether expanded or rolled back or entirely recast. And what about our deeply flawed electoral-representative arrangements? Formulas abound for improving access to the franchise or making representation more democratic, for limiting the role of money in elections, and so on.

Howard was always gently supportive of the many people who wanted to push such discussions of reform or transformation or how to get there. But he himself was deeply skeptical, both of the often-impressive academic theories that delineated the big changes and explained why they were necessary if not inevitable, and of the rather more modest strategy manuals proffered by the advocates of one or another solution.

I think he was gentle but skeptical because he was very wise. He knew about the complexities and uncertainties that bedeviled efforts at social transformation, and he knew how many had failed before us. He understood the limits of his own understanding, and knew that he couldn't be sure of the big solutions, or how to achieve them. This was not because he was really so humble, although his humble stance was surely one of his charms. Or rather if he was humble, it was not about himself but about all of us and the quandaries with which we struggle.

Howard's solution to the dilemma created by uncertainty about social transformation coupled with his moral conviction about the need for transformation was a commitment to a life of step-by-step struggle. You can see this in what Edward P. Morgan in Chapter 11 of this volume calls his "Deweyian sense of democracy as a way of life." Or it is similar to what Marina Sitrin (2011: 8) writes about when she describes "horizontalism" in Argentina's movements, a way of life that is a critique of authority and hierarchy, a way of life that is "a manifestation of an alternative way of being and relating."

So, does this make Howard an anarchist, as several of the essays in this volume argue? I would say that Howard was a radical democrat in the sense that he believed in the capacity of ordinary people to shape their own collective life, and their right to do so. By contrast, he was skeptical of arrangements for representation that delegated democratic rights to professional politicians. This was also the stance, I should note, of the radical democrats of the revolutionary era. But maybe he was also an anarchist, if we take anarchism to mean a life commitment to a struggle for democracy in which the process through which the struggle is conducted—how people relate to each other in the movement—is as important as the goals of the movement.

To me, this sounds a lot like the Occupy Wall Street movement, and I know absolutely that Howard would have been a champion of Occupy. But his enthusiasm wouldn't be because so many of the activists profess to be anarchists. Howard would have cheered Occupy because it proclaimed itself a resistance movement of the 99% against the 1%; because it announced its resistance with theatrical occupations; because it welcomed the down and out to its encampments; because Occupy's boldness and clarity and inclusiveness have stirred other groups to protest; because the Occupiers rebuffed those who scorned them for not having demands when everything they said and did actually made their demands clear; because they eschewed conventional electoral-representative politics; and because they were devoted to creating a movement that exemplified in itself their democratic beliefs.

If that is anarchism, Howard was an anarchist. But most importantly, Howard exemplified in his person the joys of an engaged and moral political life. The essays that follow will give you a sense of this wonderful man.

Preface and Acknowledgments

Agitation with a Smile is a project that began in the wake of Howard Zinn's passing in January 2010. Although the actual discussions for this volume occurred in that immediate aftermath, its genesis dates back many years. The three of us met and became friends while attending the doctoral program in political science at Boston University, where Zinn had taught from the mid-1960s through the late 1980s. In our initial discussions, we discovered a particular affinity for approaching the study of history, political ideals, and activism (not to mention musical tastes and racquetball). We soon realized that we individually chose to attend BU in part due to Zinn's association with the institution. Although he was rarely (physically) present during our tenure there, each of us has had the pleasure of his company on a few occasions in informal settings. The text that follows is a testament to his devotion to critical thinking, and to his political and social ideals.

Discussions of Zinn and his work in popular culture are too often superficial or reductionist; therefore, we took great pains to ensure that this volume is neither fawning nor unduly critical. Our intent is to present a counternarrative that assesses and analyzes his ideas and theories in a substantive manner. The concern is with history, not hagiography; analysis for the future, not animus. This is the first academic volume to offer a serious assessment of Zinn's ideas and theories.

We are fully aware that he might not have approved of such a project, especially when economic inequality in the United States and around the world is growing at alarming rates, civil-rights violations are rampant, the Arab Spring is still unfolding, and the United States is still engaged in military action in Afghanistan and Iraq, as well as countless other countries. His famous phrase, "We publish while others perish," highlights the point that an academic's time would be better spent working to change the world rather than focusing on individual gain. However, in light of the current domestic and international political and social environments, we believe that a systematic reevaluation of his methods and theories is needed. Consistently enthusiastic responses to this project from contributors, colleagues, and friends have only reinforced our conviction. We hope this text provides a useful appraisal of Zinn's political thought, situates his efforts in a contemporary context, and looks toward the nature of activism and dissent in the future.

There is a variety of distinctive features and qualities to this volume. First, the text is focused specifically on what Zinn's approach, history, and thoughts mean *for the future*. This is certainly not to say that we ignore Zinn's history. Obviously a historical framework is critical to understanding the future of Zinn's vision for activism, academia, and a political approach to the arts. Nonetheless, this text focuses specifically on questioning how Zinn should be understood in the twenty-first century, by a new generation of scholars, progressives, activists, and the public in general.

Second, we have worked specifically to include a mixture of contributors who are established and well-known, along with young, early-career authors. By working to include more-senior authors, we have voices that come from and understand the context under which Zinn operated from the beginnings of his career. And by incorporating younger academics and voices, we acknowledge the challenges for activism and approaches to academia that will be encountered by the generation just beginning their careers. These writers face a future much changed by the challenges of globalization; the digitally networked world; and a new kind of warfare complicated by international battles of ideas, information, and violence mediated not just by countries, but also by religion, resources, and class.

Third, this manuscript is devoted to achieving a difficult balance between presenting writing and ideas at a high intellectual and academic level and speaking to non-academic readers interested in a thoughtful assessment of Zinn and his activities and ideas. This is not always an easy task. However, we argue that this was one of Zinn's emphases in his own writing and that he was able to successfully straddle both kinds of audience.

Fourth, the book is multidisciplinary and international in nature. Again, we have taken our inspiration from Zinn. He was a historian who worked in a political science department and didn't shy away from addressing issues in sociology, economics, public policy, critical studies, or the arts. Arguably a book like this about Zinn could be successfully implemented only in a multidisciplinary fashion. We believe this necessity is also a strength because it creates the beginning of a conversation among disciplines that is rare and more crucial now than ever before. We include several contributors from outside of North America. We have worked to provide a perspective that is both cosmopolitan in its origins and appealing to an audience within and beyond the Americas.

Finally, a criticism of multi-contributor books is that they are inconsistent, patchy, and erratic. We were conscious of this potential problem early on and this drove us to write the framework chapter (Chapter 1) prior to the call for chapter contributors. All contributors were able to read and consider the framework chapter as they developed their own chapters. We hope that it functions to create a consistent approach and mechanism to understand and reassess Zinn.

We wish to thank the Zinn family, especially Myla Kabat-Zinn, for their interest in the project; Anthony Arnove, who was instrumental in facilitating the development of this project; Irene Gendzier for her spirited and encouraging presence throughout the entire process; our friends and colleagues in the Department of Political Science at Boston University; William Miller, Abram Trosky, and Andy Vitek for their contributions to the project during the early stages; the anonymous peer reviewers who provided useful and insightful feedback; our chapter authors, who have made this such an enjoyable intellectual pursuit; and Dean Birkenkamp and the staff at Paradigm Publishers for their commitment to implementing our vision for the book.

The three of us are equal contributors to this project and are responsible for any errors or omissions. Additionally, we would like to offer a few individual acknowledgments:

Stephen Bird: To my colleagues in humanities and social sciences at Clarkson University; my parents, Ann and Roger Bird, for encouraging arts, academia, and activism (all three!); and Mary Cabral and Lucas Bird, without whose love and support I could not have completed my part in this.

Adam Silver: To my parents for encouraging inclusive and progressive political values and social consciousness, and for creating the environment and desire to think critically and ask questions, especially of those in authority; my dad for raising me on a steady diet of Woody Guthrie and Pete Seeger; my uncle Phil for bestowing a "Free Leonard Peltier" T-shirt on his eleven-year-old nephew, prompting a quest for information to answer the many queries raised by friends who wanted to know who that was and why was I wearing that T-shirt; my friend Aimee for introducing me to Howard Zinn by giving me her copy of *A People's History of the United States*; and all the teachers—inside and outside of academia—who have guided and continue to influence my life.

Joshua C. Yesnowitz: To my parents, Arlene and Gilbert Yesnowitz, for their unconditional love and support. My contributions to this book are dedicated to the memory of my grandfather, Murray Marks, who instilled in me a love of learning and helped me to master a reverse left-handed layup.

CHAPTER I

Agitation with a Smile

A Framework for Reassessing the Contributions of Howard Zinn

Stephen Bird, Adam Silver, and Joshua C. Yesnowitz

> In a world where children are still not safe from starvation or bombs, should
> not the historian thrust himself and his writing into history, on behalf of
> goals in which he deeply believes? Are we historians not humans first, and
> scholars because of that?
> —*Howard Zinn,* The Politics of History *(1990 [1970]: 1)*

Howard Zinn was an activist, scholar, and public intellectual. In the wake of his
passing in January 2010 at the age of eighty-seven, scholars and citizens have
begun to revisit his landmark works—writings that have inspired scholars and
schoolchildren, motivated dissident movements, and been embraced by popular
culture. This book evaluates Zinn's academic and civic contributions to American
political discourse (and beyond) and considers the applicability of his political
thought to contemporary struggles. What is the potential resonance of Zinn's message, moreover, when the messenger is no longer alive to deliver it? This question
presumes that the political philosophy of Howard Zinn is heavily predicated on
personality and presentation. We do not dispute this characterization—Zinn's
scholarly efforts were often overshadowed by his celebrity—but, as demonstrated
throughout this book, a close reading of Zinn's body of work provides scholars with

an opportunity to reassess his work, most appreciably in the fields of revisionist history and democratic theory, and take serious his pleas for a more politically engaged academia.

This chapter proceeds as follows: We begin by identifying the scope of this project. There are three (intentionally broad and overlapping) spheres that encapsulate Zinn's political, intellectual, and civic commitments: (1) participation in direct forms of action; (2) academia; and (3) arts and culture. Through an examination of these pursuits, we find five conceptual themes that encompass what we term *Zinnian* political thought. The political philosophy of Howard Zinn might be synthesized to include the following thematic elements: (1) direct democracy; (2) disobedience; (3) the danger of neutrality; (4) dual convictions; and (5) disposition.

Importantly, Zinn might well have had some criticism for a project such as this one. He would care infinitely more about the application of a framework and less so about its conceptualization. He believed that an academic's time would be best spent working to change the world. That said, a thoughtful analysis of Zinn is necessary. For too long, supporters and opponents of Zinn have invoked his ideas—correctly and incorrectly—to buttress their arguments without substantively assessing the merits of their claims. By "rescuing the man from the mythology,"[1] our hope is to present a more accurate assessment of Zinn's contributions, and also provide a more inspiring (and less daunting) account for those looking to replicate his accomplishments. To treat Zinn and other progressive icons as heroes is to make their achievements less imaginable.[2] As a result, this book is designed to be a substantive account and assessment of Zinn's beliefs, ideals, and approach to collective action and, to a larger extent, the democratic project.

We intend to provide a useful appraisal of Zinn's political thought for activists, scholars, pundits, and the general public. The ultimate value of this volume is not only to offer a framework for situating his efforts in a contemporary context, but also to look toward the nature of activism and dissent in the future. What are the most effective mechanisms by which to arouse public support for seemingly radical positions? How have current technological advancements altered one's perception of Zinnian activism? More generally, though, the conclusions drawn from this project may help guide the next generation of scholars of politics—those who came of age politically under aspects of Zinn's influence—in gauging the lasting relevance and legacy of this man's ideals, concepts, and approach to effecting change on behalf of the disenfranchised and under-represented members of society.

THREE SPHERES OF ATTENTION

Democracy, for Howard Zinn, could not be realized through conventional forms of political participation such as voting or the contacting of elected officials. These rights may be considered necessary features of a democracy, but are certainly not sufficient. Throughout Zinn's scholarship and personal politics, we encounter a healthy skepticism about achieving social change by working within the political system (i.e., electoral action) in favor of direct action against the system. Zinn was fond of reminding those who thought supporting candidates would bring progressive change that what matters most is not who is sitting in the White House, but who is sitting in and marching outside of the White House. Zinn's final publication, a brief note in *The Nation* on the first anniversary of Barack Obama's inauguration, reflects this sensibility.[3] Unlike many supporters of the president, Zinn displays a lack of surprise at the prevarications and compromises of that past year and cautions readers to expect more of the same from the administration unless a mass movement develops to exert pressure on those in power.

The American two-party political system, to Zinn, has always been inattentive to the needs of the mass public—those profiled in his *A People's History of the United States* (1980)—and therefore "cannot be respected" but instead it must be "protested, challenged, or, in the words of the Declaration of Independence ... be 'altered or abolished.'"[4] Zinn's own active participation in the civil-rights movement (where he advised students at Spelman College who worked to desegregate public facilities in Atlanta, and lost his job in the process) and his role in the anti–Vietnam War movement (where his advocacy included providing covert shelter to deserting soldiers and traveling to Hanoi to secure the release of prisoners of war) demonstrate this belief in action.

The sphere of academia is concerned with Zinn's critique(s) of mainstream political science and value neutrality as a desired goal, the responsibility of academics to participate in making a better world, and his contentious relationship with university leadership. In framing an agenda for conducting historically accurate yet socially aware scholarship in *The Politics of History* (1990 [1970]), Zinn explains how those tasked with conveying a nation's history to its mass public are significant political actors—even if they resist this vocational attribute. Zinn's worldview, which he terms *radical history,* offers a corrective to traditional accounts of American triumphalism and provides an alternative to the often dispassionate analyses emanating from the academy. A revisionist account of American history aims to complicate the historical record by demystifying the American experience. By "dusting off" and remembering "forgotten" events (and actors) in American history, Zinn hopes to learn lessons applicable to present social struggles and thereby broaden the possibilities of change.

The impact of historians' interpretations and evidence, Zinn asserts, is broadly encompassing: "Historical writing always has some effect on us. It may reinforce our passivity; it may activate us. In any case, the historian cannot choose to be neutral; he writes on a moving train."[5] The recent debate by attendees to the national conference of the American Historical Association (AHA) over whether the organization should be more vocal about US involvement in Iraq and Afghanistan embodies the struggle in academia of detachment versus engagement.[6] Zinn's stance during an eerily similar debate over Vietnam forty years earlier promotes an activist, engaged, non-neutral path for members of the academy.[7] If the AHA (then and now) refuses to stipulate a position on a policy that could benefit from their trained expertise, does the organization thereby yield the debate to government officials and less informed constituencies?

A fundamental consideration throughout Zinn's scholarship (and life experience) regards the proper role of the academic in a democracy. His dissertation was recognized by the AHA (honorable mention, 1958 Albert J. Beveridge Award) and he published in academic journals as well as more popular outlets at the beginning stages of his career.[8] While all of Zinn's work might be considered progressive in orientation, much of this earlier research was traditional in presentation. As his career proceeded, and more importantly his activism became more central to this scholarship, Zinn made specific, conscious, and conscientious choices about his academic trajectory that had significant and largely permanent consequences.[9] Disciplinary colleagues became less interested in Zinn (as an academic historian) as he increasingly focused his attention on reaching non-academic readers and on his concern toward progressive ideals.

Zinn's activities in the last two decades of his life, as the "people's historian," point us toward one particular direction for applying a Zinnian approach in a new century. The focus of Zinn's writing (and by extension, his audience) expanded and changed considerably as he shifted to writing and activities designed to educate and bring the plight of the downtrodden into the world's living rooms and class-rooms. We can see this in Zinn's pursuit of the *People's History* project (in print, radio, and televised media), the embrace of drama as a political vehicle, and the production of books designed to be read by a general audience, not merely by academics. This demonstrated an understanding and emphasis by Zinn on the importance of influence and change through popular arts and culture and repre-sented a shift away from "messaging by action" (e.g., protest in the streets, actions and demonstrations, and vigorous confrontational measures).[10]

Another focus that emerges is the approach that Zinn uses to apply the lessons of history directly to current events. For instance, reading *Vietnam: The Logic of Withdrawal* during the present "global war on terror," one sees uncanny parallels between then and now. Zinn would likely remark that these equivalen-cies are not coincidental but rather illustrative of the continuity of bipartisan US foreign policy. Critics of the occupations in Iraq and Afghanistan, much like Zinn during the Vietnam era, have noted several concerns: the economic dependence of American coalition allies,[11] the simplification of the "enemy" into an "us versus them" dichotomy,[12] the willingness of media to further a "march of freedom" myth, and the dangerous precedence of a preemptive war strategy.[13] They also note the recognition by liberals (who initially supported the war) that it was a mistake to intervene but who remain reluctant regarding withdrawal because of its possible impact on American prestige abroad.[14] (Zinn's extended essay on Vietnam inspired his longtime collaborator Anthony Arnove to write *Iraq: The Logic of Withdrawal* in 2006.)

A Power Governments Cannot Suppress (Zinn 2007a), a collection of previously published essays from sources like *The Progressive* and *The Nation*, offers Zinn's historically informed perspective on current events. In contrast to *Vietnam: The Logic of Withdrawal*, whose initial readership was activist in orientation, or *The Politics of History*, which targeted academics, *A Power Governments Cannot Suppress* is written for a popular audience whose only previous encounter with Zinn's work was most likely *A People's History*, which was first published in 1980 and had sold almost two million copies at the time of Zinn's death.[15] Written in punchy prose, Zinn's writing merges the empirical and the normative in his admonitions against despair. He advises readers to think beyond present political setbacks and embrace a more historically minded view that both emphasizes past successes and provides potential lessons for future action.

Although the trajectory of Howard Zinn's life has been documented elsewhere, namely, by Davis Joyce (2003), Martin Duberman (2012), and by Zinn himself in his 1994 memoir, Figure 1.1 highlights major events and publications.[16] This biographical sketch, furthermore, provides a context through which to view Howard Zinn's contributions and intellectual development. Many of the timeline entries are discussed in detail throughout the book.

FIVE CONCEPTUAL THEMES OF ZINNIAN THOUGHT

The three spheres—action, academia, and arts and culture—manifest themselves to varying degrees in the five conceptual themes of direct democracy, disobedience, the danger of neutrality, dual convictions, and disposition. The first two themes might be considered as systemic assessments while the latter two themes might be referred to as personal affectations. The middle theme, the danger of neutrality, serves as a bridge between the macro concerns of direct democracy and disobedience and the micro nature of dual convictions and disposition. Table 1.1 lays out the components of our conception of Zinnian thought. The themes are explained in the sections that follow.

Direct Democracy

To begin an inquiry into Zinn's concerns about democratic participation, it makes sense to start with some reservations about representative government discussed by his (equally famous) colleague and friend. In *Manufacturing Consent* (Herman and Chomsky 1988), Noam Chomsky lays out a concern for the activism of the 1960s: "Large groups of people who are normally passive and apathetic began to try to enter the political arena to press their demands. . . . The naïve might call that democracy, but that's because they don't understand. The sophisticated understand that that's the *crisis* of democracy."[17] Chomsky's concern here is that democracy should normatively be functioning by other, less agitated forms of activity. For instance, one might expect a civic public to have an active, engaged, and knowledgeable sense of purpose in the political sphere, and to have that purpose extended to representatives of the polity. Further, such a concordant form of democracy is assumed to be superior to a "crisis" democracy that requires direct action, and is also assumed to be an achievable possibility of a republican state (if not the expectation for reaching that final end state). For Chomsky and others, the focus is on the health of a democratic system. If people idly sit by and do nothing, then we have a sick democracy; when citizens allow politicians to pursue wars and embrace torture as policy, it is a crisis. Direct action is energetic and vigorous; allowing these tragedies to persist without saying anything is passive and submissive.

Zinn understood popular action similarly, but with slightly different emphases.[18] People taking to the streets represent not so much a crisis of democracy,

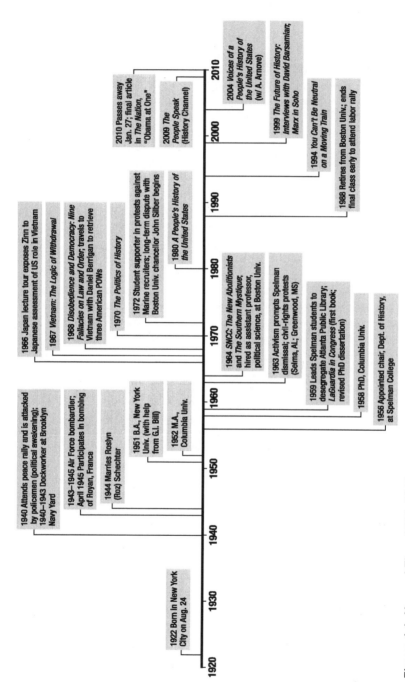

1922 Born in New York City on Aug. 24

1940 Attends peace rally and is attacked by policeman (political awakening); 1940–1943 Dockworker at Brooklyn Navy Yard

1943–1945 Air Force bombardier, April 1945 Participates in bombing of Royan, France

1944 Marries Roslyn (Roz) Schechter

1951 B.A., New York Univ. (with help from G.I. Bill)

1952 M.A., Columbia Univ.

1956 Appointed chair, Dept. of History, at Spelman College

1958 PhD, Columbia Univ.

1959 Leads Spelman students to desegregate Atlanta Public Library; *LaGuardia in Congress* (first book; revised PhD dissertation)

1963 Activism prompts Spelman dismissal; civil-rights protests (Selma, AL; Greenwood, MS)

1964 *SNCC: The New Abolitionists* and *The Southern Mystique;* hired as assistant professor, political science, at Boston Univ.

1966 Japan lecture tour exposes Zinn to Japanese assessment of US role in Vietnam

1967 *Vietnam: The Logic of Withdrawal*

1968 *Disobedience and Democracy: Nine Fallacies on Law and Order;* travels to Vietnam with Daniel Berrigan to retrieve three American POWs

1970 *The Politics of History*

1972 Student supporter in protests against Marine recruiters; long-term dispute with Boston Univ. chancellor John Silber begins

1980 *A People's History of the United States*

1988 Retires from Boston Univ.; ends final class early to attend labor rally

1994 *You Can't Be Neutral on a Moving Train*

1999 *The Future of History: Interviews with David Barsamian; Marx in Soho*

2004 *Voices of a People's History of the United States* (w/ A. Arnove)

2009 *The People Speak* (History Channel)

2010 Passes away Jan. 27; final article in *The Nation*, "Obama at One"

Figure 1.1: Howard Zinn, 1922–2010

6

Table 1.1: Summary of a Thematic Framework for Zinnian Analysis

Conceptual Theme	Definition
Direct Democracy	Popular participation and mass action. Activism is essential to improving democracy. People are the ultimate power.
Disobedience	Deliberate violation of the law for a social purpose. This action is organized and focused.
Danger of Neutrality	Impartiality can breed apathy; apathy then perpetuates the status quo. It is the responsibility of the academic and citizen to avoid neutrality, to question and challenge authority.
Dual Convictions	Antagonisms or tensions between poles: individualism and communalism; majority and minority; and skepticism of authority versus the proper exercise of state authority.
Disposition	Humor, optimism, the ability to reach people at their level, often via mass media, to make ideas broadly accessible. Decency of spirit.

but more precisely an inherent crisis, or failing, of the democratic system. Mass action in the streets was constructive, necessary, and much more benevolent to the forward movement of both progressivism and democracy. For Zinn, popular action is *always* needed as an important component of even the healthiest of democracies. Further, Zinn was suspicious to some degree of the idea that a healthy democratic end state was possible. This perspective didn't change his ongoing optimism, but rather demonstrated his concern that democratic and republican ideals will always be under attack by the rich, the powerful, and/or the sociocultural majorities.

Zinn lived his activist ideals as much as he preached them. A review of Zinn's recently released FBI files reveals constant and tireless engagement in direct action, letter-writing campaigns, and public speaking to various academic and activist organizations.[19] Throughout these activities, Zinn often maintained a wry humor when challenging authority, as depicted by the title of this book. In January 1964, for example, Zinn attended a meeting of potential participants in voting-rights efforts in Hattiesburg, Mississippi. FBI records sternly note that Zinn advocated for the "citizen's arrest" of FBI agents who failed to take action to protect demonstrators who were being physically assaulted by local police or mobs.[20] Zinn often worked to subvert state power by emphasizing and pointing out the protections that authorities ought to be providing should they be performing their role as effective guardians of civil liberties.

Zinn understood activism as an activity critical to the success of progress and change in a modern democracy. *The Politics of History* (Zinn 1990 [1970]) stipulates this view of activism. The text produces examples from his own work to demonstrate—in terms of topics chosen, questions asked, and narrative structure employed—what this historical perspective looks like in practice. The chapters on class draw upon a wide range of topics and periods in American history—e.g., inequality during the colonial and Vietnam eras (Ch. 4), the Ludlow Massacre of

1914 (Ch. 5), the legislative career of Congressman Fiorello La Guardia (Ch. 6), and the limits of the New Deal when considered in comparative context (Ch. 7)— yet each asks related questions about perspectives, possibilities, and values. The final five chapters of part two relate to nationalism, violence, and "the forgetting of discomfiting facts."[21] For Zinn, US foreign policy (in Vietnam) is not aberrant behavior—an aggressive foreign policy of an otherwise peaceful state—but rather indicative of what was feasible abroad but not similarly available in the domestic sphere (at this particular time in American history) due to (perceived) popular resistance.[22] Throughout this text, and others, Zinn demonstrates that democracy is always under pressure, and is always imperfect; it requires direct action.

This worldview is about the power and importance of activism. Zinn inherently believes that activism is an ongoing concern for scholars and citizens alike. The people should be engaged consistently in checking government action and preserving their rights and liberties, and should not wait to act until the situation reaches a crisis, as Chomsky terms it. Activism, agitation, and direct participation should be the norm; they are signs of a healthy democratic process, and democracy will always be in crisis.

A second question for Zinn's conception of the effectiveness of direct democracy involves the nature of such communication and/or action. Different forms of activism have different kinds of advantages, and potential dangers or vulnerabilities to manipulation or control. Is it grassroots-based, an accelerated form of online digital action, and/or mainstream media? To some degree, this question is related to other tensions intrinsic to Zinn's thinking (see the "Dual Convictions" section later in this chapter). On one hand, Zinn had a deep history with, and strong sympathies toward, organic "street" activism. On the other hand, his final two decades were focused more often on the dissemination of his ideas by spreading his concerns via a variety of popular media and press. Whether this represents a shift in Zinn's thinking or simply a redirecting of his focus is not clear.[23] We return to these questions in the final chapter of the text.

Disobedience

Building on his belief in the necessity of popular action, Zinn argues that the people must also be eternally vigilant. Direct action is essential to challenging authority. The people must be *dis*obedient—challenge the state and the law—to realize their interests and improve their democracy.[24]

Zinn articulates the need for disobedience in *Disobedience and Democracy: Nine Fallacies on Law and Order* (1968), a treatise written in response to Supreme Court Justice Abe Fortas's *Concerning Dissent and Civil Disobedience* (1968). Fortas echoes the oft-repeated claim that the United States is a society of laws, not men. The law, then, is more objective and less susceptible to the whims of any one individual. He insists upon the importance of the rule of law above all else.

In fact, it is precisely because men and women make the laws and are elected to serve that Zinn contends that laws are fallible. Some of these representatives are corruptible and not worthy of their position or the trust of the governed. Should we not, then, question and challenge the laws they write? Reverence for the law is dangerous because it gives "a blank check to government" and "could lead to a general contempt for all laws."[25] The most serious threat to a democracy is when the people stop questioning the laws (and challenging their leaders), and simply conform to majority rule.

Zinn inserts a moral imperative to our understanding of the law by drawing a distinction between just and unjust laws. Obeying the law may bring order and stability, but may not bring justice. Such an understanding poses the question, "Are we not more obligated to achieve justice than to obey the law?"[26] Challenging an unjust law is necessary to furthering democracy. This is an act of civil disobedience: "the deliberate, discriminate violation of a law for a vital social purpose."[27] Civil disobedience is a useful method of effecting positive social change because it provides an "organized outlet for rebellion," which "may prevent chaotic and uncontrolled reactions."[28]

Further, Zinn questions the requirement that those who violate an unjust law simply accept their punishment. Such a notion creates a passive and oppressed citizenry. Rather, "civil disobedience gives an *intensity* to expression by its dramatic violation of the law.... If we are to avoid majority tyranny over oppressed minorities, we must give a dissident minority a way of expressing the fullness of its grievance." Protest action beyond the law—that is, disobedience—Zinn argues, is essential to democracy.[29]

Zinn extends the necessity for civil disobedience by challenging Fortas's trust in American political institutions and procedures as a mechanism to remedy society's ills. This belief, according to Zinn, is a fallacy.[30] In modern American society, the rich and powerful manipulate and hide behind the law for their benefit. The law is used to reinforce inequality.[31] The system, in turn, inhibits the ability of the people to discern their adversary by obfuscating the lines of accountability. First, due to campaign-finance regulations, the wealthy have tremendous advantages in making sure laws remain favorable to their monetary interests. Second, the nature of the American political system with its checks and balances, along with multiple access and veto points, stalls momentum of change. The debate over universal health care is a prime example.[32]

The outcome of the argument is that not all disobedience to the law should be tolerated, but that absolute obedience to the law must not be either.[33] Ultimately, direct action through civil disobedience is necessary "to bring the demands of aggrieved people before the leaders of government, with minimum of turmoil and maximum of insistence."[34] Agitation in this form shakes up the status quo and must continue in perpetuity to keep leaders in check.[35]

The Danger of Neutrality

Zinn was deeply skeptical of those who would stand on the sidelines. The title of his 1994 memoir (and 2004 companion documentary), *You Can't Be Neutral on a Moving Train,* demonstrates his passionate dislike for those who could not, or would not, decide. Explicit throughout Zinn's work is the notion that values underlie all behavior; every action, including inaction, is a decision in itself and should not be overlooked (or respected). For Zinn, the danger of impartiality was similar to JFK's famous misquote of Dante: "The hottest places in hell are reserved for those who in great moral crisis preserve their neutrality."[36] Zinn saw explicit nonalignment (i.e., "preserved" neutrality) as almost worse than apathy, though both were worthy of criticism. There might be justification for apathy in some circumstances, but to work actively to preserve one's so-called impartiality, particularly operating from a position of power or respect, was highly problematic.

That is, in part, why Zinn's concern for noninvolvement was perhaps greatest among other members of academia. He believed that educators have a responsibility to motivate and encourage students to contribute to a cause greater than themselves. As Zinn describes, "knowledge is a form of power" and intellectuals should behave accordingly. Under the guise of scholarly detachment, social scientists, Zinn asserts, have all too often chosen the side of the status quo:

> Ironically, scholars have often served narrow governmental, military, or business interests, and yet withheld support from larger, transcendental values [like eliminating war, poverty, race and national hatred, and governmental restrictions on individual freedom], on the ground that they needed to maintain neutrality.[37]

Zinn's role in desegregating the public library system in Atlanta, participating in Freedom Rides, and leading protests against the war in Vietnam (while teaching at Boston University) clearly depicts the lead-by-example method. In *SNCC* (2002 [1964]), Zinn promotes the valuable education college-age activists were receiving by participating in history. Zinn contrasts this participatory approach with traditionalist Allan Bloom, who often boasted that his students remained in class at Cornell University during the tumult.[38]

Zinn's commitment to action does not preclude, as many of his critics have alleged (without substantiating textual evidence), a commitment to honest scholarship. Rather, Zinn would argue that exhortations of "objectivity" are themselves misleading:

> Surely, we want to be objective if that means telling the truth as we see it, not concealing information that may be embarrassing to our point of view. But we don't want to be objective if it means pretending that ideas don't play a part in the social struggles of our time, that we don't take sides in those struggles.[39]

The Politics of History is Howard Zinn's "methods and approaches" text—his attempt to confront these epistemological matters. In this ambitious three-part volume, Zinn outlines a research program for scholar-activists to embrace, proposes criteria for pursuing such "action-inducing" research, informs colleagues (and aspiring academics) of their professional responsibilities, and produces examples from his own work to demonstrate—in terms of topics chosen, questions asked, and narrative structure employed—what this historical perspective looks like in practice. *A People's History of the United States* (1980) represents the grand embodiment of Zinn's research agenda, and the attendant franchise (i.e., *A People's History* spinoff volumes and television series) can be seen as its culmination.

Dual Convictions

Zinn often struggled with tensions in his writings and speeches.[40] These tensions, or divergences, occur in several different arenas: between communitarian principles and iconoclastic individualism; between minority and majority concerns; between organized and spontaneous democratic action; between antagonism against the state and the needed protections of the state; and, as discussed previously, between grassroots activism and street actions and the "accelerant"[41] and broad dissemination properties of the media, arts, and popular press.

Zinn saw himself as "something of an anarchist, something of a socialist. Maybe a democratic socialist."[42] Indeed, there are components of Zinn's thinking that fit in with a variety of anarcho-communist, Left libertarian forms of thinking and that often demonstrate a variety of tensions that are not clearly resolved. Zinn describes himself in a 2008 interview as an anarchist (with no qualifications), and as someone who sees the state as a co-optive body.[43] Yet Zinn clearly was also willing to use the state as a tool for the protection of rights, and for the delivery of goods such as education or health care. In some ways, Zinn was a pragmatist whose ultimate concerns were always for the rights of the individual, however achieved. To be fair, it is not just Zinn's convictions that occasionally existed in tension with each other, but also the principles themselves that all political thinkers constantly have to mediate.[44]

The tension between majority and minority rights pervades Zinn's work. While he unabashedly supported the people (the majority), he recognized that a tyranny of a majority could be perpetrated to curb minority rights. Or, conversely, a tyranny of minority could utilize the tools of the state to disaggregate a majority whose rights and liberties were being breached by a few for their own gain. This understanding of the tension between the majority and minority led him to endorse an approach in the civil-rights movement that may seem antithetical to his belief system—positive state action. To protect voter-registration drives and other civil-rights activists in the South, Zinn recommended that the president should create a special task force of federal agents whose sole purpose would be "to defend the constitutional rights of any person against private or official action."[45] He further argued that "there is no *necessary* lessening of individual freedom with stronger central authority, so long as such authority is specifically combined to a limited field of action."[46] Similarly, Zinn embraced the presence of the National Guard to protect civil-rights workers, that is, to use state power to demonstrate against the state. Zinn notes, "I was not an absolutist on the use of the state if, under pressure, it becomes a force for good."[47]

In addition, Zinn endorsed a more proactive and aggressive use of the injunction power by the US Department of Justice. Injunctions "act to *deter* and *prevent* violations before they occur, because they are court orders, secured in advance, directing that local officials should not engage in certain activities."[48] A jury trial is not necessary, which prevents the problem of an all-white jury.

Ultimately, however, power for Zinn was almost always problematic, and his concern was almost always for an implicitly minoritarian stance. By this we mean a focus almost entirely on concerns for minority rights. In this arena, Zinn was almost always concerned with minority rights from an individual perspective, not necessarily from a group minority perspective. To some degree, Zinn's approach is similar to the philosophical concepts of "minority" and "becoming minor" developed by Deleuze and Guattari (1987). Becoming minoritarian, from this perspective, is an ethical approach developed as a manner of fascist avoidance. This approach has been conceptualized further by Connolly (2002) and Patton (2005) in their approach to modern democratic thought. Minoritarianism, while not specifically defined by Zinn as such, is the underlying idea that permeates much of his writing from *SNCC* to *A People's History*.

Similarly, Zinn's implicit sympathy with the minority finds much in common with Rousseau's concern for minoritarianism. Rousseau's various discussions of the "general will" certainly leave some ambiguities in terms of specifically how minority rights might be protected on a consistent basis. Rousseau, however, was clearly the first Enlightenment thinker to substantiate the general idea of basic human rights that should be applied on a consistent basis to all, arguing that "every authentic act of the general will obligates or favors all the citizens equally."[49] This was the essential concern of Zinn—the uniform application of consistent principles of rights to all.

Zinn's approach to activism also had a strong degree of pragmatism that reflected and responded to various tensions. In many ways, Zinn's form of activism and his pragmatic response to frictions seem to reflect the writings of John Dewey and his response to democracy. For Dewey, democracy was an evolving and deliberative activity that reflected the impossibility of eternal or consistent truths. Talisse (2005: 188) argues that Dewey's philosophical pragmatism is not "the dispassionate hunt for truths, but rather the intelligent resolution of emergent problematic situations."[50] Similarly, Zinn's approach focuses more on practice and action than on the niceties of formal ideological consistency. His concern was to pursue an outcome of justice, not to perfectly define the principles surrounding it.

Disposition

In his public life, Howard Zinn demonstrated how humor, optimism, and an even temperament can make radical ideas more accessible to a general audience. We are not claiming that for Zinn form trumps content, or suggesting that his demeanor was contrived, but rather that Zinn understood the importance of style and presentation, especially when conveying previously neglected (and often painful) moments in American history. Within his scholarly research, Zinn's positive and forward-thinking outlook also stands out. The topics he pursued and the ways in which he engaged historical material always had constructive aims; his scholarship, moreover, was solution-based. Zinn's disposition should not, therefore, simply be understood in a stylistic sense, but also as a discursive method of dissemination.

In his appreciation of Eugene V. Debs (and radicals more broadly), Zinn speaks to the importance of agitation with a smile when he argues, "We are always in need of radicals who are also lovable.... Debs was what every socialist or anarchist or radical should be: fierce in his convictions, kind and compassionate in his personal relations."[51] Hard truths about one's own country can be difficult to digest—the mass public has been conditioned to think (hope?) in a positive way about the nation—so Zinn recognized that previously unimaginable knowledge had to be communicated in a convivial manner.

We also find in Zinn, unlike in many of his peers on the Left, a hopeful spirit—or at least a lack of fatalism.[52] In *A Power Governments Cannot Suppress* (2007a), the cautiously optimistic (and often humorous) columns cover the familiar landscape of Zinn's interests in an accessible manner while the takeaway message remains—social change is always possible, but it is not inevitable. We must work for it, but if we organize we can create a power no government can suppress. Illustrative of the Zinnian approach is the 2005 commencement address that he delivered to the graduates of Spelman College, the historically black women's college in Atlanta, Georgia, from which he had been fired forty years earlier for his political activism. Combining history lesson and "pep talk," Zinn cautions "against discouragement" (the title of his speech) during this present era of war and tells a relatable historical narrative about how in the 1960s, African American students had fought a similarly insurmountable struggle in the South and emerged victorious. Here, Zinn creates a "usable past" to inspire an audience in a time of apparent helplessness. "Many people had said," Zinn reminds us, "the South will never change. But it did change. It changed because ordinary people organized and took risks and challenged the system and would not give up. That's when democracy came alive."[53]

Zinn's overall demeanor—his *agitation with a smile*—is present in his interactions with the state, in the university setting, and generally in his observations about pursuing progressive change. His disposition in the face of authority is highlighted several times in the FBI files. The reports note that his FBI interviews in 1953 were cordial, and that he "shook hands with the interviewers" but that he had not been reinterviewed because Zinn "was uncooperative in a previous interview and is in a position to embarrass the Bureau."[54]

His humorous approach showed in his willingness to make a point the hard way. Zinn was arrested in May 1970 as part of an anti-conscription demonstration outside an army base in South Boston. He was convicted but refused to pay the $20 fine and went to jail on December 2 to work off the fine at $3 per day. Nonetheless, he went to jail because he "didn't want to just be processed through like they wanted to do it. I didn't want to make it so easy for them to get rid of us. I wanted to put a little crimp in the judicial machinery."[55]

Agitation with a smile was also evident at the university level in Zinn's experiences with school administrators. This was particularly clear in his interactions with John Silber, the president of Boston University (BU) throughout the bulk of his tenure at the institution. The animosity began when Silber invited Marine recruiters to campus in the spring of 1972. In response to student demonstrations opposed to the military presence, Silber called in the police, who then escalated otherwise peaceful protests. Zinn missed the demonstrations due to illness, but penned an acerbic, sarcastic newspaper editorial, joking that "a philosopher turned university president [Silber] is best of all" to teach students about the rule of law:

If his arguments don't work on the students—who sometimes prefer to look at the world around them than to read Kant—then he can call in the police, and after that momentary interruption (the billy club serving as exclamation point to the rational argument) the discussion can continue, in a more subdued atmosphere.[56]

In response, Silber invoked the teachings of Martin Luther King Jr., which provoked Zinn to equate Silber's action with Birmingham sheriff "Bull" Connor (King's captor, and holder of the jail cell from which MLK wrote his famous letter).[57]

Throughout his life, we see Zinn constantly committed to activism and agitation, but more often than not with a broad sense of humanity, compassion, and humor, which served to provide relief from the dour gravitas of dissent against a powerful state. So often, agitation or protest is expected to be deadly serious, requiring a somber, humorless, and unsmiling approach because of the seriousness of the issues. Zinn simply wasn't willing to let solemn issues make any discussion of them similarly grim or unpleasant. As recently as 2009, he discussed the world financial crisis with comical allusions to the pope and the Red Sox:

> I remember that pope—I think it was Pope John XXIII, but one of the recent popes—I'm not up on my popes, as you can see. I'm more up on the lineup of the Boston Red Sox than I am on the popes. But it was one recent pope, and certainly not the current one, who talked about something has to be done about—and these are his words—"savage, unbridled capitalism," capitalism unregulated. . . . We need to regulate corporate behavior.[58]

Zinn's ability to incorporate laughter and wit, and maintain a lightness—even in discussions of "savage" human behavior—were his hallmarks. It contributed enormously to his ability to inspire and create hope.

APPLYING ZINNIAN POLITICAL THOUGHT IN THE TWENTY-FIRST CENTURY

What can we conceive of as Zinn's approach to progressive social change? It must preclude safely neutral scholarly work that promotes passivity, and must include radical history and "action-inducing" research.[59] In *SNCC* we see this approach directly.[60]

SNCC incorporates each of the themes represented in this study: direct democracy, disobedience, the danger of neutrality, dual convictions, and disposition. Zinn provides excellent detail of the organization and tactics of the Student Nonviolent Coordinating Committee (SNCC) as well as vivid accounts of direct-action campaigns. The civil-rights and voting-rights activists organized demonstrations in the streets to raise awareness to their cause—locally and nationally. In 1963, the civil-rights activists even attempted to run their own candidate for governor of Mississippi under the Freedom Democratic Party ballot.[61] To advance its cause,

SNCC operatives disobediently violated laws against segregation and pushed for the enforcement of others, such as registering individuals to vote. Their actions forced the government to abandon its neutral stance on repeated occasions, such as with the enforcement of the federal laws banning segregation on interstate travel and with President Kennedy's public outrage at Sherriff Connor's tactics in Alabama. The civil-rights protestors also exhibit the tension in the role of the state. Although Zinn is distrustful of state authority, he repeatedly requests state intervention on behalf of the activists. Finally, Zinn's disposition shines through in the most compelling and provocative aspects of the *SNCC* narrative, which depicts actual direct-action events and the violence perpetrated against unarmed youth by the state (i.e., the local authorities with the acquiescence of the national government). Detailing the events so plainly broadens their understanding and accessibility to those of us who did not directly participate in this movement.

The sacrifices that Zinn highlights in *SNCC* are at the core of a contemporary debate on activism and the proper place of these Zinnian ideals in movement politics. In a much-discussed *New Yorker* article, Malcolm Gladwell (2010) contrasts current forms of online-movement activism with direct action and civil-disobedience activism of the civil-rights movement. By arguing that the costs incurred with the sit-ins and voter-registration drives of the Deep South in the sixties are potentially much greater than those associated with the relative anonymity of fund drives and meet-up activities facilitated by social networks, Gladwell suggests that current-day activism is somewhat diluted.[62] Although online social networks increase a sense of political participation, he questions the real effects of what is often dismissively referred to as "clicktivism." "Facebook activism succeeds not by motivating people to make a real sacrifice," Gladwell speculates, "but by motivating them to do the things that people do when they are not motivated enough to make a real sacrifice." Rather, "activism that challenges the status quo—that attacks deeply rooted problems—is not for the faint of heart."

Gladwell's thesis engages the emerging debate over the importance and characterization of online networks (text messaging, social media, and the like) in pro-democracy movements, and in doing so questions the meaning of activism. (What is activism? By lessening the costs and motivations, does it lessen the meaning or strength of the message?) Events in North Africa and the Middle East during the Arab Spring (and Occupy Wall Street actions throughout the American Fall), however, challenge Gladwell's depiction of social networking as a stand-in for true activism; it facilitated actual protests and real sacrifice.[63] The image of a fruit seller self-immolating in Tunisia incited people to take to the streets in Egypt, Bahrain, and elsewhere throughout the region.[64] Protestors in Egypt used social networking technologies to organize mass demonstrations and publicize the events as they unfolded. This tactic proved so successful that the government of Egypt enacted a blackout of all Internet and cell-phone capability.[65] As images of Hosni Mubarak's henchmen attacking and opening fire on the peaceful demonstrators became public, observers could hardly say that the protestors incurred no costs.[66]

Although Gladwell raises appropriate questions about activism and Zinn's perspective on these issues is unclear to some degree, Zinn certainly had the prescience to move to the broad dissemination of his ideas in contemporary media in later years. They are important questions to address, however, as we relate Zinn's thematic criteria to contemporary and possibly future movements. This project fosters a more thorough understanding of Zinn and places him in a contemporary context.

OVERVIEW OF THE BOOK

Contributors to this volume have been tasked with engaging these themes—direct democracy, disobedience, danger of neutrality, dual convictions, and disposition— on topics ranging from foreign policy to civil liberties and human rights to current events and theoretical debates, all within the three overlapping spheres of action, academia, and arts and culture. As will be clear to the reader, some chapter topics lend themselves to more explicit application while others are inspired by, if not directly responding to, the framework conceptualized in this chapter.

The next three chapters comprise the "Zinn as Historian and Public Intellectual" section. In Chapter 2, "Legacies and Breakthroughs: The Long View on Zinnian History," Ambre Ivol and Paul Buhle trace the intellectual lineage of Zinn's scholarship and consider how the publication of and response to *A People's History* represented the popular culmination of a venerable tradition of self-consciously radical American historiography. Transitioning from intellectual predecessors to generational contemporaries, Ambre Ivol, in Chapter 3, "The US Left in Generational Perspective," situates Zinn's coming-of-age trajectory to examine the imprecision of group categorizations. In her remapping of intellectual generations, Ivol uses the example of Zinn to complicate the (largely accepted but somewhat arbitrary) New Left vs. Old Left binary, and by doing so provides us with a richer understanding of the World War II generation to which Zinn belongs. Paul Reynolds, in Chapter 4, examines how Zinn's historically informed yet present-oriented voice personifies a particular type of public figure—the radical public intellectual. Designating him an exemplar of this civic type, Reynolds locates Zinn within a community of critical voices drawn largely from previous historical eras and emphasizes the characteristics shared by all who have assumed this essential role.

In his ethnographic narrative of SNCC, Zinn (2002 [1964]: 7) describes the temperament of the organization as "radical, but not dogmatic; thoughtful, but not ideological." As demonstrated in the chapters that comprise the "Zinn in Theory" section of this book, this summary statement also applies to Zinn himself, the chronicler of the prominent student civil-rights group. Eric Boehme's empirically focused contribution on Zinn's "pragmatic anarchism" in Chapter 5 builds upon historical examples (from the United States) to present Zinn's argument for prefigurative politics—what Boehme calls "anarchism of everyday life"—as a compelling, more realizable form of anarchism in contrast to more revolutionary (doctrinally pure) forms of anarchism. The radical democracy endorsed by Howard Zinn, a political philosophy defined by a lack of sectarianism or absolute ideological commitments, is also the focus of Žiga Vodovnik's theory-centered Chapter 6. "The Forbidden Word: Howard Zinn as Anarchist" explores Zinn's "flexible epistemology" and suggests the consequences of Zinn's endorsement of anarchism as methodology, not ideology. Zinn's lack of rigidity, though, should not be misconstrued as an absence of serious consideration and sophistication. Christopher C. Robinson, in Chapter 7, "Politics against the Law," engages the complexity of Zinnian philosophy through an inquiry into his view of academic freedom. In his reflections on the university and the professoriate, Zinn offers, according to Robinson, an expansive understanding of citizenship that seeks to reconcile the individualist and the collective, the ethical and the political strands, of his political thought and action.

In Chapter 8, an examination of just and unjust uses of force, Patricia Moynagh addresses war as a condition to be cured. War, for both her and Zinn—a professor of hers at Boston University in the 1980s—could be ended through societal and individual choices. A close reading of Zinn's writings on the subject reveals a nuanced view of violence as possibly a just, yet unlikely to be considered a legitimate, course of action to address a grave injustice. Situating her analysis within cross-disciplinary work in history, political philosophy, and evolutionary psychology, Moynagh finds support for this argument by way of Zinn's distinction between just wars and just causes.

With their interplay between personal narrative and theoretical considerations, the contributions by Ross Caputi and Alix Olson in Chapters 9 and 10—which are grounded in their military and artistic experiences, respectively, and enhanced by their skillful integration of the relevant academic scholarship—represent a continuation of Zinnian efforts among a younger generation of scholar-activists. These chapters within the "Zinn in Practice" section embody the spirit of Zinn; moreover, Zinn the antiwar veteran and Zinn the archivist of optimism serves more as a personal than an academic inspiration for these essays. Weaving his own involvement as a Marine in the November 2004 siege of Fallujah with ruminations on the philosophical literature on the concept of collective responsibility, Caputi, motivated by the example of Zinn's misgivings about his own participation in World War II, examines the responsibility of the individual within collective actions and considers the implications of an antiwar movement that honors ethically questionable behavior and refuses to wrestle with the role of the combatant during wartime.

Reflecting on her years touring nationally as a spoken-word artist along with her present efforts studying political theory, Olson considers the role of the artist in a democratic society and argues for more collaborative interactions between radical academics and similarly minded artists. Zinn's cultural contributions (including his three theatrical plays) are examined to discover connections between academic and artistic spheres. Zinn's path of radical citizenship, particularly in its disruption of standard notions of artistic and academic roles, represents what Olson calls a "passport of possibility," an example for other academics to emulate.

In the final section, "Zinn Today and Tomorrow," Edward P. Morgan develops the idea of Zinn as "master teacher." His Chapter 11, on the transmission of democratic messages, identifies the qualities that made Zinn an effective communicator and considers the potential for "educative conversations" in current media environments. Calling for "two, three, many Zinns" who exemplify humor, hope, and an ability to "speak American" like Zinn, Morgan's chapter serves as a bridge in this final section of the text, which considers Howard Zinn's legacies and the future of activism, the subtitle of the book.

Using the Gilded Age as a basis for comparison, Irene Gendzier in Chapter 12 draws from *A People's History of the United States* and *Voices of a People's History of the United States* to highlight the continuity of elite dominance and the historical significance of labor mobilization. In her discussion of Zinn and "the 99%," Gendzier shows how Zinn approached American history through the lens of economic inequality decades before the age of Occupy. This application of contemporizing history is then extended to a description of the Arab Spring uprisings against authoritarian regimes (e.g., Tunisia and Egypt), which she asserts are also rooted in movements against income inequality.

Our final chapter revisits the major themes of the book and looks ahead to the degree to which one might consider Zinn's approach as a model of social activism, as well the degree to which that model can be successful in a globalizing twenty-first century. We argue that Zinn's methods and practices constitute a distinct type of public intellectual: the *scholar-activist*. While activism and academia are fundamentally changing, Zinn's approach remains an important consideration for activists and, perhaps even more importantly, for those of us in academia.

In the afterword, Noam Chomsky considers Zinn's legacy. His reflection, based upon his decades-long friendship with Zinn, speaks for itself, but most persuasively, Chomsky reminds us that Zinn's optimism and dedication to positive, progressive change—his agitation with a smile—remains a potent model for others to embrace.

A Note on Interludes

As Alix Olson discusses in Chapter 10, and as Zinn himself practiced as a scholar-activist, we have used artistic *interludes*—pauses in the text—as a way to merge academia and activism with the arts, a confluence of form and content. We are mindfully following Zinn's engagement with multiple forms of expression. Thus, the reader will find two poems, by Alix Olson and Martín Espada (preceding the final two sections), and song lyrics by Woody Guthrie (preceding the first section). The lyrics from Guthrie, as explained by Ambre Ivol in Chapter 3, motivated Zinn's initial interest in labor history and "forgotten" historical events more generally. Olson's poem reflects a diarist's recognition that her nation has failed to make good on the "promissory notes" outlined in its founding documents; the relationship between citizens and state had been permanently damaged. Espada's poem was originally read at an April 2010 memorial service in honor of Howard Zinn held at Boston's Arlington Street Church.[67]

Ludlow Massacre

Song lyrics by Woody Guthrie

It was early springtime when the strike was on,
They drove us miners out of doors,
Out from the houses that the Company owned,
We moved into tents up at old Ludlow.

I was worried bad about my children,
Soldiers guarding the railroad bridge,
Every once in a while a bullet would fly,
Kick up gravel under my feet.

We were so afraid you would kill our children,
We dug us a cave that was seven foot deep,
Carried our young ones and pregnant women
Down inside the cave to sleep.

That very night your soldiers waited,
Until all us miners were asleep,
You snuck around our little tent town,
Soaked our tents with your kerosene.

You struck a match and in the blaze that started,
You pulled the triggers of your gatling guns,
I made a run for the children but the fire wall stopped me.
Thirteen children died from your guns.

I carried my blanket to a wire fence corner,
Watched the fire till the blaze died down,
I helped some people drag their belongings,
While your bullets killed us all around.

I never will forget the look on the faces
Of the men and women that awful day,
When we stood around to preach their funerals,
And lay the corpses of the dead away.

We told the Colorado Governor to call the President,
Tell him to call off his National Guard,
But the National Guard belonged to the Governor,
So he didn't try so very hard.

Our women from Trinidad, they hauled some potatoes,
Up to Walsenburg in a little cart,
They sold their potatoes and brought some guns back,
And they put a gun in every hand.

The state soldiers jumped us in a wire fence corners,
They did not know we had these guns,
And the Red-neck Miners mowed down these troopers,
You should have seen those poor boys run.

We took some cement and walled that cave up,
Where you killed these thirteen children inside,
I said, "God bless the Mine Workers' Union,"
And then I hung my head and cried.

ZINN AS HISTORIAN AND PUBLIC INTELLECTUAL

CHAPTER 2

Legacies and Breakthroughs

The Long View on Zinnian History

Ambre Ivol and Paul Buhle

The "backstory" of Howard Zinn's popular and influential *A People's History of the United States* (1980) might be found in Zinn's own personal life up to the writing of the book, in his graduate training, or in the work of scholars of his generation that he admired. But we might also take a longer view: Why has the history of the United States itself, seen from a radical angle, been so persistent and relevant by contrast, for instance, to the obscurity of anything resembling European-style Marxist theory? Who preceded Zinn and perhaps set a path for what would reach large numbers of readers, educated or otherwise, and give them a different view?

There is another angle of vision useful to us: utopia and its perennial partner, dystopia. From at least the American Revolution, claims of specialness (American "exceptionalism" or "city upon a hill") seemed to exempt Americans from the woes of humankind. However, from at least the late nineteenth century, the specter of something different, a monstrous reversal of dreams into nightmares, has occupied a section of the popular radical mind. These histories of the "present as history" are an illuminating part of our story.

Socialists and anarchists, and later communists, New Leftists, and all their present-day descendants, have had to wrestle with an old Marxist conundrum. If the United States were indeed the most industrialized, modern nation in the world, why would the forces representing the working class be so weak, divided, and not especially socialistic? Populists and other radicals at large, including abolitionists, supporters of women's rights (later, suffragists), or African Americans faced the same problem, albeit from other standpoints. For all of them, it is fair to say, the American Revolution, the Constitution and Bill of Rights, not to mention the Civil War (and formal abolition of slavery) seemed to promise far more than was delivered. Indeed, iconoclasts would often conclude that the grand phrases and even the Fifteenth Amendment often provided the powerful with more opportunities to exploit the lowly. Was each grand achievement to be built upon earlier ones, or had ordinary Americans been hoaxed all along? Or was the story yet more complex and contradictory?

Socialist Gustavus Myers, whose vastly popular *The History of Great American Fortunes* first appeared in 1910, captured a mood by declaring that history had been by and large a dishonest enterprise because "private property" imposed a war between the haves and the have-nots. For better and worse, this view did not explain why so few of the oppressed, well-paid skilled workers or the impoverished unemployed opposed their Wall Street bosses with abandon. Nor did any alternative version explain why seeming democratic triumphs were never able to overcome forces of exploitation and corruption.

We might be tempted to say that native-born writers were more likely to feel the pang of disillusionment and to write a sort of *noir* history while immigrant intellectuals, hopeful about the rise of the working class around them, were more likely to write an upbeat saga of one stage of democracy following another. This schema is far too simple, of course, and the effects of the New Deal in particular seemed to have a strong influence upon nearly all radical writers of the national saga. But a division of mordant themes against hopeful ones or, seen another way, upper-class manipulation versus compliant or resistant masses, is a continuing, inescapable theme or trope. How else could it be within the grandest empire (and largest military machine) the human race has ever known?

Within this context, Howard Zinn wrote history that exemplified these concerns. His early work is somewhat closer to the expectations of academia, and his later work completely dismisses those provincial concerns in favor of a true history for the people. In both cases, Zinn's history consistently spoke to the broad concerns of America's utopian promise, its often dystopic reality, and the unfailing ability of its people (and others beyond American borders who lived under its influence) to address the two.

In this chapter, we make four broad claims. First, Zinn's history was *intentionally* and *specifically* about people's movements broadly construed, which were instigated by the various concerns of the American progressive left (as distinct from, and much broader than, Marxism). This focus was often simultaneously despairing of the actions of dominant elites and exultant in the perseverance and/or resistance of social movements (and their associated division of labor with leaders and other principal actors). Second, Zinn's historical tradition should be understood as part of a longer pattern of well-established American radical history. In essence, Zinn represents an extension and modification of a well-established history of radical progressivism. Third, Zinn's approach to protest and movements was farsighted, and provides a valuable approach to understanding and researching history. His conception of protest and agitation was that citizens who form movements do so in emergent networks, from broad, naturally occurring epistemic communities that are more nuanced than the blunt instrument of simple "class" labels. Zinn understood that observing such history from within movements provided an invaluable perspective. Fourth, Zinn's belief that aspects of contemporary American academic history were "broken" is well-established.[1] However, Zinn's approach to history—all the aspects of his oeuvre for which he was criticized by mainstream academic historians—was a specific, conscious, and arguably deeply considered intellectual approach. Ultimately, Zinn's history was not just history *about* people (in a broadly configured sense of the term), but, more importantly, history *for* people.

Assessing Zinnian History over Time

Asked about the motivations behind *A People's History*, Zinn remembered there was a "practical need" for it:

> I wanted to write a history that would be useful. So many people had approached me and asked if I could recommend a book on US history; they did not want to read specialized books, to read ten different books. That is why I was not writing for historians—because the average person doesn't want to read that many books. He wants … a bird's-eye view.[2]

His sense of this need was informed by his activist experience in the South from 1956 to 1964.

> In the South, people would say, "Tell me a good book on this, on that." People in the movement would ask me that—so I thought in a way I was writing for movement people and also for the general public.[3]

Rooted in such a special political moment, the book seemed in some ways to have acquired a life of its own. It functions as a rich collection of past struggles that later social movements in the United States have drawn from for inspiration and reclaimed as their own. Its ambition and political perspective have further disconnected the project from its original intention. Scholars have reviewed it according to academic standards, and politically minded readers have positioned themselves as left or right of Zinn's philosophy of history. An epistemological debate remains over the relevance of structuring a narrative exclusively around social struggle. There is a risk of leaving out the dense complexity of popular culture that presages periods of social polarization. It runs the risk of caricaturing the history of ordinary people.

Further, Zinn's insistence on his own interest in social movements (suggested in the original title of the book, *Struggle for Democracy*)[4] and his acknowledgments of a number of shortcomings (mainly regarding Latino and gay/lesbian history) have not put these debates to rest. This is in part because the exponentially growing popularity of the book has been interpreted either as provocation (how can such "bad" history be so widely read?) or confirmation (for the ongoing importance of radical history).

Zinn has been placed squarely within the large category of "New Left historians." This occurs despite his being remembered as an "Old Leftist" active as a teenager in the 1930s. This approach suggests that his political views, inspired by the struggles of the working class and his youthful interests in communism, set him on the path that inevitably led him to write about social movements in a certain way. Critiques of *A People's History* tend to be associated with specific schools of thought (Beardian economism, Marcusean class pessimism, New Leftist celebration of spontaneism) despite the lack of coherence or viewpoint among these different perspectives (for instance, how can Zinn be accused of being both workerist and Marcusean or of being a Beardian and a New Leftist?). Moreover, though rarely pointed to, the very assumption that Zinn wrote an inverted story of the "people" (the photographic negative print of the top-down approach) is, although intuitively sensible, in fact intellectually impractical since the new social history of the 1960s and 1970s—on which Zinn drew considerably—intended, by essence, to do away with the prevalent, centralized, and overarching consensus narrative.[5]

Far from being a fixed narrative long in planning, *A People's History* actually grew out of major social and personal changes of which the author only gradually became aware.[6]

> When I wrote the other books I wasn't as conscious about, "Oh, I am writing this from the ground up, as opposed to traditional textbooks. I am writing about people and people's movements, people's point of view." Unconsciously I was doing it, as when writing about SNCC I was writing about a people's movement.[7]

Zinn reminds us here of the importance of historicizing ideological trajectories, especially the dichotomy between the so-called New versus Old Left. Ivol argues in Chapter 3 of this book that Zinn's generational roots are usually dismissed or misconstrued. The same may be stated about the way his intellectual contribution has been studied, criticized, or celebrated.[8]

Zinn provides us with a different understanding of generational interaction within the movement by emphasizing his processing of certain experiences when he was already in his forties.

> I wasn't yet—well, by then I had already written my book on SNCC—but as I say, I was not conscious of the fact that this was what I was doing, so I had not yet developed a consciousness about what was important to write about, the social movements that generate policy. It wasn't until I sat down to write *A People's History* that I was conscious of this.[9]

Continuity and generational transmission have been convincingly demonstrated by scholars who have emphasized the influence of older mentors in the movement.[10] Less has been said about generational cross-fertilization.

Zinn's trajectory demonstrates *regeneration* in ways that remind us of what Karl Mannheim (1952) said about generations: whenever a new generation is intellectually strong enough to bring about a new understanding of the world, learning processes go both ways as the elders come to learn from the young.

Through his participation in a number of struggles, Zinn's views changed, especially regarding the relationship between intellectuals and spheres of government. Although his work always emphasized the importance of social protest and disenfranchisement, it progressed to a greater emphasis on movements in later years.

> When I edited this book *New Deal Thought,* in many ways probably the most traditional of my books, even though I was trying to look at the New Deal from a more radical point of view, I still wasn't dealing with the labor movement of the 1930s.... It was very much about national policy.[11]

New Deal Thought (1965b) was published as a collection of essays representing the wide range of solutions initiated by self-described New Dealers. Sympathetic to liberal and radical intellectuals—working as social experts for the federal government or running for office, thinking within the limits of (or beyond) the capitalist horizon—Zinn argued that although the underdog drove social change forward, intellectuals provided "theories," "ideals," and "perspectives" for nascent social movements.[12]

Such a view had previously been developed through his doctoral research on the congressional career of Fiorello La Guardia. "Obviously a part of the Establishment"[13] though "a rebel" in Congress from 1917 to 1933, La Guardia represented an original case study in the transition from the Progressive Era to the New Deal. Zinn saw this politician as constituting a prominent link that anticipated the economic planning implemented under Franklin D. Roosevelt. It is too simple to dismiss this early work as "traditional" history retrospectively untypical of Zinnian thought.[14] Published as a book in 1959, Zinn's research on La Guardia was being conducted while McCarthyism swept across universities and marginalized radical history.

Further, Zinn saw radical politics as a division of labor between leaders on one hand and mass movements on the other. His ideological interest was then structured around intellectual figures like journalist Heywood Broun and, right after WWII, Arthur Koestler (1905–1983). Political theory was assumed to emanate from the original thinking of a small number of essentially male thinkers, whose style Zinn hoped to emulate. Such a perspective was far removed from his later enthusiasm for anarchist feminist Emma Goldman, which was part of a long process that had brought him to realize the importance of female leaders within social movements, especially notable in the black freedom struggle. Zinn had expressed his admiration for SNCC adult advisor Ella Baker, to whom he dedicated his oral history of the group: "the lady ... more responsible than any other individual for the birth" of the first New Left organization.[15]

Zinn himself documented the depth of the transformation he underwent as he and his family moved from ethnically diverse Brooklyn to segregated Atlanta in 1956. In *The Southern Mystique* (1972 [1964]), a collection of essays exploring the relevance of Southern exceptionalism, he reflects upon how "total immersion" in the black community entailed deep cultural, psychological, and philosophical effects on whites:

> Not many white people in the United States had the opportunity to work and to live over a period of years ... in a predominantly Negro community. I count myself to be lucky to be one of those. This kind of total immersion is not just educational in the pallid sense of book learning; it is transformative, as real education should be.[16]

Asked by the Southern Regional Council to report on the Albany movement in 1962, Zinn developed organic links to the black liberation movement, both learning from and being solicited by younger activists as a "participant-observer" and "historian-journalist."[17] During this period he was writing about the partial victories and persistent obstacles to racial equality in the segregated South, calling for federal protection of civil rights, and later prompting SNCC activists to address the war in Vietnam. In the months leading up to the 1964 Freedom Summer, he received the following invitation from SNCC—a far cry from the supposed anti-intellectualism of the young:

> We need a Writer ... capable of doing a sound analytical study of what is going on. Someone who would be known in the country and "respected," who could ensure communication with liberal papers and all this sort of thing.[18]

Zinn was prompted to process his role as an academic first as a professor at Spelman College, then, after being fired for his political activism in June 1964, as a historian working on an oral history of SNCC (he stayed in the South for another year), and finally, from the mid-sixties onward, as a professor at Boston University. Zinn reinvented himself through the black-liberation and later anti-war movements, both as a historian and a radical thinker. In many ways, these activities spared him from the existential crisis undergone by other intellectuals of his generation.[19]

Presiding over the creation of *Dissent* magazine in 1954, Irving Howe declared, "When intellectuals can do nothing else, they start a magazine." Half-mockingly describing himself as a "loose fish, still flapping," Howe then saw his work as swimming against the current, as if deeply scarred by the entrenched minority position of the anti-communist Left. Zinn had found a role for himself (or had a role attributed to him), which led him to think of political change in increasingly clear interventionist terms. By the mid-sixties, he "was becoming increasingly frustrated by the fact that no major public figure ... dared to say what seemed so clear to me—that the United States must simply get out of Vietnam as quickly as possible, to save American lives, to save Vietnamese lives." His activism would even extend to his involvement in the Radical Historical Caucus, which largely informed his argument about the limits of the scholar-as-expert set forth in the *The Politics of History* (1990 [1970]). The latter focus essentially sought to bring the historical profession to take a collective stand against the war in Vietnam, summarized in the catchphrase "we publish while others perish."[20]

The bulk of Zinn's writings during this period (including 1974's *Justice in Everyday Life*) defines the high point of his interventionist period, which was brought to a close by the end of the movement against the war in Vietnam and the demise of most political networks making up the New Left.[21] *A People's History* both built on and moved beyond this stage, seeking to address a larger need that went beyond the practical necessities of social movements.

The project functioned as an ongoing contribution to the theories and practices of the United States Left. Asked about his proximity to Popular Front–styled narrative history, Zinn responded that his outlook never sought to identify with the nationalism of the Founding Fathers in the way that Howard Fast did. In a vein similar to Fast, historian Leo Huberman had identified the New Deal with a socialist horizon, celebrating national unity in the name of the war against fascism. Zinn did not identify with what scholars consider to be a typically Old Left analysis in which communism and Americanism were to be fused (in theory). This illusion was dissipated by the Second Red Scare.

Zinn's style as public historian—both in speech and writing—came out of a practice of testing his ideas through interactions with the larger citizenry, a tradition going back to Oscar Ameringer.[22] Moreover, his experiences set him apart from Beardian and communist historians, who tended to subsume race under class. Emphasis on such a biographical landmark allows us to relocate Zinn within a lesser-known generational current on the Left. The year 1956 is well known because of its significance for radicals who broke away from Soviet communism, though the trend was made more complicated and murky for American leftists, who had nowhere to turn to in the context of growing political intimidation.[23] It is in this light that we can situate Zinn within the framework of a broad general tradition of great radical historians and histories.

HOWARD ZINN: GRANDCHILD TO GREAT RADICAL HISTORIES

The late nineteenth century, of intermittent depressions, suddenly grown gray cities of distressed working classes, and impoverished countrysides, sets the background for the development of progressive history in the context of America's exceptional utopian promise and dystopic turn(s). Three hugely popular literary ventures prepared the scholarly and semi-scholarly saga to follow. Edward Bellamy's *Looking Backward* (1887) offered a happy tale of socialistic resolution by common consent. American society, with its innovative skills and affable neighbors, conquered all woes in a cheerful utopia. Populist leader Ignatius Donnelly delivered the opposite message a few years later in *Caesar's Column* (1960 [1890]), a degraded future America with the skeletons of victims encased in a great tower, suitably at the center of Washington, DC.

Another widely read volume, *Bill Nye's Comic History of the United States* (1894), compiled by Edgar Wilson Nye, a friend of future socialist leader Eugene V. Debs, was both cheerful and iconoclastic. It ridiculed (in caricatures by Frederick Burr Opper, as well as Nye's own words) nearly every group and famous individual from colonialism onward, for hypocrisy and what we might call business mentality, that is, personal calculation above all principle.[24]

In asides, Nye added droll, genuinely moral passages, this one after explaining how the original Rhode Island colony had freedom of religion—i.e., freedom from the Puritans of Massachusetts:

> With the advent of political opinion, the individual use of the conscience has become popularized, and the time is coming when it will grow a great size ... instead of turning over our consciences to the safety deposit company of a great political party or religious organization and taking the key in our pocket, let us have individual charge of this useful little instrument and be able finally to answer for its growth or decay.[25]

But war provided his main target. His caustic views of conquest-sentimentalism might be summed up in an aside about Andrew Jackson. Slaughtering 600 outright, he "knew full well that all the Indians ever born on the face of the earth could not compensate for the cruel and violent death of one ... American mother."[26] Possibly, he adds, Indians got their ideas of murdering civilians from the whites' practices.

Was any of this serious history? German immigrant Oscar Ameringer's *Life and Deeds of Uncle Sam* (1985 [1909]) not only earned him the cognomen of "the socialist Mark Twain," but sold more than a million copies. This expanded pamphlet of about fifty small-print pages was influenced by the satirical writings of mid-century Petroleum Nasby (David Locke) against Copperheads, and Samantha Allen (Marietta Holley) against male privilege, and then again by the brilliance of Mark Twain (Samuel Clemens) himself. None of these were historical or counter-historical, but like Nye's work, they set a pattern for how to write to plain folks with easily grasped social and political complaints.

Ameringer might have been borrowing directly from Nye's attack upon wars and war-makers: "Men will fight until it is educated out of them, just as they will no doubt retain rudimentary tails and live in trees till they know better."[27] Ameringer muckraked every political leader, including Washington and Lincoln, and the whole political process from the first European settlements onward.

He wrote, "The Puritans were a pious, bigoted and intolerant lot.... Nine-tenths of the good things told about the Puritans are lies and the remaining tenth isn't quite true,"[28] and this virtually begins the story. The American Revolution was fought for "economic interests," as slavery was begun (and ended) with the goal of crushing the Confederacy as a potential competitor to the North, and Shay's Rebellion proved that "farmers and wage-workers who had never gotten anything from this or any other government" were angry, but "nobody dared what they wanted or didn't want." The Constitution was an import, a "democracy with strings attached" to keep the power in the hands of the powerful. Ameringer closed his thoughts eloquently, looking to labor:

> If today we may still boast a higher standard of living, if the American workingman is still able to fight for a grander civilization, don't thank those who directed the ship of state, but come with me to the lonely graves of the pioneers of unionism.... Humble tools of evolution, you have done more for civilization and humanization of our race than all statesmen, warriors and priests.[29]

Ameringer was backed up, in his iconoclasm, by a newer wave of dystopian fiction, including Jack London's famed *Iron Heel* (1991 [1908]), and the once-popular *Darkness and Dawn* by George Allen England (1974 [1912]), both published on the lip of the world war and the unraveling sense of horror and socialist defeat. But Ameringer had another wind at his back: Charles Beard's *Economic Interpretation of the Constitution of the United States* (1986 [1913]), the super-iconoclastic work identifying the material interests of the Founding Fathers.

Beard and a small circle of others reset US historical understanding for practically two generations, in ways that were quite radical without being socialistic, and that in some ways successfully cut across Left and Right ways of thinking. Beard came of age during the 1890s, when dire poverty, brute imperial conquest of the Philippines (as well as Hawaii and Cuba), and successful manipulation of national elections by Wall Street's Republican Party roused young idealists to hope for something very different. Having spent a year of his youth at Oxford, Beard became convinced that American history could be seen as the struggle to overcome its class-ridden European heritage. Working people, factory workers, and farmers could lead a crusade to take control of (if not abolish) business-dominated politics and culture.

Beard was no Marxist. His critique of history was based upon "interests." He could scarcely find Indians and African Americans (slaves or freemen) as actors in his portrait of the United States. Still, as part of a generation of intellectuals bitterly disillusioned with World War I (he had first supported it), his views sharpened the focus on empire. Thus, combined with his suspicion of Washington as a center for expansionism (epitomized in Woodrow Wilson's strategies) and a tool of Wall Street, Beard appealed to an essentially non-Marxist Midwest progressivism.

So did socialist historian A. M. Simons, a former student of Fredrick Jackson Turner and author of *Social Forces in American History* (1911), which was said to have been used in some four thousand local socialist study classes. Simons, editor of both the erudite *International Socialist Review* and the short-lived *Chicago Daily Socialist,* provided a socialist and Marxist ending to his treatise. In the main, it reiterated familiar themes: The democratic countryside was being overwhelmed by international finance. Working people (whose history was described as if it had only begun in the United States) would pull the democratic irons out of the fire about to consume capitalism.

Beard had articulated themes larger than any Marxist way of seeing the American saga. This was the view that democratic-minded readers wanted to believe and the view that strengthened their will to act. They could look to a democratic triumph that included class, if not with working people necessarily in the lead. For these reasons and because he became by the 1930s one of the most prominent public intellectuals in the nation, Beard's four-volume *The Rise of American Civilization* (1927), written with Mary Beard, was the American-history book of the age. Millions of copies were sold, and scarcely an educated household lacked a copy, most often in the abbreviated edition. The Beards condemned the American corporate class as transnationalist, conducting itself as a global parasite. Most notably, it had pushed the nation into the World War I. In power, the corporate class betrayed not only workers and small farmers but the honest small-business class that added civic virtues to small-town society. In a society where military spending remained minor and regional interests were sometimes progressive (e.g., the northern Midwest), this view was at least credible. In their encompassing coverage of women's history—a special interest of Mary Beard's—they also looked toward the future of radical study.

The Beards enjoyed a shift toward faith in a certain kind of national leadership, revising their classic work as the New Deal progressed. FDR, sounding the alarm against the "economic royalists," had set a tone for democratic progress. Then came the approach of war that, the Beards insisted, would militarize society and throw back democracy in favor of Wall Street's plutocrats. As Mary Beard pursued women's history, Charles Beard threw himself against FDR's global plans, thus making himself a pariah among many left-wing and liberal anti-fascists.

Following World War II, elite-based liberal Cold Warriors attacked the Beards on all fronts, seeking to drive their reputations out of scholarly circles. They determinedly misconstrued the Beards' arguments for their own purposes. The Beards had, however, left behind legacies crucial to future generations of radical historians likewise scorned by the empire's liberals. It is also safe to say that Marxist writers for newspapers and pamphlets, across all ostensibly factional lines, continued to rely upon Charles Beard well into the 1960s: he had supplied the outlines of their framework, while overtly Marxist texts had been used to fill in the gaps.

Meanwhile, radical history had taken a new turn with the popular writings of Leo Huberman, a union educator. Illustrated by the great WPA artist Thomas Hart Benton, *We, the People: The Drama of America* (1947 [1932]) took on an importance that could not be appreciated at the time of its original publication. As with Bill Nye's volume, the picture-book quality counted for a great deal, bringing the ideas to life. Huberman's lucid prose followed the Beardian interpretation but with more optimism and an emphasis upon class, along with a "fighting narrative" that stirred the reader to action.

W. E. B. Du Bois's *Black Reconstruction in America* (1935), published within two years of another totemic volume of black history, *The Black Jacobins* (2001 [1937]) by C. L. R. James, may be said to have turned the study of American history upside down. The two writer-activists, a hugely prominent thinker and a still-obscure West Indian cricket journalist, had together stressed the power of African descendants (in the case of James's colonized Haiti, including some actually still brought from the mother continent) to act on their own behalf and change history. If African Americans had been mere victims, even to socialist historians, Du Bois insisted that their abandonment of the plantations had set the stage for the Northern victory and for Radical Reconstruction, the turning point in global race relations that did not quite turn.[30] Du Bois's masterwork, disdained by the history profession until the middle 1960s (safely after the author's death), offered paths forward for scholars of other minorities to make the case for American Indians, Asians, Hispanics, and others during the 1970s and beyond, not only as victims but as actors in the grand drama. Because Du Bois had drawn the outcome of Reconstruction and its sequel, US expansionism, as grotesque and monstrous, his view of American history was tragic.

Other iconic historians to follow, such as William Appleman Williams, with little clear view of race or Reconstruction, had nevertheless imbibed something crucial of the tragic view. In a way, the later insights of Charles Beard, so vigorously and venomously rejected by postwar liberals like Richard Hofstadter and Arthur Schlesinger Jr., could be said to have merged with those of Du Bois in particular. Prominent liberals of the same and later generations, Southern historian C. Vann Woodward most notably, raved against historical multiculturalism and the loss of narrative when they meant the loss of sunny optimism in the story of modern America. As long as the civil-rights movement had solved the basic problems of race and the United States had managed to exit from Vietnam, in this view, the rest of American history fell into place. The New Deal had sealed in the social settlement of class issues, World War II had likewise sealed in the US role in guiding the world—no minor divergences would matter much in the long run.

Although Williams's *Tragedy of American Diplomacy* (1998 [1959]) was read alongside Herbert Marcuse's *One Dimensional Man* (1991 [1965]) as the most studied books for campus New Leftists in the 1960s, Williams never reached a wide audience with *The Contours of American History* (1961). Radical views by the newer generations appeared in monographs of lower-class life, minorities, working people, and women, done through analysis of communities, their daily strivings and sufferings, and their culture, along with their economic status. Full of tragedy, it was still an optimistic history, with which Zinn's philosophy of history resonated, especially with the publication of his *A People's History*—oddly contrasting with the national shift to Reaganism.

The same intellectual urge to further investigate some of the basic tenets of Marxism—once materialistic determinism and mechanical historical progress were dismissed—was felt transnationally, including in the United States. The striking similarities in intent and tone between British historian E. P. Thompson and Zinn should be emphasized, as they point to a profound interest in self-emancipation, which both historians declared to be at the center of their philosophy of history. Wrote Thompson,

> I am seeking to rescue the poor stockinger, the Luddite cropper, the "obsolete" hand-loom weaver ... from the enormous condescension of posterity. Their crafts and traditions may have been backward-looking.... Their insurrectionary conspiracies may have been foolhardy. But they lived through these times of acute social disturbance and we did not. Their aspirations are valid in terms of their own experience; and if they were casualties of history, they remain, condemned in their own lives, as casualties.[31]

And Zinn wrote,

> In that inevitable taking of sides which comes from selection and emphasis in history, I prefer to tell the story of the discovery of America from the viewpoint of the Arawaks.... My point is not to grieve for the victims and denounce the executioners.... But I do remember ... a statement I once read: The cry of the

poor is not always just, but if you don't listen ... you will never know what justice is.[32]

Zinn closely annotated *The Making of the English Working Class* in the late 1960s, as the book was being circulated among New Left historians who saw in it "thick" social history to emulate.[33] Despite differences in the scope and scale of their work, both intellectuals were prompted to revisit their own support of communism in light of the failure of the Stalinist model. As World War II veterans turned historians, they came to feel, by the 1960s, the urgency to remap "history from below."[34]

Perhaps Zinn's most enduring contribution in the book has to do with his study of how collective interests form. Far from positing alliances between oppressed groups (he mentions how they can turn on each other), his narrative seeks to demonstrate how collective resistance through solidarity occurred in practice. In his copy of Thompson (1963: 11), Zinn underlined as follows: "Class is fluid, alive, *historical,* not a category." Such a dynamic view of how collective entities coalesce may be found at the heart of *A People's History.* In this light, the "people" form when they group through networks of solidarity. To quote another part of Thompson's argument that very much resonates with Zinnian history,

> I do not see class as a structure, nor even as a category, but as something which actually happens ... in human relationships.[35]

Zinn discusses the "fluidity" of the "people in movement" as he presents the "guards" standing for the more privileged sections of the working population. For him, the inherent political ambivalence of the middle class may tilt it either way: as "guards" buffering the status quo, or as potential joiners on the barricades.

> The new conditions of technology, economics, and war ... make it ... less possible for the guards of the system—the intellectuals, the homeowners, the taxpayers, the skilled workers, the professionals, the servants of government— to remain immune from the violence ... inflicted on the black, the poor, the criminal, the enemy overseas.[36]

Beyond his own trajectory, such insistence on potentiality places him within a larger intellectual tradition of scholars who wrestled with these difficulties over four or five generations. The "old middle class" of small property owners, in given ethnic groups and given circumstances, offered vital support for labor, radical, antiracist, and a variety of other progressive social movements. Indeed, the financial backing of fraternal groups that underlay the support of social movements depended on those less impoverished; likewise, the left-wing press could not have otherwise been sustained, and by the late 1940s it had become especially clear that government repression of the Left could not be resisted without considerable support for legal challenges, a circumstance that has hardly changed since.

Coming closer to the present, white-collar supporters of progressive political movements (ecological, feminist, and pro-labor) against conservative push-backs have been decisive, as the Right hostility toward unions of teachers, health workers, and assorted state workers along with reproductive rights has laid the issues bare. Herein lies, perhaps, the strategic intervention of *A People's History*: far from reducing the "people in struggle" to the lumpen proletariat, it points to the possibility of inclusive alliances in times of crisis, a hypothesis certainly relevant for activists and scholars today.

CHAPTER 3

The US Left in Generational Perspective

A Study of Howard Zinn's Trajectory

Ambre Ivol

Howard Zinn's strong association with the New Left has become arguably one of the central features of his characterization as both an intellectual and an activist. This chapter looks at this political delineation as a starting point rather than a conclusive statement. Drawing on recent historiographical studies addressing the need to complexify our understanding of the "New Left," this chapter points to the relevance of a larger generational framework to study Zinn's role in the "movement." Sharing with other prominent figures a common grounding in pre-McCarthyism America, Zinn represents, within the New Left and its countercultural orbit, a larger story, which contradicts the prevalent narrative positing that generational and political identities may be neatly superimposed. This chapter investigates the inadequacy of an ideological and generational prism structured around the binary opposites of the Old versus New Left. Indeed the process of political regeneration undergone by Zinn through the black freedom movement has yet to translate into the literature about the US Left. Zinn's political and geographical trajectory will thus serve as an entry point to a larger collective story, mapping out age cohorts usually missing in the fabric of the US Left. In light of the historiography, an alternative approach along more comprehensive generational lines will be suggested, with a special insistence on the misconstrued World War II generation to which Zinn belongs.

(SELF-)IDENTIFICATION WITH THE NEW LEFT

Zinn's contributions to the theories and practices of the civil-rights struggle and the movement against the war in Vietnam have been widely explored by scholars and activists. As a contemporary-minded historian, Zinn published two books on the South, including his oral history of SNCC (2002 [1964]), which was among the very first to address what Staughton Lynd came to call the "Black new left," and his Vietnam war pamphlet, *Vietnam: The Logic of Withdrawal* (2002 [1967]), constituted the first academic argument calling for immediate US withdrawal from Southeast Asia. In addition to personal testimonies about his atypical place in the movement, Zinn's autobiographical considerations have further confirmed the centrality of the sixties in his intellectual maturation.[1]

Though Zinn's politics continue to fuel argument among leftists, his generational identity is seldom taken up. Age-focused approaches are usually limited to attempts to complicate the historical concept of the New Left. Hunt (2003) and Novick (1988) both acknowledge the influence of older figures—like Paul Goodman, Herbert Marcuse, C. Wright Mills, Noam Chomsky, Staughton Lynd, David Dellinger, Dorothy Healey, Betty Friedan, and Herbert Aptheker—on younger activists.[2] Other scholars associate Zinn with a broadly encompassing Left or the more narrow Old Left. Jacoby (2000 [1987]) includes him in a larger list of "radicals and Marxists," together with William Appleman Williams, Eugene Genovese, and Christopher Lasch.[3]

Despite general acknowledgment of the strong presence of adults within the New Left, any attempt at characterizing their genealogy has yet to be conducted beyond monographs. For example, Zinn's place in SNCC as an adult advisor suggests limitations to the typical concept of "mentoring," which implies a division of labor between thinkers and activists. Together with two female advisors (Anne Braden, whom he replaced, and Ella Baker), Zinn was solicited by SNCC on the basis of common activist experiences that prompted collective strategizing. His theoretical contributions were informed by this kind of age-integrated practice.[4]

Such generational attitudes within SNCC suggest that age played out in more ambivalent and ultimately positive ways than is usually assumed for its white counterparts. Despite early organizational ties with union leaders and liberal groups (e.g., League for Industrial Democracy), "generational paranoia" arguably led to a complete break at the Port Huron meeting of Students for a Democratic Society (SDS) in 1962. The fallout stemmed from political arguments framed in age-related terms, namely, over the issue of how to relate to communism. Following an argument with *Dissent* magazine editor Irving Howe that same year, Tom Hayden concluded that "No younger generation likes to feel that it's being lectured to by its ... ideological or biological parents. Especially if [they] have a lot to answer to themselves."

This commingling of ideology and genealogy further consolidated throughout the decade, as summarized by Michael Harrington in 1967:

> Perhaps it is inevitable that young people come to the radical movement with the fervor of catechumens, and always believe that the veterans of past struggles are tired and going soft.[5]

Taken as a whole, these self-definitions furthered the sense of a generational rift expressed in cultural forms and in new modes of political agitation. Still, the presence of numerous older radicals in and around both SNCC and SDS suggests the need to go beyond such generational rhetoric.

POLITICAL USES OF THE PAST

The instrumentalization of youth as a political argument was formulated in the most comprehensive terms by Daniel Bell, who had himself grown antagonistic to student activism by the late 1960s.[6] Bell's classification entitled "The New York Jewish Intellectuals" (reproduced as Table 3.1 here) has become central to the literature about US intellectuals and the Left. Despite the overall inconsistency of Bell's logic due to the central ambivalence of the concept of "coming of age,"[7] this perspective remains a key reference among critics. It retains influence perhaps because no alternative overarching framework yet exists to replace it. This chapter argues that the changing intellectual landscape now makes it possible to conduct such a systematic remapping.

Published in the context of mainstream anti-communism, Bell's *The Winding Passage* (1980: 120–121) revisited his own social and political trajectory away from radical politics and closer to the mainstream. Himself a member of the "Second Generation's Younger Brothers" coming of age in the 1930s and early 1940s, Bell singled out *locality* (New York City), *community* (Jewishness), and *politics* (the radical critique of Stalinism by Trotskyism) as the three-sided prism through which to understand such intellectual influence.[8] Given the political mainstream informed by the Cold War, such a line of argument—coming from a sociologist having coined the phrase "the end of ideology"—was bound to be well-received.[9] More importantly, Bell's (1980: 119–137) claim to representation was simultaneously a claim to seniority. Indeed, he posited that members of his age group inherited a distinct political history, framed in terms of a precocious disillusionment with Soviet-styled communism. In other words, political independence from Stalinism represented the best of the Old Left.

Drawn to Trotskyism before the war broke out, autonomous, radical politics of the Old Left are still celebrated by critics as a sign of superior intellect—free of orthodoxy. Bender (1997) notes that Karl Mannheim's sociological concept of a "free-floating" intellectual may be illustrated by the trajectories of these New Yorkers. Their very isolation due to their attempts to go against the ideological current of their times indicates to Bender that they represent the best of what public figures should be—that is, behaving as "disinterested" critical thinkers.

Table 3.1: The New York Jewish Intellectuals

	1st Generation		2nd Generation	
The Elders	**The Younger Brothers**	**Bell's Generation**	**The Younger Brothers**
Coming of age:	Coming of age:	Coming of age:	Coming of age:
Late 1920s–early 1930s	Mid–late 1930s	Late 1930s–early 1940s	Late 1940s–early 1950s
Lionel Trilling	Alfred Kazin	Daniel Bell	Norman Mailer
Diana Trilling	Paul Goodman	Irving Howe	Philip Roth
Sidney Hook	Richard Hofstadter	Irving Kristol	Susan Sontag
	Saul Bellow	Seymour Martin Lipset	
		Nathan Glazer	
Gentile cousins:	Gentile cousins:	Gentile cousins:	Gentile cousins:
Dwight McDonald	Ralph Ellison	C. Wright Mills	Michael Harrington
	James Baldwin		
	Arthur Schlesinger Jr.		
	Mary McCarthy		
Magazines:	Magazines:	Magazines:	Magazines:
Menorah Journal	*The Nation*	*Dissent*	*Commentary*
Partisan Review	*New Republic*	*Encounter*	*NY Review of Books*
	Commentary	*New Leader*	*Partisan Review*
	Politics	*Public Interest*	

The influence of this taxonomy was further consolidated by what scholars have described as a sense of loss among critics of American intellectual life: the demise of a generic type of intellectual since the late 1970s. Deploring in their respective works the "end" of public intellectuals, Bender, Jacoby, and Dorman came to locate genuine intellectuals outside of academia and concluded that intellectual coming of age predating the *massification* of higher education guaranteed a more direct access to the public sphere. In the context of the demise of the New Left and the movements of the 1970s, the expression "public intellectual" seemed to apply best to the New York intellectuals because they conducted intellectual conversations outside of the university world, thus mapping out a public sphere composed of a constellation of reviews and journals whose legitimacy was grounded in the political prerequisites of heterodox Marxism.[10]

The historiographical ascendancy of the New York intellectuals was reinforced by the realpolitik of a postwar bipolar world and further fueled an ideological argument couched in generational terms. According to Bell, his age cohort skipped the phase of romanticized utopian values that is usually the privilege of the young and was marked by a sense of political disenchantment. In other words, association with pre-McCarthy-era communist groups signified irrelevance: in this view, "old" meant outdated.

THINKING OUTSIDE THE BOX: EXPANDING OUR
GENERATIONAL UNDERSTANDING OF THE US LEFT

Perceptions started to shift by the late 1980s, in large part due to the new social history that started to reconfigure the intellectual field. Maurice Isserman brought a fresh, novel angle to the generational bridges informing the New Left. He identified key players over the course of the 1950s (within Trotskyist, pacifist, socialist, and anarchist groupings) who facilitated the transition from "old" to "new." He also located cross-fertilizations in "moods"—especially between SDS and earlier pacifist-anarchist formations—thus chipping away at a misguiding binary framework. Isserman signaled a larger process of historiographical rehabilitation, addressing the collective role played by communist organizers over the first half of the twentieth century. More recently, chronological revisions of the civil-rights movement pointed to the need to root the black freedom struggle within the larger framework of the labor movement and the history of the US Left.[11]

A thorough study of Zinn's trajectory is a major contribution to the missing narrative of the US Left both because of his life experiences and the way he remembered them. Together with personal recollections about the impact of McCarthyism on academia (Zinn 1997b), the publication of his memoirs also signaled the larger historiographical shifts of the late 1990s—confirmed by his rehabilitation of a humanist Marxism in his second play, *Marx in Soho* (1999).

There was certainly a need to set the record straight. A superficial approach to left-wing activism in pre-McCarthyism America had led historians to claim that Zinn had "joined the [Communist] Party in his late teens." In his memoirs, Zinn clarified and expanded upon his youth experiences in Depression-era Brooklyn. Sympathetic to the economic aims of socialism, his support for the Party during adolescence remained partial. Though never a card-carrying member, he admired the courage of communist activists in the workplace. Still, he was growing weary of Soviet foreign policy by 1939. To him, the invasion of Finland by the USSR "was a brutal act of aggression against a tiny country" and none of his friends' "carefully worked out justifications persuaded [him]."[12]

Zinn's strand of independent radicalism was further reinforced by the brief friendship he developed in England with a fellow bombardier with whom he discussed the "imperialist" nature of the conflict. Although Zinn disagreed with such claims then, he came to develop similar views as the Cold War unfolded. Later, he realized such a position was representative of Trotskyism. Considering his retrospective criticism of World War II in the context of Vietnam, Zinn grew closer to Trotskyism than the New York intellectuals usually associated with it. Indeed, by the early 1940s, most New York intellectuals had aligned themselves with the United States—a position sustained throughout the Cold War.[13]

Zinn's combined critique of Soviet and US policy should be understood as part of a larger trend of autonomous radicalism developing in the 1940s. Recent literature clarifies how this played out for African Americans. According to Singh (2004: 111), "many important black radicals ... distanced themselves from the CP-USA [the US Communist Party] during World War II ... because they felt the Party was not radical enough." The betrayal of a "commitment to

black self-determination and the primacy of struggles against racism and colonialism" led a number of former members, such as Richard Wright, to move
away from the Communist Party.[14] What happened to radicals who did not fit
the simplified category of the Old Left, defined by the demoralizing practices of
a weakened, increasingly opportunistic Communist Party that adapted to Cold
War liberalism in the context of McCarthyism? Zinn's trajectory suggests that a
more complex understanding of the seminal decade of the 1940s is needed to
better remap the puzzle of the US Left beyond a dualistic prism.

Here again, dominant historiography has inappropriately paired together
generational and political considerations. Historian Stephen Ambrose (1997)
wrote about "citizen soldiers" and journalist Tom Brokaw (1998) came up with the
phrase "the greatest generation." This is the patriotic generation par excellence.[15]
According to these readings, the sociological subgroup of that generation—that
is, the soldiers who served in the war—came to represent a kind of political avant-
garde for their entire age cohort. Peter Novick (1988) explained the commitment
of scholars to the "domino theory" and to aggressive intervention in Vietnam as
stemming from the generational trauma of European isolationism, crystallized in
the Munich Accords of 1938, which strengthened Nazi military power. Arthur
Schlesinger Jr. and Henry Kissinger represented this position together with former
academics turned public servants McGeorge Bundy and Robert S. McNamara.[16]

Novick overlooks Zinn's obvious proximity in age and experience with this cohort and rather focuses on his enthusiastic identification with the counterculture of
the 1960s, to the exclusion of any other consideration.[17] Concurrently, it is precisely
because William Appleman Williams remained aloof from the cultural subversiveness expressed through student radicalism that Novick (1988: 445–446) singles him
out as an exception to the collective "Munich" mentality of his age cohort, noting
that Williams was "the single most important figure in the reconceptualization of
the history of American foreign policy" by bringing to light the responsibility of
the United States in the Cold War. Are Zinn's politics—first expressed through his
early involvement and writings about SNCC—reason enough to sever him from
his generational roots? Beyond the methodological flaw implied in any strict correspondence between a specific age cohort and a fixed set of ideas, such generational
displacement points to a larger gap in the historiography about the 1940s.

Two factors explain such a rupture: political rifts and sociological shifts.
McCarthyism manifested itself through the sudden decline in a number of tangible
networks structuring the US political Left. Ellen Schrecker (1998) insists upon
the brutal disappearance of a "generation of activists" from "the stage of history."
The combined effect of political repression (or intimidation) and ideological disillusionment (for most big- and small-*c* communists by 1956)[18] drastically reduced
access to the public sphere for leftists. At best, radicals were marginalized; at
worst, they gave up. Their trajectories were interrupted or became invisible, their
voices inaudible—at least for a time. Schrecker also emphasizes the more subtle
implications of repression by insisting upon what was *prevented from happening*:
books not written, research projects in social sciences not undertaken—in short,
a drastic reduction of the intellectual potentialities of an era, a de facto shrinking
of the field of possibilities.[19]

Such political reconfigurations of historic significance were compounded, if not submerged, by sociological transformations of unprecedented proportion. In their research on higher education in the United States, Bender and Smith (2008) emphasize the historic opportunity the G.I. Bill (formally called the Servicemen Readjustment Act) represented for a generation of veterans. Passed in June 1944, it was among the last pieces of social legislation of the Roosevelt era, which scholars have defined as the high point of the American welfare-state model. It offered veterans fifty-two weeks of unemployment allowance, better access to bank loans, health care coverage, and the funding of four years of higher education. More than eight million former soldiers benefited from the program, thus signaling the democratization of higher education.

Therefore the immediate aftermath of World War II constituted a context of exceptional changes on both levels. Scholars of generational politics have emphasized the need to restore the core ideological ambivalence of any age cohort. This is certainly illustrated by Zinn's processing of his experience of the "good war," which contrasts sharply with that of the New York intellectuals. Zinn's trajectory questions the legitimacy of such public figures as spokespersons for their generation of intellectuals.

THE "GOOD WAR" GENERATION OF INTELLECTUALS

Zinn's trajectory delineates new ways of studying two types of delay in the process of coming of age—sociological and political. Born in 1922, Zinn was a second generation, New York–bred, Jewish working-class male raised in poverty during the Great Depression. After high school he worked as an apprentice in the Brooklyn Navy Yard from 1940 to 1943, then volunteered as a bombardier to serve in the US Air Force during World War II. He survived the war, and, with financial support from the G.I. Bill, started undergraduate work in the late 1940s and obtained his PhD in history in 1958 at age thirty-six.[20]

Zinn's academic experiences differ from those of Howe, Kristol, or Bell, who attended The City College of New York upon graduation from high school (where they took part in the ideological feuds of the Left). Kristol and Howe served in the war—Kristol saw combat in Europe, while Howe was stationed in Alaska. Neither Kristol nor Howe chose the academic route after the war. As Jacoby (2000 [1987]: 7–8, 82–83) emphasizes, these New York intellectuals were not PhD holders. In this respect, Zinn's trajectory is relevant beyond its individual complexity because it expands upon the sociology of this age group by pointing to the *delayed* aspect of the coming of age—through academia—of an intellectual generation.

According to Löwy (1998: 125), intellectuals are best defined as a "social category" characterized by "noneconomic criteria," composed of individual "producers of cultural or symbolic goods—by opposition to consumers, distributors, or managers of those goods." Winock (1989: 17) describes intellectuals as figures intervening actively, consciously, and systematically in the public arena, using the means of their craft or skills. Hence scholars and artists may fit the definition, as may political persons (politicians or social activists).[21]

The experience of the war, though often shattering and traumatizing, para-doxically served as a means to integrate into US society in a way that would not have been possible for previous generations of veterans. This is especially true for young Jewish working-class males. Latent anti-Semitism tended to disappear in the aftermath of the war in the United States, as elitist institutions welcomed Jewish students and professors more systematically.[22] Obtaining his master's degree from New York University in 1952, Zinn then worked toward his PhD at Columbia University. He defended his dissertation in 1957 and published his first book, *La-Guardia in Congress* (1959) at age thirty-seven. His transition from shipyard worker to soldier, back to unskilled laborer, and then into academia occurred relatively late in his personal trajectory, thus indicating how his status as a veteran of the "good war" both postponed and permitted his incorporation into the university world, signaling the unprecedented enlargement of the public sphere.

Political Delay in the Making of an Intellectual

Until then, Zinn had intervened in the public sphere as an activist, essentially as a union organizer in the shipyards, then as a truck loader (District 65).[23] His militancy actually diversified and intensified in the late forties, as he joined the American Veterans Committee (AVC), which grew to become 100,000 members strong in 1947. The three main demands of the group (international control of atomic arms, an annual salary for veterans, and full support for racial equality), together with its support for the United Nations, were embodied in the following motto: "citizens first, veterans second," thus illustrating a certain continuity with the "social-democratic consensus" inherited from the New Deal.[24] Zinn became a key organizer for the Brooklyn group, which was among the strongest of all chapters, with three hundred members. They called themselves the "gung-ho section," directly inspired by a "Chinese rallying cry." Though their outlook was quite "radical," the group encompassed the Left's diversity, ranging from moderate progressives to communists.[25] However, the fate of the AVC was subjected to larger ideological shifts. Tyler (1966: 429) notes that the group's "experience provides a particularly tidy example of some of the adjustments in American liberalism to that ideological war after 1945." As the spirit of the times changed, a number of "concrete groups" fell apart. AVC, together with Henry Wallace's Progressive Party, was among them.

Although Zinn said surprisingly little about his political activism over those years, he does remember intimidating experiences. Some were collective, such as the Peekskill riots at Paul Robeson concerts in 1949.[26] Others were individual. Interrogated by the FBI in the early 1950s, Zinn (1997b: 37) refused to collabo-rate with the agents regarding his "subversive activities," but felt pressured into destroying his war correspondence, fearing it might be used to incriminate friends mentioned in the letters who were involved in the communist movement.

Described by Zinn as "casualties" of the Cold War, those letters represent what Schrecker has called "a good deal of trauma" that swept over all those even loosely associated with the radical Left, regardless of the fact that only a minority actually went to jail or lost their jobs. In this sense, Zinn's sparse depiction of his activism during the second half of the 1940s may be due to a certain reticence—in other words, psychological fallout from that enduring era.[27]

The rather oblique and complex implications of this culture of fear are also illustrated in Zinn's experience of academia. He studied labor history for his master's degree (1949–1952) and found sympathetic advisors in Harry Carman and James Shenton for his study of the then little-known Ludlow "massacre," which Zinn had heard about by listening to a Woody Guthrie song.[28] Interest in working-class struggles was then still deemed acceptable. George McGovern (1997: 40), for example, studied the 1913–1914 Colorado coal strike for his doctoral dissertation under the supervision of Arthur Link at Northwestern University in 1950–1951.[29] However, when Zinn suggested to his advisor Henry S. Commager that he might conduct doctoral research on the story of Industrial Workers of the World leader "Big" Bill Haywood, he was advised to "stay away from a civil-liberties issue" and to "pick a safer, easier topic" because the "atmosphere was not conducive" to promoting such themes.[30] Zinn turned to the congressional career of Fiorello La Guardia. Though Joyce (2003) identifies Zinn's dissertation as traditional history, a closer look indicates that Zinn approached La Guardia as an independent radical, whose development between the wars (1919–1932) brought his ideals closer to the Progressive Party (despite his Republican Party affiliation) and prepared the ground for the social measures of the New Deal. La Guardia's support for Sacco and Vanzetti and his denunciation of the First Red Scare in the aftermath of World War I resonated directly with Zinn's own immediate surroundings in the early 1950s.[31]

Zinn's years in graduate school can be considered politically passive (relative to his later participation). It is therefore fair to consider Zinn's rise to prominence in the late fifties through the black freedom movement as a time of political resurgence. In this light, the early 1950s may be seen as a period of political delay. From the late fifties onward, in the context of the black liberation struggle then gathering momentum, Zinn combined his academic expertise with new forms of militancy, thus rising to prominence within the public sphere in stages during the following decades (Zinn 1994: 1–12). The publication of *A People's History of the United States: 1492 to Present* (1980) marked a definite turning point. This somewhat belated intellectual coming of age can thus be explained by ideological and sociological criteria.

Retracing a Generational Constellation through Zinn's Personal Route

Zinn's trajectory in the 1950s and 1960s may help to reassess this *delay period* for other public figures of his time. He entered academia as a professor of history and political science by 1956–1957, when he moved to Atlanta, Georgia, to teach at Spelman College (he defended his dissertation a year after he moved south). Others like him reached intellectual maturity well into their thirties and forties, often because the war either imposed or prompted them to reconsider their life priorities.

Joseph Heller, Kurt Vonnegut, and Norman Mailer all interrupted their studies to serve in the war. Like Zinn, Heller (who shared with Mailer a Brooklyn background) underwent training as a B-52 bombardier and later drew extensively on his personal experience to imagine the now-mythical character of his ground-breaking novel *Catch 22*, Yossarian.[32]

Of German descent, Kurt Vonnegut enlisted in the fight against fascism. Imprisoned in Dresden, he witnessed the destruction of the city by Allied bombing in February 1945 and recounted his war experiences in his landmark novel, *Slaughterhouse Five, or The Children's Crusade* (1969).[33] Heller, Vonnegut, and Mailer all became major influences among the youth culture of the 1960s and 1970s, as former SDS activist and history professor Paul Buhle—founder of New Left magazine *Radical America*—remembered recently.[34]

William Appleman Williams features among the most notorious veterans of that age cohort who acknowledged how deeply the war experience affected his professional trajectory. A graduate of the US Naval Academy injured during World War II, Williams chose to enroll at the University of Wisconsin on the G.I. Bill. His urge to study history came from his wish "to try and make sense out of what the hell was going on—the bomb and all that.... History was the best way to figure out the way the world ticked."[35]

The centrality of the war in Williams's intellectual maturation has been thoroughly documented. However, despite the similar insistence to be found in Zinn's work about the defining nature of his experiences in the 1940s, little has been made of it.[36] Table 3.2 points to an underexplored genealogical constellation with a special focus on the World War II age cohort.

WHEN THE OLD LEFT WAS REJUVENATED

Howard Zinn's relocation—from New York City to the Deep South—corresponded to the demise of former networks of the US Left. In fact, this geographical transition coincides with a political decentering of progressive politics that was then under way. The early stirrings of the civil-rights movement were already an indicator of larger changes to come. Journalist-activist Anne Braden, herself a member of Zinn's generation, expressed it well. During McCarthyism, "there was only one thing which could not be suppressed; that was the burning desire of African Americans to be free."[37]

Zinn echoed her view by acknowledging that

> McCarthyism was plaguing colleges and universities throughout the country ... and it may well be that black colleges were a kind of refuge ... for white radicals ... and so white radicals like me, Staughton [Lynd], and others were especially welcome, and since our radicalism was expressed mostly in our views on race relations, well, that fit with the black community quite well.[38]

Zinn's immersion in the black community around Spelman College until the termination of his contract in the summer of 1963 (Zinn left the South in the fall of 1964) led to a number of encounters that map out generational connections among longtime activists (both black and white). These relationships indicate the need to expand our understanding of this intellectual generation beyond cultural

Table 3.2: New Directions in Generational History*

Coming of Age during the New Deal:

Ella Baker (1903–1986)	Bayard Rustin	Richard Wright
Virginia Durr (1903–1999)	(1912–1987)	(1908–1960)
Dwight Macdonald	I. F. Stone	Roy Wilkins (1901–1981)
(1906–1982)	(1907–1989)	Studs Terkel (1912–2008)

Coming of Age during World War II:

Ralph Abernathy	Howard Fast (1914–2003)	Pete Seeger
(1926–1990)	Fannie Lou Hamer	(1919–)
James Baldwin	(1917–1977)	Fred Shuttlesworth
(1924–1987)	Joseph Heller	(1922–2011)
Daniel Bell (1919–2011)	(1923–1999)	Kurt Vonnegut
Daniel Berrigan (1922–)	Richard Hofstadter	(1922–2007)
Philip Berrigan	(1916–1970)	Robert F. Williams
(1923–2002)	Irving Howe	(1925–1996)
Anne Braden	(1920–1993)	William A. Williams
(1924–2006)	Jack Kerouac	(1921–1990)
W. S. Coffin (1924–2006)	(1922–1969)	Whitney Young Jr.
Harold Cruse	Timothy Leary	(1921–1971)
(1916–2005)	(1920–1994)	Malcolm (Little) X
David Dellinger	Norman Mailer	(1925–1965)
(1915–2004)	(1923–2007)	Howard Zinn
Medgar Evers	C. Wright Mills	(1922–2010)
(1925–1963)	(1916–1962)	

Coming of Age during the Cold War:

Noam Chomsky (1928–)	Michael Harrington	Martin Luther King Jr.
Daniel Ellsberg (1931–)	(1928–1989)	(1929–1968)
James Forman	Amiri Baraka	Staughton Lynd
(1928–2005)	(1934–)	(1929–)
Eugene Genovese	Christopher Lasch	
(1932–2012)	(1932–1994)	

*A note about "case selection": sociological delimitations of "public figures" include artists, religious figures, and political activists. This methodology seeks to emphasize the need to bring these categories together so as to change the perception of what is "Left" in the United States In this lens, major players of the Mississippi Freedom Democratic Party are represented by Fannie Lou Hamer in the chart.

and racial lines. Scholars have recently highlighted how African American collective experiences complexify our understanding of the sociology of US intellectuals by emphasizing the different routes—somewhat indirect for blacks—that allowed them to access the public sphere in times of both de facto and de jure racial segregation. The extraordinary circumstances of Zinn's life (moving to a central place for black activism at the onset of the civil-rights movement) led this radical historian to widen his connections with other sociological segments from his age cohort, thereby deepening his understanding of a racial, gender, and cultural diversity that he may never have experienced had he stayed in the Northeast. This brought him closer to white female activist and SNCC adult advisor Anne Braden, as well as to influential novelist James Baldwin. The sheer circumstantial aspect of Zinn's trajectory (it just so happened that Zinn was hired to teach at a black Southern college) is rendered all the more significant as it sheds light on facets of this "good war" intellectual generation at best marginal to the historiography.[39]

Given the influence of black World War II figures in the Southern civil-rights movement, Zinn was bound to encounter some of them. Actually, by his very presence Zinn's role in SNCC serves as additional corroboration to the relevance of this intellectual generation in the movement, beyond racial lines. Zinn encountered Whitney Young Jr. during the first direct-action campaign led with Spelman students with the purpose of protesting racial segregation in the Atlanta public libraries. Then director of the Department of Social Sciences of Atlanta University, Young sought to develop both legal and extralegal strategies, namely, through the Atlanta Council on Human Relations, demanding that the library's board of trustees comply with the charter of American libraries, which banned racial discrimination. Pressure from black students, combined with voluntary de-segregation in other states, led the board to accept desegregation in Atlanta public libraries.[40] Zinn was unaware of their shared generational roots; Young, though, had been deeply affected by his experience of World War II, all the more so as his political coming of age occurred by taking part in the Double V campaign.[41]

Other members of his generation with whom Zinn became associated during the freedom movement include James Baldwin, whom he met during the 1963 Freedom Day in Selma. On this occasion, they both called for federal intervention to protect civil-rights activists. They also shared a common opposition to black separatism, which they expressed during an SNCC strategy meeting.[42] Zinn also became close friends with Fannie Lou Hamer.[43] Hamer is rarely viewed as a World War II generation member, although she was among the oldest members associated with SNCC, together with Ella Baker. A farm worker from Ruleville, Mississippi, Hamer joined the movement at forty-three years old as she tried to register to vote and was consequently jailed and beaten. She rose to prominence during the Mississippi Freedom Democratic Party campaign in the summer of 1964, especially after her moving public testimony of police brutality delivered to the credentials committee at the Democratic Convention in Atlantic City was broadcast nationally.[44]

If the black liberation movement started to sketch out generational connections making up the forgotten World War II generation, the onset of the Vietnam War expanded and strengthened those connections. The antiwar movement brought a number of pacifists to the fore, among them influential figures who had actually come of age during the fight against fascism: David Dellinger, William Sloane Coffin, and through their direct action, the Berrigan brothers.[45]

Zinn met Daniel Berrigan in 1967 through Dellinger when the latter asked both of them to travel to North Vietnam as representatives of the peace movement to meet with American prisoners of war freed by communist authorities.[46] Though generational proximity was not brought up (Berrigan was already a pacifist priest during the war, in contrast with his brother Philip, who volunteered and served in the infantry), the trip itself to a war-torn country served as an intense reminder of

World War II memories. During an air raid in Hanoi, as they took shelter in the hotel basement, Zinn (1994: 126) remembers thinking, "It was a new experience for me—a bombardier now on the receiving end of bombs from the air force I had been a part of. I had that taut feeling in my belly ... fear. I thought, I guess I deserve this." This trip with Daniel Berrigan would lead to a lifelong collaboration as activists and as friends.[47]

Zinn wove other friendships with members of his age cohort during this time. He developed long-lasting relationships with other prominent voices of his age only later, in particular with Kurt Vonnegut. Theirs was a deep connection, despite meeting later in life, in 1997. Zinn remembered having read *Slaughterhouse Five* in the 1960s, together with Heller's novel *Catch-22*. He recalled the "jabs of black humor poking holes in the self-righteous arrogance of the good guys fighting Hitler."[48] In contrast with how he recalled his militant time with Berrigan, Zinn consciously framed his friendship with Vonnegut in generational terms.[49]

BEYOND BINARIES: MISSING PIECES OF A LEFTIST GENEALOGY

Retrieving the forgotten "good war" generation implies that the very concept of Old versus New Left is too narrow to frame the ideological shifts of several age cohorts. Table 3.2 serves as an illustration of the way generational and ideological considerations wrongly overlap. Zinn's age proximity and early empirical similarities with those who are considered emblematic public intellectuals raise new issues about alternative political trajectories—different from the disillusioned radical routes of the New York intellectuals. Now that the latter group is losing its historiographical monopoly, new collective routes may be brought to the fore. Zinn's geographical shifts thus permit us to illuminate the *organizational* component, characterizing, in stages, the *dismembering* of observable or tangible networks on the Left, and the *resurgence* through newly formed groups of radical collective identities (e.g., SNCC).

One common pairing should be addressed specifically here. Howard Zinn and Noam Chomsky are often seen as forming a political group of two—being roughly the same age and having taken near-identical positions on a number of issues over the decades. Despite a political proximity going back to the black freedom movement and the Vietnam War, and despite Chomsky's somewhat legendarily precocious political awakening, his founding experiences occurred in the aftermath of World War II, as the United States rose to military and economic prominence with the onset of the Cold War, ushering in the era of political passivity and triumphalist expertise in academia.[50]

Chomsky shares generational roots with Staughton Lynd—another figure closely associated with Zinn, as they were both history professors at Spelman, immersed in the black liberation movement—and Daniel Ellsberg—famous for the Pentagon Papers and a close friend of both Zinn and Chomsky. For lack of a better term, these postwar public figures may be said to belong to the Cold War generation. This age cohort inherited a common political tradition, but members of this group are differentiated from their forebears because of their distinct formative experiences. Winock (1989) and Sirinelli (1989) note that French intellectuals of this age cohort were a "weak ideological link," precisely because of the overwhelming influence of "concrete groups"—with the numeric superiority of the French Communist Party—strengthened during the 1930s and 1940s, especially during the Resistance.

No parallel situation may be found in the United States; quite the opposite, as the domestic counterpart of the Cold War—McCarthyism—brought about the demise of the political Left. Jack Newfield (1966: 178–204) reinforces such a view as he provocatively terms this age group a "non generation," reaching "adulthood during the 1950s" with a "bank of ideas" void of anything but "a subpoena, a blacklist, a television tube, a gray flannel suit . . . and a blank sheet of paper." To him,

> the New Deal had used up all [its] intellectual capital, and now only slogans were left to cope with the new post–World War II problems of the anti-colonial revolution, the Cold War, nuclear proliferation, and technology and automation.[51]

Although this represents a typically defeatist view of the early fifties, it may not be accurate to conclude that such a generation is also a weak intellectual link—simply serving as a bridge to future, newer political theories rather than functioning as an innovative intellectual generation. Indeed, some African American public figures of that age group range among the most influential of the twentieth century, most obviously Martin Luther King Jr. Together with other thinkers, such as Michael Harrington—author of *The Other America* (1962)—and Noam Chomsky, this remark might point scholars of US intellectual history in another direction.

The very proximity between the founding experiences of the World War II and the Cold War generations may hint at possible crossings between the two cohorts and could indicate an inevitable blurring of lines. Indeed, wasn't Chomsky interested in anarchism as a teenager in the early 1940s?[52] Generational overlapping is accentuated if we consider the New Deal generation. Though a decade older than Zinn, Studs Terkel served in the US Army from September 1942 to August 1943. Unfit for combat because of perforated eardrums, he served in the Air Force on Limited Service and arranged entertainment for soldiers. In *Touch and Go* (2007), he remembered his "avuncular feeling" for the other soldiers, whom he referred to as "kids," who were ten to twelve years younger than he.

To some degree, it remains inevitable for age cohorts to brush against one another and for individuals to share facets of the same *weltanschauung*. However, Terkel came of age as a young adult as Franklin D. Roosevelt was implementing some of the key social reforms of the era. He studied at the University of Chicago in the 1930s and, as an aspiring actor working with the Chicago Repertory Club, benefited from the Works Progress Administration (WPA) programs. His youth experiences were thus informed by the rise of an American welfare state of unprecedented proportions. Zinn, though, came of age as the economy of the country shifted from social programs to preparation for all-out war. Emblematic of this shift, the WPA programs were terminated by 1943. Zinn found a relatively good job as an apprentice in the shipyards. He took part in building war equipment and could have been exempted from military service given the strategic importance of the shipyards in the war effort. Zinn's early work experience is therefore an illustration of the structural changes undergone during Rooseveltian governance.

In addition to the emotional and intellectual intensity of the war experience as such, the sociological specificities of his age cohort were heightened by the consequences of the G.I. Bill for the professional coming of age of a generation of young men and women.[53] Here, age made a significant difference. Zinn recalled feeling alienated from his fellow students at Columbia: "I did not have a social life at Columbia, I skipped half my classes. I already had two kids and worked loading trucks, so if one of my kids got sick, I'd stay home.... I didn't hang out in coffee shops after my classes."[54] The belated and democratized access to higher education for members of Zinn's generation is central to the intellectual trajectories of a number of its public figures. However, such a belated occurrence constitutes a distinctive characteristic of the formative years of the group, setting it apart from the generations immediately preceding and following it.

By contrast, Noam Chomsky's experience of college is of a more typical nature in chronologically formative terms. Chomsky recalled feeling isolated in an intellectual setting marked by a sudden shift in cultural paradigms. Pre–World War II admiration for European intellectual and cultural achievements had given way to a new American nationalism exacerbated by Cold War triumphalism.[55] Deeply shocked by general indifference for the human costs of Hiroshima and Nagasaki and the dangers of the arms race, Chomsky developed early on a sense of political loneliness. Contrary to Terkel or Zinn, his worldview had not been informed by the Rooseveltian social-democratic national consensus, but rather had been marked by the radical reconfigurations of the Cold War both at home and abroad, namely, by the creation of the State of Israel in 1948. The meaning of the latter event was reinforced by his personal aspirations—together with his wife Carol Schatz—to settle in a kibbutz in the early 1950s.[56] Such enthusiasm for communal life was shared by yet another member of this generation, Staughton Lynd, thus indicating a possible route to explore further in order to characterize more fully the processes of coming of age for this age cohort growing up under the sun of US economic optimism and, in the shadow of the atomic bomb, paradoxical existential pessimism.[57]

More than definite answers about the generational identities of three different age cohorts, I seek to point to new methodological directions, with a special emphasis on sociological and historical characteristics, and an insistence on the need to displace ideological considerations that too often foreground generational studies in the United States. The equivalence drawn by Novick (1988) between age and countercultural behaviors detracts from more objective considerations. Lynd and Zinn were colleagues at Spelman and shared experiences as activists in the black liberation movement in and around SNCC. (Lynd was a key organizer of the Freedom Schools during the Freedom Summer of 1964.) Their political proximity deepened in opposition to the Vietnam War, leading Novick to group these historians together because of their leading roles within the radical caucus of American historians. The landmark conflicts opposing Lynd with historian Eugene Genovese on the topic of Marxist interpretive frameworks for US history make it difficult to view these two scholars as anything but enemies. Precisely, their "furious oppositions" over the nature of the American Revolution or the societal role of the radical historian should be scrutinized as closely as political agreements. As adolescents, Lynd and Genovese were involved in the communist movement, experiencing the ultimately unbearable orthodoxy of a declining political party. These two scholars may be said to share a *weltanschauung* that led them to come down, systematically, on opposite ends of a number of matters. It is precisely because political oppositions form dynamic systems that scholars of generational history should take them seriously.[58]

Approached without ideological blinders, Howard Zinn's atypical trajectory should continue to serve as a laboratory of ideas—methodological, epistemological, and circumstantial—in the larger remapping undertaken in this study. The open-ended nature of our generational remapping (Table 3.2) suggests the nature of the larger work in progress presented here. Once simplistic categories no longer obscure our reading, the field of generational politics is open. It may be revisited, augmented, and reconfigured to the benefit of both activists and scholars who understand the importance of renewing our prism of analysis of both the theories and practices of the US Left.[59]

CHAPTER 4

Thinking the Radical Public Intellectual

The Exemplar of Howard Zinn

Paul Reynolds

It is time that we scholars began to earn our keep in this world.
—*Howard Zinn, "The Uses of Scholarship" (1997c: 499)*

The philosophers have only *interpreted* the world in various ways; the point is to *change* it.
—*Karl Marx, the 11th of the Theses on Feuerbach (1845)*[1]

The editors identify one of the purposes of this text examining the life and work of Howard Zinn as "rescuing the man from the mythology." Arguing that Zinn is an exemplar of a particular form of intellectual—a radical public intellectual—and drawing from Zinn's life and work some issues and lessons for radical intellectuals today might sound dangerously close to returning the man to a mythos. It is not. When the subject of inquiry is the radical intellectual, Zinn is valuable—in what he said, what he did, and how he lived.[2]

At a time when the idea and performance of the radical intellectual are critically scrutinized by both those who look to intellectuals for critical contributions to radical leadership and those who seek to silence them, exemplars are an important way of exploring what it means to be a radical intellectual and what we should expect from them. They are important because they embed the ideas and concepts of a "radical intellectual" within people in their particular conjuncture—space, time, and terms of political and ideological struggle—and so "humanize" the discussion. Radical intellectuals cannot be saints or ideals—indeed a common theme among traditions of radical thought like anarchism, Marxism, and feminism is precisely to avoid the idealization and reification of the human condition.

Zinn would probably have been indifferent as to such an enterprise and skeptical of its meaningfulness unless its value lay beyond intellectual retrospection or scholastic thesis. The man who famously observed, "We publish while others perish," held a qualified approach to the role and work of the intellectual, particularly within the context of the academic and media "industries" that grew alongside the expansion of the university systems from the 1950s and 1960s.[3] However, what is at stake is both intellectual and political. Contemporary politics, media, and higher education are replete with voices who claim to speak authoritatively of the needs and aspirations of the oppressed, the dispossessed, and the marginalized. The "radical intellectual" has become a space occupied by voices ranging from academics to journalists to commentators to political activists, and the consequence of this expansion has generally been an impoverishment of what is regarded as intellectual work and those who engage in it.[4]

If the radical intellectual is to play a critical role in the voicing or articulation of those who suffer from abuses of power, structured social inequalities, and political and social injustices, they have to be more than the repositories of soundbites, ill-considered opinions, and poorly conceived arguments and involvements by poseurs and imposters. The extent to which radical voices are regarded as serious interventions in a contemporary politics dominated by reactionary and conservative voices and unconvincing liberal responses is important. Understanding their impact makes a real contribution to critically assessing and enabling the accounting of contemporary politics and framing and articulating alternative agendas, and speaks directly to the authenticity and credibility of radical politics. Assessing Zinn as an exemplar provides a realistic yardstick by which to measure the claims and performances of radical intellectuals.

This discussion of Zinn is structured into three parts. First, it is necessary to say something about what a radical intellectual is and what issues and tensions are present in thinking about the radical intellectual. That scaffolding then allows for a consideration of Zinn's exemplar—in his political and academic writing and campaigning—of a radical intellectual. This leads to a closing reflection on the legacy he leaves and the inspiration for those who follow.

In doing so, the discussion will place particular emphasis on two of the three "spheres of attention" that Bird, Silver, and Yesnowitz outline in their introductory chapter—activism and academia. It will also, inevitably, speak to the thematic framework they suggest: democracy, disobedience, danger of neutrality, dual convictions, and disposition. This is a workable summary of the substance of Zinn's intellectual heritage, and so is useful in organizing an understanding of Zinn as a radical intellectual.

THE RADICAL INTELLECTUAL

Studies of intellectuals generally fall into two genres: the sociocultural and the historical-biographical. The latter focuses on the intellectual biographically, presenting intellectual endeavor within life history and/or tracing the intellectual within their historical context and the characterizing features of their time and place.[5] The concern of the author of such studies is to present an interesting intellectual life, with a greater or lesser explication of the intellectual's ideas according to how far it is explicitly an intellectual biography. Where the study is less focused on one intellectual and more on an intellectual movement or a particular historical period or movement, the intellectual is characterized and explored within that context and conjuncture.

Sociocultural studies are focused less on the intellectual than on the ideas, political movements, and intellectual context within which the intellectual worked. These studies focus far more on the political, cultural, and social impact of the intellectual's ideas and their applications in governance and policy or (more often) dissidence and protest.[6] Here, the intellectual is a conduit for ideas and action, often understood in those terms and conceptualized as a subject of debate in understanding what form the intellectual takes in particular societies and conjunctures, or what roles, functions, and characteristics the intellectual occupies and expresses.

When talking about the different forms of intellectual that might be distinguishable within a particular society or conjuncture, or seeking to develop a *genus* of intellectuals, it is the latter, more conceptually informed studies that exhibit the relevant focus. Yet exploring the individual intellectual in situ and contrasting the consideration of genus against particular lives and intellectual work are of critical importance—hence the value of appraising intellectuals like Zinn.

The radical intellectual is a particular form of intellectual that emerges with the development of Western capitalist, imperialist modernity, and becomes the subject of particular characterizations in relation to critiques of capitalist societal development. This is not to say that there were not radicals who used their intellectual labor to explicate radical ideas; organize collective mobilizations and struggles; and signpost strategies and interpretations of social trends, developments, and phenomena prior to capitalist modernity.[7] Capitalist modernity provides the basis for understanding these intellectuals within systems, structures, and categories that progressively make their role, functions, and characteristics distinctive.

The radical intellectual is invariably a *public* intellectual.[8] They generally neither constrain their analysis to within disciplinary boundaries or fields of specialization, nor restrict them to the academic setting where knowledge creation, development, propagation, and transfer are only conditionally political. The public intellectual extends their voice beyond the initial narrowly confined expertise they may have to broader questions of politics, culture, or science, often seeking to explicate the direct contribution that intellectual work can make to social and public problems. The public intellectual therefore has an awareness of—and engagement with—political activism, the cultural milieu, and the media in advancing their critical positions.

Richard Posner (2003) is instructive in his critical gaze on the development of the public intellectual and his withering critical commentary on the quality of public intellectual thought since the 1960s. Posner's concern is with the explosion of opportunities for (particularly campus-based) public intellectuals to posture and position from the 1960s onward, and the lamentable quality of a significant proportion of that discourse and absence of regulatory forms of reference or redress. Although he recognizes the heterogeneity of intellectual contributions to public debate, his caution is against the detriment of much of what passes for intellectual discourse in public, without sufficient means for intellectuals to be held accountable or responsible for scandalously poor, popularized production that seems motivated largely by markets and celebrity.

Posner concludes that mechanisms for academic judgment, such as available archives for tracing the pedigree of such intellectuals' contributions, might allow better discernment of whether an intellectual has something to say to the public.[9] Posner struggles with a definition of "public intellectual" and his general critique of quality in relation to his statistical analyses is problematic, but his general point remains extremely important—the progressive bankruptcy of the idea of public intellectuals by the decline in quality of intellectual output in the public domain.[10] It signposts a possibly inevitable decline in quality in the stretching of intellectual discourse from specialist to generalist, and with the particular forms of media cultures that articulate this public discourse—television, newspapers/periodicals, and webcasts. Increasingly, intellectual contributions become little more than transient verbiage with little credit or credibility.

The public nature of intellectual engagement presents a contradiction for the intellectual—the danger that the act of entering into the public realm can diminish the quality of their intellectual work. Where connected with the university, for example, public intellectuals risk representing their work as little more than opinion and conjecture by association, against the necessity of intellectual input into political decision and judgment, public debate and deliberation, and cultural choices and understandings. The radical intellectual would, on the level of individual choice and trajectory, be as much vulnerable to this devaluation of their work as any intellectual, and perhaps more so in hostile political environments and conjunctures. Against that, the role and functions of a radical intellectual in their political commitment and connection with the subjects of their intellectual work should provide a discipline against the temptations of superficiality.

At one level, the intellectual is inherently radical since it is the exploration, public exercise, and propagation of ideas, and the very questioning central to intellectual life, that locates the intellectual—in part at least—in a critical relationship with their social, political, and cultural norms, values, hierarchies, and orders. The cardinal exemplar often claimed for the intellectual is Socrates, represented as vocationally devoted to intellectual truth and discourse, a gadfly who questioned Greek complacency until he was finally put to death and accepted execution to act to his truth.[11]

What is different about the development of the intellectual in capitalist modernity is the development of discreet and specific functions for intellectuals within the developing political infrastructures of the representative-interventionist nation-state, public bureaucracies and corporate agencies, the expanding university sector, and the developing mass media. Intellectuals become particular (identifiable) participants within the sociopolitical system, absorbed with its service or set against it. Whereas the scholar at court, professionals (often clergy or lawyer), academics, artists, and "men of letters," and even court jesters were antecedents to the intellectual, two features of change in modernizing societies give rise to the intellectual as a particular category.

First, modernity requires the development of administrative bureaucracies and expert advice, typically within the nation-state, which gives rise to an expansion in numbers and specific roles for people engaged authoritatively in intellectual work, developing ideas, and translating them into programs of action. The expansion of public space within civil society and of the institutions that occupy those spaces and produce knowledge, typically the mass media, further expands the demand for intellectual workers. Further, there is a development and expansion of the university as an institution that provides the intellectual labor skilled for these roles and functions. In this respect, intellectuals begin to be seen as a distinct social category, most prominently in the emergence of an *intelligentsia* in Russia, *intellectuels* in France, and *gebildete* in Germany—cultural and social elites within the social structure.[12]

Second, two specific characteristics of modern intellectuals separate them from those who came before: they are progressively secularized and beyond aristocratic patronage. Although many were still domiciled within state and institution structures, their role was, by degrees, neither as prescribed nor as deferential to authority. In the interests of technological and economic progress, intellectuals in the service of the development of bourgeois capitalism were regarded as crucial in undermining traditional prejudices and values that stood in the way of modernity's progress, just as conservative intellectuals were charged with their defense. Intellectual life thus occupied a political and public as well as a social and cultural space, and correspondingly, there was greater opportunity for a plurality of voices to emerge.

The radical intellectual can be traced to the emergence of critical modern voices theorizing social and political transformation from the early nineteenth century.[13] Socialist intellectuals like Henri de Saint-Simon, Karl Marx, and Friedrich Engels developed their oppositional "science" to bourgeois liberal capitalism, while liberals like John Stuart Mill offered critical voices from within that evolving liberal democracy. The public awareness of "the radical intellectual" as a "voice of truth" was fired in Europe at the end of the century by the unstinting campaigning of the writer Émile Zola on the Dreyfus case, with his seminal open letter to the French president: *J'Accuse . . .*![14]

Marx, in his ceaseless critical engagement with worker struggles, organizations, and agitation alongside developing a corpus of critical work that constituted his political economy, provides an exemplar for the radical intellectual.[15] Whereas the most recognizable radical intellectuals were inherently political, Charles Darwin gives an example of the more diffident and even reluctant radical, following where his science took him rather than embracing and politicking for change, yet by force of argument and the public reception of his science, making a public impact. Darwin also provides for another distinction, between those intellectuals who intentionally engage in political agitation and those primarily moved by the science, reluctant progenitors of the politics it involves.

The particular subject of their intellectual discourse is said to be *radical* because it is in some way critical of and requiring transformation within the society they criticize. Hence criticisms of structural features—capitalism, class oppression and exploitation, patriarchy, racism and imperialism, homophobia— or phenomena—the Iraq War that began in 2003 (or, alternately, that reignited after a persistent policing action following the 1990–1991 war), or reductions in welfare and public spending in Western representative democracies after the 2009 financial crisis. At the same time, radicalism encompasses sustained and consistent critical positions and disparate, issue-based engagements. Rhetorically, the appellation of "radical" might range from an attractive branding of quite conventional ideas and a claim to independence of thinking that obscures self-interest to a more robust and consistent and less popular position on social trends and phenomena.

One example of this from the UK might be Anthony Giddens. His initial sociological work on Marxism and development of "structuration theory" gave way to a succession of vacuous slight polemics that sought to provide Tony Blair's New Labour with a "third way" philosophy while smoothing his way to the directorship of the London School of Economics and a seat in the House of Lords, and ultimately involvement with the Monitor Group that sought to provide legitimacy to Libya's Muammar al-Gaddafi.[16] Giddens provides an example of an intellectual who writes radically early in his career but for whom it could be argued that influence and reward denude his contribution to contemporary intellectual life of value.

At the core of radical intellectual work is the notion of critique—of a sustained and critical, questioning approach, not only to contemporary societies but to the ideological and theoretical positions that ground contemporary critique. Indeed, the role of the intellectual within radical politics is often partly seen as sustaining critical reflection on radical theory, politics, and organization. If the intellectual has a particular role within radical politics, it is precisely to act as "provocateur" to radical comrades as much as to proselytize to the public. This role might not, in times of political struggle, be as public, polemical, and visible as with the criticism of opponent and oppressive regimes, but it nevertheless remains part of the intellectual contribution—making sense of and reflecting on changing times and the terms of struggle.

Hence, the radicalism of an intellectual involves a dialectical relationship between the crafting of a critical position from which to sustain critique and a sense of engaging that same critical awareness to the critical position adopted. This position is partly constituted through a perceived relationship to truth and partly constituted as a contradictory position of being an aspect of opposition, resistance, and struggle and yet a critical voice, never quite with the unreserved commitment and zeal represented by the voice of opposition and struggle.

Lenin exemplifies the intellectual as political leader in the "vanguardist" sense, where the role of the intellectual is to propagate an oppositional politics in the context of struggle, upheaval, and revolutionary possibilities.[17] The vanguardist intellectual suppresses those critical to the service of the party and the cause, party discipline and cohesion, and the strategic imperatives of struggle in a particular conjuncture. The vanguardist intellectual propagates persuasive messages to rally support and mobilize struggles; engages in polemics in debate against ruling powers; serves the educational role of engaging in indoctrination within the party and its supporters; and plays a part in contributing to party strategy, characterization, and organization. The vanguardist's relationship to the party and its political functions mirrors the role of the intellectual in giving service to the state, conditionally and not uncritically but based on a balance of judgments (except where such intellectuals actively embrace the ideological positions and vested interests represented within the state).

Antonio Gramsci's notion of the radical intellectual—contrasting organically embedded working-class intellectuals with the more traditional intellectual, alternately detached and rarefied in iconography—extends this analysis.[18] Gramsci's intellectual occupies the role of carrier or vessel of the consciousness and constitutive history of a class and the values by which the class constitutes itself. Their intellectual work has a critical function in maintaining a sense of class belonging and struggle, and a connection with the struggles of the present and the struggles of the past.

Gramsci's intellectual is organic in the sense that this relationship reverses the categorization of the intellectual as apart from other categories of labor, and instead recognizes intellectual labor as embedded in social relations. The intellectual is a product of mediated social forces and relations, not of intrinsic intellectual qualities at variance in individuals. Intellectual labor can be extended in all, and is denied and withdrawn from them in order to maintain class stratification where those who are processed into intellectual labor through the education system are more likely to serve those institutions within which they are set—organizations with formal interests within the existing order—even if their voices can substantively question orthodoxy (as with the universities). As Gramsci observes, the intellectual's relationship to the means of production is indirect and mediated by civil society and the state.

Gramsci's intellectual is not simply organically linked to their class and that class's location within the social relations of production, but draws the development of their intellectual abilities and their connection with their class from the lived experience of working within that class, often experiencing directly forms of labor that are not intellectual and so not by their very nature detached from working-class experience. It is that embeddedness and its practice that is the basis of their fulfilling their role in a class. In a sense, the intellectual who is not engaged with their class, continually and praxeologically committed to engaging theory within practice, is diminished in their intellectual work and life. Gramsci explores how this functions in talking about the work of intellectuals in composing books, articles, and periodicals that extend their perspectives and interpretations across their class.[19]

This radical "organicism" is conceived by Gramsci within the context of party work and working-class struggle, in which the intellectual occupies a space that simultaneously defines and negates itself. Through researching, writing, and speaking, the intellectual builds and articulates bodies of knowledge, disseminates the tools of critique, and composes the continuous narrative by which struggle is contextualized in its history, philosophical principles, and political aims, mobilized to particular conjunctural struggles, and propagated to nourish class engagement.

Intellectuals whose practice approximates this Gramscian organicism include Tony Cliff, Ernest Mandel, and Daniel Bensaid, each important to Marxist parties in the UK, Belgium, and France, respectively.[20] Alternatively, near contemporaries of Zinn, Herbert Marcuse and C. Wright Mills, provide examples of radical intellectuals in a more complex relation to class struggles and political-party disciplines in the postwar period. Marcuse's intellectual trajectory came through work with the Frankfurt School, positions in the academy, and an involvement with revolutionary and particularly student movements in the 1960s. While inspiring critique and protest, there was no sustained relationship with programmatic political organization.[21] Marcuse's example emphasizes the importance of the mass media and the university as sites by which radical intellectuals could take a more intellectually independent position, driven in Marcuse by critical engagements with the vagaries of Soviet communism and party organization.

Mills, more a nomadic, maverick character, made radical contributions situated within the academy and largely according to his own independent position.[22] Mills's thinking on the intellectual is clear: the intellectual should be a critical independent voice for reason, making the link between private troubles and public issues that should ignite political consciousness. Intellectuals should aspire neither to serve the state nor to act as philosopher-kings, but rather to hone and exercise their craft—of necessity requiring a sense of dialectical interplay between political commitment and the detachment of critical independence.[23]

This criticality can be extended through the post-colonial gaze and the imperative to "let the subaltern speak."[24] For intellectuals to frame the voiceless, articulate their interests and aspirations, and expose their oppression and dispossession is part of the radical role. Nevertheless, here a sense of reflexivity is important. The intellectual should consider to what extent their propagation enables the voicing of the voiceless, and the relationship between what such voices might say and how their articulation represents it. This returns the intellectual to a critical focus on their own role and work as well as the injustices or inequalities they work on.

A claim of *independence* in thinking and voicing, often at hazard to themselves, returns radical intellectuals to the iconography of Socrates. This is Michel Foucault's *parrhesiastes,* speaking to truth without rhetorical flourish but with the commitment of positions they take ownership of and responsibility for.[25] The notion of "speaking truth" implies both a modernist element of expertise giving greater insight and a vocational commitment to the truth as something to be presented regardless of consequences. Foucault conceives of this speaking to truth within the context of archaeological and genealogical studies that destabilize existing orthodoxies and emphasize the conditionality of any bodies of knowledge, disrupting easy distinctions and so raising questions about what a radical intellectual might be.

This brief sketch of the radical intellectual highlights a number of characteristics that are central to understanding how we might make assessments of those who present themselves and their work as radical intellectuals:

- Radical intellectuals usually claim a direct *association* with what is regarded as a disempowered "minority" (often a sizable and significant population rendered "minority" only by an absence of power). They might come from being part of this "minority" or from a political commitment to its cause. This advocacy and involvement is motivated by either a deep and committed position with respect to that particular "minority" or a commitment to advancing causes such as human rights, social and economic equality, or legal and social justice that will benefit that "minority" and others similarly disempowered. They bear an antipathy to inequalities, injustices, and prejudices or political acts that bring suffering to the many. What brings these forms of voicing together is their relationship to dominant social and political interests and voices.

- The relationship between the radical intellectual and the people is a complex one because the intellectual seeks to neither parrot popular prejudices nor speak a popular voice from an often somewhat-more-privileged or -powerful position. Nevertheless, the act of articulating protesting positions binds the intellectual to the people (often characterized in terms of class, community, gender, ethnicity, and other social divisions). The claim of association, however evidenced in commitment, work, and membership, can be constituted more organically as a relationship by which the radical intellectual is constituted and sustained by an embeddedness in political struggle, the extent to which can be distinguished only by the particular balance of class forces and individual trajectories within material, historical conjunctures.

- The radical intellectual is fundamentally praxeological. The production of ideas, interpretations, and explanations and their articulation are inextricably interwoven with political action. Not only does the intellectual capacity to engage in such analysis leave a moral imperative to follow the prescriptions of that analysis in oppositional politics, but the richness of such understandings comes from embedding that intellectual work in the lived experience of those that the intellectual work seeks to enable, empower, and represent. The radical intellectual is rarely committed simply to exegesis. Participation and engagement with struggles and those who struggle are regarded as central to the maturation of the intellectual's work, the moral authority their voice carries, and the acuteness of their analysis.

- The radical intellectual plays a leadership function within radical opposition, either as propagandist, producer of political rhetoric and criticism, or strategist. These roles might be within particular organizations or as public intellectuals whose work is influential to the cause of such organizations and has prominence within public forums.

- The radical intellectual is often a subject of criticality and contradiction. The nature of intellectual work in the service of radicalism necessarily involves the possibility of the turning of critical thinking to the canon of oppositional orthodoxies as well as dominant and oppressive discourses and interests. The critical voice might be suppressed strategically at particular moments of struggle—or in the case of Lenin and the Bolshevik leadership, constrained to a prolonged political program in circumstances of revolutionary struggle—but it remains a potential source of dissent and discontent with revolutionary organization.

While such criticism can be regarded as healthy and positive, party discipline and cohesion often mitigate toward its restraint. Where it more visibly flourishes is in the radical voices outside of particular political organizations and in a more conditional relationship with political struggles, though a level of detachment might detract from the richness of the intellectual's work in its articulation of ideas to its constituencies.

These characteristics provide criteria from which some assessment can be made of Howard Zinn as a radical intellectual—not for the purpose of validation, or because the ascription is in itself valuable, but because such a discussion contributes to our understanding and appreciation not only of Zinn, but of the tradition of radical intellectuals within which he can be understood.

Zinn as Radical Intellectual

Zinn's detachment from the values of conventional academic study might have been a product of his working-class background, with his undergraduate and graduate education coming after experiences of manual labor and military service. Indeed, his higher education was sponsored by the G.I. Bill that offered working-class veterans an opportunity to study. It is precisely this sort of lived experience that may have contributed to the intensity of Zinn's commitment to intellectual work as representing and enabling others who could not speak. It might equally explain Zinn's interest in those who were neglected in 1950s and 1960s America (outside narrow intellectual and left-wing circles) or pointedly ignored until they forced their way into the public gaze. Hence the prominence of narratives of the working class, Native Americans, and black Americans in *A People's History of the United States* (1980). Such a background has a strong relationship to the idea of the organic intellectual, not from party work but from a lived connection with the people and their travails.

Zinn's intellectual trajectory is characterized, again and again during his career, by three features. First, a detailed, meticulous, and careful scholarly interest in investigation combined with a desire to reach the widest audience. This is typified by projects ranging from the detailed accounts in *A People's History of the United States* to his coverage of the Colorado coal strike of 1913 and the Ludlow Massacre of 1914 to his research on World War II and Vietnam, notably *Vietnam: The Logic of Withdrawal* (2002 [1967]). This scholarly interest is firmly directed to episodes that are neglected in canon or marginalized in their political focus. For Zinn, intellectual work is valuable insofar as it exposes exploitations, oppression, and immiseration; empowers readers to understand their place and act to change it; and provides the intellectual support for those at the forefront of political action. Zinn is, by example and by what he propagates, praxeological.

The form of much of his scholarship is revealing. While Zinn clearly has a substantial knowledge of his subject, he refuses the traditional academic style of close referencing and dense prose. Much of his writing focuses on what individuals say and do as a means of drawing in the reader. Referencing is minimized and his prose style adopts a poetic form to enable readers to be taken along with a strong narrative rather than work their way through an informative but less accessible text.

Zinn's first priority, above any academic recognition, in his writing and his ceaseless lecturing is to get the messages *out*—to be debated, engaged with, and adopted by those campaigning and those who wish to be informed in order to make informed decisions. Like Marx's writing, when Zinn's is reduced to its initial forms of publication from its collected volumes, much of the work is journalism or in the pamphleteer tradition rather than in longer academic treatises—influencing public debate and not academic discourse. In this respect, Zinn is an exemplar of a radical intellectual of the nineteenth century—a ceaseless and energetic commentator whose academic career, once established and given due care in respect of responsibilities to students and demonstration of scholarship, is subordinate to his intellectual role.

Secondly, he has a desire to make a political intervention, whether against the racial segregation and violence in the South in the 1950s or against the Vietnam War in the 1960s and 1970s. Zinn's writing is polemical and definite in its argument, notably in his being the first intellectual to devote an extended study to seeking the immediate withdrawal of US troops from Vietnam in 1967. This intervention involves participation in protest movements and in protest activity as well as writing, not in a leadership capacity but as someone delivering insight and vision from which political leaderships fashion their strategies and critiques. *Vietnam: The Logic of Withdrawal* is a leadership intervention insofar as it speaks the voice that is fragmented and veiled at the time of publication, but Zinn does not parlay it into a formal leadership role in organizational terms, and that particular form of contribution runs through Zinn's contribution to the political struggles he supports.

In a sense, this is an astute negotiation of the fine line between the intellectual as truth-teller and the intellectual as contributor to sustained political campaign. Zinn's negotiation of the contradiction between critique through party strategy and propaganda—where polemic and definite argument is required—and critique as speaking to truth is successful because throughout his working life he clearly acts without personal interest other than the political values he believes in. His relative detachment from the organizational politics of intellectual life partly explains this. For example, he clearly recognizes affinities between his work and Marxism, but he is never committedly involved in a Marxist program of campaigns (though frequently he finds himself standing with Marxists in his political work).[26] Zinn's development of a reputation for integrity and commitment to political struggles effectively carves the space for him to work successfully within this contradiction—by effectively negating the importance of *his* voice in favor of the importance of the messages he *voices*.

It is also worth noting that his concept of intellectual work is wider than lecturing, journalism, and larger research-oriented texts. In "Testifying at the Ellsberg Trial" (Zinn 1997c), he reflects on the role of expert witness as a crucial intellectual role in supporting test cases that challenge the law and its existing privileging of the powerful.[27] In this respect, Zinn recognizes the opportunity to employ public spaces for radical intellectual action.

Finally, his critical eye is consistently unsparing. It is evidenced most prominently in his persistent criticism of the tolerance of racial prejudice by the US government, the illegitimacy of its use of nuclear weapons against Japan, and the project of the war in Vietnam. At the same time, his critical writings include discussions of violence, direct action, and strategy that contradict and contest the views of his ideological allies. Again, Zinn negotiates this tension by adopting a consistent position that celebrates workers and dispossessed peoples taking power without any strict alignment to organizations other than those focused on particular goals, such as civil rights and against the Vietnam War, that contain broad constituencies of opinion. His critical eye is interesting when he incorporates himself into his historical reflections, notably in "The Bombing of Royan," where his own guilty involvement becomes a provocation to uncover the callous logistics of war.[28]

Zinn's writings might be best accessed in *The Zinn Reader: Writings on Disobedience and Democracy* (1997c).[29] Since Zinn compiled this collection and provided an editorial narrative throughout, the composition of the collection is as revealing as the individual pieces. He does not concentrate on pieces that might be most valued for their scholarly form. The pieces clearly reflect a narrative that is personal, insofar as the accompanying commentaries clearly reflect different moments in Zinn's intellectual development. Yet the collection represents in the main a selection of pieces that chart his key concerns of empowering the marginalized and key interventions in episodes like Vietnam or other historical episodes where the United States has acted unjustly. It is a political collection. It is not Zinn at his most impressive or most poetic—but as a collection it speaks of an editor who wants to stress the questions of injustice and change that have occupied him through a lifetime of scholarship.

In the introduction to *The Zinn Reader,* Zinn reflects on his own approach to the role of the intellectual in academia:

> There was never, for me as teacher and writer, an obsession with "objectivity," which I considered neither possible nor desirable. . . . Those who talk from high perches about the sanctity of "facts" are parroting Charles Dickens' stiff backed pedant in *Hard Times*, Mr. Gradgrind, who insisted his students give him "facts, facts, and nothing but facts." But behind any presented fact, I have come to believe, a judgment—the judgment that *this* fact is important to put forward (and, by implication, other facts may be ignored). And any such judgment reflects the beliefs, the values of the historian, however he or she pretends to "objectivity."[30]

Later, he observes,

> I am by profession a historian, by choice an activist, and the tension between the two was something I thought about constantly. What was the proper (or improper) role of the historian in a time of crisis?[31]

Zinn's answer in his personal practice seemed twofold: speak truth to power and voice those who have not been heard—or who have been deliberately ignored. The tension Zinn refers to did not stop him from putting politics before career when he was dismissed from Spelman College in 1963 for "insubordination" after supporting students against the college administration. It did not stop him from writing a visceral condemnation of US politics and ceremony that led to the cancellation of his column with the *Boston Globe* in 1976. He wrote the following in "Whom Will We Honor Memorial Day?":

> Memorial Day will be celebrated ... by the usual betrayal of the dead, by the hypocritical patriotism of the politicians and contractors preparing for more wars, more graves to receive more flowers on future Memorial Days.[32]

The first of the quotations on intellectual work underlines a feature of Zinn's approach to intellectual discourse that has already been touched upon. Peppered throughout his work are not intellectual references of Plato, Aristotle, or the historical cast of theorists and philosophers that populate intellectual discourse (though when relevant they are drawn upon—as evidenced in the essay that references Plato's arguments on the obligations we bear to the state, "Law and Justice").[33] Zinn's rhetorical style is to draw from literature or politics, connecting with the reader or listener through relatable figures, references, and anecdotes. Zinn might have discussed objectivity in terms of historiography or positivist science, but instead he conveys the essence of the thing—all intellectual explanations involve judgments, with the "facts" often telling less than half the story.

This rhetorical style achieves three goals: it connects the reader and the writer in "common knowledges"; the writing is of a style that reads as if spoken and so gives a sense of narrative, as the best fictional stories do; and it privileges the message over the medium—Zinn writes not to further Howard Zinn's reputation, but to make a statement he thinks important. It is a rhetoric designed for political consumption—and if that means that his illustrations and evidence are not fully referenced, that is not Zinn's primary concern.

In "The Uses of Scholarship," Zinn gives his most extended critical discussion of the role of the intellectual in the context of academia and contemporary intellectual culture.[34] Written in 1969, it is an astute condemnation of the introspective intellectual in academia. The "knowledge" industry and its power, and the culture of disinterested scholarship, objectivity, disciplinarity, and neutrality are calmly exposed and undermined:

> We might use our scholarly time and energy to sharpen the perceptions of the complacent by exposing those facts that any society tends to hide about itself.... We need to expose fallacious logics, spurious analogies, deceptive slogans.... We need to dig beneath the abstractions so our fellow citizens can make judgments on the particular realities beneath political rhetoric. We need to expose inconsistencies and double standards. In short we need to become the critics of the culture, rather than its apologists and perpetrators.
>
> Along with inspirational visions, we will need specific schemes for accomplishing important purposes, which can then be laid before the groups that can use them.... Thus, we will be acting out the beliefs that always moved us as humans but rarely as scholars. To do that, we will need to defy the professional

mythology that has kept us on the tracks of custom.... We will be taking seriously for the first time the words of the great poets and philosophers whom we love to quote but not to emulate.[35]

This represents the essence of Zinn as intellectual—in the service of the dispossessed and oppressed, where the intellectual is a praxeological figure with a mission to serve democracy and to avoid the temptations and comforts of the structures of intellectual life, where leadership is by example and not title.[36]

ZINN AS EXEMPLAR

What does Zinn offer as an exemplar, as a study of the radical intellectual? It seems to me the critical contribution he makes is threefold. First, much of his credibility comes from occupying a contradictory space—both authoritative intellectual voice and political rhetorician—with credibility and integrity. It is curious to focus first on personal characteristics, but it is precisely Zinn's transparent commitment to the subject of his endeavors and to the importance of public debate and knowledge that underlines that integrity. When reading or listening to Zinn there is a sense of singular engagement with a voice that is intellectually focused on speaking truth as it appears. Zinn's interests, affiliations, and worldview *as an individual intellectual* are detached from his voice. His voice occupies the space of the issue under discussion, in support of those impoverished by it. Zinn's lifework is not characterized by intellectual or academic ambitions; it is characterized by the work he produces, the struggles to which he contributes, the dispossessed or oppressed with whom he stands in solidarity. In an intellectual world replete with career paths, lucrative opportunities, and media exposure, Zinn is one of a small minority of intellectuals whose voice seems curiously *uninfected*—even though his political, cultural, and intellectual "footprint" is substantial—by the status or reward his role offers.

We must be careful not to reify Zinn and fail to see him as having the same human frailties and desires as others, but in considering how a pedigree and reputation in work and actions allow an intellectual such as Zinn to develop respect as an intellectual, it is difficult not to be drawn back to Plato and Aristotle and their concerns about cardinal virtues that elevate the ethical status of the actor. Perhaps one way of thinking about the contemporary radical intellectual is not to devise roles, functions, and criteria by which they are identified, but rather to focus on characteristics—through the use of exemplars—that are present in the radical intellectual. (This approach is best suited to thinking about those who show excellence in their craft.) Perhaps the best radical intellectuals arise from those characteristic virtues—and regardless of the mediums and techniques of media, for example, they cannot simply be made or produced.

Second, Zinn's engagement with politics, with communities of the unvoiced and dispossessed, is a central feature of what he offers as an exemplar. Whether within a particular tradition or political organization or with a less definite belonging, whether organic within or committed to those who are the subject of the intellectual's articulations, what Zinn exemplifies is the necessity of seeking to speak with engagement and commitment—and against the temptations of detachment and neutrality as a means of preserving status. Zinn was a praxeological intellectual, a *parrhesiastes* whose intellectual engagements are not fettered from speaking to truth as he conceived it. This truth, both in what is expressed and what relationship—organic or otherwise—it represents, is a critical feature of the intellectual and signposts the third contribution of fidelity to critique and to scholarship. In Zinn, there is the example of an intellectual who recognizes his work is valuable only if the critical capacity is sustained beyond the oppositional political targets to friends and self, in what is produced as intellectual labor, for what purposes, and in what form.

These contributions seem to suggest that a critical engagement with Zinn as an intellectual, and an approach that seeks to explore the radical intellectual by exemplar—in this case through Zinn—moves away from a political programmatic guide, or vocational or career pathway, or type of engagement with scholarship and public intellectual life. Rather, it suggests that the exemplar lives the craft of the radical intellectual because it is driven by the exemplar's speaking to truth and their sense of the craft, where such extraneous influences often impede rather than enable their work. Zinn might have identified with Etzioni's (2006: 2) recall of the Marquis de Concorcet, who claimed public intellectuals should be devoted to "the tracking down of prejudices in the hiding places where priests, the schools, the government and all long-established institutions had gathered and protected them." Or as Edward Said has observed,

> The intellectual represents emancipation and enlightenment, but never as abstractions or as bloodless and distant gods to be served. The intellectual's representations ... are always tied to and ought to remain an organic part of an ongoing experience in society.[37]

In thinking how we might encourage the development of a new generation of radical intellectuals—critical, meticulous and careful, informed speakers of truth and reflexive thinkers whose first thought is of their work—Zinn offers us not an exemplar as an ideal, but an exemplar as a craft worker whose work characterized his life. When we look to current radical intellectuals, whether the self-conscious Slavoj Žižek and his interplay of political and "pop cultural" play or Jeffrey Sachs's influential engagements as advisor and academic, it gives a sense of how difficult the role Zinn exemplifies can be. The value of his exemplar, however, is critical as a means of measuring radical intellectuals against the best traditions of their heritage—and Howard Zinn provided a worthy measure to reflect upon.

ZINN IN THEORY

CHAPTER 5

Against All Authority

Howard Zinn's Pragmatic Anarchism, Active Resistance, and Radical Democracy

Eric Boehme

For Howard Zinn, anarchism reflects the best of Left and progressive political theory and practice in the United States. Though Zinn read Marx first, it was the American anarchists Henry David Thoreau, Emma Goldman, the Industrial Workers of the World (IWW), and Sacco and Vanzetti who inspired Zinn's pragmatic anarchism. These anarchists used direct action, confrontation, and disobedience, but also claimed rights and protection from the state by publicizing the inability or unwillingness of the state to support free speech and free association. American anarchism is pragmatic, responding to the unique conditions of the American working class divided by race, ethnicity, religion, language, and skill differences. As a result, Zinn believed that anarchist history and practice showed a path for radical democracy to achieve economic and social justice.

Zinn's unique contribution to civil-rights historiography is to demonstrate how the organizing structure and the direct action of the Student Nonviolent Coordinating Committee (SNCC) reflected the local autonomy, loose networks, spontaneity, and tactics of American anarchism.[1] SNCC members lived and worked in the local communities they organized in the Deep South. SNCC is the great exemplar of an American pragmatic anarchism combining direct action and community-building based on the "activism of everyday life" with confronting the state to protect the rights of free speech and association. Pragmatic anarchism replaces a theory of revolution with a theory of anarchism in everyday life, represented by the collectivism and mutual aid shown when we rely on others, and the resistance and direct action of creating alternative institutions and culture.

Howard Zinn's anarchism is a strange sort of political theory. There are no ideological or metaphysical "theories" behind his normative ideas, just a consistent questioning of the paradoxes and problems of authority and a critical attack on imbalances and inequalities of power. His lifelong investigation of authority and power was deeply informed by a kind of pragmatic anarchism in his thought and public life. He embraced the anarchist tactics of direct action and participatory democracy; the harmony of means and ends; and the anarchist challenge to all forms of privilege, hierarchy, and inequality.

Yet Zinn's political theory and praxis often put him at odds with two key tenets of anarchism: a complete rejection of state power in all forms and a tactical argument for the use of violence as part of a theory of direct action.[2] In the great American philosophical tradition of pragmatism, Zinn argued for the use of state power to protect minority rights and create distributive justice in the economic realm.[3] Zinn's political theory relies upon the "tensions" or the "dual convictions" (which the editors identify in Chapter 1) between opposing all authority and pragmatically advocating forms of authority such as the state's protection of free speech and association. Zinn's writings on the New Deal and big government make it clear that the state ought to be used to protect minority rights and pursue economic justice. But this idea is in tension with Zinn's arguments for direct action and radical participatory democracy.

Howard Zinn's critique of liberalism and political representation, his advocacy of direct action and participation as enacting an equal society, and his suspicion of political parties and centralization all reflect anarchist themes. Yet similar to the dilemma faced by one of Zinn's favorite American anarchist groups, the IWW, Zinn's theory of radical democracy paradoxically relies upon the state to protect the rights to free speech and free association.[4]

First, Zinn's anarchism critiques liberal constitutional government and political representation as deeply flawed because they perpetuate the divisions and inequalities between rich and poor, elites and masses. Any theory of radical democracy needs, therefore, to answer two crucial questions about the superiority of direct participation to all forms of representation: How should one participate? And, why participate?[5] For Zinn and other anarchists, participation reflects both the social and the collective bonds we have with each other. Direct action forces the state to confront the demands of oppressed groups directly, not mediated through political parties. By answering the question of how to participate, Zinn again draws tactically on pragmatist arguments. Direct action, then, serves two pragmatic and realistic purposes: First, participants in direct action enact the everyday forms of anarchism present within us as humans. Second, by pressuring the state to enforce its own laws, Zinn uses anarchism tactically, to make a series of points about the relationship between the government and the people. Participants in direct action publicize the hypocritical nature of the state and pressure states to live up to their own laws. Direct action shows the irrationality, lies, and deceptions of the state. Direct action and disobedience are keys to a healthy democracy.

Direct action also serves to build anarchist institutions and culture in everyday life that reflect true relations of freedom and equality.[6] Here Zinn engages the debate about whether direct action is a means to an end or an end in itself. Direct action could be the means of pursuing revolution or pursuing justice. Or direct action could be an end in itself, either in the form of permanent revolution or enacting the already existent forms of anarcho-collectivist relations.[7] I argue that Zinn wants those who in engage in direct action to be doing so for the purpose of justice.

Unlike many anarchist proponents of direct action, Zinn does not believe in revolution.[8] As a means, direct action is a tactic and a pragmatic choice that should submit to the greater demands of justice. Here Zinn's answer to the question of "why participate?" is different than that of other anarchists, such as David Graeber (2009) or Todd May (1994), who see direct action as an end in itself. Zinn's theory of radical democracy encourages direct action both outside of the state and within it, tied to and assuming the legitimacy of the state's enforcement of its own law. Zinn's arguments for direct action saw the confrontation as creating a counterweight to the actions and truth claims of the state. Rather than seeing direct action as the end itself in enacting consensus decision-making and anarchist organizational principles, Zinn wanted direct action to be a means to the end of greater justice, equality, and liberty. For instance, Zinn might interpret the Arab Spring uprisings and Occupy Wall Street protests as groups pressuring for a stronger or reformed state and more regulation of the economy. However, an anarchist like David Graeber would see Occupy Wall Street as direct action where "one proceeds as if the state does not exist,"[9] both through pressuring the state through a "diversity of tactics" and through internal radical democracy where protestors rigorously stick to consensus and democratic participatory decision-making.[10]

Today, in a global situation characterized by conditions of disaster capitalism and recession, with the continuing war on people of color and the poor, social movements can learn from Howard Zinn's pragmatic anarchism. By combining participatory and radical democracy with minoritarian rights protected by the state, Zinn argues we can create and prefigure a just society of free and equal persons. Zinn's pragmatic anarchism continues to offer a reinvigoration of anarchist practice toward the everyday and the possible. Zinn's pragmatic anarchism is politicized and participatory, focused on specific policies and issues and willing to use the state to pursue larger aims of justice, equality, and liberty.

THE AMERICAN ANARCHIST: HOWARD ZINN'S PRAGMATIC, PLURALISTIC RADICAL DEMOCRACY

Despite his occasional support for the state, Howard Zinn's political theory is anarchist. His very definition of "democracy" is anarchistic, tempered by a pragmatism that uses the state when necessary. In public lectures or interviews, Zinn always used stories of American anarchists to highlight the need for direct action, the complicity between the government and big capital, and the individual's responsibility to actively resist all forms of hierarchical authority.[11] In his analysis of the Declaration of Independence, Zinn (2003c: 17) argues "that governments are artificial creations" beholden to the people. For Zinn (2001e: 31), the Declaration of Independence stands for the fact that government "is set up to give people an equal right to life, liberty and the pursuit of happiness and that if it fails to do this, we have a right to 'alter or abolish it.'"

Zinn consistently references activists in the American anarchist tradition, dissenters like the abolitionists and Henry David Thoreau, the workers in the railroad unions of 1877, the Haymarket and Ludlow martyrs, Emma Goldman, Alexander Berkman, the IWW, and SNCC. It is the duty of citizens to reveal the truth about governments. The people always need to be suspicious of government because, as I. F. Stone said, "governments lie." Zinn (2003c: 13) takes Stone's remarks a bit further: "Not just the US government, but, in general, all governments lie.... The anarchists have something there."

The brief stories Zinn tells about American anarchists unfairly arrested or deported for speaking or assembling reveal the inherent hypocrisy of liberal democracies. Zinn lists a series of events in which anarchists were involved, including the railroad strike of 1877, the Haymarket strikes in 1886, the IWW-led Lawrence Textile strike in 1912, and the Colorado coal strike of 1913 that culminated in the Ludlow Massacre of April 1914. Zinn reflected, "to dig into the details of the Colorado coal strike was to affirm and strengthen whatever radical criticism I had of American society. It was class struggle, American-style." Zinn's case study here shows the "intense and violent" actions of big capital supported by the state, as John D. Rockefeller used "courts and soldiers to burn and kill," the media and press to cover it up, and highlighted "the role of a liberal federal government (the Wilson administration) in cooperating with the mine owners."[12] This episode is one of the stories he most liked to recount, showing how government repression is nakedly used to uphold capitalist property relations.[13] Zinn's list of American anarchist heroes, like the lists in Walt Whitman's poetry, reflects the diversity, flexibility, and radically imaginative approaches anarchists have taken to active resistance against the state. Each figure on Zinn's list serves as a symbol. Each has a story attached, illustrating the tactics of confrontation, disobedience, and direct action against the state.

Zinn saw the government repression of radicals like the IWW becoming the blueprint for the state later to spy on, prosecute, and break up many of America's most radical and dissenting social movements, labor unions, and activist groups. He believed that the state never has respect for its own law and order; it picks and chooses which laws it wants to defend. Zinn (2002 [1968]: 24) asks, Why should we always obey the law? His answer reflects a broader "Zinnian anarchist" radical democratic theory: those outside the law must always pressure the state into a kind of tenuous balance or equilibrium. Zinn (1997c: 410–411) says, "We need to go outside the law, to stop obeying the laws that demand killing or that allocate wealth the way it has been done." He (2001e: 38) sees in American history the failures of liberalism and reform, that all the "slow steps" against slavery or exploitation of the working class never did as much as the direct action of radical abolitionists and labor unions. As he says,

> *No* form of government, once in power, can be trusted to limit its own ambition, to extend freedom and to wither away. This means that it is up to the citizenry, those outside of power, to engage in permanent combat with the state, short of violent, escalatory revolution, but beyond the gentility of the ballot-box, to insure justice, freedom and well-being.[14]

Democracy and justice can never be actualized, but always must be fought for, approximated, compromised, and struggled with—democratic citizens must be active and wary of government. Even in stable democracies, Zinn still sees the necessity for critique, dissent, and disobedience as never-ending.

For Zinn, the anarchists who dissented against war are particularly indicative of the state's power to take away and suppress free speech and association rights; he describes those anarchists as groups "the government felt they had to suppress to successfully prepare for and carry on a war."[15] The Palmer Raids and the deportations of thousands of immigrants, including Emma Goldman and Alexander Berkman; the arrest and trial of Sacco and Vanzetti; and the passage of the Espionage and Sedition Acts showed elites' fear of the threat of anarchist antiwar protest. Zinn (2003c: 53) jokes in a speech, "Anarchists in general, being antiauthoritarian and not trusting governments (I can't imagine why they don't trust governments), are instinctively antiwar." Zinn's activism against the wars in Vietnam, Afghanistan, and Iraq place him within a long tradition of anarchists protesting wars by the United States through civil disobedience. Zinn's antiwar protests put him with "Henry David Thoreau committing civil disobedience to protest the Mexican War, Eugene Debs and Emma Goldman and Helen Keller criticizing US entrance into World War I" (2003c: 62).

In 1964, Zinn called himself a "half-serious" anarchist.[16] By 2008, in answer to a question about globalization, Zinn said, "I am an anarchist, and according to anarchist principles nation states become obstacles to a true humanistic globalization."[17] Zinn's arguments for radical participatory democracy and for economic and social justice recognized anarchism as the closest approximation of a true democracy where liberty and equality worked together rather than being at odds.[18] For Zinn (1997c: 464), anarchism represents "a full democracy in which neither foreignness nor poverty would exist." In the foreword to his play on Marx, he wrote that he became interested in anarchism as a critique of Stalinist communism and classical Marxism, but also through his own personal experience organizing and participating in the civil-rights movement in the South. Zinn (2010b: 106) places SNCC within the American anarchist tradition: "SNCC, without any self-conscious theorizing, acted in accord with anarchist principles: no central authority, grassroots democratic decision-making."

Howard Zinn's pragmatic anarchism is a kind of patchwork quilt pulled together by strands of democratic socialism, Left-libertarianism, and cosmopolitan claims for recognition and protection of universal rights.[19] Free speech, free association, and disobedience are the foundations for Zinn's theory of radical democracy.

He defines democracy as not the counting up of votes but the counting of actions. At the very heart of democracy is a variety of tactics or actions taken on the part of people directly participating. In 1970, Zinn argues for a vision of democracy led by active participatory citizens. "What can a democracy possibly mean if not that people assembled whenever and wherever they can, for whatever reason, may express their preferences on the important issues of the day?"[20] Disagreement, dissent, and civil disobedience are part of how democracy improves itself. Zinn argues, "Democracy must improve itself constantly or decay."[21] Resistance through dissenting speech and disobedient associations are integral to radical democracy; in fact, disobedience and dissent mark the participation of an engaged citizen.

> Protest beyond the law is not a departure from democracy; it is absolutely essential to it. It is a corrective to the sluggishness of "the proper channels," a way of breaking through passages blocked by tradition and prejudice. It is disruptive and troublesome, but it is a necessary disruption, a healthy troublesomeness.[22]

Resistance to bullying even became the motto of his anarchist teaching. "In my teaching ... I made clear my abhorrence to any kind of *bullying,* whether by powerful nations over weaker ones, governments over their citizens, employers over employees, or by anyone, on the Right or the Left, who thinks they have a monopoly on the truth."[23] Political participation pressures the state, but it also engages individuals to act as caring citizens and moral warriors for social and economic justice. Resistance and rebellion are part and parcel of democracy and "the struggle for justice should never be abandoned because of the apparent overwhelming power of those who have the guns and the money and who seem invincible in their determination to hold on to it."[24] Struggle and direct action against overwhelming odds define the improvements democracy must make to itself.[25]

No doubt Zinn's intimate knowledge of the history of American anarchism as well as his practical activism with SNCC during his time at Spelman College influenced his pragmatism. One of the SNCC volunteers recalls, "No one really needed 'organization' because we then had a movement."[26] But like the antebellum abolitionists and the Wobblies, SNCC had to negotiate the tensions of criticizing and rejecting the state and the political system wholesale with calling on the state to protect free speech and free association. As with other American anarchists, these "new abolitionist" student civil-rights workers also developed a vibrant oppositional culture.[27] By building local communities with alternate or "shadow" institutions like the Mississippi Freedom Democratic Party, SNCC reflected the anarchist theory of "dual power" of working within existing institutions while creating new institutions where the ideas of freedom and equality were practiced every day.[28]

In American politics the conditions of local autonomy that help direct action foster autonomy can also intensify the tyranny of the majority. Jim Crow segregation in the South was a tyranny of the majority, intensified by local autonomy and the majority support given by white Southerners.[29] A recurring theme of Zinn's pragmatic anarchism is how often the federal government turns a blind eye to enforcing its own laws protecting speech and association. As Zinn lays bare in his SNCC book, civil-rights workers were being beaten and killed while federal agents stood by and watched.[30] As SNCC workers exercised their speech and association rights helping to register black Southerners to vote, their civil rights to equal protection under the Fourteenth Amendment were being violated. The "day-to-day protection" the federal government failed to provide SNCC workers showed "that the absence of central power may simply leave the citizen victim to the greater tyranny of local or private power."[31]

Zinn knew governments cannot be trusted to follow their own laws. His experiences as a young teacher and activist working with SNCC in the South gave him firsthand knowledge about the inability and unwillingness of the federal government to enforce its own laws. But Zinn also argues that an anarchist's relationship to law in America must be pragmatic. Direct participation and direct action by the people rely on speech and association to engage in any critique of the state. Yet who will protect those freedoms of speech, freedoms of association, freedoms of petition, and in general, the freedoms of dissent and disobedience vital to any thick, robust democracy? We must call on the state to protect civil liberties and apply the guarantee of equal protection under the laws. Zinn writes of his disagreement with a longtime pacifist-anarchist over whether the police should be protecting civil-rights marchers: "But I was not an absolutist on the use of the state if, under popular pressure, it became a force for good."[32] In a federalist system, popular pressure can play one branch of government against another, one level of federalism against another. For example, both states and the federal government can either protect or take away the civil liberties of individuals in protesting, organizing, or association. The history of the selective incorporation of the Bill of Rights in constitutional law reflects the push and pull of federal and state jurisdiction over civil liberties.

The IWW used the judicial branch in its free-speech fights in the Northwest and California, particularly in Spokane, Fresno, and San Diego.[33] Wobbly anarchists decided to stage a mass protest by filling the jails with workers who continued to step up onto the soapbox and get arrested for disobeying local laws restricting freedom of speech. Thus, as SNCC did, the people must engage in direct action, disobedience, and dissent to keep governments honest and display the hypocrisy and injustices of the state.[34]

Disobedience and dissent also dramatize the continuing need for society to become more pluralistic and recognize the autonomy and identity of racial, ethnic, gender, sexuality, or religious differences. Zinn (1991: 232) writes, "It is the special gift of oppressed groups to reveal universal truths." Disobedience is key to actualizing Enlightenment principles against the arbitrary exercise of power. For Zinn, our rationality makes consent and legitimate exercises of power important parts of anarchism. If the state exercises power arbitrarily—for instance, by ignoring the injustices of racism or sexism, the people have an obligation to disobey and, through the publicity generated by disobedience, shine a light on those injustices.[35]

Zinn's contribution to anarchism is to argue for a kind of equilibrium between the disruption and direct action of the people pressuring the government to recognize new needs and demands balanced with calling upon the state to protect civil liberties and even act affirmatively to provide things like social-welfare provisions. Zinn (2001e: 58) writes, "We want government, responding to the Lincolnian definition of democracy, to organize, with the efficiency that it ran the G.I. Bill, that it runs Social Security and Medicare, a system that gives free medical care to everyone and pays for it out of a reformed tax system which is truly progressive."

Zinn always maintained a positive outlook toward the chances and goals of social movements. This admonition to always be wary of the government was also a pedagogical tool. Zinn knew how to inspire students and activists into direct action: give the nuts-and-bolts basics for how to organize a social movement. Just by describing what these movements did, his books serve as organizing manuals spelling out how to mobilize a social movement. Certainly Zinn was writing "history" for the purpose of social action.[36] He was excited about the 1999 protests in Seattle and the anti-globalization movements, and he continued to see large gatherings of people as important pressure points on the political process: "Civil disobedience—protest *beyond* the law—is so precious for the rectification of wrongs in our society; because whatever the law says in theory, as applied by the federal courts, including the Supreme Court, in practice it is not a dependable shield for free expression."[37] The people themselves must act to protect those wrongs, or act to force the state to do so.

Direct Action, Active Resistance, and the Question of Revolution

Anarchism begins and ends with a fundamental animosity to representation and the state: "The larger, central theme of anarchism: the rejection of representation.... The state is the object of critique because it is the ultimate form of political representation."[38] This original and fundamental critique of representation naturally dovetails with critiques of hierarchy, authority, and the state. Zinn (1991: 254) writes that representation "has serious problems. No representative can adequately represent another's needs; the representative tends to become a member of a special elite; he has privileges that weaken his sense of concern over his constituents' grievances." Nowhere is the failure of both liberal constitutionalism and representation more apparent than with the experience of African Americans in the United States: "The history of blacks in the United States exposes dramatically the American political system. What that history makes clear is that our traditional, much-praised democratic institutions—representative government, voting, and constitutional law—have never proved adequate for solving critical problems of human rights."[39]

Democracy without struggle and direct action is only representative, with voting as the weakest form of political participation.[40] Actually, "Voting is most certainly overrated as a guarantee of democracy. The anarchist thinkers always understood this."[41] Zinn critiques liberalism and voting because of the massive disconnection people feel from the elites who supposedly represent them. Liberal constitutional government has a kind of "moral and emotional remoteness ... from the deepest grievances of its citizens."[42] According to Zinn's practical anarchism, laws where neutral procedures are (ostensibly) applied equally to everyone are not enough to protect rights. Representation and liberalism run on procedures rather than direct participation and "the rich will dominate any procedure."[43] One must claim rights if the government is not protecting or acknowledging them (as in economic rights) because the government and the state uphold the law and the status quo.

For anarchists, representation poses the problem of the development of elites, but perhaps more importantly, makes autonomous actors dependent on others for their power. Todd May (1994: 47) describes this as the "transfer of power" involved in representation. Rather than governing ourselves through action, we let someone else act for us. Colin Ward links representation to the powerlessness of individuals. For Ward (1988 [1973]: 19), "They are weak *because* they have surrendered their power to the state. It is as though every individual possessed a certain quantity of power, but that by default, negligence, or thoughtless and un-imaginative habit or conditions, he has allowed someone else to pick it up, rather than use it himself for his own purposes." Anarchist suspicions of representation and voting push them to theorize direct participation as the only way that radical democracy can flourish. Zinn (1991: 255) quotes Emma Goldman speaking to female suffragists: "Every inch of ground [man] has gained has been through a constant fight, a ceaseless struggle for self-assertion, and not through suffrage."

Direct participation is the only way individuals can overcome the problems of liberalism, with its distance from politics, its apathy and privacy, as well as the problems of Marxism with the hierarchies and top-down control of party mem-bers. Like other anarchists, Zinn believes anarchism reflects a radical democracy of direct participation, where citizens govern themselves in institutions organized around decentralized and local power. He argues that if government does not provide rights, "working people have to gain these rights for themselves. The openings ... that working people have found reside in something that they had to really enlarge and create for themselves—things like the right to strike and withhold their labor."[44]

Just as Zinn saw the strike as a tactic of direct participation, anarchists like Todd May and Richard Day argue that flexible and adaptable "tactics" are best for organizing dissent, rather than the blueprint-like rigidity and hierarchy needed to implement "strategies." May situates anarchism within a tradition of tactical political philosophy where struggle occurs across multiple sites, using a diversity of practices. Rather than focus "strategically" on taking power over a central node or institution like the state, May (1994: 11–12) argues that "there is no center within which power is to be located.... [Thus] anarchists seek political intervention in a multiplicity of irreducible struggles." Tactical activity is decentralized, local, diverse, and, most importantly, multiple in simultaneously attacking a variety of hierarchies. Prioritizing decentralized and multiple places of action and critique also means that anarchists look for revolution and change society-wide, not just in politics. Finally, as Richard Day (2005: 8–9) argues, tactics are based on anar-chist connections of "affinity" grounded in equality rather than the hierarchical relationships demanded by "strategies."

The array of tactics Zinn advocates ranges from redefining classic American myths and specific words (like American exceptionalism, anarchy, and law and order) to teaching and personal relationships as forms of activism to mass direct action against the state. Even Zinn's choice of material in his writing reflects a broad diversity of sites of struggle: everything from the macro-structural sites of antiwar demonstrations and civil-rights sit-ins to the more local struggles for democracy in institutions of higher education to the micro-local and deeply personal places of struggle waged by a teacher who "can't be neutral on a moving train."[45]

Zinn's theory of radical democracy is a flexible tactical theory, based on a diversity of practices that can be applied in various contexts and circumstances, yet linked to the ideas of affinity and decentralized equality among all participants in a kind of "everyday anarchism." Zinn's work with SNCC shows both the strengths and weaknesses of these organizing strategies while also reflecting the intense personal relationships of affinity developed by the activists as they engaged in everyday forms of anarchism. For Zinn, SNCC drew pragmatically on many elements of American anarchism. Direct action was just such an adaptable tactic. In 1964, he wrote, "Civil disobedience as a technique spread in a matter of weeks from sit-ins in restaurants to stand-ins at movies, kneel-ins at churches, wade-ins at beaches, and a dozen different kinds of extra-legal demonstrations against segregation" where "spontaneity and self-sufficiency" were the characteristics of these organizing tactics.[46] The SNCC activists engaged in two primary activities of everyday anarchism: direct action and community- and culture-building.

SNCC saw the failures of representation, specifically after the National Democratic Party refused the Mississippi Freedom Democratic Party equal representation at the 1964 convention. Zinn's disillusionment with the regular political channels echoes the anarchist tradition by arguing for the importance of direct action as a form of political participation. Zinn (1991: 258) observes that "What has worked in history has been *direct action* by people engaged together, sacrificing, risking together, in a worthwhile cause." (Emphasis in original). In an interview, he relays the story of Emma Goldman getting up in front of a crowd in Union Square and encouraging people who had no money to take food from stores as direct action:

> It's called direct action. That's what anarchists believe in. You don't sign petitions. You don't lobby. You don't visit your legislator. You take direct action against the source of your problem. That's what workers do when they go on strike; it's what women do when they take direct action against men, or against the source of their oppression.[47]

Moreover, he writes that direct action is

> a deliberate use of power to effect the most change with the least harm.... It disturbs the status quo, it intrudes on the complacency of the majority, it expresses the anger and the hurt of the aggrieved, it publicizes an injustice, it demonstrates the inadequacy of whatever reforms have been instituted up to that point, it creates tension and trouble and thus forces the holders of power to move faster than they otherwise would have to redress grievances.[48]

But direct action should not lead to revolution or mass violence. Rather, if the goal and the ends of direct action are to achieve justice and human rights, revolution and violence would create a disconnect between the means and the ends.[49]

Direct action is a set of tactics used by anarchists for particular ends. Because anarchism is essentially a moral and organizational theory,[50] the means and ends for anarchists must be in harmony. Mikhail Bakunin's break with Marx was over this question.[51] As Todd May (1994: 48) writes, "For anarchists, the goal must be reflected in the process." But what is the nature of revolutionary practice and how ought we to engage in promoting institutional change? Certainly the question of how institutional change should happen has long vexed the revolutionary traditions of Marxism and anarchism. In order to fully realize our potential as communal beings, many anarchists have argued that a full and complete revolution must take place where both capitalist economic relations and the state are destroyed.[52] However, unlike the Marxist focus on political revolution and capturing the apparatus of the state, anarchists focus on creating and advancing social revolution through everyday anarchism and building institutions of "dual power."[53] Zinn's anarchism is never utopian but is pragmatic and realistic. Like the British anarchist Colin Ward, Zinn argued that revolution is impractical and utopian.[54] In "Nonviolent Direct Action," first published in 1966, Zinn addresses the question of how institutional change happens. He analyzes war, revolution, and gradual change, finding all three insufficient. Zinn writes that early revolutions "justified the relatively small amount of violence required to fulfill them." Zinn (2001e: 36) argues we cannot look to revolutions as the chief means of social change because "the power of weapons in the hands of the ruling elites makes popular uprisings, however great is the base of support, a very dubious undertaking."

Direct action causes disruption and pressures the state, but it also engages individuals in participation where they experience real autonomy. "Direct action aims to achieve our goals through our own activity rather than through the actions of others. . . . Where it succeeds, Direct Action shows that people can control their own lives—in effect, that an Anarchist society is possible."[55] While direct action eventually confronts the state through protest or street actions, the focus is on creating new institutions and culture based on equality, mutual aid, and autonomy. An anarchist acts as if "the state did not exist and leaves it to the state's representative to decide whether to try to send armed men to stop her."[56]

DUAL POWER AND COMMUNITY: ZINN'S EVERYDAY FORMS OF ANARCHISM

Revolution is not feasible. But we do not need revolution any longer because anarchism already exists in our everyday life. Zinn understands direct action as serving two pragmatic and realistic purposes: First, participants in direct action enact the everyday forms of anarchism present within us as humans. At the same time, direct action serves to build anarchist institutions and culture in everyday life that reflect true relations of freedom and equality.[57] Through the creation of industrial democracy and workplace democracy, through the culture and community built by the Wobblies in their halls or in migrant farm-worker camps, or through the institutions of culture and community built by SNCC, people participate directly themselves in building these new institutions within the shell of the old. Zinn (2001e: 94) writes, "We are not totally free but our strength will be maximized if we act *as if* we are free." (Emphasis in original.)

For Colin Ward, anarchism reflects the underlying moral infrastructure of mutual aid and federation that naturally exists between us, covered over and twisted by capitalism and the state. Ward argues that mutual aid and federation are part of our natural tendency to cooperate. Thus there is no need for a revolution but "rather a prolonged situation of dual power in the age-old struggle between authoritarian and libertarian tendencies, with outright victory for either tendency most impossible."[58] It is through these experiences of everyday life, where we enact and engage in mutual aid and federation, radical democracy and the critique of the individual, that direct action creates alternative culture and community where "we are forming the structure of the new society within the shell of the old."[59] Ward (1988 [1973]: 14) says an anarchist society "is always in existence, like a seed beneath the snow, buried under the weight of the state and its bureaucracy, capitalism and its waste, privilege and its injustices, nationalism and its suicidal loyalties, religious differences and their superstitious separatism.... [Anarchism] is a description of a mode of human organisation, rooted in the experience of everyday life."

For Zinn, the history of American anarchism is filled with examples of the robust and lively culture and community created by people in alternative institutions within the shell of the old. It is through culture, the arts, and community where we express the nature of our true being and humanity through connection and collective action. Zinn especially admires the Wobblies and the community and culture they built. It is through the songs and poems of the Wobblies' "little red songbook,"[60] the collective persona and culture of the Wobblies built through solidarity in the jails, at the campfires of hoboes and migrant farm workers, in the polyglot immigrant cultures of organizing in East Coast factories where the internationalism and solidarity of Wobbly anarchism lies.[61] Even in populations as tenuous, mobile, and difficult to organize as hoboes, migrant workers, and unskilled immigrant workers from many different countries with many different languages, Zinn finds a vibrant, electric, individualistic-collectivist anarchist community of labor centers and Wobbly halls.

Anarchists look for those places in experience and everyday life where we exhibit autonomy, mutual aid, and equality. In his 1969 article on "The New Radicalism," Zinn echoes the anarchist impulse toward creating dual power institutions as a way of enacting or actualizing anarchist principles: "The New Left's idea of parallel organizations, as a way of *demonstrating* what people should do, how people should live, has enormous possibilities: freedom schools, free universities, free cities ... self-controlled communities. But also, free, active, *pockets* of people inside the traditional cities, universities, corporations."[62] The goal is to "create constellations of power outside the state to pressure it into humane actions, to resist its inhuman actions, and to replace it in many functions by voluntary small groups seeking to maintain both individuality and co-operation. Black Power, in its best aspects, is such an endeavor."[63] Indeed, it is anarchism's focus on community and the social revolution, and the importance of art and culture, that are reflected in the turn that Zinn takes later in his life, when he starts writing plays and engaging with the mass media and popular culture.[64] In Zinn's play on Emma Goldman, where he highlights her work in culture as she speaks on Ibsen, the family, or women's issues, he celebrates the anarchism of everyday life, the politicization of culture, where every hierarchy and every authority are challenged through the creation of alternative institutions. Truly Zinn's work and life were *against all authority.*

CONCLUSION

Howard Zinn's theory of radical democracy derives from his commitments to practical, pragmatic, and everyday anarchism. Zinn theorizes radical democracy as active, participatory, and in the best traditions of anarchist direct action. Yet Zinn also pragmatically calls on the state to protect rights, particularly for numerical or racial/ethnic minorities. For Zinn, true democracy, real democracy, cannot be representative. Democracy must include the direct participation of individuals. He believes this vision of equality, mutual aid, and autonomy is realistic and possible. He lists the decentralized, local, direct democracies in ancient Athens, the early Soviet workers' councils, and town-hall meetings and neighborhood associations as examples of actually existing radical democracies. Zinn (1991: 256) writes, "It is conceivable that a network of direct democracy groups could register their opinions in a way that would result in some national consensus" where participation and discussion would better reflect the needs of people.

Zinn sees hope in the social ontology of collectivist anarchism that looks at what we have in common.[65] Using examples of anarchism in action, like the 1871 Paris Commune and the anarchist collectives organized during the Spanish Civil War, Zinn (2006b: 10) writes that when the anarchists took over the city of Barcelona, "There was no overarching authority. There was no police state. People policed themselves. There was virtually no crime. People shared things. There was no stark inequality. People traded goods and services and took care of one another." He looks to radical democracy and anarchism for optimism and hope:

> The struggle for justice should never be abandoned because of the apparent overwhelming power of those who have the guns and money.... That apparent power has, again and again, proved vulnerable to human qualities less measureable than bombs and dollars: moral fervor, determination, unity, organization, sacrifice, wit, ingenuity, courage, patience.[66]

Zinn would approve of the direct-action strategies of the Arab Spring movement and the Occupy Wall Street protests. Zinn would see disobedience through free speech and association. He would marvel at the nonviolent overthrow of Egypt's Hosni Mubarak and be saddened by the Syrian government's crackdown and massacres of protestors. Zinn would see both the potential and the pitfalls for Occupy Wall Street's attempts to force the state to allow occupation of public areas by citizens using political free speech. Both movements are anarchistic in their self-organization and decentralized decision-making structures. And both the Arab Spring and the Occupy movement reflect the Zinnian anarchism of direct action and confrontation, publicizing and confronting the state through the rights of free speech and association.

CHAPTER 6

The Forbidden Word

Howard Zinn as Anarchist

Žiga Vodovnik

> The Wright Brothers' first plane flight lasted only twelve seconds, but the Kronstadt Commune already lasted almost a month.
> —*Howard Zinn, Speech at B-Fest film festival, Athens, Greece, 2009*

"As for my fame (God help us!) and your infame, I would be willing to exchange a good deal of mine for a bit of yours. It is not hard to write what one feels as truth. It is damned hard to live it."[1] So concluded Eugene O'Neill, the playwright and winner of the Nobel Prize for Literature in 1936, in his letter to the (in)famous American anarchist Alexander "Sasha" Berkman. It is not hard to imagine that another American radical, Howard Zinn, might have received a similar compliment had O'Neill written the letter decades later and not on January 29, 1927. Throughout his life Howard Zinn inspired many, not only with his radicalism and complete dedication to the political struggles of the day, but also because of his politics and political ideas that defied any easy compartmentalization, as confirmed by the recently released FBI files pertaining to Zinn, where he is described alternately as a communist, socialist, Marxist, and even a social democrat.[2] Yet similar difficulties with understanding Zinn's political thought have not been limited to outside observers. Many political organizations on the Left have tried to point to him as providing support for their political platform. After Zinn's unexpected

death in January 2010, similar attempts to gloss over his politics gained new ac-
celeration, with one label again missing—forgotten or omitted—in the ensuing
heated discussions. The forbidden word: *anarchist.*

We cannot really blame them since the breadth and depth of Zinn's politics
are hard to match, but it still comes as surprise that his anarchist inspirations and
aspirations have been overlooked, even though Zinn himself often described his
political philosophy as anarchism. For instance, in the foreword to his play *Emma,*
on the famous anarchist-feminist Emma Goldman, Zinn writes,

> Coming to the faculty of Boston University in the fall of 1964, I was introduced
> to another new faculty member whose field was philosophy. Learning that I was
> joining the political science department, he asked: "And what is your political
> philosophy?" I replied, half-seriously, "Anarchism." He looked at me sharply
> and said: "Impossible!"[3]

It was at Boston University that Zinn taught the seminar "Marxism and
Anarchism" for many years, and his course "Introduction to Political Theory" also
relied heavily on anarchist political thought. Syllabi for the course show that the
reading list included Peter Kropotkin's *Mutual Aid: A Factor of Evolution*, Mikhail
Bakunin's *God and the State*, Emma Goldman's *Anarchism and Other Essays* and
Living My Life, and Alexander Berkman's *What Is Anarchism? (The ABC of Anarchism)*, while Zinn's own notes include Giovanni Baldelli's *Social Anarchism* and
other anarchist titles released in the 1960s and 1970s.[4]

In this chapter, I argue that anarchism represented one of the main currents
of Zinn's political theory, although his activism and writings always defied any
simplistic leveling to a single ideological position. In his reading of anarchism,
Zinn anticipated the emergence of "post-ideological anarchism" that is nowadays
the best response to the reconfigured ideological landscape that renders doctrinal
purity obsolete. Intrinsic to this aim is an attempt to show that in Zinn's explicit
interventions in anarchist theory—e.g., Zinn's syllabi and personal notes, interviews
conducted with Zinn over the years, and Zinn's texts on anarchism—we can find
a conceptualization of anarchism as a methodology, and never as an ideology, that
without doubt speaks to anarchists in the age of Occupy.

Unlike the majority of anarchist scholars who by concentrating merely on
classical "thinkers" of anarchism neglect the creative potential of ordinary people,
Zinn's conceptualization of a (post-ideological) people's anarchism, which he kept
refining during his life, starts from the assumption that throughout history anarchism has never been merely an idea and practice of self-proclaimed anarchists.
Many times "ordinary" people have practiced anarchism without being aware of
it, or without even having heard the word.

The anarchist principles of non-authoritarian organization, direct action
and mutual aid, direct production, and direct democracy have spread to such an
extent that many social movements could be considered anarchist, although they
do not have such an identity. In contrast, many anarchists deliberately refuse to
declare themselves anarchists due to their uttermost following and consideration

of the anarchist ideas of anti-sectarianism, openness, and flexibility; in fact, full emancipation also includes emancipation from identity. In Zinn's theoretical examination of anarchism we thus find warnings that only by exceeding the rigid pursuit of a certain doctrine can anarchism remain one of the most important and most topical intellectual currents of the modern world on one hand, and the starting point for achieving social changes on the other.

In the second part of the chapter, I examine how Zinn's "anarchist" political theory informs the need for a wider epistemological and methodological transformation. According to Zinn, many political concepts and categories are too elusive for traditional disciplines, theories, and epistemologies and therefore their analyses must be founded on a new, more flexible epistemology and methodology. Zinnian epistemology hence begins with the assumption that nowadays exclusion, oppression, and discrimination have not only economic, social, and political dimensions, but also cultural and epistemological ones.[5] As opposed to past practices, political control and domination are today not grounded solely on economic and political power, but foremost on knowledge or the hierarchicalization of knowledge. By contrast, Zinnian methodology argues that activists frequently perceive processes of social and cultural changes and power relations within societies more precisely than academics themselves. It starts from the fact that also within political science the most important theoretical contributions and insights have for a long time come from the ranks of academics and activists involved in critical and reflective "co-research," "militant investigation," or "action research" with social movements.

In short, this chapter argues that Zinn's anarchist writings anticipate a new post-ideological anarchism and attest to the need for the "actionization" of theory, where the state and perspectives of anarchist political thought and epistemology are not solely understood as academic questions but also as political questions. The contemporary world is a world of conflicting interests—war against peace, selfishness against equality, nationalism against internationalism, elitism against democracy—therefore, it is both impossible and unwelcome to remain neutral. Indeed, you cannot be neutral when riding on a moving train.

At the outset, one methodological and completely technical instruction is worth noting. The British writer Alan Alexander Milne once wrote that it is practical to quote others because it saves one from the trouble of thinking. This chapter includes quotes from Zinn's works not so I can spare myself many troubles, but rather so that no one should be deprived of their own findings and interpretation of Zinn's works. In this way, I can also counter potential objections that I have misread Zinn or, at least, overemphasized his anarchist inclinations.

ZINN ON ANARCHISM

> Anarchist ideas are frightening to those in power. People in power can tolerate liberal ideas, they can tolerate ideas that call for reforms, but they cannot tolerate the idea that there will be no state, no central authority.
> —*Howard Zinn, Interview with Žiga Vodovnik, March 13, 2008*

Anarchism can be described as a socioeconomic and political theory and practice whose aim, according to Pierre-Joseph Proudhon, is to create *anarchy*—a state without a ruler. Anarchism as a socio-philosophical and political doctrine aims at a society based on justice, equality, and brotherhood, and in which all means of state and social constraints would be abolished. As such, anarchism opposes all kinds of hierarchy, exploitation, and authority, and consequently also its main forms—*state* and *capitalism*. Despite this, the public at large and even the academic community still predominantly use the term *anarchism* pejoratively, which equates anarchism with nihilism, chaos, violence, and even terrorism.

Although Zinn's interest in anarchism came relatively late, at the end of the 1950s and in the early 1960s, it was only a decade later that he had already risen to national prominence as an important anarchist thinker. It is worth highlighting that in 1971 Beacon Press invited Zinn to write an introduction to Herbert Read's collection of essays on anarchism, entitled *Anarchy and Order*. In 1979 his article "The Conspiracy of Law" appeared in Terry M. Perlin's edited volume on *Contemporary Anarchism* among contributions by George Woodcock, Murray Bookchin, Sam Dolgoff, George Lakey, and other prominent anarchist authors, and a year earlier Richard A. Falk quoted Zinn heavily in his article "Anarchism and World Order" for *NOMOS, Yearbook of the American Society for Political and Legal Philosophy*.[6] In reflecting his slow transformation from Marxism to anarchism, Zinn stresses two main factors:

> One was the growing evidence of the horrors of Stalinism in the Soviet Union, which suggested that the classical Marxian concept of "the dictatorship of the proletariat" needed to be reconsidered. Another was my own experience in the South in the struggle against racial segregation spearheaded by the Student Non-violent Coordinating Committee (SNCC). SNCC, without any self-conscious theorizing, acted in accord with anarchist principles. No central authority, grassroots democratic decision-making. In the New Left of the 1960s, this was called "participatory democracy."[7]

Zinn's epistemological and theoretical postulates reflected the imagination of the period and hence he understood anarchism not as a rigid ideological system, but rather as an ever-changing set of ideas and practices open to modification in light of new findings. Consequently, anarchism for Zinn was never a result of individual anarchist "thinkers," but rather of ordinary people who, all around the world, evolve and enrich anarchism with their own theoretical and practical contributions. Although the extraordinary contribution of the classics of anarchism should not be underrated, Zinn still highlights the fact that their ideas were also a result of, or at least bore a strong mark of, many anonymous individuals who played active roles in the workers' movement of the nineteenth century and, with their common sense and activism, created "not only the ideas, but also the facts of the future itself."[8]

Anarchist ideas need to be

> freed from the small circles that call themselves anarchist. They need to be connected with the far larger world, embracing a majority of the human race, whose instincts are anarchist without using the name.... Whenever historical

circumstances allowed, whenever human beings could break away from domination, whenever they could find spaces in which their natural instincts could have free play, they have acted in accord with anarchist principles without using the language or identifying the theory.[9]

A brief reflection on the Occupy Movement, its perception of democracy, diverse political praxes, and aspirations, confirms this thesis, as does Zinn's prediction that new anarchists should take the lessons of SNCC into account and be "radical, but not dogmatic; thoughtful, but not ideological."[10] Zinn acknowledges that through theoretical purism, the stubborn emphasizing of principles, and rejection of compromises and reformism, anarchism preserves its (ontological) radicalism, but also loses its (applied) relevance:

> Anarchism deserves to be liberated from all the ideological debris it has accumulated for over a hundred years. Anarchism, properly cleansed of myth and pretense, has never been more needed than in our time, when every system, every culture, has been corrupted by the profit motive or the hubris of leaders, and has led the people of the earth into a morass of injustice and violence.[11]

To provide the necessary future emancipatory potential and topicality that will ensure its presence also among new generations, anarchism must finally give priority to political praxis over ideology: "It is time to breathe some clean, refreshing air into the stale, nonsense-filled discussions of anarchism which have occupied the attention of people on all sides of the political spectrum—right, left, center."[12] This way anarchism will be able to transcend particular struggles bounded by a single issue or area, as well as racial, sexual, class, religious, and other differences; it will be as global as our exploitation and misery, and be as flexible as capital and our jobs. In short,

> [new radicalism] should be anti-ideological ... [b]ut it also should be—and here it has been inadequate—concerned with theory. I see three essential ingredients in such a theory. First we need a vision of what we are working toward—one based on transcendental human needs and not limited by the reality we are so far stuck with. Second, this theory should analyze the present reality, not through the prism of old, fixed categories, but rather with an awareness of the unique here and now and of the need to make the present irrationality intelligible to those around us. Finally, such a theory would explore—in the midst of the action—effective techniques of social change for the particular circumstances we find at the moment.[13]

A PEOPLE'S ANARCHISM

> Radicalism is not an ideology but a mood. Moods are harder to define. They are also harder to imprison.
> —*Howard Zinn,* SNCC: The New Abolitionists *(2002 [1964]: 274)*

Giorel Curran (2006: 2) sees "post-ideological anarchism" as the main ideological current within the alter-globalization movement and at the same time as the best response to the reconfigured ideological landscape that makes doctrinal purity obsolete. "Post-ideological anarchism" adopts ideas and principles from classical anarchism very flexibly and non-doctrinally, and simultaneously rejects its traditional forms to construct genuinely new autonomous politics. The question arises of whether it is possible to talk about a new anarchism also within the Occupy movement.

In Dave Neal's "Anarchism: Ideology or Methodology?" (1997), written years before the global initiative Occupy had reached full stride, we already find the two main positions within anarchism being identified—capital-*A* and small-*a* anarchism. If capital-*A* anarchism emphasizes the achieving of ideological uniformity and can be understood as "a set of rules and conventions to which you must abide," then small-*a* anarchism is understood as a methodology or "a way of acting, or a historical tendency against illegitimate authority."

Neal estimated that within the movement we could still find "a plethora of Anarchists—ideologues—who focus endlessly on their dogma instead of organizing solidarity among workers." A decade later, David Graeber (2004: 214) contemplated that what we might call capital-*A* anarchism still exists within the newest social movements, but it is the small-*a* anarchism that represents the real locus of creativity within that movement. In his reflection on new anarchism, he stresses that it still has an ideology but for the first time it is an entirely new one—i.e., a post-ideology essential to the anti-authoritarian principles of its praxis:

> A constant complaint about the globalization movement in the progressive press is that, while tactically brilliant, it lacks any central theme or coherent ideology.... [T]his is a movement about reinventing democracy. It is not opposed to organization. It is about creating new forms of organization. It is not lacking in ideology. Those new forms of organization are its ideology. It is about creating and enacting horizontal networks instead of top-down structures like states, parties or corporations; networks based on principles of decentralized, non-hierarchical consensus democracy. Ultimately, it aspires to be much more than that, because ultimately it aspires to reinvent daily life as whole.[14]

In "Anarchism and the Anti-Globalization Movement," Barbara Epstein (2001) also ascertains that anarchism represents the main inspiration for a new generation of activists. For them, anarchism does not represent some abstract radical ideology, but instead means

> a decentralized organizational structure, based on affinity groups that work together on an ad hoc basis, and decision-making by consensus. It also means egalitarianism; opposition to all hierarchies; suspicion of authority, especially that of the state; and commitment to living according to one's values.... Many envision a stateless society based on small, egalitarian communities. For some, however, the society of the future remains an open question. For them, anarchism is important mainly as an organizational structure and as a commitment

to egalitarianism. It is a form of politics that revolves around the exposure of the truth rather than strategy. It is a politics decidedly in the moment.[15]

In many recent reflections of contemporary anarchism we find the two main positions within anarchism that were already identified by Zinn—anarchism as an ideology and anarchism as praxis. If the former emphasizes a conscious acceptance of anarchist ideology and the identification of the subject as an anarchist, then the latter represents a sensibility or the ethical paradigm and understands anarchism rather as "a tendency in the history of human thought and practice, which cannot be encompassed by a general theory of ideology," since its contents and manifestations change over time.[16] In this case, there is also no need for interpolation of the individual into a self-conscious anarchist. By analogy with Zinn's understanding of Marxism, anarchism

> is not a fixed body of dogma, to be put into black books or little red books, and memorized, but a set of specific propositions about the modern world which are both tough and tentative, plus a certain vague and yet exhilarating vision of the future, and, more fundamentally, an approach to life, to people, to ourselves, a certain way of thinking about thinking as well as about being. Most of all it is a way of thinking which is intended to promote action.[17]

At the center of Zinn's examination of anarchism is the idea that anarchism should not be a theory of the future, but "a living force in the affairs of our life, constantly creating new conditions, the spirit of revolt, in whatever form, against everything that hinders human growth," as Emma Goldman claimed at the beginning of the twentieth century.[18] It goes without saying that many "hard-line" anarchists were appalled by such unorthodox understanding of anarchism, particularly by Zinn's idea that anarchism should not be anarchistic "just in wanting the ultimate abolition of the state, but in its immediate requirement that authority and coercion be banished in every sphere of existence that the end must be represented immediately in the means."[19]

DEMOCRACY AS A VERB

> Civil disobedience is not just to be tolerated; if we are to have a truly democratic society, it is a necessity.
> —*Howard Zinn,* Disobedience and Democracy:
> Nine Fallacies on Law and Order *(2002 [1968]: 25)*

When Zinn explains that democracy is "not just a counting up of votes; it is counting up of actions," he basically argues that we should imagine democracy in much broader terms whereby the performative dimension proves to be crucial; especially if we understand democracy outside of the political sphere (an achievement of the eighteenth century) so that it also includes a social and economic dimension.[20] However, we should add that with performative democracy Zinn does not mean practice per se, but the *praxis* or philosophical category of practice. Praxis differs considerably from the epistemological category of practice, which can mean an activity that remains entirely alienated. Although the word *praxis* is commonly used in everyday language and appears to be relatively clear and understandable since it is primarily used as a synonym for activity, creation, work, habit, experience, or training, its meaning within praxis philosophy is considerably more profound and specific.

Praxis is equated only with free, universal, and creative activity with which man creates and transforms his world and consequently himself. The key characteristic of *praxis* as a normative concept is therefore the fact that this activity represents a goal and purpose in itself. Of course, freedom in this case should not be understood in a negative sense as an absence of external obstacles and limitations, but in a positive sense whereby the creative moment of this action is emphasized. *Per analogiam* with Gajo Petrović's (1978: 64) definition of praxis, democracy as praxis "is the most developed form of creativity and the most authentic form of freedom, a field of open possibilities and the realm of the truly new. It is the very 'essence' of Being, the Being in its essence."

In stressing the importance of performative democracy, Zinn's concept closely resembles the idea of "infrapolitics" that, according to James Scott (1990: 184), "provides much of the cultural and structural underpinning of the more visible political action on which our attention has generally been focused." Infrapolitics as "the art of resistance" is as much a product of political necessity as of political choice, so we should understand it not only as a form of political opposition in the conditions of tyranny, but also as "the silent partner of a loud form of public resistance" of modern democracies. Although performative democracy, which we can find in various pockets of resistance all across the globe, is nowadays not always part of the mainstream, and many times it is hard to detect this "immense political terrain that lies between quiescence and revolt," it is still real politics "in many respects conducted in more earnest, for higher stakes, and against greater odds than political life in liberal democracies."[21] The political struggles of "illegal" immigrants in the United States, the *sans-papiers* in France, or the Erased in Slovenia are further proof of this.

Zinn warns that equating democracy with the majority vote, which we are usually taught in schools, creates a very flawed notion of what democracy is, explaining that "majorities can be wrong, majorities can overrule rights of minorities. If majorities ruled, we could still have slavery. 80 percent of the population once enslaved 20 percent of the population. While run by majority rule that is OK."[22] Graeber (2007: 342) further supports this claim and contends that majoritarian democracy, in all its forms, has been a rarity in the history of political communities because it builds on two factors that only rarely coexist: the belief that people should have an equal say in decision-making, and a coercive apparatus capable of enforcing those decisions.

Graeber claims that throughout human history it has been extremely unusual to satisfy both ideas at the same time. In egalitarian societies it has usually been considered wrong to impose systematic coercion, whereas in those polities where a system of coercion did develop it did not even occur to those wielding it that they were enforcing any sort of popular will.

We can agree with the thesis that a hegemonic notion of democracy only recuperated the word, yet at the same time renounced its content. Zinn would add that "[d]emocracy is not our government, our constitution, our legal structure. Too often they are enemies of democracy."[23] The result of this myopia that sees democracy coming through institutions alone includes, as stated by Graeber, modern liberal democracies within which nothing remotely similar to the Athenian *agora* can be found, but are undoubtedly flooded with parallels to the Roman *circus*.[24] Here architecture was certainly not the sole thing Graeber had in mind.

One might, of course, ask about Zinn's position on representation. True to his anarchist principles, Zinn argues that

> democracy would have to go far beyond the rule of parties, whether in one-party or two-party systems, and far beyond representative government. Parliaments and congresses everywhere in the world have become a facade behind which men of power make decisions, while other men delude themselves into thinking they control their own destiny because they go to the ballot boxes to make their puny choices, on prepared-in-advance ballots. People would have to be drawn into active, day-to-day participation in decision-making, instead of pulling a lever once in two years, or once in four or seven years, or once in a generation.[25]

For Zinn, the infrapolitics of the seemingly nonpolitical on the micro level is thus recognized as the crucial precondition of democracy on the social level.

Lessons from the civil-rights movement led Zinn to propound "a healthy disrespect for respectability" as the essence of democracy.[26] Democracy should not be based solely on consent, but rather on dissent since major problems of contemporary one-dimensional societies (as Herbert Marcuse described those societies without opposition) result precisely from blind obedience:

> Our problem is the numbers of people all over the world who have obeyed the dictates of the leaders of their governments and have gone to war, and millions have been killed because of this obedience. Our problem is that scene in *All Quiet on the Western Front* where schoolboys march off dutifully in a line to war. Our problem is that people are obedient all over the world, in the face of poverty and starvation and stupidity, and war and cruelty. Our problem is that people are obedient while jails are full of petty thieves, and all the while the grand thieves are running the country.[27]

It should be obvious by now that Zinn did not have abundant respect for the law. For Zinn, going "beyond the law is not a departure from democracy; it is absolutely essential to it" if we are trying to return to the spirit of the Declaration of Independence that calls for an equal right to "Life, Liberty, and the pursuit of Happiness."[28] Zinn did not expect that governments will act in the interests of the whole *demos,* so he had no illusions that administrations will change things by themselves. He knew from his work in the South that "etceteras of history," as Studs Terkel would call the ordinary people left out of the pages of history, cannot depend on government to help or support them if the government is not forced into this by social movements. The essence of democracy is, according to Zinn, "that people should control their own lives, by ones, or twos, or hundreds, depending on whether the decision being made affects one or two or a hundred."[29]

KNOWLEDGE AS POWER: ZINNIAN EPISTEMOLOGY

> Schemes and models and systems are invented which have the air of profundity and which advance careers, but hardly anything else.
> —*Howard Zinn,* The Politics of History *(1990 [1970]: 8)*

In Zinn's discourse on anarchism we can also find a call for the "actionization" of theory where the state and perspectives of anarchist political theory, epistemology, and methodology are not understood solely as academic questions but also as political questions. Zinnian ("anarchist") epistemology calls for an undisciplinary or counter-disciplinary approach that rejects all pretentions of objectivity or of formulating or consolidating a universal theory. It offers radical criticism of the idea of inter- and transdisciplinarity as they implicitly still build on and advocate the separation of disciplines and fields of research.

What we are facing is epistemological ignorance, a form of *epistemicide,* that strengthens the status quo and at the same time dismisses, discredits, and trivializes those arguments and solutions not in line with the hegemonic epistemological position—a hegemonic notion of truth, objectivity, and rationality. Zinn would agree with Santos (2004: 238), who warns that there is no global social justice without global cognitive justice. What is therefore needed is an epistemological transformation that will broaden the spectrum of (relevant) political solutions and innovations.

An outline of Zinnian epistemology can be found in *The Politics of History,* where Zinn explains why "disinterested, neutral, scientific, objective" scholarship is impossible and even undesirable. If objectivity means to pretend that ideas play no particular role in social struggles and that we should adopt specific positions within them, then, for Zinn, scholarship should be far from "objective." Objectivity is also impracticable for the methodological fact that every analysis encompasses a subjective and limited range of relevant data taken from a myriad (i.e., market) of available information. Every analysis is defined by one's own subjective belief of what is relevant and what is not, and thus already contradicts the "noble dream" of objectivity.[30]

Even if "objectivity"—understood as passivity and non-engagement—were possible, it would still be undesirable. That is to say, science should never serve only its own purpose but should contribute to the broadening of human values such as freedom, equality, fairness, and brotherhood and to solving the fundamental problems humanity faces, such as famine, warfare, and poverty. Too many of today's scholars are merely passive reporters of more or less absurd, trivial, and esoteric issues, while outside their offices and lecture rooms social struggles are taking place. Their work must rather be "consciously activist on behalf of the kind of world which history has not yet disclosed, but perhaps hinted at."[31] Of course, the "activist approach" does not suggest that some specific (historical) facts should be ignored or modified, let alone invented.

Moreover, this "non-objectivity" does not mean that the analysis of the subject matter should fail to follow scientific standards (cognitive and argumentative procedures). It merely starts from the supposition that holding certain values does not require that we find certain (desirable) answers in our research, but instead turns our attention to certain (useful) objectives and questions, particularly the consideration of "how to achieve a better world." But becoming an activist-scholar should not result from our partial and egotistic aims, but from our immersion in the struggles of "the etceteras of history": "We will be doing this, not in the interests of the rich and powerful, or in behalf of our own careers, but for those who so far have had to strive alone just to stay warm in winter, to stay alive through the calls for war."[32]

In the past, many disciplines went through radical epistemological turbulence. Within historical research, for instance, a new generation of young scholars of the New Left enabled the discipline no earlier than the 1960s and 1970s to overcome inner limitations best summed up by Henry Kissinger's thesis that history is the memory of states, and everything else is of minor importance. Radical historians such as Staughton Lynd, Jesse Lemisch, Howard Zinn, and Christopher Lasch initiated *history from the bottom up* or *people's history*, which, figuratively speaking, moved its focus from those in the White House to those picketing the White House. With this very shift, epitomized by the publication of Barton Bernstein's edited volume *Towards a New Past: Dissenting Essays in American History* in 1968, the discipline was able to detect new questions and offer new answers. For Lynd, by far the most influential piece of radical historiography is Zinn's *A People's History of the United States,* a book that alone "has probably done more good, and influenced more people (especially young) than everything the rest of us 'radical historians' have written put together."[33]

In *A People's History,* Zinn explains that in the inevitable taking of sides he prefers

> to try to tell the story of the discovery of America from the viewpoint of the Arawaks, of the Constitution from the standpoint of the slaves, of Andrew Jackson as seen by the Cherokees, of the Civil War as seen by the New York Irish, of the Mexican war as seen by the deserting soldiers of Scott's army, of the rise of industrialism as seen by the young women in the Lowell textile mills, of the Spanish-American war as seen by the Cubans, the conquest of the Philippines as seen by black soldiers on Luzon, the Gilded Age as seen by southern farmers, the First World War as seen by socialists, the Second World War as seen by pacifists, the New Deal as seen by peons in Latin America, and so on, to the limited extent that any one person, however he or she strains, can "see" history from the standpoint of others.[34]

In this reversal of perspective, Zinnian epistemology anticipates the idea of "diatopical hermeneutics" as developed by Raimon Panikkar (1999). Diatopical hermeneutics can be understood as a *détournement* of perspective that, instead of one (hegemonic) position from which we determine the relationship between equality and difference, proposes a plethora of such perspectives and "dialogical dialogue" between them. It builds on the thesis that *topoi*—places of (self-)understanding within a certain culture and tradition or, to put it differently, forms through which we think, although we do not think about them—cannot be understood with tools and categories of other *topoi,* but at least we can gain a better understanding of them by traversing between various *topoi.*

Paraphrasing Restrepo and Escobar (2005), such an epistemological transformation calls for a critical awareness of both the larger epistemic and political field in which disciplines have emerged and continue to function, and the micropractices and relations of power within and across different locations and traditions of individual disciplines. We should add that the shift would also result in the acceptance of new methodologies, research foci, and research ambitions, which would be a first step toward the pluralization and decentralization of political science. Although our epistemological position is not a sweater that we simply take off to be replaced by another, as already cautioned by Furlong and Marsh (2002), the difficult task of changing "a skin, not a sweater" is a prerequisite for the new imagining of a free society.

It follows then, that Zinn attributed an epistemological component to exclusion, oppression, and discrimination. This new understanding is in addition to their previously recognized economic, social, and political dimensions.[35] Thus, Zinn challenges past practices to recognize that political control and domination are now foremost in knowledge or the hierarchicalization of knowledge, rather than grounded solely on economic and political power. This approach does not aim at the exclusion of others. Instead, it attempts to understand the structure and constellation of political communities, and the asymmetry of power within it. In this process, knowledge plays the crucial role:

> True, force is the most direct form of power, and government has a monopoly on that (as Max Weber once pointed out). But in modern times, when social control rests on "the consent of the governed," force is kept in abeyance for emergencies, and everyday control is exercised by a set of rules, a fabric of values passed from one generation to another by the priests and the teachers of the society.[36]

Hence, we can understand why the knowledge industry, which these days reaches millions of young people in colleges and universities around the world, is becoming a vital locus of power. That is also why the traditional centers of power, which already control obvious forms of power, are trying to monopolize it.

For Zinn the epistemological transformation must always also include a methodological transformation. In his essay entitled "Historian as Citizen," Zinn urges,

> In a world hungry for solutions, we ought to welcome the emergence of the historian—if this is really what we are seeing—as an activist-scholar, who thrusts himself and his work into the crazy mechanism of history, on behalf of values in which he deeply believes. This makes of him more than a scholar; it makes him a citizen in the ancient Athenian sense of the word.[37]

Zinn did not perceive his role as an activist or as a historian as something that is separated or should be separated. Unlike the majority of scholars who neglect the creative potential of "ordinary" people, Zinnian epistemology and methodology are thus based on the assumption that activists often apprehend the processes of social change and the relations of power within society more accurately than unengaged academics. The involvement of anarchist activists/theoreticians in contemporary social struggles also results in a "collective theorization" about the most pressing and sensitive issues, as well as in a search for realistic and, in particular, credible analyses that are then offered as a gift to movements so as to partake in the success of their shared struggle. This is evident is his book on the Student Nonviolent Coordinating Committee, *SNCC: The New Abolitionists,* where Zinn demonstrates a benefit of the work is that it is not "a comprehensive scholarly book on the SNCC, but a work of on-the-spot reportage."[38]

For Zinn, there are two benefits of activist research: first, an ethnographic approach can transform scholars and enable them to "transcend their immediate circumstances by leaps of emotion and imagination"[39]; second, engagement in social struggles can enrich the scholarship of activist-scholars, enabling them to uncover subaltern infrapolitics of the hidden or seemingly nonpolitical:

> Contact with the underground of society, in addition to spurring the historian to act out his value-system, might also open him to new data: the experiences, thoughts, feeling of the invisible folk around us. This is the kind of data so often missed in official histories, manuscript collections of famous personalities, diaries of the literate, newspaper accounts, government documents.[40]

Such an attitude was also incorporated in his teaching, where Zinn admitted that he "hated grading; that was the worst part."[41] In his files you will not find samples of old tests, but rather a selection of student journals and project papers where they commented on their exploration of "justice in everyday life"—either on campus or in the wider Boston area.[42] He admitted that early in his teaching career he decided that he "would make the most of the special freedom that is possible in the classroom. I would introduce what I felt to be the most important, and therefore the most controversial, questions in my class."[43]

THE REVOLUTION OF EVERYDAY LIFE

> If we do act, in however small a way, we don't have to wait for some grand utopian future.... [T]o live now as we think human beings should live, in defiance of all that is bad around us, is itself a marvelous victory.
> —*Howard Zinn,* You Can't Be Neutral on a Moving Train
> *(2002 [1994]: 208)*

Since the contemporary world has removed the feasibility of revolutions in the old sense, and rendered customary methods of political action obsolete, Zinn predicts that in the search for new methods of social change, we should allow experimentation and imagination full play, where anarchist theory and praxis are especially helpful. For Zinn, the subversiveness of anarchism comes from its holistic approach to political change. As opposed to other socialist currents, it has never been characterized by the narrow economic reductionism that had resulted in the fetishization of economic exploitation and class antagonism. In Bookchinite terms, anarchism has operated with the concept of domination, which consequently detected and included exploitation that may not even have an economic meaning at all. Instead, anarchism raises a much broader and more important question—not only the question of class antagonism, but of hierarchy and domination as such. Anarchists do not perceive revolutionary change as something that concerns an alternation in hegemonic economic and political arrangements only, but, as Zinn puts it, they see

> revolutionary change as something immediate, something we must do now, where we are, where we live, where we work.... Squelched in one place, it springs up in another, until it is everywhere. Such a revolution is an art. That is, it requires the courage not only of resistance, but of imagination.[44]

Consequently, what we need are "tactics short of violent revolution, but far more militant than normal parliamentary procedure, it seems to me. It will take systematic, persistent organizing and education, in the ghettos, in the universities, plus coordinated actions of various kinds designed to shock society out of its lethargy."[45]

Through his activist work Zinn learned that when someone gets into working through electoral politics they begin to corrupt their ideals. The solution is therefore prefigurative politics as an attempt to create the future in the present through political and economic organizing alone, or at least to foresee social changes to which we aspire. It is indeed an attempt to overcome current limitations with a construction of alternatives from the bottom up since it foresees a renewal of the political power of local communities, and their federation into a global nonstatist network as a counterbalance to nation-states and corporate power.

Although many Left intellectuals are losing too much energy with their theoretical disputes about the blueprint of the future society to even start "experimenting" in practice, Zinn still argues that it is worth presenting ideas, but one should always maintain her/his flexibility. Discussions about the future are therefore useful only so long as they do not obstruct our immediate goals and our small steps toward remaking the social/political/economic order.

The other crucial aspect of political strategy/tactics that Zinn highlights is that the means of political action correspond to the ends or, to put it differently, that we organize ourselves in such a way as to create that kind of human relationship that should prefigure future society. For Zinn, that would mean

> to organize ourselves without centralized authority, without charismatic leaders, in a way that represents in miniature the ideal of the future egalitarian society. So that even if you don't win some victory tomorrow or next year in the meantime you have created a model. You have acted out how future society should

be and you created immediate satisfaction, even if you have not achieved your ultimate goal.[46]

But in the struggle for social change, "there is no act too small, no act too bold" (Zinn 2012). Zinn does not deny the importance of what we shall call revolutionary reformism. His experience with the G.I. Bill, which enabled him to enroll in New York University and later to continue with graduate studies at Columbia, resulted in the provocative idea that in every system of domination and control it is still reasonable to achieve its change within the limits it allows; when the system itself becomes an impassable obstacle to progress the solution is, of course, a conflict, a fight, and revolutionary changes. He saw the possibility of and need for government intervention to solve the precarious situation of the ordinary American—with this term including all immigrants, documented or undocumented—and to rebuild the levees to defend them from the deadly flood of the "financial Katrina." It is in this way that we can defend pockets of resistance, even empower them, so in the long run we can indeed overcome this anachronistic institution we know as the nation-state. Even the present social/economic/political framework could be reinterpreted in a fashion that is "moving away from the deification of precedent":

> Why should not the equal protection clause of the Fourteenth Amendment be applied to economics, as well as race, to require the state to give equal economic rights to its citizens: food, shelter, education, medical care.... Why should not the "cruel and unusual punishment clause" of the Eighteenth Amendment be applied in such a way as to bar all imprisonment except in the most stringent of cases, where confinement is necessary to prevent a clear and immediate danger to others? Why should not the Ninth Amendment, which says citizens have unnamed rights beyond those enumerated in the Constitution, be applied to host of areas: rights to carry on whatever family arrangements (marriage, divorce, etc.) are desired, whatever sexual private activities one wants to carry on, so long as others are not harmed (even if they are irritated).[47]

If such a stance is denounced as social-democratic reformism at best, then this is indeed revolutionary reformism that transcends the binary position of revolution versus reform. It clearly builds on the pragmatism and realism much needed in contemporary anarchism. Zinn's pragmatism captures the spirit of Gustav Landauer, who early on in the twentieth century revealed that for political emancipation we should overcome the negative fetishization of the state since people do not live in a state, but are performing and creating the state.[48] The state is not something that can be destroyed by means of a revolution, which is why it is necessary to build libertine enclaves next to it, or to postulate a revolution as a "peaceful and gradual creation of counterculture" opposite from the idea of "a revolution as a violent mass rebellion." It is impossible to attain a free society merely by replacing an old order with a new one since it can be attained only by spreading the spheres of liberty to such an extent that they finally prevail over all social life. If the state is in all of us, then we can only abolish it by revising our behavior.

A table can be overturned and a window can be smashed. However, those who believe that the state is also a thing or a fetish that can be overturned or smashed are sophists and believers in the Word. The state is a social relationship; a certain way of people relating to one another. It can be destroyed by creating new social relationships, i.e., by people relating to one another differently.... We, who have imprisoned ourselves in the absolute state, must realize the truth: *we* are the state! And we will be the state as long as we are nothing different; as long as we have not yet created the institutions necessary for a true community and a true society of human beings.[49]

That is also why Zinn believes the difficult task of defying authority within as well as without, of consistently refreshing our radical politics from the spring of anger and love, still lies ahead of us.[50] Taking Zinn's metaphor of the moving train seriously means not postponing our demands for "another word" until the objective (pre)conditions are ripe (the maturity of historical circumstances, or the formation of some coherent subject or class), but it builds on the supposition that every individual can—in the here and now—change this world and create it anew. It is only in this way that we will not be torn between the tragic past and the impossible future.[51] It is only in this way that our vision will not be blurred by some grand utopia squelching our immediate goals. It is also only in this way that we will see the subversiveness of Zinn's infrapolitics of the seemingly nonpolitical:

Let's not speak anymore about capitalism, socialism. Let's just speak of using the incredible wealth of the earth for human being. Give people what they need: food, medicine, clean air, pure water, trees and grass, pleasant homes to live in, some hours of work, more hours of leisure. Don't ask who deserves it. Every human being deserves it.[52]

CHAPTER 7

Politics against the Law

Howard Zinn on Academic Freedom beyond the Academy

Christopher C. Robinson

Liberties are not given, they are taken.

—*Aldous Huxley*[1]

To be neutral is to collaborate with whatever is going on, and I as a teacher do
not want to be a collaborator with whatever is happening in the world today.
—*Howard Zinn,* You Can't Be Neutral on a Moving Train *(2002 [1994])*

Was Howard Zinn a liberal advocate of individual rights or a communitarian
whose primary political values were equality and collective action? This intriguing question illuminates some internal tensions in Zinn's political thought, and
it can be answered (at least provisionally) by examining his autobiographical
reflections on where he stood on the political spectrum, his more formal inquiries
into and interpretations of the US Constitution, and/or by studying his regard
for academic freedom. Not to show my hand completely at the beginning of this
chapter, but we notice immediately Zinn's celebrations of such liberal freedoms
as free speech and thought for the individual are suffused with notions of community, social solidarity, and economic equality as an expression of dignity and
political effectiveness.

In political theory, individual liberty and social equality are staged as irreconcilable differences. One doesn't have to be Walt Whitman to know that we can live comfortably while living out and acting upon these logically and ideologically opposed beliefs. Indeed, such conceptual tensions can be a creative force for citizen and community alike, even as they find temporary reconciliation in the demands of political action. If nothing else, these contrary beliefs function to dissolve the tendency toward ideological dogmatism in the person. If such a tension exists in the Constitution—think of the freedoms of the individual adumbrated in the First Amendment and whether they can be harmonized with the equal-protection provisions of the Fifth and Fourteenth Amendments—then the result is a document that defies coherent interpretation and exposes continuously the poverty of strict constructionism (described by Zinn as "legal fundamentalism"). As I will argue, and as the editors of this volume describe in terms of spheres of action, Zinn found, and achieved personally, this conceptual cooperation of individual liberty and communal equality in his notion of academic freedom as it was forged through conflict with administrators at both Spelman College and Boston University.

Howard Zinn was a scholar, as well as a political activist.[2] Commitment to scholarship has a way of challenging and softening the more fixed aspects of a life guided by ideological frameworks that, in turn, guide political action. That is, as scholars, we know we need to be reflective about the way we see the world and frame political issues precisely because each way of seeing also entails a form of blindness. It is the scholar's job to recognize the limits of the ideologically contoured perceptual stance, and Zinn's work is a model of this kind of effort. At the same time, there is no escaping the contours of ideology, unless we want to pretend to have access to an omniscient perspective. Moreover, ideological foci (e.g., socialism, queer theory) that stand in opposition to the mainstream help to illuminate dimensions of political life (e.g., class, heteronormativity) that can go unnoticed. Zinn was particularly effective, progressives will agree, in pointing out the blindness entailed by an enclosed narrative of American exceptionalism, laissez-faire liberalism, racism, militarism, and classism. Indeed, he was more comfortable describing the blindness entailed by these worldviews in terms of deafness to the voices of those marginalized and victimized by power. This happened most often in those writings and lectures where he endeavored to let the subaltern speak. In doing this work, he followed and cultivated a particularly robust account of academic freedom. This is key to understanding his perspective on the constitutional grounds of free speech, and the concurrent responsibilities that attend citizenship.

The engine that drove Howard Zinn had both causal and teleological features. On the causal side, he was driven by the friction of his individual and egalitarian commitments. Teleologically, Zinn's vision of a more just and peaceful society remained rich, compelling, and attainable to the very end of his active yet academic life.

ZINN ON ACADEMIC FREEDOM AS A KEY TO HIS THOUGHT

What was the ideal classroom and the ideal campus for Howard Zinn? The short answer is the sort of public space for the free exchange of ideas that drove his conservative detractors crazy.[3] The longer answer must refer to classrooms without walls, and campuses conceived not as islands of learning apart from political society, but as open spaces that invite reflective discussion and debate that promote learning in a continuum with the struggles for peace and justice that are part (or that should be part) of the everyday life of the citizen. This image of the campus as part of political life, so vital to the understanding of Howard Zinn as a person, professor, and activist, poses some significant problems for the way the relation of academic freedom to constitutionally protected speech is usually presented.

We can get at these problems with two interrelated questions that expose the spatial limits of the freedoms associated with campus speech: What happens to academic freedom when professors speak, teach, and act off campus? What happens to the freedom of speech guaranteed by the First Amendment when professors offer public lectures at their local universities?[4] The boundary between campus and political society is at best porous and blurry. Yet the way academic freedom is framed conventionally and described by even its most ardent proponents entails a careful distinction between its foundations in professional standards and campus governance on one hand, and the individual character of freedom of speech as it is protected by the First Amendment on the other hand.[5] In making this case, these proponents present an impracticably dichotomous image of the professor as scholar and as citizen. This tension is played out in Finkin and Post's *For the Common Good* (2009), one of the finest histories of academic freedom available:

> We argue that the concept of academic freedom proposed by the 1915 Declaration differs fundamentally from the individual First Amendment rights that present themselves so vividly to the contemporary mind. The profession's claim to academic freedom is grounded firmly in a substantive account of the purposes of higher education and in the special conditions necessary for faculty to fulfill those purposes. In essence, academic freedom consists of the freedom to pursue the scholarly profession according to the standards of that profession.[6]

This point is clear, but we sense immediately that the lived division between academic freedom and freedom of speech is not experienced so cleanly by academics who are also active citizens. "Academic freedom," the authors continue, is conventionally understood as having four distinct dimensions: freedom of speech and publication, freedom in the classroom, freedom of intramural speech, and freedom of extramural speech.[7] Intramural speech—speech pertaining to matters and issues in the institution and its constitutive disciplines—is clear and protected enough, but what is the governing speech protection when the scholar travels off campus and engages in "extramural" speech (speech on broader political and social issues, beyond one's discipline and campus)? At the very least, we need to note an ambiguity or area of overlap (conceived by Zinn in terms of complementarity) that Finkin and Post (2009) wish to ignore for purposes of conceptual and professional clarity.

The way Zinn lived and taught amounted to an existential and pedagogic challenge to this spatially divided image. He sought to underscore the areas of overlapping characteristics shared by these freedoms. Nevertheless, in academic freedom he saw a model for the way free speech should be conceived and defended by citizens. That is, free speech ought not to be regarded as a gift handed down to the *demos* by the founders and by the Supreme Court; rather, it should be a democratic achievement that is struggled for and defended by the community.

For Zinn, the enemies of free speech and education are forces seeking to perpetuate the status quo and those people who lead lives fearful of change and fearful of the power of ideas. He thought it his job as a teacher to challenge this kind of fearful defense of order and stability.

> In my thirty years of teaching—in a small southern college, in a large north-eastern university—I have often observed that fear. And I think I understand what it is based on. The educational environment is unique in our society: It is the only situation where an adult, looked up to as a mentor, is alone with a group of young people for a protracted and officially sanctioned period of time and can assign whatever reading he or she chooses, and discuss with these young people any subject under the sun. The subject may be defined by the curriculum, by the catalog course description, but this is a minor impediment to a bold and imaginative teacher, especially in literature, philosophy and the social sciences, where there are unlimited possibilities for free discussion of social and political issues.[8]

The sort of discussion Zinn was alluding to is free in the sense that it may drift outside of the bounds of one's area of academic expertise to express a political perspective or opinion even as it advances the purported mission of higher education.[9] While this teaching may on occasion challenge the formal parameters of academic freedom based in professional standards and perhaps raise questions about whether the teacher is teaching or indoctrinating her or his students, it also betokens the benefits of active, discussion-based pedagogy that serves to highlight the more pervasive political agenda that works in the direction of political quietism.

Zinn used his pedagogical experiences to illuminate the ideological conflicts occurring in higher education:

> I have no doubt that I was taking a political stand when, in the early 1960s, I expressed respect for my students who missed classes to demonstrate in downtown Atlanta against racial segregation. In doing that, was I being more political than fundamentalist Allan Bloom, at Cornell, who pointed with pride to the fact that the students in his seminar on Plato and Aristotle stuck to their studies and refused to participate in the social conflict outside the seminar room?[10]

Where Bloom's approach celebrated the case for the insularity of the academy from political influence and pressure from the outside, for Zinn it was an expression of conservative ideology at work indoctrinating students into the principles of elitism and conformity. To be sure, academic freedom protects both Zinn and Bloom, but the price paid by Bloom and his students is the acceptance of injustice as something that occurs outside the boundaries of the campus and therefore exceeds their personal and professional responsibility and is only a distraction from the true goal of education: personal advancement. In Bloom we get a clear view of academic freedom detached from the First Amendment and at its unreflective and elitist worst because this cultivation of insularity blinded Bloom and his students to grave threats to their romanticized image of education in the humanities occurring not as a result of the voices of diversity and radical politics they denigrated and feared, but rather because of the subverting and antihumanist forces of corporatism and militarism. If these threats were at all visible to Bloom and company, they were perceived (indeed welcomed) as forces of order. The price paid by Zinn took the form of rebukes by administrators (he was fired at Spelman, for example) and by the history profession (*A People's History of the United States* was denounced as a form of subjectivist history).[11]

Zinn was most concerned with revealing the fiction perpetrated by more conservative professors and pundits of the university as somehow protected from political and economic interests that flourish outside its walls and yet designed to prepare students for a future of servitude to this corporate state.[12] Zinn could see what Bloom could not or would not: as he struggled to make the university a democratic institution supportive of democratic actions and movements in this country and abroad, the institution was being transformed by corporate and military intrusions.

> Boston University, where I taught for many years, is not too far from typical, with its panoply of military and government connections—ROTC chapters for every military service, former government officials given special faculty posts, the board of trustees dominated by corporate executives, a president eager to curry favor with powerful politicos. Almost all colleges and universities are organized as administrative hierarchies in which a president and trustees, usually well connected to wealthy and important people in the outside world, make the critical decisions as to who may enjoy the freedom of the classroom to speak to the young people of the new generation.[13]

These internal threats to academic freedom were, for Zinn, embodied by the administration of John Silber at Boston University. It is important to note at the outset that while Zinn had the protections of tenure, his academic freedom was definitely imperiled by Silber's tactics. Nevertheless, the storied struggle between Zinn and Silber would never have occurred if Zinn had been vulnerable to the whims of presidential power experienced by untenured faculty members on the campus.[14]

Upon taking his position as president of BU in 1972, Silber invited the Marines to recruit on campus. Students from the antiwar movement organized a protest that was by all accounts peaceful. It was a sit-in organized on the steps of the building where the recruiters had set up shop, and it was indeed an obstacle—symbolic and physical—to keep people from meeting with them. Silber called the police and actually led the phalanx of officers with a bullhorn as they moved on the students to make arrests. The headline for the BU paper the next day read, "Disruptive Students Must Be Taught Respect for Law, Says Dr. Silber."[15] Zinn was not on campus for the protest. From his sick bed, he wrote a description of and response to the event that made clear that what John Silber thought was the educational mission of the university was not shared by at least one member of the faculty:

> It is true that one crucial function of the schools is training people to take the jobs society has to offer.... But the much more important function of organized education is to teach the new generation that rule without which leaders could not possibly carry on wars, ravage the country's wealth, keep down rebels and dissenters—the rule of obedience to legal authority. And no one can do that more skillfully, more convincingly than the professional intellectual. A philosopher turned university president is best of all. If his arguments don't work on the students—who sometimes prefer to look at the world around them than to read Kant—then he can call the police, and after that momentary interruption (the billy club serving as exclamation point to the rational argument) the discussion can continue, in a more subdued atmosphere.[16]

Zinn's sarcasm was not lost on Silber, who claimed that he had given the student protestors the opportunity to be arrested for their beliefs in the tradition of Martin Luther King Jr. Zinn responded,

> How odd that a man whose own behavior that day more closely resembled that of Birmingham's Bull Connor—replete with police dogs, hidden photographers, and club-wielding police—should invoke the name of Martin Luther King, who would have been there on the steps with the students.[17]

It is worth recounting this incident and the exchange between Zinn and Silber in full because it shows the power of the confrontation on Zinn's thinking about the university and academic life. Silber pushed him in this direction at a time when Zinn was focusing his civic and scholarly energies on the antiwar movement, which itself belied any claim about the separability of campus from the political movements animating the larger society. It may be too much to say that Zinn became the anti-Silber, but the diametrical quality of their disagreements can be gleaned from Silber's reflections on his philosophy of education. "As Jefferson recognized," Silber wrote in an op-ed for the *New York Times,*

> There is a natural aristocracy among men. The grounds of this are virtue and talent.... Democracy freed from a counterfeit and ultimately destructive egalitarianism provides a society in which the wisest, the best, and the most dedicated assume positions of leadership.... As long as intelligence is better than stupidity, knowledge than ignorance, and virtue than vice, no university can be run except on an elitist basis.[18]

Zinn adds, "on another occasion, Silber said, 'the more democratic a university is, the lousier it is.'" This kind of conservative vision of the university as the city on the hill dedicated to the education of future elites was the perfect foil for Zinn. It demanded the kind of dissent that was both the hallmark of Zinn's pedagogy and the conduit for reconciling academic freedom and freedom of speech.

DISSENT IS BASIC TO ACADEMIC FREEDOM
AND TO THE FIRST AMENDMENT

As noted, historians and commentators are usually careful to distinguish academic freedom from the freedoms guaranteed by the First Amendment. By contrast, Howard Zinn knew that dissent was essential to the expansion and perpetuation of both. Moreover, his concept of academic freedom had an idiosyncratic character insofar as it was moored not so much in the relation of professors to the standards of the profession, but rather in the relation of professors to their students, which he conceived in terms of liberation. The emphasis on formulating dissent in the form of substantiated argument as a pedagogic goal engendered the conceptual space for Zinn to reconcile the individual and collective strands of his identity as citizen and scholar. This account of academic freedom is a window into Zinn's character as a public intellectual because the population who counted as students of Howard Zinn far exceeded the seating capacity of the halls where he taught.

The scope of any freedom guaranteed by the Constitution depends ultimately upon the Supreme Court for definition and defense. Free speech can be thwarted by a crowd bent on shouting down or beating up those who express opinions they find odious or un-American. At the very least, the threat of violence has a chilling effect on anyone who wishes to protest a governmental or social policy. These two limits—springing from democratic and elitist sources—converge often in the lead-up to and during the initial popular phase of any war. For Zinn, then, it is incumbent on the dissident to conceive of freedom of speech in political rather than legal terms. That is, speech carries with it great risks of imprisonment and/or bodily harm—even in a nation that prides itself on its democratic openness—and so the dissenter must respond with courage (bolstered by solidarity) and an understanding that freedom and civil rights are created and strengthened by political (democratic) struggle and not by law.

Democracy, defined in radical and agonic terms as against the strictures of law, is the underlying reason why scholars and defenders of academic freedom have been and are so careful to note its distinctive foundation in professional norms and its independence from the First Amendment. This strategy freed the principle from the vicissitudes of judicial opinion, enhanced the autonomy of the campus as a self-governing community, and gave the American Association of University Professors' (AAUP's) 1915 and 1940 *Statement of Principles on Academic Freedom and Tenure* applicability to both public and private institutions of higher education. However, while this bifurcated approach to the freedoms of the campus achieves both conceptual clarity and historical accuracy, it begins to fray when confronted with contemporary political reality.[19] For the purpose of this chapter on Zinn's pedagogical and political defense of academic freedom and free speech, an examination of the 2006 case *Garcetti v. Ceballos* can be sufficient to illuminate the areas of overlap and friction between academic freedom and the law. These areas of imbrication are where Zinn directed his teaching and his political action.

The case is relatively straightforward. Richard Ceballos was a deputy district attorney for the Los Angeles County District Attorney's office. He was asked by a defense attorney to examine some apparent inconsistencies in an affidavit that was used to obtain a search warrant. Ceballos engaged in a personal investigation, found several problems with the affidavit, and wrote a memorandum to his superiors requesting dismissal of the case. At a subsequent meeting with his superiors, which was described as "heated," Ceballos's request was denied and the case proceeded. At trial, he was called to the stand by the defense attorney, and Ceballos once again described the problems with the affidavit. The trial court did not consider his testimony substantial enough to accept the challenge to the warrant. Following the memorandum and the testimony, Ceballos was assigned to a new position, transferred, and denied promotion. He considered these actions to be retaliations for his opinion on the affidavit and sued his superiors. His case was dismissed by the district court, but he won in the Court of Appeals based on earlier rulings that recognized the First Amendment right of a public employee who spoke "as a citizen upon matters of public concern."[20] This right would protect, for example, a public-school teacher's right to criticize a budgetary policy of the local school board or school administrator.

In his concurrence, Judge Diarmuid O'Scannlain set the tone for the eventual reversal of the decision by the Supreme Court. He argued that the Court of Appeals was bound by precedent (*stare decisis*) to rule as it did. He contended that those earlier cases should be "revisited and overruled," and the new principle for deciding cases of speech by public employees should be predicated on the distinction "between speech offered by a public employee acting *as an employee* carrying out his or her ordinary job duties and that spoken by an employee acting *as a citizen* expressing his or her personal views on disputed matters of public import." (Emphasis in original.) The implication of such a standard for academic freedom is a blurring of the kind of division between principle and constitutional law the framers of the 1915 *Statement of Principles* sought to secure conceptually and rhetorically. The standard also entails an attenuation of the role of the professor as employee.

In the Supreme Court, Justice Anthony Kennedy, writing for the majority, argued that Ceballos's remarks regarding the affidavit were made pursuant to his duties and could be restricted because it was a matter of an employer's exercising control "over what the employer itself has commissioned or created."[21] Justice Kennedy responded to concerns over the decision's "ramifications for academic freedom" by asserting that the activities of teaching and scholarship are protected by "additional constitutional interests," and left the matter to be adjudicated in future decisions. However, a subcommittee of the AAUP's Committee A on Academic Freedom and Tenure observed three such future cases where lower courts employing the *Garcetti* rule undermined the assurances of Justice Kennedy and denied claims of protected faculty speech.[22] The subcommittee went on to note the chilling effect these rulings have on faculty speech (both intramural and extramural), on their involvement in university governance, and how the decisions reveal a disturbing ignorance on the part of the judiciary regarding the roles and work of the professoriate. Once a complaint by a professor or university official leaves the confines of campus and becomes part of a legal proceeding, the terms of academic freedom require acceptance (in the forms of precedent and discretion) by the judiciary to be employed effectively.

The implications of the *Garcetti* rule for academic freedom and the candor required for effective campus governance are clear. Moreover, the AAUP report shows that *Garcetti* and related cases[23] demonstrate a clear trend toward increased contentiousness in questions of campus governance, especially, and not surprisingly, in this post-9/11 age of increasing neoliberal and national-security influences on curriculum and pedagogy. These cases redefine the status of the professoriate from an independent voice in the classroom and a citizen of the campus to that of a mere employee bound by loyalty to the rules of the employer. It is an eclipse of the idea of the university as a space for the exchange of ideas on even the most controversial of public issues, and a redefinition of university administration as an agent of the state and beholden to the views of private and public funding sources.[24] According to the AAUP draft report,

> What has emerged from these rulings is a negative or inverse correlation between the scope of a professor's (or a faculty's) role in shared governance and the breadth of potential protection for expressive activity.... In brief, as the cases stand now, one could argue that the less of a stake you have in your institution's shared governance, the freer you are (as a First Amendment matter) to criticize how it is governed, and vice versa.[25]

Howard Zinn was never guilty of expecting justice or enlightenment from the judiciary, although there were judges, decisions, and principles in landmark cases he admired. He would contend that academic freedom is strengthened when it is used as a platform from which political pressure can be exerted on the courts to expand the freedom of speech and inquiry, and not only for the privileged who study and forge careers on the campuses of the nation.[26] That is, Zinn thought the courts an imperfect avenue of redress and conflict resolution, where argumentation is performed by a small class of experts employing a technical vocabulary that equates law with order and justice. Even when the victims of an injustice win in court, it does not translate into the kind of empowerment experienced by those who foster change through democratic political action. Democratic demands for judicial reforms expose the anti-democratic character of the courts as a form of corruption. The legitimacy of the court system is not anchored in the sovereignty of the people; rather, the court's legitimacy is anchored in the Constitution, and justices conceive themselves the last and best interpreters of the document, hence the court system's vulnerability to corruption defined classically as rule in one's self-interest rather than in the interest of the whole.

While teaching in the Jim Crow South, Zinn was well positioned to see the corruption of a judicial system (backed by the police) bent on perpetuating apartheid. This experience nourished his equation of law with disorder and injustice. The path to justice was, for him, direct political action against laws that justify exclusion and inequality, empower the police to break up peaceful demonstrations, send young people to war, and demand unreflective loyalty. In reflecting on the relation of law to democracy, Zinn turned to the language of the Declaration of Independence:

Law is only a means. Government is only a means. "Life, Liberty, and the pursuit of Happiness"—these are the ends. And "whenever any Form of Government becomes destructive to these ends, it is the Right of the People, to alter or to abolish it, and to institute new government."[27]

The tenor of this claim takes us back to our original reflection on whether Zinn was motivated by communitarian politics or a liberal ethics, by the question of the just life of the citizen or the good life of the individual. He was always careful to distinguish himself from Marxism; and while he acted against state-enforced injustices, Zinn (1997c: 614–618) believed that the state could be reformed and turned toward constructive ends. This ambition for the just employment of state power, and occasionally state protection, distinguished him from the anarchists he often marched with and for whom he professed admiration.[28]

Dissent in Academia

For Zinn, dissent was intrinsic to what it means to be a good citizen. He was dedicated to being a good citizen on these active grounds and extended this idea to include being a citizen of the campus community. Thus, even when Zinn described himself in revolutionary terms, the revolution he spoke of was personal and did not entail the overthrow of the state or any act of violence. Rather, you pressure the state with symbolism and mass movements to act on behalf of oppressed minorities seeking change. You change the world, however, by changing yourself. In this, Zinn thought of himself as a follower of Emma Goldman (and wrote a play about her).[29]

The dissenting actions Zinn engaged in strengthened and expanded both academic freedom exercised on campus and free speech as it appears in the First Amendment. Dissent was the nourishing source for both. This causal historical and principled relation must never be forgotten, warned Zinn. Moreover, these ideals are only steps along the way to the ultimate goal: from dissent would spring vital and popular democracy, Zinn believed, and on campus this would be the fulfillment of "the idea that students and faculty should have a decisive voice about the way education takes place."[30]

When there is administrative resistance to this ideal, as in the case of John Silber's reign at BU, then the correct response for the faculty, according to Zinn, is to bring the politics of the street onto campus and unionize.[31] At BU this union was formed "under the auspices" of the AAUP. Clerical workers, librarians, and building and grounds workers soon followed with their own union actions. When the Silber administration refused to recognize groups or to negotiate, and reneged on agreements, strikes ensued. By Zinn's account there was great solidarity among all unions and all members of the BU campus. And the solidarity extended beyond the campus, too. When Zinn and four other faculty members refused to cross the picket line of clerical workers, Silber began proceedings against them, citing the terms of their contract. The immediate effect was a proliferation of petitions originating from MIT and Harvard that circulated around the various campuses of Boston, demanding that the harassment of the "BU Five" end, and that Silber be fired. Alumni began filing complaints and demands for Silber's firing too.

With solidarity came polarization. Silber had the backing of a majority of the Board of Trustees, who were grateful for the favors he showed the banking and utilities interests they represented. It was this group of elites, the face of the corporate university, squared off against the various groups composing the campus and its students, the true university. Zinn's (1997c: 613) chronicle reads like a perfect storm stirred up by the power of dissent against fundamentalism in education in league with the fundamentalisms of politics and law:

> The fundamentalists of politics—the Reagans and Bushes and Helmses—want to pull the strings of control tighter on the distribution of wealth and power and civil liberties. The fundamentalists of law, the Borks and Rehnquists, want to interpret the Constitution so as to put strict limits on the legal possibilities for social reform. The fundamentalists of education fear the possibilities inherent in the unique freedom of discussion that we find in higher education.
>
> For today, the names involved in the conflict may have changed, but the terms of the struggle have not, even as they have expanded well beyond BU to characterize the contemporary American university in general. With the decline of tenure and funding for basic scientific research as indicators, it is clear that the fundamentalists are winning.[32]

CONCLUSION: WHAT WAS HOWARD ZINN?

I began this essay with a question about Howard Zinn's politics. Was his political thought grounded in individualism or egalitarianism? I think it fair to say that Zinn was big enough to embody the contradictions between working within Constitutional parameters set out by courts and scholars and challenging these parameters through political action.[33] But I think we get at something far deeper about his political thinking by conceiving of Zinn as a proponent and a powerful embodiment of academic freedom. Politics for Zinn was a matter of directing the power of the community to enhance and defend the liberties and dignity of the individual, particularly the individual subjected to the pains of abjection. We would probably not see Howard Zinn playing the ACLU attorney and defending the freedom-of-speech rights of conservatives. Rather, he worked to cultivate communal regard for the value of the free exchange of ideas.[34] In this, we sense the deep consonance between Zinn's activism and the communal terms of justice and campus governance at the heart of academic freedom.

Effective employment of the terms of academic freedom will both strengthen and broaden its parameters. That is, paradoxically, the more creative you are in taking advantage of academic freedom for pedagogic and scholarly ends, the greater your chances of being criticized for violating its terms and its underlying professional standards, and for turning the classroom into a site for indoctrination rather than learning. Conservative critics of Zinn leveled all of these charges against him.[35] What did Zinn do to earn these criticisms? He pushed the idea of the professor as citizen and officer of the university in terms consistent with the language of the 1940 *Statement of Principles,* to the consternation of the Silber administration.[36] He expanded the plurality of voices normally heard in classes on American history, constitutional law, and political theory. His syllabi offered a reading list to his students that allowed the politically marginalized to speak to a new generation. He expressed a definite point of view in his lectures and discussions that challenged the pieties of the pro-market, pro-military majority and the two-party system, while responding to student questions and counterarguments with respect. His popularity with the students of Spelman and BU testifies to this. And he published books and articles that continue to be read widely, used in classrooms around the country, and criticized and praised by peers, and that contributed to the literature on peace and justice in twentieth-century America. In this, he was a dedicated scholar and teacher.[37]

Reflection on academic freedom created for Howard Zinn the intellectual conditions necessary to reconcile the individualist and egalitarian strains of his political thinking.[38] What the principle of academic freedom calls us to is a life dedicated to learning, which can be conceived as a matter of personal benefit. But we are to use this lifetime apprenticeship in scholarship to teach students to think critically, communicate effectively, cultivate the responsibilities of citizenship defined in terms of dissent as opposed to superficial patriotism, and achieve some sense of personal fulfillment. Perhaps this integral unity of liberalism and socialism could be achieved in the beliefs and actions of social democracy, but political programs tend to be anchored in the logic of coherence and consistency that limit the kind of intellectual experimentation invited by academic freedom. This pragmatic quality of the 1915 *Statement of Principles* was an expression of its principle organizer, John Dewey, and the vital and generous impulse of academic freedom that actually welcomed challenges to its claim as a principle of order and professional standards by those, like Zinn, who argued for the primacy of freedom.

In the end, Howard Zinn came to see academic freedom as a communal model of what the First Amendment should be. He aimed to present this to his students as a way of life. But he also saw that higher education is a privilege not extended to everyone in this country. His books, articles, and speeches were designed to communicate the power of this conception of freedom of thought and inquiry to those whose workdays preclude the time and thrill of classroom discussion. It is this extension of academic freedom—in the form of extramural speech as in a continuum with the educational goals of the university—that will be Zinn's legacy to us, his colleagues and students.

Dear Diary

Alix Olson

Dear Diary,
I'm soooooo in love with my country! All for now.... My country's taking me to a parade!

Dear Diary,
Everywhere I turn, I hear people extolling the virtues of my country and telling me how lucky I am to be with her. Even though I admire a lot of things about her (for example, she has a remarkable music collection, fascinating stories, and a real natural beauty), it's still beginning to feel a little claustrophobic!

Dear Diary,
Today, I found out that my country has been telling people to tell me about how great she is! Kinda immature, don't you think? I had guessed she was a little insecure (she's younger than a lot of other countries), but doesn't my country trust me to think for myself? So, I assured her that I value countries for their kindness, compassion, honesty, and ability to have a sense of humor about themselves. She looked uncomfortable. My country would never admit it, but deep down I don't think she thinks I'm worthy of her love.

Dear Diary,
I'm getting a little worried about my relationship with my country. You see, as much as I want to love, support, and nurture her, the one-way giving is starting to feel unhealthy. When I struggled to explain, for example, that I need to feel celebrated, not just tolerated, she went "uh-huh, uh-huh," but I got the distinct impression she was only pretending to listen. And I've noticed that sometimes my country takes my

checkbook when she thinks I'm not looking and spends it on stuff like new missiles for her and her friends. And then she lectures ME about independence! Something doesn't feel right.

Dear Diary,
Today my country had a huge fight with her best friend, Church! Secretly, I was glad because Church always looks at me weird, like he wants to take control of my body or something, and I just know he's dying to get in bed with my country. I suggested maybe she and Church should cool it for a bit, have a trial separation. My country looked at me like I was crazy. "I need Church's support right now," she said. Whatever. I think Church should go get laid.

Dear Diary,
I asked my country today if she'll love me when I'm old and gray. She said, "As long as I don't have to go helping you out or nothing." That hurt my feelings because I work hard to provide for my country. Heck, I even pay my country's bills. Still, we made up when she told me to take off my clothes and lie spread-eagle on the bed. Then she took pictures and posted them on the internet. But then she said, even though she liked it, it made me a dirty whore. My country sure does give some mixed messages!

Dear Diary,
My country claims she's suffering from multiple-personality disorder. She claims she hears two voices in her head; she calls them "blue" and "red," but I personally never see any changes in her when this happens. So I confided the symptoms to my psychologist friend, who diagnosed her as clinically bipartisan. My country is going on Prozac.

Dear Diary,
Today, my country accused me of betrayal when I was simply pointing out another country's virtues. This, of course, segued into the topic of nonmonogamy, and so I finally felt the courage to tell her that I thought we should open up our relationship. I explained maybe I wasn't the type to settle down with one country. That even if we lived together, I didn't belong to her, that I have allegiances that surpass just one country! First my country pleaded with me, even dragging out the flag as a reminder. When I refused to back down, my country went ballistic—I mean, completely narcissistic, screaming that she was #1! and that I was a free-loving commie and that I've been flirting with Canada right in front of her face. I reminded her that she is always going around meddling with other countries, invading their personal space and ultimately breaking their hearts. I learned that my country sure does not enjoy hearing the truth told right up to her face like that. She completely shut down, cracked a beer, and turned on the news—the kind that only she likes to hear— these meaningless platitudes that massage her ego and justify her aggression. It's incessant. I feel powerless. I want constructive discussions as equals: me and her. But it seems like all my country is looking for is a cheerleader!

Dear Diary,

Today my country and I broke up. It's like a war swept through our relationship, rendering it irreparable. For all her talk of core family values, she's completely unreliable, completely undependable. And I can't be in love with a country I don't trust. But me and some friends of Zinn's—we're planning on staging a critical intervention.

Signing off for now,
Grieving American Citizen

ZINN IN PRACTICE

CHAPTER 8

War Is a Condition in Need of a Cure

Patricia Moynagh

One does not make wars less likely by formulating rules of warfare.... War cannot be humanized. It can only be abolished.

—*Albert Einstein*[1]

I am not a pacifist. I'm against war.

—*Gino Strada*[2]

Violence can be justifiable, but it never will be legitimate.

—*Hannah Arendt*[3]

My hope is that your generation will demand an end to war, that your generation will do something that has not yet been done in history and wipe out the national boundaries that separate us from other human beings on this earth.

—*Howard Zinn, "Against Discouragement" (2005)*

Two years before he died, Howard Zinn said, "It's time to accept that war, like tuberculosis, like cannibalism, like slavery, is something that should be put into the past."[4] This statement is deeply principled. It equates war with sickness, moral depravity, and institutional evil. If it can be so described, and I think it surely can, then it follows that we have an obligation to do away with it. It is thus that I see war as a condition in need of a cure. This essay honors Howard Zinn's legacy by reflecting upon this most astute historian's hope for the future. I see no greater way to pay homage to his immense body of work, and to the man himself, than to foreground one of his primary visions for the future.[5] For Zinn, war must become a thing of the past.

I believe his vast knowledge of history, and his telling of a people's history in particular, puts him in a privileged position to envision where he thinks we are capable of taking ourselves. Extremely well acquainted with past struggles for social justice, he is famous for chronicling numerous examples of "a power governments cannot suppress." Through his mining of history, Zinn demonstrates that we have reason to believe it is not only deeply desirable, but also possible, to reject war. It is clear: We must work together to render war a thing of the past, or suffer the consequences of living with its wretched results for who knows how much longer. He not only hopes that we, the people of the world, may one day refuse war once and for all; he argues it is only we who can do so. As he often claimed, any semblance of democracy and liberty we experience is the result of people's struggles for greater social justice. A war-free world will occur when people demand it. Just weeks before he died, Zinn told *New York Times* reporter Bob Herbert (2010) what he had told so many of us over the years: "If there is going to be change, real change, it will have to work its way from the bottom up, from the people themselves. That's how change happens."

If the past is indicative, then we cannot rely on governments to accomplish this great feat. It is their business to wage wars and win them, not enlist new ideas to think beyond them. Yet, we must contest the military mind-set. This means exposing the myths and lies that surround war as well as discussing and disseminating the consequences of war. It also means challenging governments whenever they plan for war. The old cliché "war is hell" is often uttered with despair, drowned out by resignation. But we must take on this defeatist mode of thinking as well and look to the research and history that, as Zinn shows, produce no compelling evidence to suggest that war is natural, and therefore destined to remain part of the human condition. On the contrary, governments make great efforts again and again to bring a nation to war. Zinn provides numerous instances to support this claim. For example, he recounts important information about the US government's efforts to lure soldiers to fight in World War I. When Woodrow Wilson was campaigning for president in 1916, he said he would not support the war, knowing it would be unpopular to do so. Once elected, Wilson started to mobilize for war, but it was no easy task. Zinn writes,

> Despite the rousing words of Wilson about a war "to end all wars" and "to make the world safe for democracy," Americans did not rush to enlist. A million men were needed, but in the first six weeks after the declaration of war only 73,000 volunteered. Congress voted overwhelmingly for a draft.[6]

Zinn makes these points about how populations need to be coerced, cajoled, or otherwise enticed into fighting wars. If the government's use of propaganda and coercion does not work, then punitive measures are used, including the draft and jail. Zinn documents all kinds of governmental inducements and threats to mobilize young people for war. Even once in the military, there are many soldiers who have revolted against their military commanders for unfair treatment or challenged the morality of their assignments. This has occurred since the beginning of the nation's founding until the present day. Soldiers have resisted in all times in various ways and for different reasons. From mutinous troops in the Revolutionary War, who grew angry as they were "suffering in the cold, dying of sickness, watching the civilian profiteers get rich,"[7] to "fragging" (soldiers using grenades or other explosives against commanders) in Vietnam, to the current Iraq Veterans Against the War—whose founder, Kelly Dougherty, said about her experiences in Iraq, "I'm not defending freedom; I'm protecting a corporate interest"[8]—voices of resistance emerge. Zinn excavates what happened in 1781 to some of the mutinous Revolutionary War troops, an event that is no doubt hardly known today. In the eyes of Washington, the execution was an example for others who might resist:

> Six hundred men, who themselves had been well fed and clothed, marched on the mutineers and surrounded and disarmed them. Three ringleaders were put on trial immediately, in the field. One was pardoned, and two were shot by firing squads made up of their friends, who wept as they pulled the triggers. It was "an example," Washington said.[9]

Zinn's accounting of these episodes, like so many others he provides, documents how official commanders, in this case the future first president of the United States, use the most brutal violence on those who resist their conditions. There are numerous examples of dissent and revolt against military leaders across this land and others.

But the belief in the instinct for war prevails for many, and it is very well entrenched, not easily undone, despite there being no scientific proof for it. Zinn draws on many disciplines, including the biological sciences, and finds no compelling evidence for people wanting to go to war and risk their lives doing so. To those who interpret the sociobiologist E. O. Wilson's work, particularly his book *On Human Nature,* as supporting war as natural, Zinn notes that even though Wilson spoke of a propensity for aggression, he also concludes that environmental circumstances determine if people act on it. Moreover, Zinn also emphasizes that there are many ways to channel aggression. It need not translate into war and violence.[10] Thus, one can surmise that altering our conditions, indeed improving our environments to render them more peaceful, is likely to beget less violence.[11]

Furthermore, Zinn draws on anthropology and shows that conditions help determine a group's proclivity for bellicosity or more peaceful behavior. So there seems no inherent inclination for war. Indeed, governments have continuously propagandized wars, tried to justify them in the name of some greater good, offered enticements to people if they join the military, and so on. But wars cannot occur without the willingness of people to fight them. Zinn claims this is why wars are sold as good wars, fights for democracy and freedom. Wars must be cloaked in noble causes. Zinn observes it is a tribute to people's basic sense of decency that if governmental leaders told the truth, it would not be possible to get people to fight in wars. Governmental leaders lie to achieve their purposes. Zinn says it is a failure of American education that the citizenry does not know more about the history of wars. Zinn (2007a: 194) says, "When you look at the history of wars, you see how war corrupts everyone involved, how the so-called good side behaves like the bad side, and how this has been true from the Peloponnesian War all the way to our own time." With greater memories of past wars, including the steps national leaders take to justify them, there might well be greater resistance from the beginning; and this resistance could also be less likely to wane, despite efforts by governmental leaders to weaken it. With time, but tremendous human losses, populations eventually turn against wars.

Wars have served military and economic expansion. This was as true in 1848, when the United States took half of Mexico, as it was in 1898, when it won Cuba from Spain (and later gave it conditional independence). It is also true of William McKinley's war in the Philippines at the end of the nineteenth century and of Woodrow Wilson's occupying armies in Puerto Rico and Haiti. Mark Twain's observation that history does not repeat itself but that it surely rhymes is easy to invoke here. Each of these historical events is discrete, circumscribed, and contained by its own contingency, to be sure. One is not the other. The point is not to conflate them, but rather to discern a likeness among them. If the general sequence of events is similar enough, it can be called a pattern. Indeed Zinn, a great admirer of Twain, quotes him for giving voice to the scenes that unfold once leaders have decided on a military action. As Zinn (2011a: 128) puts it, Twain describes "the process by which wars that are first seen as unnecessary by the mass of the people become converted into 'just' wars." It is the turn of the twentieth century as Twain observes the US wars in Cuba and the Philippines. Capturing this historical moment in his short story "The Mysterious Stranger," Twain writes,

> The loud little handful—as usual—will shout for the war. The pulpit will—warily and cautiously—object—at first; the great, big, dull bulk of the nation will rub its sleepy eyes and try to make out why there should be a war, and will say, earnestly and indignantly, "It is unjust and dishonorable, and there is no necessity for it." Then the handful will shout louder. A few fair men on the other side will argue and reason against the war with speech and pen, and at first will have a hearing and be applauded; but it will not last long; those others will outshout them, and presently the anti-war audiences will thin out and lose popularity. Before long you will see this curious thing: the speakers stoned from the platform, and free speech strangled by the hordes of furious men who in their secret hearts are still at one with those stoned speakers—as earlier—but do not dare to say so. And now the whole nation—pulpit and all—will take up the war-cry, and shout itself hoarse, and mob any honest man who ventures to open his mouth; and presently such mouths will cease to open. Next the statesmen will invent cheap lies, putting the blame upon the nation that is attacked, and every man will be glad of those conscience-soothing falsities, and will diligently study them, and refuse to examine any refutation of them; and thus he will by and by convince himself that the war is just, and will thank God for the better sleep he enjoys after this process of grotesque self-deception.[12]

As these expansions were accompanied by noble language, so was the US invasion of Afghanistan in 2001. First called "Infinite Justice" and then named "Enduring Freedom," this invasion was packaged, in part, as a mission to free women. It was no such thing, of course, but selling it this way was an attempt to gather support for worthy aspirations. That wars are cloaked in noble-sounding causes is, as Zinn says, a salute to people's sensibilities to want to fight for good purposes. Zinn says Americans should stand behind freedom and democracy. These are commendable goals. But these are goods that cannot be developed through the force of arms.[13] Latching on to so-called good purposes, however, can lead to horrifically violent results to attain the espoused goal, especially if one fails to think through what one is doing to achieve them.

Drawing upon his own experiences as a bomber in World War II, Zinn shares an insight that deserves great reflection. Referring to a mission that was testing a new kind of bomb made from "jellied gasoline," later referred to as napalm, Zinn recounts dropping bombs that destroyed a German encampment and left a blaze that killed many inhabitants of a nearby small French town called Royan. About his direct involvement, Zinn testifies,

> I don't remember having any hesitation about releasing those fire-bombs. And since that day I have never doubted that all of us are capable of the most atrocious acts—not because our intent is evil, but because it is so good. We set laudable ultimate goals, and these enable us to proceed to the most ruthless acts without scrupulously making sure they lead to those goals.[14]

Zinn's personal war experiences that led to his subsequent thoughts about evil invite a comparison both to Hannah Arendt's concept of evil and to Simone de Beauvoir's concept of refusing freedom through elevating a *cause* to the detriment of people's real needs. Arendt, like Zinn, developed her thoughts on evil out of her reaction to World War II. Arendt coined the phrase "the banality of evil" to capture her emerging responses to Adolf Eichmann's trial in 1961. Observing and reporting upon his trial, she concluded that the kind of evil performed by Eichmann was not akin to the stark malevolence of a Shakespearean villain such as a Richard III, Macbeth, or Iago.[15] Evil intent runs through the veins of these literary characters and the Bard's audience can readily grasp the presence of malice. Self-evident monsters are easy to name, and they are rare. But Eichmann's evil was "terrifyingly normal" in that he was without motive except for his own job promotion and wanting to make it to the higher rank of lieutenant colonel. He did not even know what the Nazi Party stood for, but he needed a job. Once employed, he carried out some of its worst crimes. Arendt claims that Eichmann's evil was wrought from a "remoteness from reality" that came from not really thinking about what he was doing.[16]

Unlike Zinn's position, which suggests we are all capable of doing atrocious acts from good intent, Arendt's take on Eichmann is that he had no motive at all. However different Zinn and Arendt are on conceptualizing evil, they converge in one important way. Monstrous, premeditated wickedness is not necessary for great evil to occur. Either way, the lesson from World War II is troubling in that evil actions are all too common and do not spring from evil intentions. Whether from good intent (Zinn) or lack of any particular intent (Arendt), we all may be capable of atrocious actions. One need not be villainous to do evil (Arendt). One can even mean well (Zinn).

Beauvoir's concept of freedom, and how any of us can refuse it in many ways, is useful to discuss in the context of Zinn's claim that evil actions can readily flow from good intentions. In *The Ethics of Ambiguity*, Beauvoir (1948: 47–52) discusses what she calls "the serious man," to show how any of us can lose ourselves in a cause, be it "science, philosophy, revolution, etc." I think we can relate this insight to Zinn's personal experience. If a cause becomes greater than anything else, including people, then whole villages, in Zinn's case Royan, can be destroyed. For Beauvoir, the cause takes the place of freedom, nothing is questioned, and this is perilous. She writes,

> But the serious man puts nothing into question. For the military man, the army is useful; for the colonial administrator, the highway; for the serious revolutionary, the revolution—army, highway, revolution, productions becoming inhuman idols to which one will not hesitate to sacrifice man himself. Therefore, the serious man is dangerous.[17]

Of course, Zinn would become an ardent spokesman against war. It is crucial that we recognize, with Zinn, that it "isn't the population that demands war. It's the leaders who demand war and who prepare the population for war." That war is part of human nature relieves governmental leaders of their responsibilities for driving nations into wars and blames citizens for this calamity. Zinn likens this inversion to faulting poor people for being poor, rather than seeing that wealth is distributed very unequally.[18] Both are insidious examples of ideology flowing from the dominant political interests. I am reminded of Karl Marx's observation that the ruling ideology in every epoch is the ideology of the ruling class. With education and courage, it can all be challenged.

Of all Zinn's positions on politics and history, his universal rejection of war as a way to solve any human problem has, in his own words, "undoubtedly aroused the most controversy."[19] To reject war categorically is to take away the possibility that some wars are just and others not. There is an enormous literature and history on just and unjust wars dating back to the Middle Ages, but Zinn thinks this distinction cannot be credibly drawn and it is misguided to do so. Indeed, Zinn says that the worst legacy of World War II may well be that it has been deemed "a good war." This thinking enables governments to claim this elevated, yet dangerously deceptive, status for subsequent wars. Denying that such distinctions can be made is a crucial step for Zinn, and he urges that we all take it with him.

It is important to see that Zinn once believed this distinction sustainable. It is also important to appreciate his evolution in thinking about war. He was not, in his youth, antiwar; he became so after he began to question his own role as a once-enthusiastic bombardier in World War II. His repudiation of all war grew out of his reflections upon his own war experiences, followed by his deep reading of the history of war and militarism. If one renounces all war, then there is no way to categorize some as good, others bad; some just, others not. For Zinn, this is precisely the most salient point, one that he shared numerous times in his writing and speeches.[20] Zinn questions how good "this good war" could be if it took at least fifty million lives, most of them civilians. It isn't that fascism wasn't worth fighting against or that genocide shouldn't be stopped. These are honorable and just causes, and he is adamant that they be so recognized. But a just cause does not mean a just war. And the two should not be confused.

Long after World War II, in the wake of 9/11, Zinn drew this contrast between a just cause and a just war. Zinn takes to task some progressives who were willing to support military action in Afghanistan for confusing just causes with just wars. Three months after 9/11, Zinn's piece "A Just Cause, Not a Just War" appeared in *The Progressive*:

> I believe that the progressive supporters of the war have confused a "just cause" with a "just war." There are unjust causes, such as the attempt of the United States to establish its power in Vietnam, or to dominate Panama or Grenada, or to subvert the government of Nicaragua. And a cause may be just—getting North Korea to withdraw from South Korea, getting Saddam Hussein to withdraw from Kuwait, or ending terrorism—but it does not follow that going to war on behalf of that cause, with the inevitable mayhem that follows, is just.[21]

Zinn draws a crucial distinction here that allows one to recognize that a cause can be just while war is not. But why not use militarism to fight on behalf of a just cause? The answer lies in the corrosive consequences of war and what military force does to people. The reality of the many innocent deaths must be confronted, and it is not acceptable to dismiss such deaths by calling them "accidents."

Zinn uses a powerful analogy to argue against NATO and US assurances that bombing in Kosovo was justifiable. Zinn convinces readers that civilian casualties are not accidents by comparing these bombings to a reckless driver in a school area. He first shares his own actions as a bombardier. Even though he didn't intend to cause civilian deaths, it is not an accident that they occurred. He doesn't accept that the civilian deaths are accidents, even though one doesn't intend them. One knows ahead of time that there will be unacceptable civilian casualties:

> One day in 1945, I dropped canisters of napalm on a village in France. I have no idea how many villagers died, but I did not mean to kill them. Can I absolve what I did as "an accident"? Aerial bombings have as inevitable consequences the killing of civilians, and this is foreseeable, even if the details about who will be the victims cannot be predicted.[22]

Zinn says, "When you make war against a tyrant, the people you kill are the victims of the tyrant." This is clearly applicable to the invasion of Iraq that began in 2003. As of the end of 2011, 145,800 civilians and approximately 20,000 combatants were killed as a direct result of the war.[23] Zinn (2003b: 288) writes, "It is sad to see how, in so many countries, citizens have been led to war by the argument that it is necessary because there are tyrannies abroad, evil rulers, murderous juntas. But to make war is not to destroy the tyrants; it is to kill their subjects, their pawns, their conscripted soldiers, their subjugated civilians." War wreaks unimaginable havoc on innocent people, a good many of them children. It should be clear how and why Zinn concludes that war, at least in its modern incarnation, is reckless and its consequences far too grave to ever be justifiable. Given the inevitable and colossal loss of lives, war should be rendered something of the past.

If mayhem is too great a price to pay, even for a just cause, and if we refuse, with Zinn, to endorse any war, then must we support pacifism? The refusal of war may be the only absolutist position Zinn came to hold, suspicious of absolutes as he remained. But Zinn's antiwar stance does not mean he is a pacifist. He begins a piece entitled "Pacifism and War" as follows:

> With the world immersed in the turmoil of war, it may be useful to examine the idea of pacifism. I have never used the word "pacifist" to describe myself, because it suggests something absolute, and I am suspicious of absolutes. I want to leave openings for unpredictable possibilities. There might be situations—and even such strong pacifists as Gandhi and Martin Luther King believed this—when a small, focused act of violence against a monstrous, immediate evil would be justified.[24]

Although Zinn's refusal of war is categorical, it is clear that he reserves the possibility for the use of violence to combat "a monstrous, immediate evil." Such a focused act of violence would be justified. The sequence of words "monstrous, immediate evil" is key in this passage because it provides criteria for evaluating when violence may be justified, if not legitimate. The farther away a threat, the less compelling it is. This is why the preemptive-war doctrine is wholly unjustifiable. It is using violence because of some potential future danger. The danger must be monstrous and immediate. Here I am reminded of Arendt's useful analysis on violence. She writes,

> Violence can be justifiable, but it never will be legitimate. Its justification loses in plausibility the farther its intended end recedes into the future. No one questions the use of violence in self-defense, because the danger is not only clear but also present, and the end justifying the means is immediate.[25]

What about humanitarian intervention? Zinn writes,

> Strada rejects the idea of "humanitarian intervention," as I do.... I can accept that there may be rare situations where a small act of force might be used to halt a genocidal situation—Darfur and Rwanda are examples. But war, defined as the massive and indiscriminate use of force (and technology dictates that any large-scale use of force cannot be focused on a particular evil-doer) cannot be accepted, once you understand its human consequences.[26]

Zinn agrees with Gino Strada, an Italian war surgeon who has performed operations in many war-torn countries, including Afghanistan, Iraq, Bosnia, Somalia, Eritrea, and Cambodia. Like Zinn, Strada aims to bring light to the atrocities on civilian populations. (The percentage of civilian deaths during wartime is alarmingly high, 40–90 percent depending on the particular conflict.[27]) He founded Emergency, a non-governmental organization that provides medical care to war victims. His position did not start out as a political one, but grew out of the work he did on operating tables. Strada and Zinn teamed up together and appeared in public to denounce military "solutions" to our problems.

This raises the question of using violence in the service of a just cause. Is this permissible? I think Arendt was on to something when she maintained that "violence can be justifiable, but it will never be legitimate." Violence can be defended, but it will never truly be quite right. Violence is a failure of human relations. However, this does not mean an absolutist position of nonviolence is sustainable. Zinn puts the matter this way:

> An absolutist position of nonviolence is logically hard to defend, it seems to me. If people are ruled by a powerful and unrelenting oppressor, nonviolence might compel them to forego social change. They would thus be condemned to a permanent cruelty that might be ended by a violent but brief rebellion.[28]

Zinn continues to explain that a small act of violence "may be required to prevent a larger one." Formulating his position in the late 1960s, he provides several examples to convey such a justification, such as "the removal of a malignant tumor by surgery; the possible assassination of Hitler to shorten World War II; and the action of a Negro mother, alone with her children, whose home in Georgia was about to be invaded by a mob of armed white men, and who fired her shotgun through the door, killing one and dispersing the rest."[29]

These examples are easy to follow, and yet Zinn worries that "the rationalization is so easy and so frequent that once we give up a position of absolute nonviolence, the door is open to the most shocking abuses." He then affirms that "our starting point should always be the premise that violence is to be avoided and other methods of achieving change should be sought." He concludes with this claim:

> If violence is ever to be justified, the evidence must be overwhelming and clear; the greater the proposed violence, the greater must be both the magnitude of the social goal and the certainty that it will be achieved. Certain other principles are also essential; that the more closely the violence is focused on the social malignancy—as in precision surgery—the greater likelihood that it can be justified; that the persons who pay the price (since cost must be measured against gain) are the ones who decide whether violence will be used. Self-defense, involving direct action by the persons attacked and against the attacker, meets both these principles.[30]

Captain John Brown's use of violence to fight against slavery is an interesting case study to test the Arendtian claim that violence can be justifiable, but not legitimate. Brown's violence is also useful to think through because it allows us to examine Zinn's (2002 [1967]: 64) claim that "Violence as a means of achieving social change is a very complex problem." Brown tried to end slavery by using violence, starting on October 16, 1856, when he and his men killed five people who were aligned with pro-slavery forces during what came to be called the Pottawatomie Massacre. The term "Bleeding Kansas" (1854–1861) would be used to describe what became a battleground for pro-slavery and abolitionist contingents fighting in the Kansas Territory and Missouri over whether Kansas would join the Union as a free or slave state.

In 1859, Brown led eighteen men in storming the arsenal at Harpers Ferry, Virginia, with the aim of starting a slave insurrection. Most of these men were in their twenties and "had written farewell letters to family and lovers. Five of them were black, including a fugitive slave and a freedman whose wife and children were still in bondage. Two others were the Captain's sons."[31] This effort was fated to fail, given how entrenched slavery was at the time. Henry David Thoreau, in his "A Plea for Captain John Brown," describes Brown in glowing terms, claiming that he "had a spark of divinity in him," and that he was "an angel of light" and "the bravest and humanest man in all the country."[32] Thoreau had great sympathy for Brown and thought it unjust for him to be executed. For Thoreau, Brown's resistance to authority was admirably principled. I agree.

The country would suffer much more violence during the Civil War, which brought slavery to an end. Brown's last words powerfully capture the injustice of class. One month before his hanging, he said,

> Had I interfered in the manner which I admit, and which I admit has been fairly proved ... had I so interfered in behalf of the rich, the powerful, the intelligent, the so-called great, or in behalf of any of their friends, either father, mother, brother, sister, wife, or children, or any of that class, and suffered and sacrificed what I have in this interference, it would have been all right; every man in this court would have deemed it an act worthy of reward rather than punishment. This Court acknowledges too, as I suppose, the validity of the law of God. I see a book kissed here which I suppose to be the Bible, or, at least the New Testament. That teaches me that all things "whatsoever I would that men should do unto me, I should do ever so to them." It teaches me, further, to "remember them that are in bonds as bound with them." I endeavored to act up to these instructions. ... I believe that to have interfered as I have done, as I have always freely admitted I have done, in behalf of His despised poor, was not wrong, but right. Now, if it is deemed necessary that I should forfeit my life for the furtherance of the ends of justice, and mingle my blood further with the blood of my children and with the blood of millions in this slave country, whose rights are disregarded by wicked, cruel, and unjust enactments, I submit, so let it be done![33]

Zinn, in *The People Speak: American Voices, Some Famous, Some Little Known* (2004a), followed this speech up with that of Frederick Douglass, who in 1881 gave a talk at a college in Harpers Ferry. Douglass paid tribute to Brown, saying,

If John Brown did not end the war that ended slavery, he did at least begin the war that ended slavery. If we look over the dates, places and men for which this honor is claimed, we shall find that not Carolina, but Virginia, not Fort Sumter, but Harpers Ferry and the arsenal, not Colonel Anderson, but John Brown, began the war that ended American slavery and made this a free republic. Until that blow was struck, the prospect of freedom was dim, shadowy and uncertain. The irrepressible conflict was one of words, votes and compromises. When John Brown stretched forth his arm, the sky was clear.[34]

Douglass finds honor and courage in John Brown, as did Thoreau and others, including Ralph Waldo Emerson, but many others branded him insane. About this episode, Zinn (2007a: 139) writes, "Shortly after John Brown was hanged for killing people, believing he was advancing the cause of freedom for slaves, the US government engaged in a war, presumably to abolish slavery, and 600,000 died on the battlefields. Would anyone dare to refer to the US government as 'dangerous' and 'insane'?"

I think Brown's violence, used for a most just cause, was justifiable, but it cannot count as legitimate. This is because using violence, even for a justifiable purpose, is a sign of failed human relations. A legitimate action is somehow thoroughly right and requires no justification. Brown's use of limited violence to fight against a far greater violence requires justification and, as I said earlier, I think his actions are justifiable. Because slavery was violent to the core, and institutionally defended, Brown was more than justified in his actions to confront it with force. Moreover, Brown's violence was in response to a "monstrous, immediate evil," to use Zinn's criteria. It is justifiable by this measure. It was an act of force, not an indiscriminate use of force that would wipe out innocent people. But unlike Brown's violence, which can be defended, that of modern warfare is not justifiable. For, as Zinn says,

> Modern warfare has certain fundamental characteristics which make it the least defensible use of violence in achieving any social goals: It is massive, indiscriminate, not focused on the evil-doers; its human cost is gigantic; it violates the principle of free choice on two counts, because it is fought by conscripts, and against people who did not decide to be involved (civilians).[35]

Zinn (2003b: 296) says, "Those of us who call for the repudiation of massive violence to solve human problems must sound utopian, romantic. So did those who demanded the end of slavery." This sentiment leads Zinn to question the possibility of military victories in modern warfare.[36]

The invasion of Afghanistan, now one of the longest wars in US history, will likely end in US military withdrawal, as has the war in Iraq. This after the unnecessary suffering of the many and the monetary enrichment of a few. Another war with no clear victory is the 2006 conflict between Israel and Hezbollah, deeply entrenched in Lebanon. Neither side emerged a winner here either, but there were enormous human costs. The Iran-Iraq War (1980–1988), which resulted in no border changes or victor ended in a truce after 1,500,000 deaths on both sides, mostly civilians. What came to be known as "the war of the cities" killed thousands indiscriminately on both sides, as the capital cities of Tehran and Baghdad exploded bombs on each other's capitals and border towns. The war in the former Yugoslavia (1992–1995), which ended in the Dayton Accords, killed 102,622 civilians and military personnel, of which 55,261 were civilians.[37] In this case, the United States brokered a settlement, but there were no winners. Between 1945 and 2000, it is estimated that 41,000,000 people have been killed in wars.[38]

Zinn could have despaired in the face of the enormous obstacles that stand in the way of achieving a better world. Military and corporate interests are formidable forces to fight. But the *people's historian* remained optimistic. He could draw upon many examples from our past about amazingly brave and humane movements. And it is because of this that he remained hopeful to the end—so hopeful that he could say what probably very few would. To the graduating seniors of the college where he held his first full-time teaching job, where he was also advisor to the Student Nonviolent Coordinating Committee (SNCC), he said,

> My hope is that your generation will demand that your children be brought up in a world without war. If we want a world in which the people of all countries are brothers and sisters, if the children all over the world are considered as our children, then war—in which children are always the greatest casualties—cannot be accepted as a way of solving problems.[39]

That Zinn delivered these words at Spelman College years after he was fired for insubordination—Zinn angered the administration for marching with his students for civil rights in the 1960s—was not an irony lost on him, to be sure. But it is also an indication that Zinn's ideas are gaining the credit they deserve. Those who continue to resist his work and activities do so because their ideology blinds them to historical truths or their interests are entangled with forces that need to be dismantled, given what Zinn advocates.

Zinn knew who the real heroes of American history are and he made a whole generation aware of them. In "Unsung Heroes," Zinn (2007a: 57–61) remembers the many voices who should replace the war-makers and military leaders. *They* are the giants, whether well-known or not, who took action in one way or another for which the rest of us remain their beneficiaries. In the American pantheon of heroes, Mark Twain towers over Theodore Roosevelt, Helen Keller over Woodrow Wilson, Frederick Douglass over Abraham Lincoln, William Penn over George Washington. Along with these stand millions of other ordinary yet extraordinary Americans, who fought in ways big and small to develop a more just society. These Americans, like Zinn himself, are a constant source of strength.

Zinn reminds his audience that lest we think war will always be with us, we can point to other monumental social struggles, such as abolition, that eventually prevailed over a formidable apparatus. To some, it must have seemed a utopian wish. But abolitionists persisted and the dream became a reality. This is deeply inspirational. In repudiating war, even so-called just wars, Zinn doesn't recoil from just causes. Indeed, his own life can be seen as encompassing one just cause after another. In actuality, he aligned himself with groups and often took leading roles in social struggles. He fought against many injustices: segregation, the Vietnam War, apartheid, and economic inequalities, among others. As we have seen, he accepts that there are instances in which a just cause may require force to combat a great wrong. Protecting Rwanda and Darfur stand out as profound examples. But while force may be justifiable, war (most especially in its modern incarnation) will never be just. The injustice of war is, above all, revealed in its consequences—namely, that too many of its victims are civilians, and so many of them children. Zinn (2007a: 195) was right in claiming that wars waged by nations "are a hundred times more deadly for innocent people than the attacks by terrorists, vicious as they are." As this chapter has reminded us, the statistics demonstrate this point overwhelmingly. This is a fitting quote by Zinn with which to end this chapter given our current historical moment, in which our governmental leaders fight the so-called War on Terror without really examining the *terror of war*. War is a condition in need of a cure. The cure resides in the people's will.

CHAPTER 9

Howard Zinn

A Moral Example for G.I. Resistance

Ross Caputi

There are some harmful actions that can't be blamed on a single individual. Some harms can only come about when many people contribute, even though each person's actual contribution may seem small and insignificant. Imagine a working mother who buys a daily coffee and throws her styrofoam cup away when she's finished, a college graduate who takes a job that makes money over a job that does good, and the many Americans (and citizens of the "coalition of the willing" nations) who watched their country wage an unjust war. When these individual actions and inactions are multiplied by a population, they can result in enormous amounts of harm. When my former military unit, 1st Battalion 8th Marines, laid siege to Fallujah, Iraq, in November 2004, we forced 200,000 civilians to flee their homes, we killed hundreds (possibly thousands) of civilians, and we destroyed large portions of the city.[1] There isn't one person from my unit whom I can point my finger at and say he alone is responsible for the atrocities that ensued; everyone played a role.

My experience in Fallujah taught me one clear lesson: it is not enough that we refrain from committing individual acts of harm; we have to refrain from participating in harmful group actions as well. I didn't know it then, but what I came to believe in is called "collective responsibility," a controversial (and, I would argue, radical) ethical concept. A proper understanding and application of collective responsibility was completely lacking during my experience in the Marine Corps; surprisingly, I also found it lacking when I joined the antiwar movement. I believe that this concept makes clear why the antiwar movement failed to end the occupation of Iraq.

COLLECTIVE RESPONSIBILITY AND HOWARD ZINN

Howard Zinn played an important role in developing my belief in collective responsibility. When I got back from Iraq I was lost, torn between what was expected of me as a Marine and the guilt I felt for what we did to Fallujah. Around that time I read Howard Zinn's *A People's History of the United States*. Few books have had a greater impact on my life. Howard Zinn's words had a moral clarity about them that immediately rang true to me, and they did so at a time when I needed them most. It was because of him that I began to trust my instinct that what we had done to the people of Fallujah was wrong, and I gradually built up the courage to leave the Marine Corps.

I eventually joined the antiwar movement, but its message, the positions it took, and its tactics often frustrated me. In an effort to grow in numbers, the antiwar movement tried to appeal more to Americans' self-interest and sense of patriotism than to their sense of morality. It focused on informing Americans about the impact that the occupation was having on the economy instead of focusing on the destruction that it had brought to Iraq. To not risk being called anti-troops, it treated American servicepeople as victims of larger circumstances—like propaganda, the economic draft, and deceitful politicians—rather than as people, good and bad, who made a choice, consciously or not, to be part of something terrible. The antiwar movement spoke out against the atrocities that were committed in Iraq, but when it came to talking about who committed the atrocities its language got vague and its analysis became muddled. The antiwar movement blamed the government; it blamed the corporate media; it even blamed war itself. However, it did everything in its power not to blame the troops.[2] To me all of these positions and tactics appeared to be calculated appeals to patriotism and self-interest, and came in stark contrast to *A People's History of the United States,* which had appealed to me on a moral level.

A slogan often used by various veteran-led antiwar groups is "honor the warrior, not the war." This slogan epitomizes the type of thinking that often bothered me about the antiwar movement, and that Howard Zinn helped me break free from. If one thinks about it, it is difficult to imagine how one could be deserving of honor for participating in something dishonorable. Yet this slogan pops up again and again at veteran-led antiwar actions, and the antiwar movement doesn't consider its meaning. This slogan confuses the American public, it misrepresents how soldiers actually conduct themselves in war, it doesn't challenge the alleged honorable position that veterans hold in our society, and it makes real solidarity with Iraqis difficult, if not impossible.

Many people get nervous whenever they hear "blame" and "veteran" in the same sentence. The antiwar movement during the Vietnam era was accused of unjustly blaming veterans, and was harshly criticized for this. Most likely the antiwar movement of today wants to avoid a similar reaction from the public, so it tiptoes around the subject of veteran responsibility.[3] But it is of the utmost importance that we think about what our veterans did in Iraq and describe their actions honestly. If they harmed innocent civilians, we may have no choice but to blame them. If they did honorable things and truly deserve to be honored, then we should honor them. It should be noted, though, that veterans may not deserve blame or honor; the truth may be more complex, and we shouldn't let patriotism or a political agenda color our judgment on this issue or cause us to avoid it altogether.

Whether some veterans are deserving of blame—and if so, how much and for what specifically—is a side issue that will be discussed only briefly in this chapter. The issue at hand, broadly, is collective responsibility and what this concept has to offer to the activist, revolutionary, and average citizen. Collective responsibility was a big part of Howard Zinn's moral reasoning, and it shaped his approach to activism and academics. Of immediate consequence is what collective responsibility can teach us about how to resist war and occupation, and Howard Zinn's beliefs on this matter provide all of us, but veterans in particular, with a strong moral precedent. The antiwar movement's message and tactics have lacked clarity and have not addressed issues in American moral culture.[4] Consequently, it has failed to protect Iraq from our government, though not for a lack of good intentions and hard work.[5] In light of this failure and as members of the antiwar movement, we owe it to Iraqis to be self-critical. An understanding and application of the concept of collective responsibility will clarify our message and improve our tactics.

The Theory Behind It All

Contemporary ethics has traditionally focused on the causal and moral responsibility of individuals. The dominant belief in this field is that *individuals* are moral agents (assuming that they act under free will, they are capable of deliberating about reasons for acting, they are conscious of what they are doing, and they understand the consequences of their actions).[6] Moral agents are held to be morally responsible for their actions, and they are ascribed with praise or blame for those actions. Thus, moral responsibility is different from causal responsibility. In the eyes of many philosophers, collective responsibility is a controversial concept because it judges *groups* to be either causally or morally responsible for *collective* actions.[7] As a concept it is ardently both attacked and defended. Some deny that it is even sensible, while others claim that it is a common sense concept that most people use every day.

Those who reject collective responsibility usually do so because they believe that the intentions that lead to an action are the correct basis for moral evaluation. They claim that groups, unlike individuals, don't have the necessary center of consciousness or free will to be capable of intending to do something. Therefore, collective responsibility is something like a contradiction in terms. They believe that what might appear as a single group action is really an aggregate of individual actions, and is better termed as group "behavior."[8] Those who support collective responsibility either argue that collectives can form intentions[9] or that the scope of morality involves more than just intentions.[10] For example, people tacitly invoke it when they make statements like "Monsanto pollutes," "the Winter Hill Gang ran South Boston," or "the US military laid siege to Fallujah." Many philosophers do accept collective responsibility; however, its nuances and implications are still very much debated.[11]

Consider a group of people in which each person commits an act that doesn't interact with any other group member's action. Compare this to a group of people who act in concert with one another, and each person's action supports or interacts with all the other contributing people's actions. When these individual actions are related in such a way, they take on a character that wouldn't have been possible otherwise. The first example is just an aggregate of individual actions, and each person is responsible for his or her own individual actions. The second example is a collective action, and each person in the collective is responsible for his or her contributing action or actions, but the collective itself also bears additional responsibility.

A real-life example of the first case might be when 100 military personnel each perform a single military task independently of one other—tasks such as carrying a radio, firing a weapon, standing post, manning a checkpoint, and so on. Separately each one of these actions has little moral significance. Carrying a radio that isn't connected to air support is neither harmful nor useful. Standing post doesn't make any sense if you're not attached to a military and don't have a mission. However, when 100 military personnel perform the same military tasks together and their actions support, act in concert with, and interact with everyone else's, their actions become a collective action, which is greater and more significant than the sum of all their contributing individual actions. Carrying a radio and standing post are no longer isolated acts; they now have moral significance in the context of the collective action. The 100 military actions are now something more—they are a mission, an assault, a siege, or something of the kind—and the 100 military personnel may be blameworthy or praiseworthy as individuals for their contribution to this collective action. Additionally, the 100 military personnel are something more; they are a platoon, a battalion, or some other type of collective, and that collective may be blameworthy or praiseworthy itself.

This distinction between a group of people acting independently of one another and a group of people acting in concert with one another is typically ignored in the ethics literature, yet it is of great importance. It is this distinction that separates group behavior from a collective action, and the moral implications of this are significant because being a member of a group is a very big part of life.[12] Our families are groups, the people we work with are a group, and our society is a group. Understanding morality from the perspective of individuals, as it has been traditionally understood, is insufficient because it leaves a large part of our lives unexamined. Collective actions can be good or bad, and because the effects of collective actions are always more than the sum of all the contributing individual actions, enormous amounts of good or harm can result when groups act. In the globalized world that we live in today, where a single person's actions can have effects on the other side of the planet, it is more important than ever that we understand collective responsibility, be aware of the collective actions that we contribute to, and feel empowered by the good that we can achieve when groups act.

There are many different types of collective action that may warrant collective responsibility. One type is when every member of a group engages in a collective practice, but only the action of one member results in any good or harm. In such cases, we might ascribe collective responsibility to the entire group.[13] Imagine a community where everyone drinks and drives, and one night a drunk driver runs over a young child crossing the street. Even though it is only that night's driver's fault that leads to any harm, we might be inclined to ascribe blame to the entire community.[14]

Another type of collective action is when every member of a group contributes to a collective action. We can even make distinctions within this category. Consider, for example, when large numbers of people act without any communication or coordination between them (e.g., in a riot or by creating pollution). Or when a number of people jointly and cooperatively undertake a collective action (e.g., a military assault or a revolution). Or when harm or good is caused by some feature of the culture consciously endorsed and participated in by every member of a group (e.g., a society that endorses slavery or universal human rights).[15]

There may be some disagreement with these subcategories. For instance, someone might say that a society can't be held collectively responsible for pollution, since the polluters weren't acting as a group but rather as individuals with no cooperation or communication between them. True enough, most people in Western society don't get together and communicate and cooperate on how to pollute. However, most of us are aware that we pollute; we are aware that others pollute; we are aware that our pollution and everyone else's pollution is adding up at an alarming rate; and we are aware that our pollution is contributing to disease, climate change, and the extinction of entire species. Yet we continue to pollute, fully aware that we are acting with others and that together our actions will have a harmful effect. Whether or not the individuals in question intended to act together is irrelevant. The fact that they *did* act together is what makes their actions a collective action.

A group could even be collectively responsible for collective *inaction.* Imagine a society that has a government that lies to them, unjustly awards their tax dollars to multinational corporations, and allows only a very limited amount of democracy. If members of that society decided to rise up against its government, they could potentially overthrow it, but instead they remain docile.[16] The society as a whole might be blameworthy, but the individual citizens could hardly be blamed. After all, it can only be considered heroic to risk being jailed, or worse, by one's government, and surely morality doesn't require so much from us. However, the whole group had it within its power to overthrow their government, and did nothing.[17]

Howard Zinn's writings have a lot to offer us on this topic even though he never explicitly wrote about collective responsibility. Zinn never felt a need to ground his moral judgments in one or another moral theory. He didn't need the theories of Kant or Hume or any other moral philosopher to oppose slavery or to speak out against war. His moral judgments came from a place of common sense and empathy for others. Collective responsibility was most likely a tacit component of Zinn's moral reasoning, because it is implicit in his writings on history, justice, and peace. One can see this in the title of his autobiography, *You Can't Be Neutral on a Moving Train*. Employing this metaphor, Zinn (2002 [1994]: 8) means "that events are already moving in a certain deadly direction, and to be neutral means to accept that." War, occupation, social movements, apartheid, and pollution are collective actions, and Zinn clearly believed that we can't pretend that our actions are neutral, that they don't contribute, to these "events" around us. We can either oppose these collective actions or embrace our collective responsibility for them.

Collective responsibility also is implicit in his writings to the extent that it's implicit in a class analysis of society. You invoke collective responsibility when you claim that there is a group of people who unjustly maintain an economic and social system that favors them at the expense of everyone else in their society. (When the Occupy movement blames the 1%, it invokes collective responsibility.) Furthermore, Zinn believed that we all have a moral obligation to take direct action against injustices. This obligation falls on the individual rather than the collective, but it is not your traditional obligation to refrain from individual acts of harm or to do individual acts of good. The obligation is derived from the individual's status as a member of a collective (e.g., a citizen in a society, a soldier in an army, a member of the human race) and the responsibility that such a status places on the individual to oppose harmful collective actions (e.g., wars, pollution, oppression) and to participate in benevolent collective actions (e.g., social movements, protests, marches).

The Problem with Blaming

One contentious point in the debate about collective responsibility concerns blaming. Many philosophers become outraged at the idea that someone might be blamed for something that other people in their group did. However, this concern reflects a misunderstanding of collective responsibility. If the individual who is being blamed for the actions of others in his group truly did nothing, most likely he or she didn't participate in a collective action. Related to this issue is how we define group membership in a theory of collective responsibility. Collectives need not be defined along the lines of race, religion, nationality, or anything of the sort. These groups do not always act as a whole, and when they don't, they should be considered ancillary to a theory of collective responsibility. The type of group that is relevant to a theory of collective responsibility is the group of individuals who participate in a collective action. Those who should be held responsible for that collective action are only those who participated in it. Hence, group membership should be defined by participation in a collective action. If group membership is defined any other way—such as by race, religion, or nationality—and entire groups are blamed for the actions of just a few of its members, this would be terribly unjust.

Margaret Gilbert (2006: 109) formulates this concern better when she asks, "What does the blameworthiness of the collective's act imply about the personal blameworthiness of any one member of that collective?" The answer she gives is that "from a logical point of view, the short answer is: *nothing*. Everything depends on the details of a given member's particular situation."[18] Those details may include the precise amount that the individual in question contributed to the collective action. Or whether the individual knew that the collective action was immoral. If the individual was unaware, and that person's ignorance was in no way blameworthy, then he or she can't be blamed for the act in question.[19]

Collective actions are phenomena that transcend the individual contributions of each member. Similarly, the identity of the collective transcends the identity of its members. By participating in a collective action each individual becomes a member of a collective, an entity that is something more than the sum of all its individual members, a thing that we can speak of separately from its members, a thing that we can ascribe moral judgments to and that its members can feel pride or shame in. Also, individuals who have participated in a collective action often do hold separate moral judgments for themselves and for their collectives. All of these reasons indicate that the collective itself is capable of bearing moral responsibility that does not distribute to its individual members. For example, many veterans of the occupation of Iraq can truthfully say that they themselves are not responsible for war crimes in Iraq; however, no one who has been a member of the US military from the start of the occupation to its end can truthfully say that *we* are not responsible for war crimes in Iraq.[20] If they aren't ashamed of their own individual actions, they should, at the very least, be ashamed of the US military's actions.

This brings up an important question. What if our employer, our university, our country, or some other group that we belong to is doing something immoral? What is required from us as individuals? Based on the questions raised by Juha Räikkä (1997: 95–96), we might ask ourselves a similar set of questions when considering what we should do when we believe that a group we belong to is committing harm:

- Can I oppose the collective action without serious risk of being killed or tortured?
- Can I oppose the collective action by appealing to shared values accepted by the group and to factual knowledge readily available to its members?
- Is there no reason for believing that opposing the collective action would be completely futile?
- Should I accept the collective action without opposing it?

If our answers to the first three questions are yes, then our answer to the final question should be no.

Räikkä notes that we need to be more specific about what it means to oppose an immoral action or practice. If one's criticism or act of resistance is late, if it could have been made more effectively, or if it ends up being counterproductive, then it can't be considered genuine opposition.[21] Räikkä concludes that the only way to "disassociate" ourselves from collective responsibility is to oppose the collective action in question and cease *all* support of it.[22] He believes that there are real-life examples of people who oppose harmful collective actions but continue to contribute to them in some way, and who can still be considered blameworthy. Imagine a scholar who opposes how American society pollutes the environment, but the only way he can oppose that practice and be taken seriously is to fly in jets to speak at conferences on the topic. So the only way this scholar can oppose America's practice of pollution effectively is by polluting the environment with jet exhaust. Alternatively, imagine an activist who opposes American society's practice of exploiting the developing world and consuming its resources. But this activist can't oppose this practice without exploiting these nations at least a little bit. This activist can't realistically reject American living standards completely. It would mean being an outcast from society, and few people would take the activism of an outcast seriously.[23]

This raises important questions about what is required of each one of us to oppose our groups' harmful collective actions. Does morality require of us that we immediately stop polluting and reject all the comforts of a Western lifestyle? Should we be considered blameworthy if we do not completely convert to a sustainable and non-exploitive lifestyle so as to not be complicit in the crimes being committed against the developing world? Certainly action is required from us to move toward sustainability, but morality would hardly require from us sacrifices that are beyond our means. Those who do manage to completely disassociate themselves from the collective responsibilities of pollution and exploitation go above and beyond the call of duty. This brings to mind the heroic story of Brian Haw (1949–2011), who gave up everything, left his wife and children, and camped out in Parliament Square in London to protest his country's involvement in the occupations of Afghanistan and Iraq.[24] Brian Haw died after ten years of camping in Parliament Square. His dedication to justice and human rights is nothing short of heroic, and people who fall short of his example cannot rightly be considered blameworthy. It is often difficult to know precisely where to draw the line between what counts as opposing a harmful collective action and what counts as being complicit in it, but perhaps it is less important to know exactly where to draw the line than it is to draw one.

Some philosophers have even gone as far as to say that collective responsibility is not just a poor concept, but that it is actually dangerous. One such argument comes from Mark Reiff, who writes,

> Attributions of collective responsibility have led to the wholesale murder, displacement, and oppression of entire peoples often enough that it should be obvious that a belief in collective responsibility cannot easily be controlled—given human nature, we must regard it as always presenting an invitation to evil.[25]

Challenging a common analysis of terrorism that it is a "war-like instrument for advancing a political agenda," Reiff (2008: 210) argues that terrorism is often more than just a means of coercion—some terrorists consider their acts to be retribution for past harms. He notes that terrorism is often "a means of exacting punishment on a political community the terrorist believes is collectively responsible for grievous wrongs certain members of that community have committed."[26] Reiff reasons that since terrorists believe in collective responsibility, arguments that show that collective responsibility is both dangerous and wrong might help to end terrorism. Therefore, he sets out to "attack the notion of collective responsibility on which the terrorist relies."[27]

Reiff's account of terrorism as retribution may be correct, but his assumption that terrorists justify their crimes with rational argument rather than irrational hate may be mistaken. Reiff worries that collective responsibility doesn't protect the autonomy of the individual, unlike competing notions of individual responsibility. He sees this issue as part of a larger issue between communalism and liberalism—where communalism considers the basic social unit to be the community (a group or collective) and liberalism considers the basic social unit to be the individual.[28] Reiff cites Sayyid Qutb's book *Milestones,* which he claims is one of the "most important statements of the purpose, nature, and scope of the Islamic fundamentalist conception of *jihad.*"[29] Here he points to references to the Muslim community for evidence that terrorists are communalists, suggesting that terrorism is carried out only by Muslims.

However, individualists are just as capable of committing terrorism as communalists are, as are Christians, Jews, Buddhists, and atheists. I, myself, a secular Westerner, participated in terrorism against Muslims during the second siege of Fallujah, and I didn't need collective responsibility to justify it. The second siege of Fallujah was to a large extent retribution for the victory of the resistance in Fallujah over the US military during the first siege seven months earlier.[30] After that victory Fallujah became a symbol of resistance throughout Iraq and throughout much of the developing world. What Fallujah symbolized and the hope that it inspired in Iraqis became extremely dangerous for the US military, especially when there started to be indications that various armed resistance movements across Iraq were going to unite against the Americans.[31] The purpose of the second siege of Fallujah was threefold: to destroy the strongest armed resistance group in Iraq, to mend the US military's tarnished image with a clear and widely broadcast victory over the militants who had once embarrassed it, and to inflict such pain and suffering on the entire population of Fallujah that it would discourage others from trying to follow in their footsteps.[32] The second siege of Fallujah was both terrorism as coercion and terrorism as retribution. The hundreds of civilians who died in this siege from the weeks of aerial bombardment and siege by ground troops, the entire neighborhoods that were either bulldozed to the ground or bombed into rubble,[33] the use of indiscriminate and illegal weapons such as white phosphorous, the use of indiscriminate and illegal tactics like reconnaissance by fire,[34] the 200,000 refugees that the siege created, and the continued suffering of the people of Fallujah today are all evidence that this siege is an example of terrorism.[35]

Reiff's assumption that only Muslims are terrorists is ahistorical, and the fact that some people have *tried* to justify their awful crimes against entire groups by claiming that they were collectively responsible is not a reason for thinking that the concept of collective responsibility is flawed, nor is it a reason for thinking collective responsibility will inevitably lead to collective punishment and terrorism. Many good ideas have been twisted, abused, and used for evil, but the evil has never been inherent in the ideas themselves. Collective responsibility can be more reasonable and more nuanced than as described by Reiff. It applies to bad collective actions and good ones as well, and even though Reiff focuses on the issues of blame, this concept is just as much about praise. But even beyond praise and blame, there is yet another side to collective responsibility that is often ignored in the ethics literature, and completely ignored by Reiff. It is the side that Howard Zinn would have preferred.

Keith Graham (2006) notes that we have very different moral responses to cases of imposing collective responsibility as opposed to cases of embracing collective responsibility. Imposing collective responsibility goes beyond blaming a group for some harmful collective action by distributing that blame among the group's members. Graham notes that imposing collective responsibility often elicits "moral repugnance," whereas cases of embracing collective responsibility are very different. People are often inspired when they see individuals or groups voluntarily take responsibility for, own up to, take action against, or make amends for some collective action for which they feel partly responsible.[36]

I joined the Marine Corps because I wanted people to call me a hero. I joined because I wanted to see combat. I wanted to be part of a big dramatic gunfight, just like in the movies, and I wanted my friends back home to "ooh" and "ahh" as I told them stories about it. I joined the Marine Corps for money, adventure, and respect, and I got all of those things. I gave no thought to Iraqis or what our occupation was doing to them. My decision to join was all about me, and my moral reasoning was as individualistic as it gets. I knew that our occupation of Iraq was more about stealing oil than it was about freedom and democracy, but I felt no obligation to consider the bigger picture of what I was participating in. I reassured myself that the war was the fault of corrupt politicians, and as long as I minded my own individual conduct once I got to Iraq, I wasn't to blame.

During the second siege of Fallujah, I saw women and children fleeing into the desert from our "liberation" of their city. I saw the dead bodies of resistance fighters lying in the streets. I saw us bulldoze homes and drop white phosphorous from the sky, but I didn't see what any of that had to do with me. My job was to carry the radio. I didn't force civilians from their homes with my own two hands, or shoot anyone, or bulldoze anyone's house. I kept blaming all the horrible things that I was seeing around me on the few bad apples in my unit, the generals who dreamed up the mission, and the corrupt politicians who put me there in the first place. I convinced myself that I was not to blame. I told myself that I didn't want to be there, that I was obligated by contract to follow orders, and that I was just doing what I had to do to get back to my family. But the truth was that I chose to be there. Everyday that I decided to follow orders, I made a choice, and I chose to follow orders because it was in my own best interest. I couldn't see how carrying a radio allowed someone else to call in an air strike or to bulldoze houses. I couldn't see myself as being complicit, and I imagine that is how most of the guys in my unit saw themselves, too.

My intentions were to come home a hero and bask in the glory of being a combat vet, not to liberate Iraqis, and I knew perfectly well that we were hurting innocent people. For a while I was able to ignore all of this and convince myself that I had done nothing wrong, but at some point that changed, and even though I never shot anyone or forced anyone from their home, the fact that I played a role in what we did to Fallujah became more shameful than I could bear.

The other men in my former unit, though, may have believed that the war was just and that our mission in Fallujah was just. They may have been fooled by propaganda, and they may have been unaware that we were harming civilians. They also may have had the best intentions. Perhaps they were ignorant about the harm we were causing the people of Fallujah; however, were they *culpably ignorant*? Was information about the harm that we were causing easily available to them and they just chose not to look at it, or chose not to believe it? Can someone be blameworthy for choosing to believe lies over an inconvenient truth because the lies are more psychologically salient? What if the belief of the men in my unit that we were doing the right thing was the result of media deception, an incredible amount of pressure from what society expected of them, pressure from what their command was ordering them to do, and a complicated psychological mechanism that tainted their judgment? Are they blameworthy?

Psychology has taught us about the mechanisms that can cause otherwise-decent people to "morally disengage" and commit atrocities.[37] These psychological mechanisms explain our behavior in Fallujah well. We used sanitizing language, like "collateral damage," "pacifying the city," and "taking down . . . a sanctuary for the insurgents,"[38] and our command told us that we were "liberating" Fallujah and described our mission as a moral one against a great evil. This allowed many of the people in my unit to perceive their actions as benevolent. We told ourselves that everything we were doing was for the people of Fallujah; even the destruction of their homes and their forced exodus was for their safety and their freedom.[39] At the same time we dehumanized the people of Fallujah. We denied them a voice, we ignored their will, and we rejected their right to defend themselves against our aggression.[40] We jumped through psychological hoops to cognitively reconstruct our behavior as moral and just.

Understanding these psychological factors that led me and everyone else in my unit to do what we did is important, but how far can they go in exonerating us from responsibility for our actions? This is a question I don't pretend to have an answer for. Ascribing blame and praise in real life is far more complicated than it is in the abstract. Identifying intentions and beliefs that lead to an action is never as simple in real life as in philosophy because of the complexities of human psychology. These issues are complicated and intimidating, but they are also extremely important, and we shouldn't simply dodge them, as the antiwar movement has done. If American society is ever going to come to a clearer understanding of these issues and act more responsibly because of it, we need to discuss this in an intelligent way.

That all the men from my former unit are causally responsible for what we did to Fallujah is unquestionable. But I can't pretend to know what was in each person's head at the time that the operation began; therefore, I can't come to any conclusion about whether any of them are blameworthy as individuals. I can only say with certainty that *I* knew we were causing harm to civilians, but the fear of being called a coward for refusing to participate any further and the prospect of going home as a war hero with money in my pocket got the better of me. Fear and self-interest kept me from doing what I knew in my gut was right, and I know that these psychological factors cannot relieve me of blameworthiness. I don't believe that I am the only blameworthy individual from my unit, but the majority of the people in my unit were misinformed, misguided, and manipulated by our leaders and our society. However, I also don't believe that anyone from my unit, with full knowledge of the harm we caused and with full understanding that our justifications were false, could still look proudly at being a former member of 1st Battalion 8th Marines. I believe that shame is the appropriate response to *our* actions, which is not to say that any of the individuals in my unit are shameful. I hold us collectively responsible.

Howard Zinn had a skill for addressing hard truths and delicate topics in a conciliatory manner, and perhaps it was the collective responsibility in his moral reasoning that allowed him to speak about atrocities and address all affected parties fairly, to fully express complicated moral issues without minimizing the suffering of one side and without carelessly laying blame on the other. The purpose of such an approach is not to punish one side, but, hopefully, to encourage it to embrace its collective responsibility while pursuing justice for the other. I hope that acknowledging the lies that were told to my former unit and fully describing the "atrocity producing situation"[41] that we were thrown into—while not minimizing the suffering, death, and destruction that we visited on the people of Fallujah, and not minimizing each individual's moral agency—will help others from my former unit to embrace their collective responsibility too.

APPLYING COLLECTIVE RESPONSIBILITY

In *A People's History of the United States* (2003 [1980]), Howard Zinn preferred not to lay blame on the individuals who carried out atrocities. Instead, he focused on the individuals who embraced their collective responsibility and felt compelled to resist and speak out against oppression, unjust war, and racism, and he described them as heroes. Throughout his years as an academic and an activist he often expressed eloquently and poetically his belief that we must fight against harmful collective actions:

> More and more in our time, the mass production of massive evil requires an enormously complicated division of labor. No one is positively responsible for the horror that ensues. But everyone is negatively responsible, because anyone can throw a wrench into the machinery. Not quite, of course—because only a few people have wrenches. The rest have only their hands and feet. That is, the power to interfere with the terrible progression is distributed unevenly, and therefore the sacrifice required varies, according to one's means. In that odd perversion of the natural which we call society (that is, nature seems to equip each species for its special needs) the greater one's capability for interference, the less urgent is the need to interfere.
>
> It is the immediate victims—or tomorrow's—who have the greatest need, and the fewest wrenches. They must use their bodies (which may explain why rebellion is a rare phenomenon). This may suggest to those of us who have a bit more than our bare hands, and at least a small interest in stopping the machine, that we might play a peculiar role in breaking the social stalemate.

This may require resisting a false crusade—or refusing one or another expedition in a true one. But always, it means refusing to be transfixed by the actions of other people, the truths of other times. It means acting on what we feel and think, here, now, for human flesh and sense, against the abstractions of duty and obedience.[42]

Howard Zinn blamed the government, not the soldiers, for the atrocities that have been carried out against Native Americans, African Americans, Filipinos, Japanese, Vietnamese, Afghans, Iraqis, and many others. That is, he put the moral responsibility on our government, though he did acknowledge the causal responsibility of our soldiers. He never publicly blamed veterans, nor did he demand that they accept responsibility. Instead, he led by example and held himself, a veteran of World War II, to the highest standard of accountability.[43] On several occasions he wrote with regret about his participation in World War II. His words express embarrassment for his naïve enthusiasm in joining the war,[44] and remorse for his victims.[45] It is unclear whether he held his actions as a bombardier to be blameworthy; nevertheless, he felt a responsibility for the rest of his life to educate others about the injustice that is inherent in war.

Howard Zinn joined the Army Air Corps in 1943 when he was twenty years old. He got involved late in the war, and ended up flying some of its last missions. One day he was briefed for a bombing mission over the French town of Royan, of which he wrote,

At our bombing altitudes—twenty-five or thirty thousand feet—we saw no people, heard no screams, saw no blood, no torn limbs. I remember only seeing the canisters light up like matches flaring one by one on the ground below. Up there in the sky, I was just "doing my job"—the explanation throughout history of warriors committing atrocities.[46]

This bombing mission more than any other moved Zinn to question the necessity of war, because years later he and his wife traveled to Royan and spoke to survivors of the bombing and "rummaged through documents."[47] Zinn was horrified to learn that his mission had claimed the lives of over a thousand French civilians.[48]

The British, American, and French officers involved in planning the mission all excused their actions by appealing to the unfortunate consequences of war.[49] In essence they blamed war itself. Honor the warrior, not the war. Their justifications for the hundreds dead in Royan were completely unacceptable to Zinn. He occasionally blamed war throughout his life as an academic and activist. However, there is a large and important distinction between Howard Zinn saying that "war poisons everyone who is engaged in it"[50] and the military officers who planned the assault on Royan saying that bad things happen in war. Those officers were blaming the collective action of war to relieve themselves of responsibility. They are claiming that the blame does not fall on the agents who carry out the action, but instead on the action itself.

Most philosophers agree that *agents,* not actions, are the type of thing that can be blameworthy or praiseworthy. So to say that war is wrong presupposes that those who go to war are wrong to do so.[51] The slogan "honor the warrior, not the war," seems hardly antiwar in this light. Yet this slogan goes even further than saying something like, "bad things happen in war, but those who go to war aren't to blame." This slogan attributes honor to those who participate in a collective action that they admit is dishonorable. "Honor the warrior, not the war" seems to be as morally bankrupt as the officers who ordered the bombing of Royan.

Zinn's blaming of war might be seen by some moral philosophers as an analytical departure from collective responsibility, but Zinn would likely laugh at the idea that all of his language should be coherent with one or another moral theory. He was far more concerned with acting morally and encouraging others to act morally than he was with adhering rigidly to doctrine. Zinn's intention behind blaming war seems to be to posit a moral responsibility to refrain from war, not to wash anyone's hands of responsibility. He is saying that war is bad because it is inevitably destructive and indiscriminate, and that those who participate in war often behave in the most horrid ways because of the nature of war, the atmosphere it creates, and the means of destruction that it employs. He is not removing the agency of the individuals who fight wars, nor is he disregarding the circumstances under which the people who fight wars act. He is not looking for any special treatment for being a veteran, nor is he pointing his finger and blaming anyone. He is simply trying to inform people that war is a harmful collective action, something in which we should never participate.

Most of us can benefit from reading about ethics from time to time, whether it be from a religious text or a philosophy book. But that doesn't mean that moral theories should be dogma for us to live our lives by. I don't pretend to have given a fully explanatory, predictive, or descriptive theory of collective action and collective responsibility. I only hope to show the intuitive appeal of these ideas, and to encourage others to think about what they are contributing to when they act. We all get lost from time to time, and I hope that when people are faced with moral dilemmas, the concept of collective responsibility might bring them clarity. From the soldier in the unjust war to the citizen in the corrupt society to the movement within the unjust system, collective responsibility can help show us the right way forward.

CONCLUSION

When seen through the lens of collective responsibility, the antiwar movement's message appears confused, and consequently its tactics don't sufficiently address important issues in our moral culture. To a limited extent the antiwar movement encouraged Americans to end the occupation for moral and principled reasons. However, to a much greater extent it tried to get Americans to do a cost-benefit analysis and determine that the occupation wasn't worth it. It chose to emphasize that the invasion and occupation of Iraq were devastating to the economy, that American servicepeople were sent to die for lies, and that it all has been counterproductive to national security. In doing so it minimized the important facts that the invasion and occupation were devastating to *Iraq*'s economy, that our occupation may have killed over one million *Iraqis,*[52] and that it all has been counterproductive to *Iraq*'s security. The antiwar movement blamed the invasion and occupation on George W. Bush and the corporate media when it should have been raising awareness about all the ways that our society is collectively responsible—from our inability to control our government to our cultural support for militarism—and it should have been encouraging Americans to take action and make changes for a more peaceful, just, and responsible society. The antiwar movement should have challenged Americans to stop honoring the people who committed atrocities against Iraqis. Only when this happens will solidarity with Iraqis be possible.

Most importantly, antiwar veterans need to stop organizing around self-exonerating slogans and attack the false belief in our culture that veterans automatically deserve honor and esteem. The esteem that our society gives to veterans causes children to idolize veterans and follow in their footsteps, and it discourages public criticism of our military. Veterans have a moral obligation to renounce their own hero status. The power that veterans have to end these wars is, perhaps, best articulated by Michael Prysner (2008), a veteran of the occupation of Iraq and cofounder of *March Forward!*, who gave one of the most powerful and moving testimonies at the Winter Soldier hearings:

> While all of those weapons are created and owned by this government, they are harmless without people willing to use them. Those who send us to war do not have to pull a trigger or lob a mortar round. They do not have to fight the war. They merely have to sell the war. They need a public who is willing to send their soldiers into harm's way and they need soldiers who are willing to kill or be killed without question. They can spend millions on a single bomb, but that bomb only becomes a weapon when the ranks in the military are willing to follow orders to use it. They can send every last soldier anywhere on earth, but there will only be a war if soldiers are willing to fight.

Clear moral reasoning is an indispensable guide to the activist, revolutionary, and citizen. Few have reasoned so clearly and have set such an uncompromising moral example as Howard Zinn did. His ethical beliefs, embodied in his words and actions, illuminate where we have erred in the past and provide us with a path forward. As activists, revolutionaries, and citizens, as members of the antiwar movement, we need to look critically at our failure to end the occupation of Iraq, and think about what we could have done differently. Our tactics have done little to change American culture and challenge Americans to think in more moralistic terms. We have not gotten the majority of society to understand that shock-and-awe bombing is just wrong, that invading another nation is wrong, and that placing sanctions on other nations is wrong. Instead of appealing to traditional American values, we should have been trying to create a revolution in our moral culture. We should have acted as the moral compass that our country needed.

CHAPTER 10

Archivists of Optimism

Zinn and the Arts

Alix Olson

The roster of artists with social consciences is endless. I point to a few to represent so many, because their work, their commitment, encourages and sustains me, and I want it to encourage and sustain others.

—*Howard Zinn (2001c)*

I first met Howard Zinn in Berkeley, California, in April 2001, at a conference called Speak Out: An Evening of Art and Politics. I was performing spoken-word poetry and Howard was presenting a preview of his play *Marx in Soho* and engaging in a discussion with poet Aya de Leon about art as resistance. I recall clearly Zinn's emphatic message that evening, which he went on to document in *Artists in Times of War* (2003c). He notes that while political power is the domain of the corporate elite, the arts are a locale for a unique type of guerrilla warfare; artists must "look for apertures and opportunities where they can have an effect."[1] In other words, where corporate media fails us, artists have the ethical responsibility to raise challenges, to interrogate injustices, to reaffirm history, and, just as importantly, to risk failure. Further, Zinn suggested that evening that carrying these stories of a political victory or struggle from one town to the next might be the only kind of true democratic media we have in this nation.

For me, a young, queer, feminist, spoken-word artist having newly embarked upon a touring life and deeply invested in the radical potential of the oral tradition, Howard Zinn's message struck a compelling chord, and throughout the next decade of my career, I carried with me the questions it provoked: Who decides what trail of evidence is left behind to show us how we have lived? How might artists take seriously a responsibility to document everyday resistance and what legacy of survival might we work toward? How might we record an alternative kind of historical memory, and thus imprint upon the next generation "an upside down world" (Zinn 2003c) with a new or different set of heroes? How might we best serve as political witnesses of the present, working to sustain the optimistic momentum required in pursuing a better world?

I did not anticipate at the time that I would return to these same questions a decade later, this time as a political scientist looking to connect the radical potential of academic and artistic spheres. In this chapter, I pursue the question of how artists and scholars, if we are to use both grassroots art and intellectual writing as "guerrilla warfare," might work to support one another in spotting "apertures" and sites for discursive intervention(s). In other words, how might we mutually fortify our progressive movement with a renewed and *collaborative commitment* to Zinn's emphasis on disobedience, risk-taking, and the commitment to serve as what I call *archivists of optimism*? Through exploring these connections, I argue that we move toward a deepened radical citizenship, not only in our individual commitments but also as a community of thinkers devoted to movements. My understanding of radical citizenship is not one that can claim a fixed identity, an institutional infrastructure, or even a specific set of practices; it may allow us, though, to share the passport of possibility. Here, I take my cue from Zinn's grassroots investigation of history, exploring the notion of radical citizenship from the ground up.

It is in this spirit that I first offer some personal reflections upon working as a touring grassroots poet, exploring how I came to see disobedience, risk, and investment in others' stories as integral to the practice of radical citizenship. Next, I reflect upon artists, in their unique role as archivists of optimism, interrogating performance spaces as crucial for fomenting and conducting alternative discourses. Finally, turning to the academy, I consider how social scientists dedicated equally to understanding the formation of political consciousness and to social change might not only take seriously the work of artist-activists, but risk new alliances with these potential collaborators. How might this work entail contesting "authority" to coauthorize our radical artists? How might the project of expanding our political imagination benefit from incorporating or at the least reflecting each other's interpretations, dilemmas, and contributions? I argue that by connecting artists and academics, and disrupting the discursive and symbolic borders between them, we may begin to work toward a more powerful version of the radical citizenship Howard Zinn's legacy begs of us. In my view, it is these kinds of commitments that will keep the legacies of Howard Zinn and Emma Goldman in their dancing shoes throughout the next generation.

"I See You" (Revolution): Serving Disobedient Witness

> There are experts in little things but there are no experts in big things. There are experts in this fact and that fact but there are no moral experts.
>
> —*Howard Zinn (2003c: 10)*

> Those of us who have been forged in the crucibles of difference ... know that survival is not an academic skill. It is learning how to stand alone, unpopular and sometimes reviled, and how to make common cause with those others identified as outside the structures in order to define and seek a world in which we can all flourish.
>
> —*Audre Lorde (1984: 112)*

Like many of us who went on to tour as spoken-word poets, the slam-poetry community was largely responsible for shaping my identity as a political artist. The format of a slam-poetry contest, in which audience members, mostly poets themselves, are randomly tapped as "judges," was designed to make poetry palatable, engaging, and accessible to everybody. In this way, the genre not only allowed poetry to be re-democratized, but also provided it with an ironic anticapitalist and antiestablishment flair. Anyone could do it, anyone could be good at it, and the "winner" was not in the hands of "experts" or "literary critics," but rather at the mercy of the sundry and often exuberant crowd. Poetry should, Adrienne Rich (2001) argues, break the silence, forcing us to ask, "What kind of voice is breaking the silence, and what kind of silence is being broken?" To be sure, the genre of slam poetry produced a bold and unique pool of artists challenging silence on all fronts: rules about who should speak, the ways of speaking that hold value, and, importantly, what should or should not be said. In this way, I have from the beginning understood my own work as both a "hijacking" of poetry from formal elitism and a "confiscation" of the corporate media's claims to legitimacy in truth-telling.

Throughout my years of touring, however, I have learned that the practice of radical citizenship demands more than toting around a set of progressive ideas; the first and perhaps most important lesson was about claiming the job of active disobedience. This has sometimes entailed a willingness to accept accusations of being out of touch with reality, a loony tune, even a traitor. I have been followed to my car after shows, been "blackballed" at a few venues, and acquired my own little bundle of hate mail. For Zinn, however, the most perilous act within a democracy is "civil obedience" or "the submission of one's conscience to authority."[2] The very act of speaking out publicly, he claims, designates a refusal of silent participation. My first major US tour began smack in the middle of the plague of nationalism that was the post-9/11 atmosphere. As the United States accelerated its ferocious military stomp across the globe, I continued to listen intently to the assessments offered by Zinn and other political thinkers—critiques that gave substantive form to the inchoate values I felt deeply but had yet to articulate. Deeply critical of what was (and still is) passing for US justice, their formulations penetrated the predictable political script articulated by politicians and coursing through the veins of the corporate media. Mainstream reporters, as Chris Hedges (2011) put it,

in moments of crisis become clinicians. . . . We make facts conform to our perceptions of ourselves as Americans and human beings. We work within the confines
of national myth. We make journalism and history a refuge from memory. The
pretense that mass murder and suicide can be transformed into a tribute to the
victory of the human spirit was the lie we all told to the public that day and
have been telling ever since.

As political artists invested in exercising radical citizenship, many of us felt
the responsibility to tell different stories. I named my first post-9/11 tour the "I
See You Revolution," a phrase that I felt encapsulated two ways of bearing political witness. First, as a symbolic gesture to the Bush administration (and its new
PATRIOT Act)—to demonstrate that citizens are just as capable of surveilling,
studying, and critiquing the government (and its actions) as the government is
of doing those things to us; and second, to let individual people know that their
dissenting voices were being documented, that the emotional tenor of the country
was being recorded in ways counter to jingoistic reports.

It was on this tour that I began to consider creative ways to disseminate
alternative analyses like Zinn's and I began to experiment with integrating his
powerful words with my poetry. It is one of the unique capacities of art, I have
discovered, to animate debate simply by creatively challenging the very terms of the
discussion. Sometimes simply by oddly synthesizing disparate narratives, people can
be startled into awareness. Reflecting upon Zinn's concept of "stealing the truth"
back from the media, I wrote a piece called "Pirates." It was a direct accusation
of the US government's lies to its citizens in its reasons for going to war: "Enron
gives millions to the Taliban to build a pipeline through Afghanistan / and the
corporate scam of evil is buried deep beneath the sand / Transporting the blood
of children in Palestine, Iraq, Iran." I began performing "Pirates" over a recorded
recitation of the PATRIOT Act; looping underneath, the following audio excerpt
from Howard Zinn (2003c: 11) would break the silences: "It takes only a bit of
knowledge of history to realize how dangerous it is to think that the people who
run the country know what they are doing." I hoped that pairing the poem with
Zinn's unassuming but equally stark challenge to question one's government might
work in tandem to interrupt the chilling discursive authority of the PATRIOT Act.

One of the most common questions asked of me, and, I suspect, of many
political artists, has been which I prioritize: my politics or my poetry. It is a question that I would venture is not asked of mainstream entertainers, artists typically perceived as politically "neutral" but whom I would categorize as serving a
highly political function as preservationists of the status quo. As Zinn argues, "in
a world already moving in certain directions . . . neutrality means accepting the
way things are now."[3]

In any case, in my view the very idea that poetry and politics can be at
odds with each other denies the interpretive dialectic between art and the world.
Indeed, interpretation of the world is an unparalleled companion to changing it.
In creative expression, we have the power to erode the credibility of mainstream
rhetoric by framing that rhetoric as something different. In other words, artists

can (sometimes quite literally and other times linguistically) shift the frame in a way that exposes preprogrammed patriotism and dogmatic certitude.

Edward Said (2004: 142) argues that the selective recording and/or erasure of history has always been a strategic weapon of the powerful, "the invidious disfiguring, dismembering, and disremembering of significant historical experiences that do not have powerful enough lobbies in the present and therefore merit dismissal or belittlement." The intellectual, he continues, "is perhaps a kind of counter-memory with its own counter discourse that will not allow conscience to look away or fall asleep." So too, Zinn reminds us, is the political artist. While the historian has the ability to re-invoke history with its missing, and most important, chapters of resistance, art has the potential to accompany us through a process of revising the official text as it is written.

Moreover, art contains an ability to move people, to entice them toward critical thought and then perhaps political action. In Judith Butler's (2010: 73) analysis of prohibitions on wartime photography, she argues that state control operates "on the field of representability, in order to control affect—in anticipation of the way affect is not only structured by interpretation, but structures interpretation as well. What is at stake is the regulation of those images that might galvanize political opposition to a war." Indeed, as Zinn (2003c: 90) reminds us, it is this more candid rendition of the world—made possible by filmmakers, poets, and writers who represent the stories of "war, class conflict, and who controls what; government lies, broken treaties and official violence"—that allows us to see our present more clearly.

Bertolt Brecht posited that "art is not a mirror held up to reality, but a hammer with which to shape it." I would argue also that it is often the power of holding up a mirror to reality itself—in the face of so much false and contorted "mirroring"—that forces an urgency to raise our own hammers.

ARCHIVING OPTIMISM IN THE CREATIVE COUNTERPUBLIC

> The idea that hope alone will transform the world, and action undertaken in that kind of naïveté, is an excellent route to hopelessness, pessimism, and fatalism. But the attempt to do without hope, in the struggle to improve the world, as if that struggle could be reduced to calculated acts alone, or a purely scientific approach, is a frivolous illusion.
> —*Paulo Freire (1995: 2)*

> When we're all poets, the politicians will have to look for a day job.
> —*Bob Holman (1998), cofounder of slam poetry*[4]

In "Artists of Resistance," Howard Zinn (2001c) says, "Whenever I become discouraged (which is on alternate Tuesdays between three and four) ... I lift my spirits by remembering: The artists are on our side!" Zinn was claiming for "our side" grassroots artists who—provocative, unabashedly direct, and sometimes in political disagreement with one another—nevertheless assign themselves the role of the colorful (often cheerful) gadfly in the face of monochromatic power—those who engage with the world in irreverent ways, who foster laughter in the face of dismal prospects, who "wage the battle for justice in a sphere which is unreachable by the dullness of ordinary political discourse." Perhaps most importantly for Zinn, these artists understand that they are one more vertebrae adding to the spine of persistence—that they are not simply part of a political legacy, but always in the middle of comporting a movement of resisters.

A common accusation hurled at political artists is that we are simply "preaching to the converted." It is an indictment that has always read to me as an attempt to deflate us, to derail our sense of purpose. As grassroots artists, however, we are generally under no illusions that we are reaching huge audiences, much less single-handedly engineering a social movement. Rather, I began to think of my performances the way that Zinn characterized his speaking engagements: as "a little pep talk" for like-minded folks, a way to keep the radical snowball rolling: "Truth is," Zinn (2004b: 59) explains (fittingly, in *Failure to Quit: Reflections of an Optimistic Historian*), "converts need constant reinforcement, and fresh inspiration so they can go out and add to our numbers."

Moreover, in Zinn's experiences of traveling the country, he reports that many activist groups simply did not know about one another and so, "while they persisted, they did so with the desperate patience of Sisyphus endlessly pushing that boulder up the mountain." Smiling, he would remind his audiences that "they, the very people who were disheartened by the absence of a national movement, were themselves proof of the potential for such a movement."[5] For Zinn, it is the fact of possibility itself that is always the reason to hope, and hope, in turn, that allows us to persist. Pessimism, by contrast, "reproduces itself by crippling our willingness to act." If we see only our depression, Zinn reminds us, it is as if "we have lost our historical perspective and then it is as if we were born yesterday."[6]

It was Zinn's framing of possibility that helped me to understand how political artists might serve as *archivists of optimism.* Just as artists like me thrive creatively on the revitalizing histories of Zinn and others, so can we document as it happens the bold noncomplicity and perseverance of the present—upon which both current and future activists rely during dark times. The political artist is a professional excavator of the present, working to retranslate the disheartening and to mine for current resistance. Translating those artifacts of rebellion into poems, dances, or songs, whether performing at protest rallies or coffee shops, the political artist reminds those of us self-positioned as outliers of, or cast as outlaws from, dominant political thought that we are not alone. In this way, creative spaces might be seen as a constellation of disobedient counterpublics,[7] sites in which prevailing notions of patriotism are often irreverently disrupted and from which new forms of critical consciousness and oppositional discourse emerge. With grassroots artists as traveling witness to this radical imagination, they work to report upon and help circulate optimism among this "imagined community" of indefinite radical citizens.[8]

In *Artists in Times of War,* Zinn (2003c: 15) describes with admiration how the writer Mark Twain "stepped out of his role as story-teller" and "jumped into the fray," acting as a lead protester against the war in the Philippines. Conversely,

I became a political storyteller precisely in the hope that my art might enter new narratives into what Bonnie Honig (2001: 10) refers to as "the interpretive fray" of retellings. In my job, the possibilities for engaging with stories of resistance were all around me. Zigzagging my way around the country, I couldn't help but stumble into them. Still, as I became more actively invested in and curious about other people, their experiences, stories, and ideas, I took that responsibility more and more seriously: scouring the local newspapers and tuning in to local radio stations, talking to people at coffee shops and bars, incorporating their ideas about the war, their political and personal losses, fears, and triumphs—as well as my own observations—into the next evening's show. Sometimes I simply reminded the gathering in Lincoln, Nebraska, for example, that I had witnessed a similarly fueled crowd the week before in Tucson, Arizona. During some of the particularly vicious political moments through which I toured, making these small connections was the contribution I felt I could make to coaxing us another inch toward a more humane moment.

Certainly throughout the Bush years, the arsenal of information at the creative disposal of artists came as quickly as the suffering those years brought. The world became its own crazy script, all in dire need of redescription, as it unfolded in front of us. Writing and performing took on a new requirement—the pairing of outrage with a particular brand of sanity-maintaining satire and parody, a tactic that Lipsitz (2001: 16) argues works to "uncrown power." The very act of laughing together at the insanity of the current political order provokes an intimate and immediate form of solidarity. Laughter, like poetry and like politics, has both a timeless and a deeply contingent quality.

I reflect here upon attending a George Carlin (2008) *It's Bad for Ya* concert, wiping tears from my eyes as Carlin irreverently, needless to say "disobediently," summarized how so many of us feel about the need to replace fervent nationalism with what Zinn (2002: 52) called a "declaration of interdependence among peoples in all countries of the world who are striving for the same thing":

> "God bless America!" Once again, respectfully, I say to myself: "What the fuck does that mean?" ... Let me tell you a little secret about God, folks: God does not give a flyin' fuck about America.... There are 200 countries in the world now! Do these people honestly think that God is sitting around picking out his favorites? Why would he do that? Maybe it's because he heard we have eighteen delicious flavors of Classic Rice-A-Roni? ... You know what these "God Bless America" people oughta do? They oughta check with that Jesus fellow they're so crazy about.

In our outrage, but also importantly in our humor, we were able to recognize in each other a common longing for a better, sweeter world. It is through recognition of this collective desire that we cultivate resilience. These brief empathic, even mutually sardonic, connections are tangible evidence that we are not alone, an awareness that we can tuck into our spines for the tougher days ahead. In opposition to nationalist political culture, then, the artist can work to connect and mobilize this dissident citizenship.

Zinn's own archiving of optimism, of course, often took the form of documenting the courageous acts of others, many times those of artists: Pete Seeger, Eartha Kitt, Paul Robeson, Langston Hughes, Zinn's student Alice Walker. Zinn writes, "The roster of artists with social consciences is endless. I point to a few to represent so many, because their work, their commitment, encourages and sustains me, and I want it to encourage and sustain others."[9] For example, the late antiwar, feminist-lesbian poet Adrienne Rich is one among countless examples of radical citizen artists who have risked their livelihoods, their careers, even their lives to speak out against injustice. Rich was the first poet to decline the National Medal of Arts, the most prestigious award granted to artists by the United States government. Instead of claiming praise, Rich used her authority as an "honored" artist to claim solidarity with those radically dishonored by the Clinton administration. In a letter to the National Endowment for the Arts and published in the *New York Times,* she wrote that art, as she understood it, was simply "incompatible with the cynical politics of this administration. As such, a President cannot meaningfully honor certain token artists while the people at large are so dishonored.... Art ... means nothing if it simply decorates the dinner table of power which holds it hostage."[10]

Zinn was himself an artist of the nondecorous variety. As a political playwright, Zinn aimed to "transcend orthodoxy, transcend the word of the establishment, to escape what is handed down by our culture." Whereas "ideas and facts" might prompt individuals to "examine the world anew," he attests, art "lend(s) a kind of spiritual element to reality ... an intensity that a simple matter of recounting facts will not accomplish." His eventual decision, as he remarks in the introduction to his trio of plays, to "move outside the boundaries of the discipline (to refuse to be disciplined)" was inspired by the "life-long" desire to experiment with this unique form of political mobilization.[11] It is in the spirit of this refusal to be disciplined that I turn to radical citizenship in the academy.

RADICAL CITIZENSHIP IN THE ACADEMY: THE AUTHORITY EFFECT

> The strongest bulwark of authority is uniformity; the least divergence from it is the greatest crime.
> —*Emma Goldman (1940)*[12]

> The work of an intellectual is not to mold the political will of others; it is, through the analyses that he does in his own field, to re-examine evidence and assumptions, to shake up habitual ways of working and thinking, to dissipate conventional familiarities, to re-evaluate rules and institutions and to participate in the formation of a political will (where he has his role as citizen to play).
> —*Michel Foucault*[13]

When I decided to return to graduate school, Zinn was encouraging but offered a caveat: "Take your ferocity with you and please don't lose your sense of humor." Zinn was well known for his critical stance toward the "disinterested" scholar, his perpetual warning of that intellectuals "publish while others perish." I too was nervous about displacing my passport of purpose, of ingesting wholesale a new academic jargon that might force my political commitments if not into hiding, then at least into an odd-fitting discursive outfit—one that only other academics window-shopping in the same boutique-like journals would recognize. Still, I was excited about pursuing the study of political theory, so much of this work having influenced my art. I also quickly discovered the countless scholars, committed to the project of real social change, similarly concerned about the view of the academic world as barred from broader political accessibility.

Importantly, this is a struggle with which, I can attest, political artists invested both in craft and "world-making" are quite familiar. Political artists may be, in many ways, the guerrillas outside of the fold willing to take risks that others cannot or will not, but that "outside" can sometimes feel like a self-limiting location. In other words, in some real sense both artists and scholars constitute spheres of radical citizens frustrated by what Michael Warner (2002a: 158) calls the "language game of the public sphere." However, since much of this work is itself aimed at a rethinking of democratic politics—locating and interpreting counterhegemonic practices and writing against the political indoctrination of dominant narratives, doesn't the next logical step call for a communicative nexus of these two realms?

In *Artists in Times of War,* Zinn contends that it is the job of artists "to think outside the boundaries of permissible thought and dare to say things that no one else will say." But intellectual scholarship, Zinn argues, must do the same. Rather than political theorists wiling away their days *positing* "transcendental visions of the good society," Zinn insists that we have a responsibility to "*act* transcendentally."[14] Thus, if Zinn is correct that we "surely need more practice in challenging intellectual authority of all kinds,"[15] why not experiment with contesting our own epistemological authority within the social sciences? What would it look like to forgo the corporate model of claiming a monopoly on scholarship and resources? Indeed, if we are to accept Zinn's legacy, actively combating the stereotype of the disinterested intellectual, might we consider that the time has arrived to practice using everything within our reach to render the world intelligible for people, to experiment with radically new combinations of tactics—for initiating political change? It was not the academy, after all, but Woody Guthrie's song "Ludlow Massacre" that sparked Zinn's own intellectual curiosity about labor strikes. Thus, if we are to use both grassroots art and intellectual writing as "guerrilla warfare," it is our individual and collective responsibility to intervene in our very present, spotting sites for discursive and creative disruption(s), bolstering one another's efforts and magnifying our conjoined political effect.

As Pierre Bourdieu (2010: 128) argues, "the authority effect has to be fought with an authority effect." In my view, it is an act of radical citizenship to use one's authority to share one's authority. How might scholars be crucial for engineering these coups d'état of radical citizenship, working to mobilize collective conversations between artists and intellectuals, respecting the role of artists as an integral part of our grassroots media and working to mobilize their stories? How might incorporating poets, filmmakers, songwriters, and musicians into our curricula, classrooms, and scholarship allow us to transcend the boundaries of expertise in ways we may not have anticipated as productive—or even possible? As Zinn's former student Alice Walker (2000: 48–49) writes, "Each writer writes the missing parts to the other writer's story. And the whole story is what I'm after." Might this kind of dialogic model for the pursuit of knowledge inform these alliances? What kind of political imagination would bridging the gap entail?

For Zinn (2001c: 124), freedom of expression within the academy is contingent upon taking risks, specifically those involved in the creation of a "genuinely free marketplace of thought and culture." This is particularly true in light of the ways that, as Zinn (2004b: 94) argues, the system delimits free expression within even its artistic and cultural institutions, allocating art its "special space" while exerting financial control over its size and thus its reach. Indeed, the way that the spheres of artistic culture and higher education are maintained as discrete entities is itself a pernicious and powerful form of monitoring both realms. Though Zinn has a fairly derisive view of Plato as a canonical figure, there may be an important lesson here in assessing just how far from Plato's Republic, and its philosopher-kings, we might situate our own discipline and its "guardians of traditional education."[16]

What entrenched patterns of canonical authority might need to be challenged if we were to support the circulation of artists' ideas through using them in our work, in our citations and references? What view of political science might need to be disturbed if we were to regularly publish political poetry in our journals—not as simply decorative art but rather as equally authorized critique? What if we were to include powerfully creative explanations of disenfranchisement alongside the study of institutions and voting patterns in our American-politics curricula?

To borrow from James Jasper's (1997: 138) argument about the link between intellectuals and protesters, I contend that the more we pay scholarly attention to political artists, the more we facilitate their capacity "to be taken seriously as strategic actors, to encourage their participation in democratic conversations." In this light, perhaps it is time to assess what kinds of radical alliances we are potentially sacrificing if we do not take these opportunities to visibly support the work of our radical artists. For example, Amiri Baraka, a black revolutionary poet, was fired from his honorary post as New Jersey's poet laureate for the public performance of his 9/11 poem "Somebody Blew Up America": "All thinking people oppose terrorism / both domestic and international.... But one should not / be used / To cover the other."[17] On his website, Baraka called his firing a "confirmation of the ignorance, corruption, racism, and criminal disregard for the US Constitution."[18] However, while other artists came to Baraka's defense, virtually nothing was written within the academy about this blatant injustice. In other words, academics failed to use this opportunity to act as radical citizens, to use their authority to defend the "disobedient" voice of the artist. Edward Said (2004: 140) characterizes "the intellectual as lookout" whose job it is "to discern the possibilities for active intervention, whether we then perform them ourselves or acknowledge them in others who have either gone before or are already at work." If the intellectual is to accept this task, how might we encourage political scientists to pay more acute attention, for example, to the ways the state works to obstruct some of our most important political messengers?

What I mean to suggest here is that intellectual scholarship, choice of curricula, and the direction of university resources all have a crucial role to play in expanding the ways we think about doing and studying politics—and thus, expanding the grounds of politics itself. For Zinn (2009 [1997]: 674), this clearly entailed rethinking and reclaiming the stakes of what it means to write, work, and live as scholars when "so much of what is called 'intellectual history' is the aimless dredging up of what is and was rather than a creative recollection of experience pointed at the betterment of human life." Perhaps, then, tapping into our creative counterpublics might push us to engage in our collective political imagination in ways that—in Zinn's words—entail our lives as scholars to be lived a little closer to "out of order."[19]

Blind obedience to the protocol of the academic establishment, after all, in some ways resembles the kind of dangerous patriotism about which Zinn warns us. As Zinn's work and his own personal history demonstrate, anyone who takes steps against the status quo will be held up as an example by that status quo for the purposes of intimidation. Zinn himself was fired for "insubordination" from Spelman College for supporting student civil-rights protesters, risked his tenure at Boston University for speaking out against the war, and, as was recently disclosed by the FBI, had garnered a 243-page file over his twenty-five years of "disobedience." Perhaps the most incredible display of Zinn's optimistic commitment to rebellion was his arrest for (literally) "the failure to quit." Alice Walker (2010) aptly summarized Zinn's view of these charges: "'Yes,' he would later say, with a classic Howie shrug, 'I was guilty.'"

Zinn writes, "I am not sure what a revolution in the academy will look like, any more than I know what a revolution in the society will look like.... More likely, it will be a process, with periods of tumult and of quiet, in which we will, here and there, by ones and twos and tens, create pockets of concern inside old institutions, transforming them from within."[20]

In my view of critical political science, if we are invested in transformation and movement-making, we must devote equally critical attention to what actually *moves* people. Artists have always served as a rich undergirding of social movements, crucial to sustaining activist momentum—particularly in dark political moments. In my experience, this (re)fueling is an unparalleled source of energy in the battle against atomization, combating the burnout, fears, and exhaustion of political activism—the very real human desires, fears, and even consequences of radical citizenship that political science tends to ignore in the study of politics.

For some, it may seem paradoxical to think of political scientists as deliberately engaging in this messy border-blending. The alternative, however, is not only lost opportunity for advancing understanding of political dissent, but also an impoverished community of both current and potential political dissenters. Contrary to notions of a politically "apathetic youth," for example, I have found the new generation of students—both in my audiences and now in my classrooms—bright, inquisitive, and unafraid to voice their opinions about the world. Many of these views, they tell me, they have attained through art; they are all eager cultural consumers (and some even producers) of hip-hop, spoken word, comedy (particularly of the satirical variety), and documentaries. But they fail to see the commensurate potential of these types of art and what is in their view this humdrum enterprise called political science; between creatively challenging authority and the possibilities of conceptual innovation and contestation offered by political theory. Given what often appears to be the epistemologically impenetrable structure of the social sciences, I find it difficult to blame them.

As writers and teachers committed to coauthorizing artists, might we follow the lead of artists who help to mediate the work of thinkers like Zinn? One example, among many, of Howard Zinn's circulation among artists is his liner notes for the Ani DiFranco and Utah Phillips *Fellow Workers* (1999) album, in which Zinn writes, "The songs on this disk, the stories told in Utah Phillips' extraordinary style, bring back the history, but even more, the feelings of people struggling together for a better life." Though he is referencing Mother Jones, the Wobblies, and all of the thousands of women and men who have formed and organized unions, "who struggled and fought back, and changed lives," this message also speaks to the "collaboration, defiance, and solidarity" between DiFranco and Phillips as artists and Zinn, the historian.

Frankly, in my view, intellectual analysis without some sort of creative bedrock provides not only a flat analysis and a monochromatic approach to living, but also a politically unsustainable one. According to the *Oxford English Dictionary*, an achromatic lens is a composite lens in which two (or multiple) lenses with different properties are combined to prevent distortion, to help us see the world more clearly. In bringing together the lenses of the artistic and the intellectual, I foresee the chance to directly engage a generation not only prepared to disrupt the monochromatic political narrative with critical questions, but to fill it in with new colors, and possibilities.

CONCLUSION: TOWARD AN OPTIMISTIC FUTURE

> I believe the world is beautiful
> and that poetry, like bread, is for everyone.
> And that my veins don't end in me
> but in the unanimous blood
> of those who struggle for life,
> love,
> little things,
> landscape and bread,
> the poetry of everyone.
>
> —*Roque Dalton (1995 [1975]: 39–40)*

It is almost certain that Zinn would balk at any categorization of himself as an inspiration; in this "topsy-turvy" world, however, where optimistic disobedience performs the work of setting things rightside up, the designation applies. At its core, Zinn's message was about generating hope. Zinn asks, "What does it take to bring a turnaround in social consciousness? We desperately want an answer, because we know that the future of the human race depends on a radical change in social consciousness."[21] Certainly, social consciousness requires the research and dissemination of information about injustices, but just as importantly for Zinn

(2004b: 88) it is the collective "job of democracy" to generate excitement about possibilities for moving forward differently. Consider James Oppenheim's poem "Bread and Roses" (1911), originally intended to document the Lawrence Textile strike; the words have been recorded by numerous artists and used to bolster countless political movements:

> As we come marching, marching, unnumbered women dead
> Go crying through our singing their ancient cry for bread.
> Small art and love and beauty their drudging spirits knew.
> Yes, it is bread we fight for—but we fight for roses, too!

For Zinn, not only do artists have the capacity to articulate a collective ethical vision and to reach our moral intuition, but they may also help us to imagine, perhaps even momentarily practice, a different kind of radical citizenship in these mobilizing spaces. Like many of us now engaged in documenting, directly participating in, or otherwise working with(in) the Occupy movement, it is simultaneously heartwarming and heartbreaking to reflect on what Howard Zinn's creative and intellectual contributions might have been. I feel confident, however, that he would have been elated by the artistic presence at the sites, by the ongoing and passionate conversations about the intersections of democracy, art, and social justice that Occupy continues to generate.

Perhaps partially fueled by his own artistic calling, Zinn was unique in his appreciation of progressive artists, and acutely aware of the powerful impact of his call to support them: "So when I or others get some of that history and talk about the relationship between art and social change, it is encouraging to artists who are maybe a little tremulous and uncertain about what they're doing, because what they're doing runs so contrary to the mainstream and the commercial world [and that world] is likely to come down on them."[22] His consistent use of poems in lectures, references to musicians and novelists in essays, and invitations to performers to present at his gatherings, embodies the kind of coauthorization I have in mind.

It is clear that Zinn's moral calling entailed an almost poetic fusion of political commitment and personal fulfillment: "Politics is pointless if it does nothing to enhance the beauty of our lives."[23] Like artistic expression, provocative intellectual rhetoric can help us to imagine the world otherwise, which, vital to any political project, may entail simultaneously experimenting with how to (co)inhabit our current one differently. Seen in this light, radical citizenship is necessarily dialogic and may require a creative commitment to polyvalence. Without expanding the modes of political voice, categories of institutions, and social actors we cultivate a limited and limiting grasp of politics. However, by attending to the role that artists play in catalyzing radical citizenship, we may open up new avenues of understanding protest and mobilization, developing better tools for understanding social movement and political change. Moreover, if we are not content to simply write about political change, then it is our obligation to transcend these barriers and work in new ways to create it.

Howard Zinn left us a legacy of risk-taking, disobedience, and optimism. He also left us with a tall order: progress, learn your history, progress, *agitate with a smile,* progress. And, as we "zig-zag towards a more decent society," don't let the present repeat.[24] What I am attempting to advance in these brief reflections is that identifying as radical scholars and artists by virtue of displaying a set of identifiably progressive *beliefs* is simply not the kind of risk that can compel us to move forward. Rather, it is my optimistic assertion that by employing our political imagination, adopting the practice of mutual authorization, and building a constellation of radical citizens, we might inspire one another toward the kind of action that *itself represents* "the possibility of sending this spinning top of a world in a different direction."[25] Indeed, Zinn's own embrace of archiving optimism, and thus of movement(s), moved the man himself at an almost dizzying pace: from outspoken war veteran to historian, from professor to public intellectual, and finally to playwright and artist.

For Zinn, "outrageous feminist anarchist" Emma Goldman, the protagonist in his own guerrilla theater intervention, represented "the best of the revolutionary idea: not just to change the world, but to change the way you live, now."[26] Indeed, perhaps a *New York Times* review of Zinn's *Emma* is a prescient description of the kind of collective work I have been calling for: "Despite some awkwardness," the reviewer attests, the production "builds up quiet power," and "with a bit of humming, a little foot-tapping, a few bars of music" the separate figures in the play "become before our eyes a revolutionary cadre."[27] Only in this way can we work to ensure that "the roots of one era branch and flower in subsequent eras,"[28] moving the next generation closer to the one "modest" proposal that Zinn had in mind: to change the world.[29]

Walking

Martín Espada

For Howard Zinn (1922–2010)

> I go two steps closer, she moves two steps away. I walk ten steps and the
> horizon runs ten steps ahead. No matter how much I walk, I'll never reach
> her. What good is utopia? That's what: it's good for walking.
> —*Eduardo Galeano (1995)*

You walked alone, away from the city writhing in flames and jellied gasoline,
away from the canisters of napalm dropped by your bombardier's hands,
away from medals and ribbons stuffed in a folder with the words *never again*;
walking the backroads in a country of Confederate flags, shoes baked in mud,
shuffling on the picket line with dark-skinned sharecroppers, teachers, organizers
who hungered for the ballot box and sang all night to keep their jailers awake;
walking with apparitions, the escaped slave reading the compass of the moon
between the trees, the anarchist in spectacles who made of the crowd a roaring sea,
the union man on trial for subversion of the draft, who confessed the crime
and told the judge with open hands, *while there is a soul in prison, I am not free*;
walking through the metal detectors of courthouses and airports, smuggling
manifestos in your head from the slave, the anarchist, the unionist, words freed
as a magician frees doves flown to the rafters from the great stage of the world;
walking through schoolrooms, the smooth oval of faces tilted up, astonished
by your words as they floated down like parachutes of milkweed on the wind;
walking by the river with the fugitive poet-priest who sang of *the risen bread*,
as agents of the government hunted for the poet everywhere but the river;
walking through the mace that hissed in your eyes at the march against the war,

156

the cuffs that clicked, the billy clubs that jabbed the ribs of your thin body;
walking in the circle of the peace vigil on the town common at noon,
past the jeers and staring of the onlookers who know that nothing changes;
walking when your legs trembled in the storm of nerves crushed by the spine,
when you knew you would never arrive, that the world was too bright with ice
for a fistful of sand and careful steps, and yet your fingers still tapped out
the messages of dissidents as you spoke, darting with the delirium of sparrows,
walking with thousands beside you now, a roaring sea, down the road to a city
where they greet you with blackberries that grow wild in the ruins, where scars
of liquid fire dissolve into the skin, where the bombs will never fall again.

ZINN TODAY AND TOMORROW

CHAPTER 11

Two, Three, Many Zinns

Media Culture and the Dilemmas of Democratic Transformation

Edward P. Morgan

Recalling the assassination of Malcolm X, Harlem leader A. Peter Bailey described that moment as the loss of a "master teacher," a voice that gave important inspiration and hope to an entire community.[1] In many ways, Howard Zinn was a master teacher whose voice was an important source of hope and inspiration, particularly for a broad community of Americans, over the last fifty years.

In this essay, I draw on distinctive qualities of Zinn's voice to consider the contemporary dilemmas facing efforts to move the United States (and the world) in a fundamentally more democratic direction. The democratic uprisings that emerged all over the planet in 2011 suggest to me that we have arrived at a historic moment that trembles with possibility but is full of hazards. My argument draws on my own work, which addresses how mass media interacted with the social movements of the 1960s era to influence the sixties trajectory and help move the United States away from democracy to the market-dominated neoliberal world we confront today.[2] I argue that the social movements of today need to incorporate the very qualities that made Zinn such an important historical figure in his own right. Thus my title references Che Guevara's famous 1967 quote calling for the spread of revolution in Latin America—"two, three, many Vietnams"—echoed by Tom Hayden's 1968 essay calling for the spread of campus uprisings—"Two, Three, Many Columbias."

While many of Zinn's former students have reflected on the powerful ways he influenced their lives and their political consciousness, I knew Zinn as a master teacher largely through his speaking and writing as a public intellectual addressing a wide audience.[3] This volume asks us to reflect on what made Howard Zinn's political voice so compelling. The qualities I enumerate here are, I contend, crucially important if today's social movements are going to achieve a democratic transformation.

I would first suggest the quality that made Zinn's voice so *necessary*—namely, the fact that his speaking and writing brought to wider audiences an incisive and consistently radical criticism—was a perspective on American history and contemporary society that lies outside the normal fare to which most Americans are exposed in the mass media and their schooling experiences. From *A People's History of the United States* and related projects to his active schedule as a speaker on the nation's campuses to the innumerable times he spoke to local activist groups or at mass protest rallies, Zinn provided a perspective that helped to explain why this nation has faced such disturbing problems.

I would add four qualities that enabled Zinn's radical critique to *reach and be heard by* wider audiences, to expand the base of those drawn to more progressive ideas and a more radical understanding of institutional forces. These were fundamental to what has made Zinn's voice so distinctive, and so greatly missed.

First, Zinn not only addressed committed activists, but he spoke and wrote directly to a general audience. Far from relying on mass media to communicate his message to wider audiences, Zinn devoted considerable energy to direct, often unmediated communication, perhaps most successfully through his *People's History*, but also through his plays, talks at conventional sites like public libraries, and projects like his collaboration with Anthony Arnove, *Voices of a People's History* (2004) and the related 2009 film, *The People Speak*. (I will return to the importance of this Zinnian quality later on in this chapter.)

Second, Zinn drew on a leftist understanding but consistently "spoke American." The language he used was free of the more doctrinaire terminology that has long been associated with rhetoric on the radical Left, particularly within sectarian divisions of the Marxist or neo-Marxist Left.[4] It was also free of academic jargon, and, as he put it, "I didn't pretend to an objectivity that was neither possible nor desirable."[5] While infused with a keen sense of class inequality, Zinn's speaking and writing was always grounded in the everyday injustices that people struggled with, and *A People's History*, of course, told the story of those struggles throughout the American past. One needn't have been exposed to a history of Marxist thought to "get" what Howard Zinn was speaking and writing about.

Third, what came through particularly in person was the wry, gentle humor that permeated Zinn's speech. Invariably, while speaking of what were often extremely disturbing topics, Zinn made his audiences laugh. His "agitation with a smile" could pierce the absurdity of elite rhetoric that legitimized prevailing conditions without invoking a harsh personal animus against those who used it. Most of all, while Zinn clearly took the injustices people experienced very seriously, his humor conveyed the sense that he didn't take himself too seriously. That is, it was more important for his audiences to understand the broader picture than to get caught up, one way or another, in the personality fixations of the mass media culture. At the same time, Zinn's humor was implicitly a way of recognizing the importance of establishing a relationship with his audience. In contrast to modes of address more commonly found in the intellectual Left, Zinn made serious radical inquiry *inviting* rather than off-putting to general audiences encountering him for the first time. As Emma Goldman once famously declared, "If I can't dance, I don't want to be part of your revolution."[6]

Finally and perhaps most importantly, by drawing on his important reading of history and through the compelling example of his own actions, Zinn brought hope to his audiences. Without this sense of hope, people rarely engage in the kinds of collective action that bring about political change. Zinn drew on innumerable examples of the American people taking history into their own hands; that history, in turn, helps to empower contemporary Americans by connecting their struggles with the many important breakthroughs brought about by people like themselves in the past. As Zinn (1994: 208) has written in his fittingly titled memoir, *You Can't Be Neutral on a Moving Train,* "To be hopeful in bad times is not just foolishly romantic. It is based on the fact that human history is a history not only of cruelty, but also of compassion, sacrifice, courage, kindness. What we choose to emphasize in this complex history will determine our lives." Furthermore, through the example of his own participation in civil disobedience and other forms of political activism, Zinn provided the inspiring example often characteristic of master teachers.

In combination, I would suggest, these qualities that Howard Zinn embodied provide a kind of metaphorical guide to the contemporary struggle to take the United States, and the world, from the "bad times" induced by so-called free market politics to a genuinely democratic culture. If that effort is to succeed, it must understand how the governing neoliberal ideology not only cannot resolve the enormous problems facing populations the world over, but also provide a rationale for the very system that has produced many of these problems. Neoliberalism has produced astonishing levels of inequality that have grotesquely enriched the very few while the working and middle classes struggle to make ends meet. Corporate and personal wealth exercise unprecedented power over a distracting election spectacle, subsequently dominating the agenda of government.

Americans who feel aggrieved and disempowered are ripe targets for the manipulative "affective empowerment"[7] of advertisers, whether these are pushing political candidates or a "better life" of consumption. Meanwhile neoliberalism and capital flight undercut political efforts to confront the deepening ecological crises facing the globe, and an imperial American foreign policy persists despite public opposition to American wars in Iraq and Afghanistan. What passes for political discourse in the mass media plays on the fears and antipathies of Americans while offering "solutions" to problems that are at best symbolic. As economist Robin Hahnel wrote in November 2010,

Both the economic and ecological crisis are real and huge. Both require bold, serious policy responses. Those who got a boost in the midterm elections not only have no solutions for either problem, they will work tirelessly for policies that will predictably aggravate both crises considerably.... Only progressives, nobody else, has [*sic*] solutions. Neither Washington nor the major media will be discussing real solutions for the foreseeable future.

The economic crisis that erupted in 2008 was a key catalyst for two paths of public resistance to perceived elite power. The first of these, and thus by far the more formidable of the two, was the latest chapter in a long-running saga in which elite funding and attacks on "big government" have succeeded in turning the frustrations of millions of aggrieved Americans against "liberal" uses of government. Energized by traditional pitches for tax relief and the neoliberal mythology that tax cuts for the wealthy generate productive job growth for the American people, the Tea Party was mobilized against the Obama administration's allegedly "socialist" health care reform. As it had for more than thirty years, the attack produced Republican electoral gains in 2010 and helped to cow potential Democratic opposition.

The second path of public resistance, however, arose in response to the consequences of the first. Buoyed by major electoral gains at both state and national levels in 2010 and enabled by state-level fiscal distress (produced most immediately by inadequate governmental responses to the financial crash of 2007–2008), the reinvigorated Right launched its latest campaign against socially beneficial uses of government and one of the last remaining political resources that helps to produce these uses of government: public-employee unions. Vowing "no new taxes" while often offering new corporate tax breaks, governors and/or Republican-captured legislatures in states such as Wisconsin, Michigan, Ohio, New Jersey, Indiana, Florida, Pennsylvania, Montana, and New Hampshire introduced dramatic cutbacks in state funding for education, health care, children's services, employee retirement accounts, and even sustainable energy development and environmental protection. Most acutely in Wisconsin, Ohio, Florida, and Michigan, they proposed and/or enacted new legislative restrictions on the collective-bargaining rights of public-employee unions. Several also launched new voter-identification requirements that would likely reduce voter turnout among vulnerable populations prone to voting Democratic: the poor, racial minorities, and the young. These initiatives typify the kinds of policies that have long been advocated as part of the campaign to turn the United States to the Right, away from the liberal sixties.

The dramatic, overt nature of these attacks on public-employee unions and valued public expenditures produced instantaneous resistance by broad sectors of the public, often sustained by the organizational prowess of public-employee unions, producing what Zinn called "the sudden coming to life of a flame we thought extinguished." Or, as he went on, "The isolated acts [of indignation, protest, and resistance] begin to join, the individual thrusts blend into organized actions, and one day, often when the situation seems hopeless, there bursts onto the scene a movement."[8] Inspired by these initial public uprisings (and by the Arab Spring), the Occupy Wall Street movement burst onto the political landscape in September 2011 and spread across the nation and much of the world.

I propose that this recent history of public resistance contains the potential of an aroused public not only reversing this latest neoliberal assault, but of generating an *ideological* or *consciousness shift* that opens the door to more fundamental democratic change—a potential ideological shift that reflects Howard Zinn's radical message. One reason for this potential is that there is growing evidence in all media that people around the world are rising up and resisting the dominant neoliberal model and the repressive regimes that serve it—from the Arab Spring to the American state protests to, most recently, mass actions in nations including Greece, Spain, Great Britain, France, and Italy. Mass media coverage has helped to generate what George Katsiaficas once called the "eros effect,"[9] in which mass protest spreads as people in far-flung regions act out their sense of connection to the "life force" represented by popular protest activities elsewhere. The Occupy movement followed suit. Progressive and social media alike have helped immeasurably to connect these disparate actions.

Second, attacks on state-government expenditures, in particular, produce tangible effects likely to arouse both public awareness and antipathy. As opposed to domestic federal-government cutbacks that are for a variety of reasons relatively invisible—in part because the populations adversely impacted are often highly marginalized in the media and political mainstream—state cutbacks directly affect populations that most people have some direct contact with: school teachers, nurses, police, and firefighters. And these populations have been highly visible in the protests against cutbacks. Friends and neighbors of a wide swath of the population may well be among those adversely affected. Coupled with the tangible nature of cutbacks, the attack on public-employee unions provides an opening for an aroused public to become more ideologically conscious of the inherent flaws of the entire neoliberal fabric that has dominated not only American but global politics for decades. To a degree, the Occupy movement reinforced this consciousness with its symbolic claim to represent the 99%.

Before considering the application of "two, three, many Zinns" to the potential alive in the present moment, I would contend we need to give careful consideration to the forces that produced the neoliberal world and the dominant myths that sustain it. It is in a Zinnian sense of exposing the important hidden history of our recent past that I have written and taught about the social movements of the 1960s era, and most recently about the way that past has been distorted and trivialized in the mass media. I contend that there is much to learn from this past of relevance to today's grassroots struggles. Yet those connections are severed in the public memory that is preserved for us by our mass media culture—what commonly passes for "history" in our society. These are the very same media that, following the journalistic norm of "objectivity," consider their stance to be "neutral" toward political events.

MEDIA CULTURE AND THE BACKLASH AGAINST DEMOCRACY

The present moment occurs in a historical context in which the United States traveled from a hopeful era of rising democratic social movements to one in which politics has been repeatedly denigrated and market capitalism elevated as the favored framework for addressing all political issues. Although grassroots mobilizations repeatedly crop up in opposition to various ills and injustices generated by neoliberal politics,[10] voices like Zinn's have often labored to overcome a widespread sense of despair on the part of progressives.

My own recent work documents the way that mass media culture helped to usher in this neoliberal era by distorting the turbulent era of the 1960s through both the ideological discourse of political backlash and the market imperatives of commercial exploitation.[11] For upwards of thirty to forty years, something called "the sixties" has been scapegoated by a lavishly funded corporate and right-wing campaign to move American political discourse to the Right. Simultaneously, a variety of sixties representations—images, music, personalities, and events—have been widely exploited by commercial forces in ways that have effectively converted the contagious political activism of the sixties era into the culture of consumption and entertainment. The result has been what political theorist Sheldon Wolin (2008) has called "Democracy Incorporated," in which public participation has been increasingly privatized and neutralized.

The two versions of the sixties—one overtly ideological, the other commercial and seemingly "neutral"—play off each other in a discourse that helps to sustain the persuasiveness of rightist attack, at least for a significant proportion of the electorate. Noteworthy examples of convergence between ideological and commercial media include the bellicose anti-sixties rhetoric of Ronald Reagan and the sixties representation in the popular 1983 film *The Big Chill.* Or Newt Gingrich's 1994 attack on the alleged "McGovernick-Countercultural" politics of the Clinton administration playing off the sixties representations of the 1994 blockbuster *Forrest Gump.* The never-ending commercial exploitation of sex, advertisers' appeal to the latest manifestation of "hipness," entertainment media's quest for the edgiest new story line, and an increasingly dumbed-down, dramatic news media all provide references and vehicles that are useful to interests who appeal to the conservative values of those alienated by this culture. In turn, the political impotence fostered by corporate domination of neoliberal policy and endless attacks on "big government" reinforces the allure of commercial media's "affective empowerment" and the retreat into privatized entertainment. Advertising, consumption, entertainment, and the expressive politics of the media spectacle all appeal via the feelings of empowerment they offer the public.

The turn to neoliberalism was facilitated by a faux populism that evolved out of the turbulent 1960s. Essentially, corporate and right-wing campaigns beginning in the 1960s and continuing through the Reagan years up to the current moment have used a variety of media-conveyed trigger points or hot-button issues to characterize liberal [conveniently labeled "big"] government as elitist and counter to the values and interests of a wide swath of the American public—not only traditional small-town and conservative populations but, crucially, former elements of the New Deal Coalition, notably the white South and the Catholic white working class. Along with "permissive" parents and university administrators, and eventually "tenured radicals," liberal government has been repeatedly blamed for causing many of the ills that have been loosely associated with images, personalities, and events of the sixties era that these populations found highly alienating. Over time, as this discourse has become entrenched, sixties references have somewhat receded, supplanted by more-recent attacks on "liberal media" or a "socialist" Obama administration. With the aid of mass media discourse, public attention has thus been diverted from awareness that many of these very ills are rooted in the acquisitive capitalism unleashed by neoliberal politics.

Where did the images, personalities, and stories that have energized this faux populism come from? They evolved from the interaction between social movements of the long sixties era, mass media, and the policies and repressive practices of government. In my work on the mass media's relationship with the sixties during and since the sixties era itself, I have distinguished two structural characteristics of the nation's mass media that influenced the trajectory of the sixties and did so in ways that helped to bury this powerfully democratic past while actively assisting the transformation to today's neoliberal world. Both derive from the fact that American mass media are preeminently responsive to capitalist rather than democratic imperatives. They are relevant to contemporary democratic struggles in two ways: (1) in their interaction with sixties social movements, they provide important insights into the forces that can distort, impede, and ultimately derail contemporary social movements; and (2) in the role they have played in facilitating the turn to neoliberalism, they provide insight into the kinds of cultural forces and political myths that contemporary movements invariably confront. Therefore, they speak directly to the need for "two, three, many Zinns."

The first media characteristic, variously described and widely documented by several media critics,[12] is that the word-based texts of mass media fall within ideological boundaries; that is, the interpretations and explanations found in mass market media are framed in ways that reinforce rather than challenge the dominant ideological beliefs and myths of American society. In his study of mass media coverage of the war in Vietnam, for example, Daniel Hallin found that mass media discourse about the war fell into two domains: (1) the "Sphere of Consensus," in which basic characterizations of the war and the purpose of US foreign policy remained unchallenged, and (2) the "Sphere of Legitimate Controversy," in which public debate over the war was "defined primarily by the two-party system." In the former sphere, journalists largely acted as "patriots," whereas in the latter, they were more likely to follow the professional norms—the alleged "neutrality"—of journalism. *Not* included in mass media discourse were those views that reflected a fundamental stance of many in the antiwar movement: that the war was a fundamentally immoral US assault against the people of Vietnam. These were confined to the "Sphere of Deviance, the realm of those political actors and views which journalists and the political mainstream of society reject as *unworthy of being heard*."[13] Similar spheres of discourse applied to each of the social movements of the sixties era—and they continue to do so.[14]

Social movements were, and are, able to gain access to wider publics, however, through the other defining quality of mass media—namely, its commercially driven emphasis on evocative visuals, dramatic action, conflict, charismatic personalities, and violence or the threat of violence. Reflecting the market's imperative of attracting a wide audience, these qualities became profoundly and increasingly significant as television moved to the fore as the primary source of news for most Americans during the long sixties era. Visual imagery became an important means through which sympathetic audiences could glean meanings that more conventional media prose simply could not or would not capture—as they did, for example, when images of state violence against nonviolent civil-rights protests in Birmingham (1963) and Selma (1965) had profound effects in conveying the meaning of the Southern struggle to the rest of the nation. Imagistic meanings could also transcend, if not contradict, the official explanations offered by "legitimate" sources in the mass media—as, for example, did images from Vietnam ranging from countless poignant photographs revealing the brutality experienced by Vietnamese civilians to more shocking images like the naked Vietnamese girl running from a napalm attack or the civilian corpses produced by the American massacre in My Lai.

When it came to social-movement protest, however, the two media characteristics converged to produce effects that worked to alienate wider sectors of the public, isolated the era's social movements, and ultimately eroded their potential to build a movement for more radical democratic change. In effect, mass media helped to spread the era's social movements, but did so in ways that ultimately isolated and contained those movements, setting in place the dynamic of backlash and co-optation that followed. Protests that utilized collective defiance or economic non-cooperation—most notably the Montgomery Bus Boycott—were themselves able to generate significant leverage against the beneficiaries of the status quo. Most direct action protests, however, had at least two significant targets: the powerful decision-makers themselves *and* wider audiences who might be moved to feel more sympathetic to the protesters than they did toward the target of protests. The latter were crucial to protests' ability to spread as well as to reach wider audiences who might engage in supportive political activity.

The difficulty lay, first, in the fact that mass media news coverage of protest activity was invariably about the protest itself as a political and social phenomenon, not about the protest's *argument*—except as the latter was interpreted by "credible" political actors or could be conveyed visually or in pithy slogans or soundbites. As a result, a whole range of argumentation and supporting evidence that animated a great deal of protest activity about racism, class, poverty, war, foreign policy, education, gender, sexuality, and American culture remained effectively constricted, if not outright absent, in the texts of media discourse. At the same time, of course, dramatic action and confrontation, evocative symbolism, flamboyant behaviors and personalities, violence or the threat of violence, unusual attire and individualized motivations, and, of course, significant (and growing) numbers of protesters—these were the stuff of "newsworthy" events given wide and central coverage by press reports and television cameras. These images, in turn, conveyed quite different meanings to different media audiences.

I have suggested elsewhere that these characteristics of mass media's protest coverage created a particularly telling dynamic of "exit" and "voice," to use Albert O. Hirschman's (1970) terminology, for protest participants. In effect, the mass media discourse *invited* physical and visually symbolic expression while interpreting the meaning of that expression in more conventional (and system-reinforcing) liberal and conservative terms. As John Sanbonmatsu (2004) has observed, the turn toward "expressivism" took off in the mid-1960s, significantly at the very time social movements began to target national institutions and policies. Whereas it often became a kind of "affective empowerment" for protest participants when their activities were captured by the media's cameras, *their* voices and meanings could not be grasped by the wider public unless these were conveyed by the media imagery. Finding their meanings excluded from mainstream discourse and reframed (often pejoratively) by both establishment liberals and conservatives was—along with experiences of demeaning racism or sexism, government policy retrenchment, and state repression—profoundly alienating for many, and often radicalizing for young activists.[15] Experiencing themselves as "outsiders" in mainstream discourse reinforced tendencies to seek community with like-minded others, including, of course, alternative media that spoke their language and corroborated their meanings. Along with the course of events, the restricted range of "legitimate discourse" fueled inclinations to "exit" into what Sara Evans and Harry Boyte (1992) have called "free spaces" linked to black nationalism, radical (or cultural) feminism, educational experimentation, New Left collectives, communal living, and the broader counterculture.

At the same time, for some, the urgent desire to have political voice, to generate political change, was responsive to the cues available in the mass media. Flamboyant behavior or attire and forms of militant confrontation increased the chances of being "heard" (noticed) by the media's cameras.[16] Like advertising, the mass media spectacle offered a shortcut to personal "empowerment." Simultaneously, of course, the more radicalized elements of the era's social movements found their claims falling on deaf ears, the more they sought militant ways of making their political point, particularly as the violence in both Vietnam and the United States continued to escalate. Indeed, militancy was the only form of "radicalism" the mass media seemed capable of comprehending. It also fueled increasingly effective forms of backlash.

Two brief examples illustrate these dynamics at work. In one case, in the aftermath of the fiery Watts riot in 1965, one young black male remarked, "We won, because we made the whole world pay attention to us." He was right in one sense: the urban insurrections of the sixties era definitely caught the nation's attention. But from Barry Goldwater's 1964 presidential campaign through the "law and order" campaigns of Richard Nixon and George Wallace in 1968, these same riots provided fuel for a concerted backlash campaign against Great Society liberalism, and eventually against something called the sixties. In the latter instance, antiwar protesters outside the Hilton hotel in Chicago during the 1968 Democratic Convention chanted, "the whole world is watching" as club-wielding police attacked them; they were confident the viewing public would be appalled by the police attack. Later, however, public-opinion polls revealed that the majority of Americans, viewing the convention protests through the mass media, sided with the police. Indeed, as early as 1965, individual antiwar protesters found a conveniently potent symbol for expressing their defiant outrage and alienation from the American war: they flaunted Viet Cong (National Liberation Front) flags at antiwar protests. Mass media cameras invariably zeroed in on the inflammatory symbols, while with some visual persuasiveness, political officialdom and media commentators were quick to label the antiwar movement anti-American, if not traitorous.

The combination of visually dramatic symbolism, rising militancy, and political backlash that used these images and personalities to delegitimize all "outside" criticism—and to blame liberals for its existence—produced a profoundly polarized population and provided the foundation for corporate America's turn toward neoliberalism. The isolation and denigration of "outsiders" also had deleterious effects on the dynamics occurring within the era's social movements, particularly in cases where youthful identity formation was vulnerable. Retrospective accounts of the civil-rights and black-power movements, the Black Panther party, the women's movement, and the Weather Underground have testified to occasions on which internal group dynamics became more authoritarian and abusive, emphasizing purity of thought as a criterion of group membership.[17] Fragmentation of the era's social movements became almost epidemic during the latter years of the sixties era, generating lasting impediments to broader political organizing on the Left. With its invitation for expressions of visible group identity and capitalism's market segmenting response to diverse audience tastes and niches, mass media culture has gone a long way toward institutionalizing the balkanized society.

Indeed, greatly enhanced by the Internet, the media culture is full of opportunities for expressive empowerment. In its seductiveness and power to distract the public, this is arguably one of the factors that impedes effective political organizing. Another, of course, is the pervasiveness of neoliberal ideology and the way propaganda about sixties-related phenomena has hamstrung the nation's political discourse. A third, ironically, is that liberalization produced in the sixties and neoliberalization produced in response have left systemic forces as the preeminent causes generating the profound problems that Americans and the rest of the world face. In confronting systemic forces, political organizing encounters a mass media culture that systematically excludes serious consideration of those very forces. While political organizing and a richly vital discourse focusing on these forces flourish on the Left, these activities remain largely isolated from the mass media culture the vast majority of Americans tune in to. In short, the same dynamic of political protest that affected the sixties trajectory remains in place today, despite the enormous diversity of media that are readily available via the Internet. Not surprisingly, mass mobilizations over the past twenty or more years have drawn mass media comparisons to the sixties, with all the predictable range of subjective responses those references arouse.

TWO, THREE, MANY ZINNS

This is where Howard Zinn—and this sixties-resonating phrase—comes in. Quite clearly my argument is grounded in the view that radical or systemic change is imperative. Indeed, I believe that something like the democracy that animated Zinn's life, as well as generated the social movements of the sixties era, needs to be at the center of both the movement for change and the imagined vision that inspires it. People need to be—and they need to feel—empowered to bring the wider social order into accordance with their values even as they engage in an educative public conversation about the meanings and applications of those values. While Zinn never spelled out a democratic political theory, his life is a kind of testimony to this Deweyian sense of democracy as a way of life.[18] I suggest the attributes he brought to his life's work provide strategic guidance to the organizing efforts of the democratic left.

Zinn's notion that public resistance can "be ignited by some surprising circumstance into tumultuous change"[19] underscores the fact that crises produced by the prevailing system are important opportunities for organizing mass mobilizations, if not mass social movements. And the last decade has produced its share of such crises. The so-called "war on terror" and the invasion of Iraq, the Abu Ghraib scandal, the BP gulf oil spill, growing awareness of critical tipping points in climate change and other eco-erosion trends, and the near-meltdown of the Fukushima nuclear facilities are all examples of such crises, each of which provided impetus for renewed grassroots organizing, mass protests, instant but short-lived mass media saturation, and a wealth of radical analysis and debate outside the boundaries of mass media discourse. While these have all been fundamentally important to spreading public awareness of systemic flaws and generating new reform initiatives, mass media discourse has been reflexively constricted by immediate economic pressures, corporate or governmental damage control, and right-wing attack propaganda—ultimately and with astonishing speed turning each crisis into yesterday's news. Indeed, the system has proven remarkably adept at marginalizing discourse that addresses the institutional roots of crises like these. In effect, much like the *Titanic,* society plows forward amid arguments over who gets to sit in the deck chairs.

Crises will, of course, continue to erupt, perhaps with far greater destructiveness, providing more fodder for incisive radical analysis. For the democratic Left, a crucial strategic question is *how to engage the wider population in that radical understanding to the point that the neoliberal ideology loses its persuasive power and becomes politically marginalized.*[20] Here, I think, we confront the fact that mass public action and local grassroots organizing in response to crises, while necessary, are clearly insufficient.

As innumerable community organizers have recognized, people who feel relatively powerless and/or distracted by the pressures of everyday living need to be drawn into a kind of political engagement that builds a sense of community with others at the same time that it enhances both their political awareness and their sense of empowerment. It is possible today to draw on a rich community-organizing literature and a variety of training institutions that have built on the earlier work of organizers like Saul Alinsky. With its bottom-up emphasis, community organizing is a fundamentally important component in building for a democratic future.

Yet community organizing is also limited by the fact that it is essentially localized. There is truth to the maxim that "all politics are local," for people tend to experience institutional effects at the local level, and it is at the local level that active citizenship is most meaningful and accessible for most of the population. Indeed, although selectively applied, right-wing ideology owes some of its persuasiveness to its pitch for "local control." Thus, I would argue that the crucial conundrum facing the democratic Left is how to make effective connection between local, grassroots engagement and the broader institutions that impact localities and ultimately shape our collective future.

This conundrum has both organizational and cognitive or ideological dimensions. The organizational dimension revolves around building effective organizational linkages across a range of localized populations that can exercise political power at the level of broader national and global institutions. Political parties have traditionally been the means for organizing such linkages. Yet mainstream political discourse is dominated by an exchange between a corporate Democratic Party that pays lip service to its populist constituencies and a corporate Republican Party that has been largely captured by those who pledge to "free" people from "big government" but only deliver continued deterioration of social and ecological conditions while increasing the size and authoritarian quality of government—both losing options from the vantage point of democracy. Thus it is no surprise that activists on the American Left have often agitated for "third parties." Yet the structural and political impediments to third-party success in the American winner-take-all political system are enormous, particularly given the persuasiveness of "lesser of two evils" pragmatism (a theme the more liberal mass media accentuate whenever a potent third-party campaign is launched from the Left). As Robert McChesney (2010: 16) has argued, "An emerging consensus connecting activists across labor and the entire progressive community is that labor and progressives need to develop an independent body, unattached to the Democrats, which will only support candidates who are on board with a progressive platform."

My primary concern here, however, is with the application of Zinnian qualities to the crucial need to build cognitive and ideological awareness across the range of groups and localities adversely affected by the dominant political economy. Mass political action is and will remain an important dimension of raising public awareness of and resistance to institutions and policies that adversely affect diverse living populations as well as the ecosphere itself. However, as long as the mass media remain ideologically bound—which, indeed, they are likely to as long as they are corporations shaped by elite and market forces—actions that aim to influence both political decision-makers and wider publics through these media seem likely to succumb to the forces that shaped sixties-era social movements to their detriment.[21] Still, my emphasis here on the impact of mass media discourse on this aspect of democratic movement-building adds urgency to organizing efforts that aim to transform the corporate media—efforts that are, of course, ongoing on a number of fronts.

My emphasis on Zinnian qualities in the context of mass media discourse, however, brings me back to what I consider a crucial feature of democracy as a way of life: namely, the spread of political consciousness through building relationships and understanding *across* disparate sectors of the population (and, importantly, across the balkanizing features of the Internet). Many forces in contemporary life, not the least of which is the mass media culture itself, draw people away from attending to this dimension of building movements for social change. Yet this relationship-building seems particularly necessary if an "outsider" understanding is to spread, and, I will suggest, it is particularly pertinent to the current moment in social-movement history. Howard Zinn's sense of humor and his use of everyday "Americanese" implicitly honored the relevance of relationship between Zinn and his audience. And, as John Dewey (1966 [1916]: 87) has argued, a democratic way of life is grounded in a growing conversation across wider groups in which neither party is "master" or "slave"—Dewey's way of referring to a conversation based on mutual respect. Out of such a conversation grows awareness of common interests or common good, grounded in the wishes of the people rather than the rhetoric of the elite. I have argued, for example, that it was through exchanges grounded in close relationships during the 1960s era—between blacks and whites in the early days of SNCC, between children and their parents regarding the war in Vietnam, and between women and men regarding the pervasiveness of sexism—that minds were changed and personal growth enabled, even if painfully. This is the stuff of democracy writ small.

How, then, does this dimension pertain to the contemporary moment in which state budgets have been slashed by neoliberal, rightist governors and legislatures, public-employee unions have been openly attacked and to some degree curtailed, and a still-evolving Occupy movement has clearly injected issues of inequality and corporate-dominated politics into the nation's political discourse? My suggestion is that the two distinct movements—state-level resistance and Occupy—each bring an important dimension relevant to the democratic path forward.

First, the state-level attacks on public service expenditures and on labor unions have long been central to the success of the right-wing agenda and the supremacy of neoliberalism, going back most directly to the Reagan administration's attack on social-welfare programs, "Reaganomics," and President Reagan's overt assault on the air-traffic controllers' union. The mobilization of the Tea Party has played a significant role in this latest round of attacks. Second, while the Tea Party has been mobilized by highly affluent Americans who stand to benefit directly from its impact on government, it is essentially the latest round in a long-running saga in which millions of Americans with legitimate grievances about their declining economic standing have had their anxieties and resentments turned against "government"—which has always meant liberal government, and never militaristic government. In the latest round of this artificial populism, enormous (and legitimate) resentment toward the massive government bailout of Wall Street and the nation's banks was spun into Tea Party opposition to the Obama administration's "socialist" (i.e., more government spending) health care reform. The actual reform, in fact, only confirmed the Democratic Party as a corporate as opposed to a populist party.

In attacking state and local budgets and the collective-bargaining rights of public-employee unions, however, rightist politicians aroused a new wave of public resistance that has already demonstrated its potential to stem this latest advance against democratic uses of government. As some in Wisconsin have noted, these attacks awakened a "sleeping giant"—both organized labor and the wider public. In addition to immediate mass protests in most states where these cutbacks were threatened, rapid shifts in public opinion have been recorded, recall elections have been partially successful in Wisconsin, an Ohio referendum to repeal the law that curtailed public employees' collective-bargaining rights succeeded by a 61 percent to 39 percent margin, and local populations have protested against educational cutbacks in Pennsylvania and elsewhere. Public-opinion polls have indicated that the majority of Americans opposes state cutbacks targeting education and public health, opposes restrictions on the collective-bargaining rights of public employees, and even favors *raising taxes* to meet state budget shortfalls.[22] What all this evidence seems to point to is that the neoliberal agenda has been pushed too far. Significantly, it was relatively easy for the public (and local reporters) to *see* and understand the deleterious impact this latest round would have, especially as people like themselves were protesting against this assault.[23] A movement aiming to "save the middle and working classes" is inherently a majoritarian movement.

Of course, it must be said that majority public opinion has, mass media coverage notwithstanding, often contradicted the neoliberal creed or rightist creed—even supporting tax increases to achieve public-policy objectives related to equalizing opportunity or providing effective environmental protection.[24] Typically, however, a rightist or corporate propaganda attack zeroes in on a specific policy or program, creates distorted perceptions of that policy and/or the "intent" of its supporters, and thus sways sufficient public and media opinion to shift the debate. Lavishly funded media-based electoral campaigns can be anticipated in each of the state battlegrounds where this latest issue has arisen. At the same time, the participation of public-employee unions that can muster both funding and electoral turnout raises the potential for effective public resistance to this latest round—a key reason, of course, these organizations have come under attack.

Drawing on my work on mass media and sixties-era social movements, I contend that the state and local battlegrounds provide a crucial opportunity for progressive activists and allies to apply Zinnian guidelines via a range of direct, face-to-face (as well as electronic) conversations with their fellow citizens (as occurred, for example, in the Wisconsin recall and Ohio repeal campaigns). Although these movements may generate greater awareness of and interest in systemic reform targets, by themselves they are only likely, at best, to stem the advance of neoliberalism at the state level.

While still a movement in progress, Occupy Wall Street, on the other hand, provides an important counterweight to the state-level movements in that it has thus far raised awareness of some of the systemic underpinning for rightist initiatives like the attack on state-level programs and public employee unions. As of this writing, Occupy is moving through a time of transition, with its future unclear. Yet, not surprisingly, mass media coverage of the Occupy movement around the country has echoed the kind of media coverage sixties-era social movements received—although, it must be said, today's "alternative" (social) media provide a vastly more immediate and widely dispersible range of images and discussions reflecting movement perspectives. Once police violence and mass arrests occurred at Occupy Wall Street, the mass media took notice and began to scrutinize the Occupy movement, especially when it spread rapidly to other cities. Media images of pepper-sprayed victims figured prominently in this spread, as, increasingly, did images of a potpourri of participants who did not look like the "legitimate" shapers of the political and economic order.

As in the sixties, "something was happening here," and the media were determined to figure out what it was. Yet mass media coverage was predictable. In some manner the issues of inequality and corporate domination of politics could be understood within these media—especially on the more sympathetic liberal side; much like the war in Vietnam, many media professionals could understand that "this isn't working." Thus, as more and more viewers witnessed Occupy in the media, the proportion of the public who felt there was a "strong conflict" between rich and poor grew significantly.[25] At the same time, mass media coverage consistently sought definable, narrow "demands" that would help them convey the "meaning" of the Occupy protests, and media images fed "deviant" characterizations of Occupy participants. After a brutally violent January 2012 police action cleared an abandoned building occupied by the Oakland arm of the Occupy movement, sporadic acts of mayhem and the burning of an American flag by individuals reacting to the police action were prominently displayed in mass media accounts. Both the coverage and the angry acts of "expressive" defiance echoed the dynamics of protest in the 1960s.

I would contend, then, that future actions need to bring together the strengths of these two movements. By most accounts from Wisconsin, the emergence of Occupy was an important catalyst for the enormously successful effort to gather signatures to recall Governor Walker. It has also emboldened organized labor, and the November shutdown of the Port of Oakland involved the concerted efforts of Occupy and the International Longshore and Warehouse Union. But just as the state-level actions need to engage broader, more structural targets if they are to overcome the impediments to state-level support for a variety of public goods, the Occupy movement, in my opinion, needs to pursue a far more sustained and direct engagement with local political groups and the wider public in their respective communities, even as it works out an articulate and shared vision of what needs to change. One option might be to pursue a variant of the We Are Wisconsin organization in each Occupy locality. Still, the two poles of the sixties media debacle—withdrawal into political irrelevancy (e.g., the counterculture) versus public-alienating, backlash-targeted forms of "expressive politics"—remain hazards Occupy faces as it strives toward democratic transformation. In my view, the long road ahead requires both democratic forms of leadership and a major organizational effort.

One approach that might well guide movement activism would be to *reverse* the dynamic through which the mass media conveyed sixties social movements. If the mass media exclude radical or institutionally critical argument while highlighting militancy and volatile expressiveness as "radical," the content of a Zinnian message would be radical and historical, while its delivery would be direct, interactive, and relationship-building. The message would also reveal hidden history: for example, clearly and concretely explaining how rightist, neoliberal policies, part of a decades-long campaign in which the national Democratic Party has been far too complicit, have produced the state-level budget "crisis." Perhaps the most salient myth to address in the current context is the neoliberal claim that tax cuts aimed at corporations and the wealthiest sectors of the population—and their contemporary correlate, domestic budget cuts—produce job growth.

As an educative conversation with other sectors of the population, the message should be clear and, as much as possible, uncluttered by a host of related progressive causes, even as alliances with a variety of progressive groups would naturally be pursued. However, an ongoing conversation could begin to present evidence and explanatory reasoning that makes the wider connection between neoliberal budgetary priorities and rightist mythology on one hand and unpopular American wars, the eroding ecosphere, and attacks against vulnerable groups on the other. A great deal of modern American history has been massively distorted by mainstream media, so demythologizing the recent past is invariably part of this conversation.[26]

Most fundamentally, the conversation would be grounded in building relationships at the same time that it aimed at specific political targets. The correspondence between public-opinion majorities and a host of progressive priorities would be an important point of connection with much of the wider public. I have argued that community-organizing tactics and, at times, conflict-resolution practices are relevant to the effort to reach across the borders of polarized America,[27] but the "master teacher" role also highlights the need for patient but persistent voices that link immediate issues and conflicts with larger institutional forces in ways that enable others to understand these.

Yet, to *be* an ongoing conversation, at least two things have to happen. To *reach* and build relationships with these wider publics, activists need to be seen as people who are in some way like those they converse with, or at minimum are *respectful* toward them. They need to listen to the grievances of those they encounter, even as they aim to demythologize Tea Party arguments. In addition, these wider publics need to be drawn in by a sense that their participation can make a difference; they need to feel the invitation to participate. These dimensions were crucial to the participation of wider populations in sixties-era social movements. Young media viewers, in particular, saw others like themselves (or, as Robert Moses put it, others who "looked how we felt"[28]) engaging in making a difference—indeed, making history.

Concluding my study of media and the sixties, I suggested,

> In the end, the effort to build a democratic alternative to an increasingly ominous corporate future is, like many moments experienced during the long sixties era, one that can be powerfully self-sustaining. In addition to enabling people to see the forces that impinge on and repress their full humanity, it awakens in people the awareness of possibility that people of very different backgrounds and orientations can come together and discover their common humanity. The latter discovery is one of democracy's most powerful rewards, the sense of breaking through preconceptions about differentness to come to an understanding of the other that brings with it a rich, emotional connection.[29]

Practices that embody a democratic way of life, while time-consuming, can also be enormously gratifying, giving meaning to people's lives. Clear articulation of a democratic vision and the quest for what Cornel West called the "possibility of universal connection"[30] can help disparate groups caught up with their own interests and identities envision their place in a social movement that—for now, at least—concentrates on the implications of neoliberal economic policy. Howard Zinn's voice could be heard, understood, and appreciated by a wide array of social groups.

CHAPTER 12

For Howard Zinn

The Things That Count and Cannot Be Counted

Irene Gendzier[*]

Wall Street owns the country. It is no longer a government of the people, by the people, and for the people, but a government of Wall Street, by Wall Street, and for Wall Street. The great common people of this country are slaves, and monopoly is the master. The West and South are bound and prostrate before the manufacturing East. Money rules, and our Vice-President [Levi Parsons Morton] is a London banker. Our laws are the output of a system which clothes rascals in robes and honesty in rags. The parties lie to us and the political speakers mislead us.[1]

[*]I want to thank the three editors of this volume—Joshua Yesnowitz, Stephen Bird, and Adam Silver—for their initiative and commitment to its publication. I also wish to thank some of those former students at Boston University and friends of Howard Zinn who sent testimony of their appreciation on the occasion of the memorial for Zinn organized by members of the BU Political Science Department and other faculty on March 27, 2010, including José Velasco Cruz, from Mexico; Rachid Tlemcani, from Algeria; Bill Hansen, from Nigeria; and Danny Schechter, from New York.

Being a millionaire in Congress is nothing special—just about half of all members are one. The legislative process works less operatically, but the result is pretty much the same: legislative gridlock punctuated by occasional blatant special-interest legislation. Banks are rescued; the unemployed are left to their own devices. The housing market is left in free fall, with the bailed-out banks mostly still left to call the tune on foreclosures.[2]

One percent of the nation owns a third of the wealth. The rest of the wealth is distributed in such a way as to turn those in the 99 percent against one another: small property owners against the property-less, black against white, native-born against foreign-born, intellectuals and professionals against the uneducated and unskilled. These groups have resented one another and warred against one another with such vehemence and violence as to obscure their common position as sharers of leftovers in a very wealthy country.[3]

The above statements have a decidedly contemporary character. They address the most severe manifestation of the crisis of American capitalism since the era of the Depression. They are at the root of the nationwide protests sparked by the Occupy Wall Street movement and their analogues across the world, including in the Middle East, whose Arab Spring many believe to have been its inspiration.

But consider the following: The first statement, by the populist Kansas orator, Mary Elizabeth Lease, was written approximately 121 years ago. The second was posted by Professor Thomas Ferguson of the University of Massachusetts–Boston on October 15, 2011; and the third was written by Howard Zinn, in an essay titled "The Coming Revolt of the Guards," which appeared in *A People's History of the United States,* in its 1995 edition.

What do they have in common? All three address the relationship of money and power, its profoundly corrupting influence on politics, its exposé of the harsh and unspoken realities of the practice of American democracy. All three implicitly address the question, "Who rules?" and "In whose interest?" And all three, written at different periods and from different vantage points, are in accord that he who has the gold rules, as Ferguson aptly put it, echoing the voice of Mary Elizabeth Lease in her denunciation of Wall Street's monopoly of power, and seconding Howard Zinn's attack on the origins and consequences of a rampant inequality whose human no less than its political legacy has long been ignored and marginalized in the orthodox telling of American history.

By 2011 the gap between the 1% and the rest was increasing in more drastic proportion than what Zinn (1995: 619) had observed when he decried "the reality of that desperate, bitter battle for resources made scarce by elite control." There was nothing hidden about the record, at least not in 2011. The record is open and accessible to those in a position to examine the facts that government sources provide. According to the Congressional Budget Office report, "the top 1 percent of earners more than doubled their share of the nation's income over the last three decades."[4] As the same report confirmed, "government policy has become less distributive since the late 1970s, doing less to reduce the concentration of income."[5]

The sources that exposed the concentration of economic power provided evidence of its rude translation in national politics. In a work exposing the

"Logic of Money-Driven Political Systems," Ferguson (1995: 7) described the existing Democratic Party as one "run by investment bankers and their allies," a condition he warned could be particularly dangerous at a time of slow economic growth, rapidly increasing unemployment, and a severely limited political base. Sixteen years later, the same condition was responsible for the open purchase of political office, such that "among legislatures in the developed world, our Congressional parties now post prices for key slots on committees."[6] The lesson was neither subtle nor hidden. Cash flow determined access to political office and with it, the unchallenged opportunity to influence the political order. In this formula, there was no doubt as to the origin of the cash flow or its destination.

Where was resistance to this deeply rooted phenomenon to come from? In 2011 labor unions that at one time had "represented a third of American workers … now represented only some 12 percent."[7] The 1 percent at the top of the pyramid controlled 40 percent of the nation's wealth.[8] As Joseph Stiglitz (2011) reported,

> Virtually all US senators, and most of the representatives in the House, are members of the top 1 percent when they arrive, are kept in office by money from the top 1 percent, and know that if they serve the top 1 percent well they will be rewarded by the top 1 percent when they leave office. By and large, the key executive-branch policymakers on trade and economic policy also come from the top 1 percent.

Further evidence was published in the justly titled "Income Gaps between Very Rich and Everyone Else More Than Tripled in Last Three Decades, New Data Show." The authors explain how

> the gaps in after-tax income between the richest 1 percent of Americans and the middle and poorest fifths of the country more than tripled between 1979 and 2007 (the period for which these data are available), according to data the Congressional Budget Office (CBO) issued last week. Taken together with prior research, the new data suggest greater income concentration at the top of the income scale than at any time since 1928.[9]

Zinn would not have been surprised by the evidence of the hegemony of power in the hands of capital, nor would he have failed to recognize the importance of the tax structure as an indicator of class structure, even as "government spokesmen have tended to perpetuate the myth of classlessness."[10] As he wrote in a discussion of inequality in America, "the class nature of the American economy is reflected in the tax structure, but this is hidden from those without the time or training to study taxes."[11] And as he wrote in a work published in 1970, "five-sixths of the income tax comes from the lowest income-tax bracket, the 20 percent bracket."[12] He reminded us that the administration of John F. Kennedy had recommended a "tax cut," omitting an explanation of what it meant: "Everybody passed very quickly over the really crucial questions: how much of a cut for the rich, how much for the poor, how much for corporations, how much for families earning under $4000 a year." To talk of taxes in general terms, as Zinn pointed out, was all but meaningless, an attempt to blur the reality that

> Taxation is loaded intrinsically with tensions of class, but these are concealed in newspaper reports and public statements, behind vague, general phrases which make no class differentiation. More than anyone, it is the low-income groups which are kept in the dark about the tax structure. The middle class has gone to college and can figure things fairly well. The upper class hires blue-chip accountants to do its figuring.[13]

What then was to be done? The systemic origins of inequality perpetuated in the existing tax structure exposed the veritable nature of politics in contemporary America. But it was not tax reform to which Zinn was to devote himself but rather the struggle against the underlying politics of inequality.

Zinn's (1995: 619) response to "that desperate, bitter battle for resources made scarce by elite control" influenced his commitment to writing the history of those who had been ignored and made voiceless, and in his commitment to the struggle against racism, war, and "elite control."[14] Resistance against such conditions, their origins and their perpetuation, but above all, their human cost, permeated Zinn's dedication to what he termed, in a different context, "ultimate values"—namely, "that war, poverty, race hatred, prisons, should be abolished, that mankind constitutes a single species; that affection and cooperation should replace violence and hostility."[15]

The "bitter battle" over resources frightened political elites faced with popular resistance that dared to question its legitimacy. The process was transformative. It revealed "the enormous capacity of apparently helpless people to resist, of apparently contented people to demand change."[16] In a world in which, as Mary Elizabeth Lease had said, "people are obedient while the jails are full of petty thieves, and all the while the grand thieves are running the country," such acts of disobedience were justified.[17] Overturning such conditions, Zinn argued, was a prerequisite to meaningful resistance among "people all over the world who have obeyed the dictates of the leaders of their government and have gone to war, and millions have been killed because of this obedience."[18]

Those familiar with Zinn's work will recognize the major ingredients of it in the above themes of resistance to injustice and inequality rooted in an economic system benefiting the few, reproduced through an unrepresentative electoral system, and perpetuated by the effective containment and repression of discontent, the better to avert the risks of democracy.

Zinn's intellectual and political engagement was no less marked by his personal experience, by his "upbringing in a family of working-class immigrants in New York, by my three years as a ship-yard worker, starting at the age of eighteen, and then by my experience as an air force bombardier in World War II, flying out of England and bombing targets in various parts of Europe, including the Atlantic coast of France."[19] The experience of bombing Royan (a town that Zinn had known only as a bombardier, and to which he returned later in life) never left him. It informed his relentless and implacable condemnation of war and its atrocities in the killing of innocent civilians, as in Hiroshima during World War II, in Vietnam, and in the wars that followed, and it explained his demystification of the notion of "just war." It was also the experience of Royan that forced the question of responsibility from which Zinn never wavered.

When he returned to the United States after his military service, Zinn went to study under the G.I. Bill, eventually obtaining a doctorate at Columbia University and joining the faculty at Spelman College in Atlanta. If Royan explained Zinn's antiwar militancy, the experience of Spelman was at the heart of his passionate participation in the civil-rights movement that transformed the South and the United States as a whole. But there was another lesson to be drawn from this experience—namely, that the ongoing struggles over segregation in Atlanta and other urban and rural landscapes in the map of Southern racism were missing from mainstream accounts of American history. The record of sordid brutality, degradation, and heroic resistance that marked the daily life of Southern blacks was off the record.

It was at Spelman, Zinn wrote, that he "became aware of how badly twisted was the teaching and writing of history by its submersion of nonwhite people. Yes, Native Americans were there in the history, but quickly gone. Black people were visible as slaves, then supposedly free but invisible. It was a white man's history."[20]

Others similarly engaged, such as Paul Lauter, professor of English, who was to transform the field of American Studies, learned that American literature was an exclusive white man's terrain from which American Indian and African American males and females were excluded.[21]

Zinn recalled,

> From elementary school to graduate school, I was given no suggestion that the landing of Christopher Columbus in the New World initiated a genocide, in which the indigenous population of Hispaniola was annihilated. Or that this was the first stage of what was presented as a benign expansion of the new nation, but which involved the violent expulsion of Native Americans, accompanied by unspeakable atrocities, from every square mile of the continent, until there was nothing to do but herd them into reservations.[22]

Why was this chapter of American history so little known? Who determined what appeared and, more pointedly, what didn't appear in academic texts? Was there a formal policy of censorship or a consensual agreement on what justified inclusion as history? The results shaped what people came to accept as history, but what of those missing pages? How were they to know what they didn't know? As Zinn maintained, "there were themes of profound importance to me that I found missing in the orthodox histories that dominated American culture."[23] They moved Zinn to consider the nature of the "knowledge industries" and the relationship of knowledge to power. Knowledge is important, he emphasized,

> because although it cannot confront force directly, it can counteract the deception that makes the government's force legitimate. And the knowledge industry, which directly reaches seven million young people in colleges and universities,

thus becomes a vital and sensitive locus of power. That power can be used, as traditionally, to maintain the status quo, or (as is being demanded by the student rebels) to change it.[24]

It is regrettable that Zinn did not live to read an account of the principal of a school in Somerville, Massachusetts, who was reported to have "opened fire on cherished American holidays, blasting legendary explorer Christopher Columbus for 'atrocities' and saying 'we need to be careful' about celebrating Thanksgiving."[25] Principal Anne Foley was quoted as saying that "when we were young we might have been able to claim ignorance of the atrocities that Christopher Columbus committed against the indigenous peoples," but it was no longer possible to do so. "For many of us and our students celebrating this particular person is an insult and a slight to the people he annihilated." The Somerville principal's stand was a sign that things had changed. But the questions to which Zinn's reflections led remained valid. As he maintained, the omissions in the accepted canons of American history not only distorted the past; they "mislead us all about the present."[26]

Among the missing subjects that Zinn aimed to restore to popular knowledge, in addition to those dealing with race and class, was the role of labor, its organization, and its resistance to corporate control. The Ludlow Massacre of 1914, in which the strike of some 11,000 miners against their working conditions led the operators and owner of the mines to retaliate, eventually bringing in the National Guard, led to the massacre of strikers and their families. Why was the Ludlow Massacre not in history books, Zinn asked, pointing to the omission of any reference to Rockefeller interests that were directly involved. Yet, the role of John D. Rockefeller in the establishment of the Standard Oil Company was favorably reported in conventional histories of the United States. What explained the omission of Ludlow? Zinn explains,

> There was no secret meeting of industrialists and historians to agree to emphasize the admirable achievement of the great corporations, and ignore the bloody costs of industrialization in America. But I concluded that a certain unspoken understanding lay beneath the writing of textbooks and the teaching of history: that it would be considered bold, radical, perhaps even "Communist" to emphasize class struggle in the United States, a country where the dominant ideology emphasized the oneness of the nation—"We the people, in order to ... etc., etc." and the glories of the American system.[27]

To ignore the history of labor in the United States, however, as Zinn recognized, deprived people of the record of struggles that were responsible for improving conditions of working-class life. *A People's History* aimed to provide this history, or at least some part of it. It offered an account of labor-organizing and resistance, as well as repression, with the views and voices of those involved across a broad span of time that extends to the late twentieth century.

One instance of the history that Zinn vividly recaptured was that involving the organizing experience of white farmers in 1877 that spread across the country, leading to the establishment of cooperatives and collective action. The Farmers'

Alliance was an expression of the Populist movement that supported labor, and by 1889 had some 400,000 members and was promoting candidates for office. Branches of the Alliance included parties that were antiracist, such as the Texas People's Party, established in 1891, that was "interracial, and radical."[28] In 1886, *The American Nonconformist and Kansas Industrial Liberator*, created by Henry Vincent, declared, "this journal will aim to publish such matter as will tend to the education of the laboring classes, the farmers and the producer, and in every struggle it will endeavor to take the side of the oppressed as against the oppressor."[29]

Brief as Zinn's historical reconstruction of the Populist movement was in *A People's History*, it was sufficient to reveal the movement's extraordinary efforts "to create a new and independent culture for the country's farmers. The Alliance Lecture Bureau poured out books and pamphlets from their printing presses."[30] It was reported to have some 35,000 lecturers and was in the process of rewriting history and related fields of study, including law and government. Had it not joined with the Democratic Party, its history and that of the United States might have differed, argue those whom Zinn cites.

A People's History and its accompanying *Voices of a People's History of the United States* effectively restored some of the missing pages of American history, such as the record of the mobilization of activists against the World Trade Organization (WTO) in Seattle in December 1999. Police repression was unable to stop

> an estimated 25,000 activists, mainly union rank and file, [that] marched into downtown from a rally at Memorial Stadium, joining the ten thousand or so direct action activists who had seized control of the city. The demonstrations displayed a level of diversity rare in American movements, as anarchists, environmentalists, and vegan hippies marched side by side with teamsters, steelworkers, and social justice activists.[31]

ZINN AND THE 99%

In 2011, the Occupy Wall Street movement brought together an even more diverse array of protesters. Earlier, Zinn (1995: 619) had declared his intention of writing for and about those who were voiceless and powerless: "I am taking the liberty of uniting those 99 percent as 'the people.' I have been writing a history that attempts to represent their submerged, deflected, common interest." The 99 percent to whom Zinn addressed his work were Americans, but the conditions against which they struggled and to which he responded were not unique to the United States. The reflections that follow consider Zinn's legacy in relation to the movement that emerged more than a year after his death, the Occupy Wall Street movement, and its inspiration in the Arab Spring, particularly the Egyptian example. To consider Zinn in this context is to recognize the underlying humanist values that animated his work and his sense of international solidarity with "the wretched of the earth," to take the title of Frantz Fanon's book.[32]

In September 2011, the evidence of the ever-increasing inequality in a society whose ruling class was sold out to the highest bidder inspired nationwide protests.

The Occupy Wall Street movement, at once decentralized and broad-based, spread across the United States, generating widespread support in the United States and abroad, notably in the Middle East, where militants of the Arab Spring expressed their solidarity.

The Occupy Wall Street movement that began in New York's financial district in September 2011 issued its own survey that included the following statement of its objectives:

> Occupy Wall Street is a people-powered movement that began on September 17, 2011 in Liberty Square in Manhattan's Financial District, and has spread to over one hundred cities in the United States and actions in over 1,500 cities globally. #OWS is fighting back against the corrosive power major banks and unaccountable multinational corporations wield against democracy, and the role of Wall Street in creating the economic collapse that has caused the greatest recession in nearly a century. The movement is inspired by popular uprisings in Egypt and around the world, and aims to expose how the richest 1 percent of people are writing the rules of a dangerous neoliberal economic agenda that is stealing our future.
>
> Occupy Wall Street is a leaderless resistance movement with people of many colors, genders, and political persuasions. The one thing we all have in common is that We Are The 99% that will no longer tolerate the greed and corruption of the 1%. We are using the revolutionary Arab Spring tactic to achieve our ends and encourage the use of nonviolence to maximize the safety of all participants. This #ows movement empowers real people to create real change from the bottom up. We want to see a general assembly in every backyard, on every street corner because we don't need Wall Street and we don't need politicians to build a better society.
>
> We know from history that social movements grow when they have a broad base of support. We are thankful that this movement has attained such a dramatic level of support in a short amount of time. We are hopeful that this people's movement will continue to grow.[33]

In mid-October, protesters in Chicago issued a newsletter under the name "The People Speak." Its first page concluded with "a few words from Zinn":

> To omit or to minimize ... voices of resistance is to create the idea that power only rests with those who have the guns, who possess the wealth, who own the newspapers and the television stations.... [P]eople who seem to have no power ...—once they organize and protest and create movements—have a voice no government can suppress.[34]

Occupy Boston initiated a series of lectures that were designed to engage academics to enter into a dialogue with the participants of Occupy Boston "on issues of economic, political, and social justice." And, as the same posting asserted, "we propose to call these lectures the Howard Zinn Memorial Lectures at Occupy Boston in honor of the late, great Boston Historian."[35]

Within weeks of its inauguration, the New York Occupy Wall Street movement was notified of support from the labor movement: "Local 100 of the Transport Workers Union say they 'applaud the courage of the young people on Wall Street,' and are planning to turn out their members next week."[36]

As though in response to the Occupy Wall Street movement that had acknowledged the uprising in Tahrir Square as one of its sources of inspiration, "Comrades from Cairo" (2011) sent a message of solidarity that affirmed their common struggle. But it did more. It provided a history of the origins of the recent protest movements in "years-long struggles by people and popular movements" in Egypt and the Middle East that were little-known in the United States. Howard Zinn's name was not invoked in this statement, yet it is difficult to witness the uprisings across the Arab world and not think of "how he would have welcomed this evidence of the power of people to act directly, to change the very direction of the world," as Marilyn Young observed.[37]

There is another dimension of Zinn's work that is relevant to how the Arab Spring was covered in the US media and in official circles. It takes us back to his writing on history. The very elements that Zinn had found lacking in conventional histories of the United States—namely, the lives of ordinary people and their role in protest movements, including labor movements—were relevant to Arab experience and missing from conventional accounts and mainstream media coverage.

Mainstream coverage of Middle East politics was marked by an emphasis on religion and, more particularly, on Sunni-Shiite differences as causal factors explaining the nature of Arab politics. Religion, identity, ethnicity, and an exclusive focus on the state and its security apparatus, where it was acknowledged, dominated media coverage and academic discussion of the Arab world in the United States. In this context, developments surrounding the popular revolts that shook the Middle East from the winter of 2011 were met with skepticism and fear in policymaking circles and in the media. The skepticism and disdain were directed at the ability of Arabs to comprehend—let alone implement—democratic regimes, while fear reflected the reaction of policymakers whose concern was the demise of pro-Western regimes.

In practice, the events of the winter of 2011 thoroughly undermined the myths of Arab politics.

> The fantasy that the Arabs are passive and unsuited to democracy has evaporated in weeks. Arabs have overthrown hated authoritarian regimes in Tunisia and Egypt. In Libya, they have fought a sclerotic regime in power for forty-two years that has refused to listen to their demands, facing extraordinary violence, hundreds of deaths, untold injuries, mass exodus and generalized chaos. In Algeria, Morocco, Bahrain, Yemen, Jordan, Iraqi Kurdistan, the West Bank, and Oman, Arabs have taken to the streets in cast numbers.[38]

Writing from Algeria, political scientist and journalist Rachid Tlemçani (2011), a former student of Howard Zinn's, described developments across the Arab world as representing a unique phenomenon:

Marginalized, representing more than 70 percent of the population, the younger generation took over public space without the authorization of bureaucrats. The populations no longer fear corrupt police states. The abuse of obedience to an arbitrary power was suddenly transformed into a revolt.... This democratic movement will inevitably cause the downfall of these regimes, one by one, earlier than we imagined.... It is the first time in history that a social revolution is in process in the Arab world and in the Muslim world as a whole.

As to the meaning of self-immolation, which occurred in Tunisia and proved to be the spark that set off the Tunisian revolution, it had nothing to do with religion. It represented, as Tlemçani explained, an act of utter desperation intended to expose the indifference of the state to the extreme conditions it imposed on its people, whether in Tunisia or elsewhere in the region.

Insofar as Algerian conditions were concerned, American officials in the country had an acute sense of what was wrong, which in no sense affected US-Algerian relations. But US cables revealed that there was

precious little discussion about how to address long-standing political alienation and social discontent throughout the country. Housing is woefully short, while unemployment and underemployment are endemic (at least 50 percent among young people). In a relatively new phenomenon, many young people are trying to flee the country, by small boats if necessary.[39]

The hike in food prices was leading to strikes by "different labor groups almost weekly.... Algeria's young people do not see the political system as having any relevance to addressing their problems."[40]

It was not in Algeria but in Tunisia that the Arab Spring broke out, in the midst of winter. The spark was the desperate act of Mohammed Bouazizi, who burned himself to death in response to police action that claimed he had no permit to sell his wares as a street vendor. Bouazizi's self-immolation act was to inspire the "Letter to a Dead Man about the Occupation of Hope," that was a celebration of his memory in global terms.[41]

This act galvanized a population whose discontent and frustrations with the corrupt regime were rapidly turned into a spontaneous movement demanding the president's exit, and the opening of the country to democracy and elections, which were held in October 2011. The causes of massive discontent included the prolonged unemployment of youth; the increasing cost of food; the skewed nature of the economy; the political corruption of the regime, and its family ties to business and the press; and the efforts of the regime to co-opt independent unions long identified with the nationalist movement in Tunisia. In the midst of such conditions, Western officials lauded the stability and modernity of the Tunisian regime, while the Tunisian military, like its far more important Egyptian counterpart, was the beneficiary of US military sales.

What was immediately striking in Tunisia and to outside observers was the extent to which the revolt against Tunisia's president, Zine al-Abidine Ben Ali, mobilized every sector of society, "students, lawyers, bloggers, artists, hackers, housewives, children, doctors, professors and shopkeepers—each group harboring specific grievances and using its own symbolic vocabulary, but all united in overall purpose."[42] But critical to the movement's success was the role of organized labor in a country in which the labor movement had a long history of political activism through the period of French rule and the nationalist movement that followed, and continued through the regimes of Habib Bourguiba and Ben Ali.[43]

It was Egypt, the pivotal center of the Arab world, that demonstrated the critical role of labor in the events leading up to the fall of the Mubarak regime, as Egyptian journalist Hossam el-Hamalawy explained:

> We might ask, where were the workers at the beginning of the revolution? The workers participated in the revolution from the beginning in areas of Suez, in areas like Mahallah, areas like Kafr el-Dawwar.... These areas are working class areas. So when you hear that tens of thousands—and at times there were hundreds of thousands—of people [were] protesting in these cities, I think it's understood that the vast majority of them were workers. But the workers were taking part in these demonstrations as demonstrators, not as workers. They were not acting as a separate force. Number one, because this was an uprising and all of them were there in the street; number two, because the workers were either in the street or in the popular committees that were protecting the neighborhoods. But as soon as the government tried to restore "normal life" once again in Egypt in the week prior to the fall of Mubarak, the workers returned to their factories, returned to their companies, and began to talk to each other and discuss the country's affairs. And it was on Monday, Tuesday, and Wednesday that was the turning point. The strikes began. The workers began to act as a social bloc.[44]

The world that el-Hamalawy described was not one that Howard Zinn knew, but it is surely one that he would have supported.

In an interview he gave to the *Boston Globe* in 1974, Zinn observed that there was a change in how history was being written. There is "more history from below," he wrote, attributing it to the "tumult of social movements in America" over the course of the preceding fifteen years.[45] But how Zinn viewed such a change transcended American experience. "We have believed too long in our own helplessness, and the new history tells us how, sometimes, movements of people who don't seem to have much power can shake the rich and the powerful."

To read this in 2011 is to imagine Zinn (1993: 164) addressing the people of the United States, Egypt, and the Middle East, and telling them, with hope, that "the future is not certain but it is possible."

CHAPTER 13

Reassessing Zinn

Critical Reflections on a *Scholar-Activist*

*Stephen Bird, Adam Silver, and
Joshua C. Yesnowitz*

In Howard Zinn—activist, academic, and artist—we see a central figure of the
twentieth-century American Left who embodies broad goals of progressive social
change. As we think about Zinn's legacies, however, it is not clear to what degree
his philosophical principles simply reflect a pragmatic, leftist "politics of and for
the times" or a more enduring set of intellectual ideas that remain applicable over
a longer period of time. In this final chapter, we address these concerns with a
particular focus on his methodological contributions to the practice of history
and contemporary events, especially his commitment to direct action and other
forms of activism. In addition to highlighting Zinn's continued influence, we
engage critical appraisals of his work. Some observers have expressed concerns
that Zinn's presentation reflected over-simplification or marginal appreciation to
historiographical shifts in focus. Other assessments relate to a lack of conceptual
clarity and an inattention to identity politics.

We claim that Zinn's approach demonstrates the compromises necessary
to balance the dual roles of scholar and activist. While this may epitomize the
descriptive term *public intellectual* (particularly as discussed in Chapters 2–4), we
propose that Zinn's experience represents a subtype or category of that broader

term: the *scholar-activist*.[1] This characterization is useful because it clarifies and explains four important observations. First, while not unique, the scholar-activist is a generally rare combination within academia.[2] Both Frances Fox Piven and Noam Chomsky come to mind (this is one of the many reasons we asked these notable scholar-activists to write the foreword and afterword, respectively). Generally, though, academics and activists are more like oil and water: difficult to mix.[3] The challenges inherent to this type of public intellectual are enormous, and Zinn managed the balance with aplomb throughout his career.

Second, Zinn's role as a scholar-activist is the explanatory factor for the concerns that critics lay against him. That is, the popularizing function of the scholar-activist requires a degree of narrative license (to maintain fluid prose and accessibility) that is avoided in traditional academic writing. These concerns, which primarily come from the academic Center-Left, are separate in both tone and scope (and less personally disparaging) from the ideologically motivated criticisms on the Right. In the following pages, we outline some of these concerns from academia, but also demonstrate that they follow from the specific challenges of any scholar-activist.

Further, the role of scholar-activist for Zinn may contribute to a "lack of sectarianism" in his political thought.[4] Making expansive statements about a "Zinnian" approach will always be somewhat speculative and inexact. Many of Zinn's objectives parallel reform efforts within political science that call for increased societal relevance. These aims have been summarized by Schram (2003) as a "return to politics." Whether we are speaking of the *Perestroika* movement in favor of methodological pluralism or the more forthrightly political Caucus for a New Political Science, which was founded in 1967 amid the earlier critique of the "narrow parochialism" of the behavioral revolution, Zinnian attitudes have long held an important (yet all-too-often-peripheral) place within the discipline.[5]

Third, the balance between scholar and activist shifted over time for Zinn; what began as a career slightly more balanced toward the concerns for scholarly and intellectual issues moved to an emphasis on progressive agitation and education largely manifested beyond the walls of academia.

This leads to our last observation, for which we argue that Zinn provided a model of agitation to follow and arguably a theoretically coherent method of activism that will have continuing relevance for the future. Throughout his career, Zinn retained a worldview of *optimistic concern* that is refreshing among academics and public intellectuals. We maintain that in many ways, his style and temperament are almost more important than any well-articulated political philosophy. Further, we argue that his particular combination of sustained attention to injustice combined with an unwavering degree of optimism was one of Zinn's most enduring legacies. When Eric Foner was asked to comment on Zinn's contributions in the wake of his passing, the eminent historian focused on these personal attributes rather than any specific intellectual output:

> The way he inspired people, to me, is his legacy, rather than his interpretation of the Jacksonian era or the Gilded Age or the New Deal.... He really was an important figure in the public vision of history.[6]

As discussed in the introduction to the book, three broad spheres of attention—activism, academia, and arts—have driven the discussion of Zinn in this text. Within each chapter, the authors have attempted to discuss the challenges intrinsic to key aspects of his approach. Themes include inconsistencies within democratic theory, questions about how best to practice agitation and disobedience, cautions against neutrality, and the contradictions that can emerge in attempting to adhere to a progressive worldview when principles are in conflict.[7] In the next sections, we draw upon the preceding chapters, and Zinn's scholarship, to synthesize a framework that can enhance our understanding of political movements past, present, and future.

Contributions to Academia, Activism, and the Arts

The Zinnian Method

In *The Politics of History* (1990 [1970]), Howard Zinn first proposed and implemented a self-described "radical" method to serve as a corrective to the prevailing accounts of American triumphalism and exceptionalism.[8] Zinn applies a revisionist account of history to demystify the American experience through a focus on the plight of the oppressed and the role of the people in general.[9] If history is written by the victors, or the elites, Zinn sought to tell the story of the masses, those who were victimized by the powerful and had to struggle to improve their rights and conditions.

Although this radical lens is prevalent throughout Zinn's canon of writings, speeches, and activism, he does not fit neatly into a set ideological schema or academic pedagogy. Rather, as the contributions to this volume attest, he is a complex figure in regard to his activism and philosophy. Specifically, Zinn approached his studies both *inductively* and *deductively*, with an emphasis on the former. While empirically driven scholars studied history and movements predominantly by deductively reaching conclusions based upon a broad set of evidence, Zinn added to this by inserting himself into the events and directly observing the actions of the actors. Zinn could then both combine broad deductive analysis and inform it by his inductive participation in the movement itself.

This approach was apparent in Zinn's emphasis on the concepts of "history from below," "history of the poor," and "historian as citizen." These methods and perspectives, which emerged quite overtly in *A People's History*, had their beginnings in his dissertation research on Fiorello La Guardia.[10] His approach and concerns for the study of history have now been institutionalized and adopted for use in several distinct approaches to history.[11] Aspects of his perspective are apparent in the Annales School of history, social history, and labor history. Zinn learned from, contributed to the advancement of, and reinforced the importance of these historical schools and approaches to the study of history. Indeed, one of Zinn's strongest contributions as a scholar-activist was to reinforce the importance of these new models for historical research, and to function as one of the most successful and early practitioners.

Zinn's fundamental approach, in which historical events and actors are depicted from the vantage point of the oppressed, is fully realized in *A People's His-*

tory. The success of this standpoint and method has spawned a cottage industry in publishing, historical themes, and other subjects. Numerous topics, including the American Revolution, the Supreme Court, Christianity, sports, and the world, have been the focus of volumes written from this perspective.[12] Zinn's methodological perspective has brought renewed focus and alternate voices to well-known topics. This legacy has not been well acknowledged.

Zinn's approach to history is also potentially useful for current movements such as Occupy Wall Street. A fully developed Zinnian analysis of that movement is beyond the scope of this project, although Irene Gendzier's considerations in Chapter 12 provide a fine starting point. Nonetheless, there are several aspects of the still-nascent movement that Zinn would likely appreciate. For instance, Occupy has ambitious transformational goals. This is in contrast to the Tea Party, which Zinn would see as insufficiently radical because most of its stated objectives have been electoral in nature. Specifically, Occupy entertains radical possibility, it promotes historical literacy and social consciousness, it rejects elections as endpoints of achievement, and it demonstrates the utility of artistic and cultural contributions in political movements. Structurally, it represents an effort at meaningful democratic conversation and illustrates the promises and drawbacks of consensus decision-making. Occupy is a model of prefigurative politics where citizens are acting according to the ideals of the society in which they hope to live, not the one in which they currently find themselves participating.

Zinn assessed social movements from the joint perspective of an activist and radical historian. This populist (or radical) Zinnian approach to the study of social movements invokes a normative perspective, particularly when linking contemporary movements to others throughout history. Through his direct participation in the movements, we glean an intimate understanding of the motives and pressures acting on participants as well as a unique perspective on the struggle between inside and outside strategies. His method informed his activism and vice versa, an estimable blend of vocation and avocation.

The Normative Approach

The derision toward Zinn because of his political "bias" (a criticism he considered a term of respect) lacks merit. For Zinn, value neutrality was a chimera—investigating topics or proposing questions without considering "what ought to be?" amounted to disciplinary malpractice. One can pursue objectivity in assessing evidence, but judgment does and must factor into topic selection and perspective.[13] Moreover, by not applying research findings to contemporary problems, scholars are in effect endorsing the status quo. Choosing to be an academic historian does not exempt one from civic responsibilities—in fact, scholars, because of the critical-thinking skills that are required to attain such status, are primed to participate. Incorporating normative aims into historical study still requires appropriate empirical research methods and evidence to substantiate the analysis.[14]

The disagreement between scholars who support a non-normative approach and those who adopt a value-laden perspective to their intellectual pursuits permeate most academic disciplines. It may be best reflected, however, in a debate that has taken place in sociology. The Weberian view, as explained by Abend (2008), proposes a decidedly non-normative (empirical) approach to sociological pursuits. Two main principles guide this paradigm: (1) the concepts of objective truth and falsehood do not and cannot be applied to moral judgments; and (2) sociological pursuits should be non-normative. In other words, the researcher must not ascribe any of his/her own values to the observations.[15]

The competing perspective, Durkheim's *science de la morale,* challenges these assumptions by arguing for the inclusion of, and reference to, values in academic pursuits. By accepting that moral truths exist, a Durkheimian approach, in this sense, promotes normative judgments in the study of political and social phenomena.[16] While this reflects an intradisciplinary debate, the principles are easily applied to all social sciences. Further, and of importance here, the latter ideal type (Durkheimian) is precisely what serves as one of the foundations for Zinn's distinctive place among academics and public intellectuals.

Zinn viewed historical and contemporary events through a prism of republican principles and the application of justice. To Zinn, the people—the citizenry—are the ultimate power in any society. This was an enduring faith in (broadly defined) democratic action brought to bear in the pursuit of justice. He defined *justice* as "the fair treatment of all human beings, the equal right of all people to freedom and prosperity"[17] and *democracy* as the absolute right of self-determination of the people, not of the state or political leaders, to determine "how they will defend themselves, how they will make themselves secure, and how they will achieve justice and freedom."[18] This could include pursuing justice through electoral and institutional mechanisms, but Zinn also advocated actions that often challenged the system—*civil disobedience.*[19]

Obeying the law may bring order and stability, but may not bring justice. Such an approach presupposes an understanding that the relationship between law and order and justice is tenuous. No matter how hopeless it appears, the struggle for justice must never be abandoned.[20] Zinn recognized that not all actions *of the people* that are committed in the name of the people are in fact just. They must adhere to a concept of justice in principle. Furthermore, the process matters. Means that are inhumane or unjust must not be employed, irrespective of how just and desirable the ends may be.[21]

Zinn's concern for the supremacy of justice in assessing popular movements and state actions is important. It reinforces the underlying necessity for all social movements to be assessed from the perspective of justice. Not all movements fit in with a Zinnian ideal of justice for the people; some may have more specific or narrowly defined self-interested goals. This central idea serves as a foundation from which to assess movements, actors, and the state.[22]

The Link between Movements Past and Present

Zinn articulates his radical approach in *The Politics of History* and uncovers the myths surrounding state action, the connections between wealth and power, and the effects of such action that enhance a privileged minority. Zinn argues that

> [history can] add depth that time imparts to an idea. What one sees in the present
> may be attributable to a passing phenomenon; if the same situation appears at

various points in history, it becomes not a transitory event, but a long range condition, not an aberration, but a structural deformity requiring serious attention.[23]

This understanding of history is precisely what makes Zinn's methodology pertinent to the study of current social movements: first, in the highlighting of historical events that are not commonly discussed; and second, in the linking of characteristics and actors from past movements to their present-day counterparts.[24]

Zinn acknowledges, "There is no such thing as impartial history." Bias appears less in outright lying than in the selective emphasis or de-emphasis of certain facts and data.[25] He cites the absence of the Ludlow Massacre from his school textbooks as a prime example. In illuminating this underreported incident, Zinn challenges the reader to apply the themes of the Massacre to contemporary events, including the relationship of the national government to business and labor (or its people), the use of violence by the state against its people (or its serving as an accomplice when perpetrated by business interests against its employees), and the very nature of the federal system itself.[26] Zinn asks the reader not to view the Ludlow Massacre and similar events from a narrow perspective of the incident itself, but through a broader lens:

> If [the Ludlow Massacre] is read as a commentary on a larger question—the relationship of government to corporate power and of both to movements of social protest—then we are dealing with the present. Then we see a set of characteristics which have persisted, not only in American history, but in the history of all nations, although the forms vary.[27]

Moreover, his study of SNCC demonstrates his ability to link movements across time. As the title suggests, *SNCC: The New Abolitionists* compares the organization and its cause to abolitionists of the nineteenth century. Although their demographics differed,[28] these new abolitionists were similar to those of the 1830s and 1840s in their tactics.[29]

Comparing movement participants from the early to mid-nineteenth century to those of the mid-twentieth century provides the reader with a point of reference to study the contemporary movement. In addition, and perhaps more importantly, this Zinnian tactic humanizes the political actors. Comparative-historical case-study analysis offers insights into current movement activities, strategies, and actors. It provides a perspective on the prospects of success of the current movements. This kind of linkage highlights recurring themes and struggles to discover similarities and differences in actual events and participants, but also discerns trends in movement strategy and state response throughout American history. For Zinn, the past is never past. The role of a contemporary-minded (presentist) historian is to deconstruct and question a nation's historical narrative and how its civic religion and customs influence modern understandings of itself.

Direct Involvement and Participant Observation

Zinn's actual participation in direct-action campaigns provides granular-level insight into the feelings and actions of movement actors as well as how a movement unfolds in real time. This is directly evident in his work on/in the civil-rights movement.[30] In chronicling the sit-ins of the early 1960s, Zinn captures a growing change in the demeanor of the participants:

> *Impatience* was the mood of the young sit-in demonstrators: impatience with the courts, with national and local governments, with negotiation and conciliation, with the traditional Negro organizations and the old Negro leadership, with the unbearably slow pace of desegregation in a century of accelerated social change.[31]

Arguably, his most valuable contribution in this area, however, is in the portrayal of SNCC activists conducting voter-registration drives in the Deep South, such as in McComb, Mississippi, from the summer to early fall in 1961.[32] Zinn's reporting illuminates internal organizational discussions on the debate over leadership, the sensitive issue of race in SNCC, and the future direction of the movement.[33]

One of the intriguing aspects we can glean from Zinn's insertion into movement activity is his view of the dynamic between leadership and rank and file. He is widely considered to be the "people's" historian, but what comes across here is the belief that the leaders must act and the people will go along. However, we don't want to overstate the role of elites. The masses must create the impetus for change. As Zinn argues when observing civil-rights activity, the white population (masses) would most likely acquiesce to the goals of the movement if their leaders helped to create an atmosphere open to change.

The aforementioned examples suggest that this form of activism yields an intimate portrayal of the psychological strains preying upon the actors in the movement and in the larger political environment. Such an account of past movement actors contributes to our understanding of contemporary actors and movements. His immersion in the movements and subsequent activism enhance the authenticity of his voice.

FORCE AND VIOLENCE

Zinn's method for the study of historical events and social movements has internal and external dynamics. However, the use of force is a question in both. Civil-rights demonstrators, antiwar activists, and groups protesting economic inequality (e.g., the Seattle WTO protests in 1999 or the Occupy movement from 2011–present) all struggle with how best to advance their claims. Civil disobedience and direct action form the core of any challenge to the state and the status quo. Critically, what is the best tactic to *persuade* those in power to address the movement's grievances? Is violence, either against property or persons, ever acceptable? Further, if the state or oppressing population perpetrates violent acts against the movement, can these victims respond in kind? Zinn's answer to the questions of how far an agitator should go in use of force remained vague throughout much of his career.

Certainly Zinn abhorred war and state military action, but he recognized that an absolutist position against the employment of force is untenable. He also did not dismiss the positive role the force of a state can play in protecting minority rights. Both Eric Boehme and Patricia Moynagh tackle this tension in their contributions to this volume. In assessing Zinn's anarchism, Boehme (in Chapter 5) asserts that Zinn's allowance for the positive deployment of state power puts him at odds with anarchist theory. Moynagh (in Chapter 8) takes this further by unpacking Zinn's belief in the possibility for the complete elimination of war, but understanding that force is sometimes proper or necessary. She raises the distinction between just and unjust causes, and examines the idea that simply because actions may stem from good intentions, they may not be just or even legitimate. For example, stopping Hitler in World War II and coercing Saddam Hussein to leave Kuwait in the early 1990s may be just causes, but the subsequent wars may not have been just.

This distinction is explored further by considering the abolitionist activities of John Brown. His violent acts have been well documented, and he did have contemporary admirers such as Frederick Douglass and Henry David Thoreau. Yet the larger question persists: is violence acceptable in such egregious circumstances? Zinn offers a possible answer by accepting the use of violence in limited circumstances to prevent a larger, more reprehensible act of violence. In her contribution, Moynagh argues that while Brown's violence may have been justifiable, it was not legitimate. Her assessment echoes a Zinnian approach by levying a normative judgment on Brown's actions.

This paradox highlights the debate over the acceptable use of violence and serves two purposes. First, it depicts Zinn's normative, or Durkheimian, approach to events and actors. For example, when discussing the war in Vietnam, he considers the war and its perpetration of violence from a moral perspective.[34] Under what conditions is it permissible for a people or state (the United States) to employ force against another state (North Vietnam)? Zinn's analysis makes clear that regardless of the projected justice of the cause (involvement in Vietnam, which Zinn considered illegitimate), the use of violence by a government's armed forces can occur only in the face of overwhelming and clear evidence of greater violence by an opposing force. Second, it suggests Zinn's methodological legacy. Moynagh, and, to a lesser extent, Boehme employ the Zinnian method by assessing the use of force and violence from a normative perspective.[35] They assign values to the action by asking what is just or legitimate, and, thereby, moral.

CRITIQUES

Zinn and the Historians

Sometimes the most revealing forms of self-identification occur when they are ancillary to the main topic at hand. In his introduction to *Three Plays*, written toward the end of his life, Zinn says, "Why would a historian move outside the boundaries of the discipline and decide to enter the world of the theater?"[36] Zinn clearly self-identified as a historian first and foremost, despite his employment for much of his career within a political science department. Despite this, Zinn's identity and performance as a historian were often criticized. He was characterized as a radical, New Left, or progressive historian by mainstream historians (although not *always* as a criticism). These labels arguably have different subtexts—alternating as stamps of approval, disapproval, or sometimes simple identification.

Often these forms of radical history could be used as a convenient straw man that other historians could use to provide as a counterexample to a more subtle but perhaps less instructive perspective. For instance, O'Reilly (1982: 638) character-izes the rise of the FBI under FDR as a relatively innocent exercise, contrasting his explanation with Zinn's and using Zinn as a convenient counter to his analysis. However, one could argue that O'Reilly misses aspects of the subtlety inherent in Zinn's approach to some degree. Zinn's history often demonstrated not just overt forms of injustice, but the more subtle and particular biases that end up reinforcing the power of dominant elites or interests. These kinds of responses to Zinn are not dissimilar to the treatment of Charles Beard's historical-economic perspectives on the founders by many mainstream historians.[37]

That said, Zinn himself sometimes simplified history, or aspects of the historical and academic enterprise. As Christopher Phelps (2010) describes in his otherwise admiring essay,

> Professional historians have often viewed Zinn's work with exasperation or condescension, and Zinn was no innocent in the dynamic. I stood against the wall for a Zinn talk at the University of Oregon around the time of the 1992 Columbus Quincentenary. Listening to Zinn, one would have thought historians still considered Samuel Eliot Morison's 1955 book on Columbus to be definitive. The crowd lapped it up, but Zinn knew better. He missed a chance to explain how the social movements of the 1960s and 1970s have transformed the writing and teaching of history, how his *People's History* did not spring out of thin air but was an effort to synthesize a widely shared shift in historical sensibilities.

Phelps's concerns have some validity. Zinn often made the broad accusa-tion that American historical memory was subject to many facets of historical simplification or omission that allowed the forgetting of inconvenient truths. However, Zinn was occasionally guilty of a similar simplification in his discussions of historians, politicians, and academics. As Ambre Ivol and Paul Buhle argue in Chapter 2, Zinn's contribution is that he is one of the few to "intentionally and specifically" present history from a popular perspective, the movements of and for the people. While Zinn may not have had an ongoing dialogue with most main-stream historians, the field was changing; he may have popularized social history, but the field and approach are certainly more than him. Zinn sometimes didn't acknowledge the changing tradition he was building upon and/or joining. Real progress has been made in the discipline of history (and in other social sciences). Zinn could have acknowledged this. Even further, he could and should have taken credit for helping to inspire it.

More recently, Michael Kazin has characterized Zinn's over-simplification of the American Left, particularly in *A People's History,* in the context of his own book, *American Dreamers* (2011). He claims that Zinn produces "a simplistic propagandistic understanding of American History."[38] He continues,

> In Zinn there's a kind of condescension, and a refusal to recogni[z]e the gains that the left has made.... [H]e's much more simplistic and reductionist than Marx. Marx understood that capitalism was improving living standards, for example.

Kazin's critique in *American Dreamers* asserts that Zinn created a historical world in which conservative right-wing elites are an unchanging monolith, and in which the "little guy" never wins.[39] Further, he contends that Zinn never asked the most vital question: Why did Americans accept the legitimacy of their capitalist republic?[40] To some degree, Kazin's critique misunderstands Zinn's approach. Zinn's understanding of popular acceptance of capitalist legitimacy was not the question. Indeed, the degree of scholarship discussing the acceptance and entrenchment of liberal capitalism has been examined extensively by David Potter (1954), Louis Hartz (1955), and Barrington Moore (1966), among others thereafter, and includes aspects of American exceptionalism, and the use of an array of conventional tools for dominance that Zinn actually outlines in his history. The use of force, intimidation, propaganda, xenophobia and nationalism, misinformation, and "divide and conquer" strategies by dominant elites permeate his writing. For Zinn, the question wasn't "Why is empire accepted?" but rather "What do we do about it?" Further, his answer was simple: we must provide the appropriate counternarrative and education, and agitate for change, because it can succeed.

Identity Politics

Zinn devoted the vast majority of his scholarship to the politics of class, race, and war to the detriment of the politics of identity (e.g., feminism, gay rights, and reproductive rights), Hispanics, and environmental/ecological concerns. In Chapter 2, Ivol and Buhle note that Zinn's focus was toward issues of class early on, and later on issues of race (arguably as related to class). While there is an absence of attention to identity, the environment, and other post-material concerns, Ivol and Buhle argue in Chapter 2 that Zinn's approach allowed for an inclusive alliance of different sorts of progressive political movements.

There is no evidence to suggest that Zinn was unenthusiastic in his support for any of these issues of identity, but rather we are acknowledging (as Zinn did himself) that his engagement with—or theoretical consideration of—identity politics is underdeveloped. To some degree, this may reflect the broader debate among leftists over the prioritization of "the politics of redistribution" (which focuses on class and economic injustice) versus "the politics of recognition" (which focuses on identity and cultural injustice).[41]

In large part, though, one can understand Zinn's lack of attention to these areas as one of both context and simple omission. His agenda did not lack for concern for these issues; they do receive occasional attention. For instance, in an interview with David Barsamian, Zinn notes that part of what excited him about

Emma Goldman was "her powerful feminism."[42] Rather, Zinn's likely attention to these issues were otherwise occupied by his interests—based on his own formative experiences—in class, race, education, and empire. Further, in the afterword to the 2005 edition of *A People's History,* Zinn specifically discusses his "serious omissions" in attention to Latino history and the mobilizations for gay rights.[43] As a member of the progressive left, Zinn could not devote his knowledge and action to all issues, and some subjects unavoidably received little or no attention. Any "sin of omission" here, though, should not be misconstrued as indifference.

Optimism

Was Zinn's optimism unjustified or naïve to some degree? There are compelling reasons to be skeptical about the prospects for progressive change. Increased income inequality in the United States from the 1970s until the present and reduced wages for over 70 percent of Americans in the same period is unprecedented.[44] The impacts of anthropogenic global warming are expected to soon reach crisis levels, a predicament that sober-minded experts and a vast majority of climate scientists have declared as the "point of no return."[45] A Democratic president has continued—and in some cases escalated—George W. Bush–era executive powers such that the ACLU has criticized the Obama administration for "establishing a new normal" regarding the government's growing use of the War on Terror as a justification to infringe upon civil liberties and undermine due process constitutional provisions.[46] In many ways, therefore, it is unclear whether the United States and/or the rest of the world can be characterized as moving forward, moving backward, or in stasis in terms of the advancement of social justice and democratic goals.

In the context of this humbling reality, Zinn's optimism and his faith in the power of agitation and civil disobedience may be regarded as naïve, trite, or lacking in seriousness. His optimism should not be interpreted as complacency. Rather, it is an effective way of channeling strong feelings in response to injustice. His demeanor was key to his style. Zinn provided facts and analyses about the oppressed with cheer, a smile, sometimes humor, or slight dark cynicism (see Alix Olson's poem in this volume for an analogous voice). Zinn's lack of overt emotional outrage or anger was the strength of his approach, not the weakness.

Consequently, Zinn's optimism is complex. For instance, Kazin, in addition to criticizing Zinn's methodology (as discussed earlier in the context of historical accuracy), disputes this characterization of optimism. In Zinn's narrative, Kazin argues that progressives "keep getting defeated. . . . Somehow the 99% always lose, even though they're the great majority. . . . The argument that America has always had an undemocratic, exploitative and oppressive system is undermined by the fact that the majority of Americans basically support the system."[47]

For Zinn, though, the struggle is perpetual. If injustices are being perpetrated against other populations (and they always are), then the fight is not over. The focus must remain on injustice, not necessarily celebrating the advancements. Thus, from 1950 to 1980 there was, as Kazin correctly asserts, real progress in a variety of civil-rights and social-justice issues, many of which Zinn contributed to. However, Zinn felt there was little to be gained from basking in the successes of the civil-rights movement in 1967–1968 because of other continuing injustices targeting workers, immigrants, and women, as well as an imperialist war being waged in Vietnam. Zinn's optimism, therefore, is perhaps rooted not in the movement of progress, but in continuing the fight, regardless of success or failure. It is an optimism based on hope, which is perhaps best articulated by Zinn when highlighting actors who acted *as if* change was possible even in the face of danger.[48] It is the constant struggle by (and on behalf of) the oppressed that will yield a more just society.[49]

THE FUTURE OF ACTIVISM

Is a Zinnian model for the future of activism possible? As this manuscript was being prepared, the Arab Spring was changing the nature of the Middle East and North Africa, and the Occupy Wall Street movement was seemingly reawakening Americans to the concerns for the dominance of unrestrained corporate capitalism. On its face, sympathy for these movements would demonstrate an enormous degree of support for Zinn's approach to agitation: essentially nonviolent, street-based, grassroots, focused on opposition to dominant and/or authoritarian interests, and deeply concerned with participation and egalitarianism.[50] However, there are some components to these events, and of the nature of activism itself in the twenty-first century, that may require a reexamination (a reboot?) of Zinn's approach to social movements, namely, the rise of so-called digital activism.

Stefan Wray (1999: 207) contrasts digital activism ("electronic civil disobedience") with "traditional action" by using Zinn's description of 20,000 activists (and 14,000 mass arrests) against the Vietnam War in Washington in 1968. In many ways we can conceive of Zinn's conception of social activism (and, relatedly, social movements and progressive agitation) as an essentially conventional or traditional idea of protest. Wray (1999: 109) notes that "just as capitalism has become increasingly nomadic, mobile, liquid, dispersed, and electronic, so resistance must take on these attributes."

So, how does this affect Zinn's approach to activism? Do Zinn's conceptions of social action, protest discourse, and agitation remain applicable? To consider these questions it is useful to conceptually distinguish between two aspects of social protest in the digital realm. The first is the use of the digital world as an improved and/or different form of communication for the support of protest. In other words, the digital world exists as a virtual "place" where protest, concerns, information, and plans of action can be discussed and/or implemented. It *enables* communication and information dissemination for agitation in additional ways that are new, and perhaps better.

The second is the use of digital protest—for instance, the hacking of government emails, the distributed denial-of-service attacks on websites, or the release of State Department or US military data by WikiLeaks to advance aims of transparency. The publication of the US Army field reports by WikiLeaks in 2010 confirmed fears about the lack of US response to known torture, and high civilian death counts.[51] The group Anonymous has been involved in Internet "raids" on the websites of various government agencies and corporate websites.[52]

The degree of impact and change for activism in the digital and social-media era is hotly debated, and remains an unresolved topic. Earl et al. (2010) conclude that the more "active" a protest website is online, the greater the likelihood that the site will alter the dynamics of movement activism. This will then require new understandings of and approaches to the assessment of movement formation, maintenance, and success. At the very least, online social-networking tools do seem to have positive effects on movement activism. However, to what degree does a protest website affect long-term maintenance and agitation of a movement? Here the answer is less clear. Certainly Zinn would be concerned with the lasting impacts of online activism, but he undoubtedly recognized the beneficial effects of such activity. Given that Zinn wholeheartedly embraced a set of broader media (radio, Internet, television, theater, film) in the last two decades of his life, it is unlikely that he would disdain the potential efficacy of digital tools. Rather, he would view that traditional activism is (potentially) heightened by the tools of the digital era.

At the same time, however, Zinn might be skeptical of these tools of the digital era, especially in regard to "clicktivism" or "checkbook activism." This is not simply because success rates (the ends) are still unproven, but more because of what is missing in the process. This is primarily the concern that a lack of personal connections can limit long-term organizational impact. Zinn describes the development of relationships within movements and the cultivation of solidarity across groups that can be sustained over time. "Liking" Barack Obama on Facebook, signing an online petition calling for the capture of warlord Joseph Kony, or altering one's Twitter avatar to the color green to show support for the Green movement in Iran may be personally rewarding, but those activities remain sedentary and individualized.[53]

The increased speed of the mobilization process may be an additional consequence of online activism that would alarm Zinn. This faster process could hinder the longer-term effectiveness of movement. Maturation (organizational capacity) takes time, energy, and focus. The development of social networks, the growth of civil society, and the building of strong organizational ties are processes that cannot be rushed. As Zinn saw in his own study of movements, the stages of development cannot be skipped without attendant costs. If this process goes too quickly, collective work may not be long-lasting—longevity and institutionalization may be threatened.[54] We cannot simply celebrate what is possibly gained with new media without considering what might also be lost.

The "Dark Side" of Digital Activism: Social Change versus Social Control

One question is how Zinn would respond to the movement of activism to digital networks, and whether such migration would fundamentally change his approach to activism. In part, one of the reasons that Zinn might be suspicious of the ability of the Internet or digital communication to enable activism and progressive improvement of society is because of the concern that its advantages for activism and social movements are also available to dominant powers and interests. Simultaneous to "digitally enabled social change" is the concern for "digitally enabled social manipulation." One of the chief concerns of Morozov (2011) and other digital skeptics is that the digital era provides better, broader, and often more subtle means of social control by governmental or corporate interests.[55] These forms of social control have two distinct forms: overt digital interference and less-direct systems of citizen control in the form of distraction and a dominating societal message.

Overt digital interference is simply interference with online networks through key control or brokerage points in networks. Examples include data-mining of US network feeds by the National Security Agency (NSA), Egyptian control of RSS feeds or the monitoring of Facebook sites during the Arab Spring, and Chinese censorship of the Internet. These forms of governmental control have the potential for overwhelming, distinct, and (usually) obvious governmental control. This type of digital oversight has the long-term potential to shield citizens from information concerning government action.

Second, and potentially more difficult to counteract, is that the digital world provides a useful mechanism for corporations and governments to either distract or manipulate the potential for activism. Many have optimistically characterized the introduction of the Internet (as well as cell and cable network systems), in combination with globalization, as an improvement in which increased access to information by almost anyone provides a significantly improved access to opportunity, unparalleled in history.[56] Yet Zinn would likely have been the first to note that the Internet and digital eras of the last fifteen years have suspiciously coincided with distinct increases in income inequality throughout the world.[57] An extensive discussion of hegemonic manipulation of social discourse (or the distraction of citizens from any social discourse) is beyond the reach of this discussion. Nonetheless, extensive evidence exists to demonstrate that the vast majority of Internet traffic and content is devoted to the "soma" and distractions of our times, not to concerns or activities addressing social justice. Zinn would certainly be worried about the increase of the Internet and digital communication, and its correlation with documented increases in conspicuous consumption and decreased literacy and civic engagement.[58]

Finally, Zinn would have concerns about the digital divide. Earl et al. (2010) discuss the relative inclusiveness of movements mobilized through the Internet. Websites with exclusively online activism tactics have some different economic advantages and tactics than ones with a combination of online and offline tactics.[59] Although intellectual property and LGBTQQ protest actions are exclusively waged through online activism, those of labor, immigration, and homelessness are waged through a combination of online and offline forms. Given the ongoing realities of the digital divide and the disparity of high-speed Internet access in the United States and elsewhere, this would certainly give Zinn pause. There is a definite class-biased quality to high-speed Internet access, and Internet ability and facility. As a result, the community-organizing and face-to-face contact endorsed by established social-movement scholars such as Marshall Ganz might be more effective for "poor people's movements."

How would Zinn react to the simultaneous threat and potential of digital activism in the twenty-first century? For Zinn, the issue is mobilization and access. Is the movement truly a people's movement if certain affected populations are not represented? Is the population adversely affected by the object of the movement being adequately reached or mobilized—via the Web or another mechanism? These are the operating questions he would have. They are the underlying questions that Zinn would apply to any movement, and will continue to have relevance in the future.

Using the Arts

Much like "digital utopians" when discussing their Web platform, advocates for the arts emphasize their educational function. The social consciousness of otherwise-disengaged constituencies can be activated through personal experience with artistic expression. Zinn's discussion of why he started to write for the theater and arguably why he expanded his work into the arts is multifaceted. In the introduction to his *Three Plays* (2010b), he includes several answers. First, there is the happenstance of having a family involved in theater. His son's career was immersed in the theater. He goes on to talk of "the power of drama in conveying a message of social significance,"[60] the unmatched excitement in producing drama, how a play becomes a collective and emotional experience, and "working with all these other people, intensely, in close quarters, with a warmth and affection foreign to academe. People arrived for rehearsal and hugged one another."[61] He also argues that theater (and other visual and aural media) allows viewers to identify emotionally and viscerally with historical events in a way that standard history and political writing cannot.[62]

The arts were a critical component of Zinn's work, particularly in his later years, but arguably they should be considered slightly differently than the other two points of our conceptual pyramid (activism-academia-arts). In many ways, Zinn subsumed his dedication to the arts (and also to academia) under his broader dedication to activism, and all three combined to the general goal of social justice.

Zinn's use of the arts in combination with his activism was not unique. There are extensive examples of political art throughout history. Rather, it was the intersection of the three spheres Zinn encompassed that we believe was substantively unique. A scholar-activist who also incorporates artistic media into agitation and analysis is particularly rare.[63]

Further, Zinn had no fear for the use of celebrity as a method of increasing the reach of the audience for his work. He had little concern for "selling out" or co-opting the legitimacy of his message by collaborating with popular figures in music, theater, and the arts.[64] He partnered with actors Matt Damon (also his neighbor) and Ben Affleck, and musicians such as Pearl Jam, Bruce Springsteen, and Pink.[65]

As Alix Olson demonstrates in Chapter 10, there are significant risks in pursuing artistic freedom and activism in an academic context. Consider, for example, Larry Summers's lack of appreciation for Cornel West's spoken-word rap albums at Harvard, and West's subsequent departure. Embarking on ventures in the academic and artistic realms simultaneously can have adverse consequences to one on the academic career path. Yet Zinn confronted these risks, and in doing so, presents a possible model. For Zinn, the artistic context was the forum in which to humanize and breathe new life into his academic and activist interests, and, in turn, reach a wider audience.

THE FUTURE OF THE SCHOLAR-ACTIVIST AND THE LEGACIES OF ZINN

Descriptive labels are in abundance when we consider Zinn's public life. They include the following, many of which Zinn used for self-description: historian, philosopher, intellectual, political scientist, anarchist, academic, agitator, optimist, socialist, leftist, progressive, and activist. We contend that *scholar-activist* most accurately captures Zinn's broader (and less descriptive) role as a public intellectual. It provides the right balance between granularity and comprehensiveness.

Most importantly, it is a role that he successfully balanced—arguably a difficult thing to do. Richard Hofstadter argues that Charles Beard's career was ruined because he "geared his reputation as a historian so closely to his political interests and passions that the two were bound to share the same fate.... [I]n the end he lost."[66] Although Zinn has certainly faced his share of criticism, a similar fate has not befallen him. This is arguably for two reasons. First, Zinn's extraordinary success as a scholar in the public (as opposed to the academic) realm has reinforced the legitimacy of his voice. Though some scholars see mainstream commercial success and impact as essentially weakening the authority of Zinn's intellectual contributions, the success story of *A People's History* and Zinn's degree of personal fame and association with celebrity helped cement his standing.

Second, Zinn's career trajectory occurred in different historical context than Beard's. Zinn has undergone criticism for historical bias and a lack of objectivity, but his work can also be seen as a significant contribution to new ideas concerning pedagogy, learning, and practicing history. Trends within teaching currently make much of what Zinn argued for legitimate and truly applicable today. "Service learning," active learning, immersive history, history from the ground up, and citizens' history are all relatively new forms of teaching and learning in high school and postsecondary education designed to improve the learning process and student engagement. Zinn has been part of a movement that has encouraged students and citizens to more carefully examine and situate themselves in the history of the masses. Through these techniques they can more carefully understand the interaction between citizen and government, and begin to question how power is manifested.

This development also appears within academia itself. Zinn was fortunate that much of his activism was influenced by the emergence of postmodernism. The questionable goals of true neutrality and objectivity were seriously challenged in the 1970s and 1980s. Certainly, this is not to make the case that much of Zinn's work is subjective. He would argue forcefully that much of his history was a rebalancing of the narrative, a correction to the lack of analysis and omissions of conventional history. Over the last fifty years, efforts in sociology ("public sociology"), political science ("new political science"), and history ("progressive history") have acknowledged the concerns for a lack of methodological pluralism and the inability to achieve objectivity. This contributes to a "ground up" vision of academic analysis that merges with Zinn's approach.

Finally, one of the most provocative aspects of Zinn's legacy is that of self-reflection. Zinn clearly champions democracy as a participatory (contact?) sport. For a democratic society to achieve justice, the people must constantly engage the system and challenge those in power. However, an inherent aspect of this understanding is that the people must also question and challenge themselves. In *The Southern Mystique* (1972 [1964]), Zinn articulates this point by asserting that the South is not unique in regards to its views and handling of race. In fact, the rest of the country is just as complicit. By equating the behavior of the rest of the country with that of the "backward" South, Zinn forces us to confront our own behavior and accept a measure of responsibility.

Ross Caputi, in Chapter 9, takes this Zinnian mantle by asking us to do similarly when considering military action. Caputi assesses various theories of collective responsibility in an attempt to answer the question of how much blame an individual or group bears for the actions of its rulers in a given society, especially a democratic one. Although the answer is not easily attained, this speaks directly to Zinn's unrelenting faith in the people as the ultimate arbiters of power. Only the polity can achieve and maintain a just society, and they must be vigilant and active in working toward that goal. Honest and unrelenting self-reflection and criticism are key components of this path.

Challenges in Academia

Zinn's experiences in the academy serve as an example of the challenges facing those who intend to follow his path of the scholar-activist. Throughout his career, Zinn defied academic orthodoxy by abandoning neutrality in the classroom (but not engaging in indoctrination), encouraging his students to seek an education outside the classroom through participation in direct-action campaigns, and inserting himself into movement activities.[67] A serious concern today is whether this Zinnian model is possible. Challenges include the neoliberal corporatization of the university,[68] the weakening of academic freedom,[69] threats to the tenure system,[70] and the general critique of the "relevance" of higher education.

In the classroom setting, Zinn embodied an expansive role of the educator. Rather than simply lead his students through various texts, he encouraged them to get an education outside the classroom, to take time off to engage in activist pursuits in the community—to get involved. Only through such activities could individuals attain a true education of the world around them. Edward P. Morgan's discussion in Chapter 11 explores these various modes of learning and demonstrates Zinn's role as a "master teacher."

Zinn also chose not to hide his personal views on any issue. As discussed by Paul Reynolds in Chapter 4, objectivity was, and is, neither possible nor desirable. Moreover, by attempting to project an air of neutrality, the educator does a disservice to the students. The presentation of facts is always subjective because one is choosing which facts to include; to maintain a stance of either one belies judgment. Therefore, instead of focusing on an impossibility—complete objectivity—he deemed it essential for the students to be challenged and given the tools to question accepted dogma and, most importantly, be *expected* to do so. Finally, he led by example. Not only did Zinn encourage his students to get involved, but he showed them how. It is no accident that his last act as a full-time professor was to end class early in order to attend a rally on behalf of school of nursing faculty.[71]

Overall, Zinn represents academic freedom in its purest form, in and out of the classroom. Christopher C. Robinson, in Chapter 7, argues that Zinn's ideal classroom is one without walls and in which the free exchange of ideas is paramount. Zinn's concerns for academic freedom and the challenges in attempting to follow an academic path similar to his are significantly greater than ever before.[72] In many universities, professors are criticized as being *too* political, they have their email hacked by partisan operatives,[73] and they are constantly under pressure to prepare their students for the "job market" rather than to educate well-rounded members of society. How is academic freedom balanced against job security? The recent Occupy movement has witnessed the active participation of a number of professors.[74] This is a potentially risky activity unless those professors are tenured, and can influence whether one actively participates in the movement or encourages students to do so. There is a "chilling" in the academy in which educators may feel constrained from speaking their mind or engaging in material that counters prevailing opinions.[75]

Further, there is a serious concern for once again linking the role of academic and activist, creating participatory research, focusing on participant observation, and integrating the roles of research and agitation. Recent work by Croteau (2005) examines the tension between scholarship and activism and whether one can make an impact in both worlds. He concludes that a dual role is possible, though deeply challenging, and one in which the academic role is always diminished.

In the end, we are concerned that Zinn's model of scholar-activist, which challenged the academy in such a direct and effective manner, may be seriously threatened. The decreased availability of tenure-track positions and the resulting rise in the use of adjunct faculty and other forms of contingent labor[76] hinders faculty activism. Robinson notes that these shifts also increase the degree of intellectual conformity.[77] Academics restrain themselves from strong pronouncements or intellectual pursuits that are outside of the mainstream or confront the status quo. Zinn straddled (or perhaps obliterated) the line between the public academic and private intellectual in a manner that is becoming more and more difficult today.[78]

FINAL THOUGHTS

In the last two decades of his life, Zinn made a seemingly conscious effort and switch toward books with a distinctly broader audience. Zinn's early years often focused on specific actions, or speeches in the context of slightly more limited communities (academia, union, civil-rights, or antiwar movements)—later he transitioned to more generalized commentary on questions of activism, agitation, social justice, and a "people's history." This included a significant expansion of his activities in different forms of media. *A People's History* was expanded into radio, staged readings, and television. He devoted more time to the production of his plays. It also represented a shift of much of his time and attention to more general and all-encompassing concerns for social activism and history from below.

One potential argument for this trajectory toward more expansive audiences is that it is simply a reflection and natural evolution of Zinn's increasing popularity and public presence over time. While Zinn would arguably have been concerned for and skeptical of embracing the digital world as the savior of social activism and justice, he would have recognized the use of digital information as simply another form of activism, albeit with exceptional powers for dissemination and collective action, and more significant concerns for the building of solidarity, social control, or co-optation.

As this text was being written, Zinn's influence and legacy were evident in a wide variety of arenas. Zinn's model of the scholar-activist has been emulated by professors in the battles in Wisconsin over unions; with students in protests over public-university tuition hikes in Quebec, California, and New York City; in the fight for same-sex marriage; and by activists in the Arab Spring and Occupy movements. Teaching, history, and politics have been integrated in all of these arenas, with the most prevalent concerns focused on basic social justice, just as Zinn would have liked. Ultimately his influence and perspective can best be summed up by Zinn himself:

> I don't think it's too soon to talk about a legacy. I think we should have started talking about it a long time ago, maybe when I was ten years old. A Zinn legacy. What do I leave? I think the best legacy one can leave is people. I can say, I would like to leave a legacy of books, and yes, there are writings that have an effect on people and it's good to think that you've written something that has made people think, and think about their lives. When I say legacy is people, I guess I mean people have been affected by reading, by your life, or people you've encountered. The best kind of legacy you can leave is a kind of example of how one should live one's life, not that I've lived my life in an exemplary way, but let's put it this way, people should be very selective about what they look at in my life. If I were to single out, as I would be prone to do, only the good things, I would think of the necessity to work at changing the world and at the same time maintain a kind of decency towards all the people around you. So that what you are striving for in the future is acted out in the present in your human relations.[79]

It is the citizen who makes history and agitates for justice. Howard Zinn knew this implicitly, and made it the overarching message of his life. He did this constantly, providing an unwavering model of optimist, intellectual, and agitator (with a smile) for all of us.

Afterword

Howard Zinn's Legacy
of Words and Action

Noam Chomsky

It is not easy for me to write a few words about Howard Zinn, the great American activist and historian.[1] He was a very close friend. Our families were very close too. His wife, Roz, who died not long before him, was also a marvelous person and close friend. Also somber is the realization that a whole generation seems to be disappearing, including several other old friends: Edward Said, Eqbal Ahmad, and others, who were not only astute and productive scholars but also dedicated and courageous militants, always on call when needed—which was constant. A combination that is essential if there is to be hope of decent survival.

The country and the world have changed a great deal since Howard Zinn boarded his "moving train" many years ago, first as an industrial worker and labor activist, then on to becoming a leading figure in the great revival of activism in the 1960s. During those years there have been many crimes, many horrors, many acts of courageous struggle and resistance, and many victories for justice and freedom. And not least, looming challenges, ranging from domestic economic travail to literal threats to survival of the species. There are few better ways to gain a clear understanding of what has been happening over these years, and what can be done to face the critical tasks for tomorrow, than by reading Howard Zinn's eloquent words, and pondering the fascinating story of his crucial and intimate participation at every point, in thought and action.

I have just had the opportunity to read a collection of Zinn's speeches, recently published.[2] In doing so I almost felt that I was once again hearing his voice, as I had often done during the more than half a century that I was fortunate enough to know him well. Even in the written word the unique appeal comes through—his stunning pitch-perfect ability to capture the moment and the concerns and needs of the audience, whoever they may be, always enlightening, often stirring, an amalgam of insight, critical history, wit, blended with charm and warmth and hope. I have heard him speak to tens of thousands at demonstrations, to small groups of homeless people, to activists enduring brutal treatment, and at many other times and places. Always with just the right tone and message, always inspiring, a gift to all of us to be treasured, and with lessons that should not be forgotten.

Howard's remarkable life and work are summarized best in his own words. His primary concern, he explained, was "the countless small actions of unknown people" that lie at the roots of "those great moments" that enter the historical record—a record that will be profoundly misleading, and seriously disempowering, if it is torn from these roots as it passes through the filters of doctrine and dogma. His life was always closely intertwined with his writings and innumerable talks and interviews. It was devoted, selflessly, to empowerment of the unknown people who brought about great moments.

While teaching at Spelman College, a black women's college that was open mostly to the small black elite, Howard supported students in Atlanta who were at the cutting edge of the civil-rights movement in its early and most dangerous days, many of whom became quite well known in later years—Alice Walker, Marian Wright Edelman, Julian Bond, and others—and who loved and revered him, as did everyone who knew him well. And as always, he did not just support them, which was rare enough, but also participated directly with them in their most hazardous efforts—no easy undertaking at that time, before there was any organized popular movement and in the face of government hostility that lasted for some years. Finally, popular support was ignited, in large part by the courageous actions of the young people who were sitting in at lunch counters, riding freedom buses, organizing demonstrations, facing bitter racism and brutality, sometimes death.

A few years later he wrote the standard work on the Student Nonviolent Coordinating Committee (SNCC), the major organization of those "unknown people" whose "countless small actions" played such an important part in creating the groundswell that enabled Martin Luther King to gain significant influence, as I am sure he would have been the first to say, and to bring the country to honor the constitutional amendments of a century earlier that had theoretically granted elementary civil rights to former slaves—at least to do so partially; there is no need to stress that there remains a long way to go.

As a reward for his courage and honesty, Howard was soon expelled from Spelman College. Howard came to Boston, and spent the rest of his academic career at Boston University, where he was, I am sure, the most admired and loved faculty member on campus, and the target of bitter antagonism and petty cruelty on the part of the administration—though in later years, after his retirement, he gained the public honor and respect that was always overwhelming among students, staff, much of the faculty, and the general community.

While at BU, Howard wrote the books that brought him well-deserved fame. His *Vietnam: The Logic of Withdrawal,* in 1967, was the first to express clearly and powerfully what many were then beginning barely to contemplate: that the United States had no right even to call for a negotiated settlement in Vietnam, leaving Washington with power and substantial control in the country it had invaded and by then already largely destroyed. Rather, the United States should do what any aggressor should: withdraw, allow the population to somehow reconstruct as they could from the wreckage, and if minimal honesty could be attained, pay massive reparations for the crimes that the invading armies had committed, vast crimes in this case. Protest had been virtually nonexistent. Howard Zinn was one of the few exceptions, from the earliest days until the war officially ended—though it has far from ended for the victims. The book had wide influence among the public, although to this day its message can barely even be comprehended in elite educated circles, an indication of how much necessary work lies ahead.

One of many memorable occasions for me was a meeting on the war in April 1975 when the two of us shared a platform (as often before). While Howard was speaking, a young man raced down the aisle shouting "the war is over." As always, Howard had just the right words—celebration, but also warning. Significantly, among the general public by the war's end, 70 percent in a Gallup poll regarded the war as "fundamentally wrong and immoral," not "a mistake," a remarkable figure considering the fact that scarcely a hint of such a thought was expressible in mainstream opinion. Howard's writings—and, as always, his prominent presence in protest and direct resistance—were a major factor in civilizing much of the country. It is worth recalling how long that took. Even in liberal Boston, public meetings against the war, even in churches, were attacked by counter-demonstrators (with the support of the media) right through many years of horrifying atrocities. A popular movement did finally develop, but at a time when the respected Vietnam specialist and military historian Bernard Fall, no dove, wrote bitterly that "Vietnam as a cultural and historic entity ... is threatened with extinction ... [as] ... the countryside literally dies under the blows of the largest military machine ever unleashed on an area of this size," referring to South Vietnam, in 1967.

In those same years, Howard also became one of the most prominent supporters of the resistance movement that was then developing. He was one of the early signers of the Call to Resist Illegitimate Authority and took part in the sanctuary actions that had a remarkable impact in galvanizing antiwar protest. Whatever was needed—talks, participation in civil disobedience, support for resisters, testimony at trials—Howard was always there.

The solidarity movements of the 1980s opened new paths in the history of opposition to imperial violence. Many even went beyond educational efforts, protest, and resistance, and went to live with the victims, to offer help, and also, by their presence, to provide at least some limited protection against state and paramilitary terror. Few had ever contemplated living in a Vietnamese or Algerian village under brutal attack by their own state. The international solidarity movements that developed from these roots have since spread to large parts of the world, compiling a very honorable record of courage and dedication. In the same years, popular movements concerned with the threat of possibly terminal nuclear war became an enormous force that could no longer be ignored. Popular opposition to shocking Central American atrocities directed or supported by Washington was broad and deep—and once again, surprising no one who knew him, Zinn was prominent and influential in sustaining these currents of protest and organization.

Even more influential in the long run than Howard's antiwar writings and actions was his enduring masterpiece, *A People's History of the United States,* an incomparable achievement that literally changed the consciousness of a generation. Here he developed with care, lucidity, and comprehensive sweep his fundamental message about the crucial role of the people who remain unknown in carrying forward the endless struggle for peace and justice, and about the victims of the systems of power that create their own versions of history and seek to impose it. Later, his *Voices of a People's History,* now an acclaimed theatrical and television production, brought to many the actual words of those forgotten or ignored people who have played such a valuable role in creating a better world.

Howard's unique success in drawing the actions and voices of unknown people from the depths to which they had largely been consigned has spawned extensive historical research following a similar path, focusing on critical periods of American history, and turning to the record in other countries as well, a very welcome development. It is not entirely novel—there had been scholarly inquiries of such topics before—but nothing to compare with Howard's broad and incisive evocation of "history from below," compensating for critical omissions in how American history had been interpreted and conveyed.

Howard's dedicated activism continued, literally without a break, until the very end. Even in his last years, when he was suffering from infirmity and personal loss, one would hardly know it when meeting him or watching him speak tirelessly to captivated audiences all over the country. Whenever there was a struggle for peace and justice, Howard was there, on the front lines, unflagging in his enthusiasm, and inspiring in his integrity, engagement, eloquence and insight, light touch of humor in the face of adversity, dedication to nonviolence, and sheer decency.

Forty years after John F. Kennedy launched the war against South Vietnam, George W. Bush invaded Iraq. Unlike the attack against South Vietnam, in this case it was understood that it would be necessary to rally public support, and major efforts had been put in place to terrify the population. Memories of 9/11 were still fresh, and could be exploited to stir up war fever, and to mobilize the frightened public in perceived self-defense against the predicted "mushroom clouds" in New York if we did not quickly destroy the maniacal force bent on world conquest. Nevertheless, for the first time in the history of Western imperialism, there were huge and unprecedented protests against the war even before it was officially announced, not delayed until many years later when the targeted country was "threatened with extinction."

The protests did not avert the war, or the humanitarian catastrophe that it caused. But it is likely that opposition and dissent were a significant factor in limiting the means employed. There was no B-52 saturation bombing of the countryside, or chemical warfare to destroy crops, or mass slaughter of the kind unleashed against Indochina. Further, the invaders could not achieve many of their unstated goals, unlike in Indochina, where primary goals were attained (though not maximal ones). Iraq goes down in serious history as "a defeat"; five years after the invasion the Bush administration was still demanding publicly that in any final settlement US combat forces must be free to operate from military bases in Iraq, and that US investments must be privileged in the energy sector, finally conceding publicly what had been the goals all along. All of those demands were withdrawn in the face of Iraqi nationalism, a major defeat for imperial ambitions.

By 2011 popular uprisings in the Middle East and North Africa were threatening Western control over regions that had long been recognized to be pivotal for global dominance. These dramatic developments were a major inspiration for the Occupy movement that began in New York, with independent counterparts in Europe, and soon spread to hundreds of American cities.

Whatever their outcome, as always unpredictable, these popular uprisings have achieved important successes, which should be lasting. Despite many differences, there are some common themes. In one or another way, they are in substantial part reactions to the harmful effects of the neoliberal policies of the past generation, the IMF–World Bank–Treasury "Washington consensus," based on a form of "markets" designed to privilege concentrations of private wealth and power. Egypt and the United States, though of course very different societies, illustrate the pattern in their own ways. In Egypt, the neoliberal policies of the United States–backed Mubarak dictatorship greatly enriched a corrupt few who were linked to the state apparatus, while the large majority suffered. The international financial institutions were praising the government for its grand achievements virtually to the day of the January 2011 uprising that was in large part a protest against these measures.

On the domestic US front, we see a similar lead-up to these recent events. In the background is a major shift in US economic history. From the earliest days, the trajectory was toward development and industrialization, often in quite ugly ways and with many ups and downs, but the general tendency persisted. Even in such dark periods as the Great Depression, after the first few years there was a mood of hopefulness, a sense that working together, we will somehow escape from this disaster. And there were grounds for that belief in CIO organizing and other popular actions, legislation passed under public pressure that improved conditions and offered hope—though it wasn't until the huge wartime economic stimulus that the Depression ended and a period of unprecedented economic growth ensued, relatively egalitarian, through the 1960s, again relying heavily on contributions of the dynamic state sector that led decades later to the information technology (IT) revolution.

During the 1970s, a substantial change was initiated, accelerating under Reagan and beyond. The economy shifted toward financialization and offshoring of production, setting off a vicious cycle of greater concentration of wealth (increasingly in the financial sector) and with it inevitably greater concentration of political power and legislation to carry the cycle forward: fiscal measures, deregulation, rules of corporate governance, and much else. It no longer comes as a surprise to read in the morning paper at the year's end that new workers are receiving much lower salaries with little chance for advancement, and that working people new and old are so beaten down by unemployment that they barely object, glad to have any work. And in the same pages, to read that "the stock market's rebound from the financial crisis three years ago has created a potential windfall for hundreds of executives who were granted unusually large packages of stock options shortly after the market collapsed," thanks to the way tax laws are written (Kocieniewski 2011). Meanwhile what remained of functioning democracy was shredded as the cost of elections skyrocketed, driving the political parties deep into corporate pockets, the Republicans so enthusiastically that they scarcely resemble a traditional political party, the Democrats—now mostly what used to be called "moderate Republicans"—not far behind.

The Occupy movement that spread rapidly in the fall of 2011 is the first major popular reaction to these harsh processes. They quickly achieved substantial successes, placing firmly on the agenda of public concern topics that had been too easily displaced, not displaced from awareness but from sustained public discussion and planning. Not least, they brought people together to create vital living communities with common purpose, which developed modes of mutual support and democratic interaction ("horizontalism," as it was called during the Argentine rebellions a decade ago). This alone is a very significant achievement in a society that has been highly atomized, contributing to hopelessness, subordination, and despair.

It should also have surprised no one that the libraries that were spontaneously assembled in the occupied spaces featured Zinn's books. Or that Howard Zinn memorial lectures quickly proliferated. Or that he was recognized everywhere as an animating spirit. While there is naturally no single source for the complex and multifaceted processes that have led to the Occupy movement, and the others that have sprung up elsewhere, they are a graphic testimony to historical currents that Zinn highlighted and brought to general awareness in his work, and contributed to so impressively in his life of engagement and dedication.

The changes that owe a great deal to the dedicated activism of the past half century are indeed dramatic. It is hard even to imagine how many young people's lives were touched, and how deeply, by his achievements, both in his work and his life. As I mentioned, the country has become far more civilized as a result. Just to give one personal illustration, at about the time Zinn began his teaching career at Spelman College in Atlanta, I joined the faculty at MIT in Cambridge. Walking through the halls at the time, one would have seen neatly dressed white males, immersed in their work, with hardly a sign of concern for the troubles of the world beyond. In the same halls today half the students are women and a third minorities, formalities have given way to much easier interactions; there is lively interest and engagement in a wide range of human problems, with many impressive cultural and political initiatives. The experience is replicated throughout much of the country. There is a long way to go, and the process has hardly been without regression, but the accomplishments are real, and instructive.

There are people whose words have been highly influential, and others whose actions have been an inspiration to many. It is a rare achievement to have interwoven both of these strands in one's life, as Howard Zinn was able to do. His writings changed the consciousness of a generation, and helped open new paths to understanding the actual course of history and its meaning for our lives. He was always on call, ready to contribute his share and more. When the time came for action, he was always on the front lines, an example and a trustworthy guide. And he remains so after he has passed away.

It has been a wonderful privilege to have been able to join Howard on his "moving train" on many occasions over these years of challenge, inspiration, torment, and persistent and all-too-reasonable concern over impending catastrophe. Like everyone who knew him, I was constantly struck by his enduring optimism, which went well beyond "optimism of the will" to challenge the "pessimism of the intellect" that complements it in the slogan that Gramsci made famous. Howard's life and work remain a persistent reminder that our own subjective judgments of the likelihood of success in confronting serious problems are of little interest, to ourselves or others. What matters is to take part, as best we can, in the small actions of unknown people that can stave off disaster and bring about a better world, to honor them for their achievements, to do what we can to ensure that these achievements are understood and carried forward. Howard Zinn's life and work are an unforgettable model, sure to leave a permanent stamp on how history is understood and how a decent and honorable life should be lived.

Notes

CHAPTER 1

1. This phrase comes from the headline of Peniel E. Joseph's (2011) astute review of Manning Marable's (2011) deservedly praised biography of Malcolm X.

2. Michael Eric Dyson (2011) has spoken about the humanization of Malcolm X in Marable's work. In presenting this "hero as human," the reader remains motivated to action yet is not intimidated by comparisons to an idealized image.

3. Zinn (2010a).

4. Zinn (2007a: 42).

5. Zinn (1990 [1970]: 35). This appears to be the first usage (in print) of the aphorism that would become the title of Zinn's (1994) memoir some two decades later.

6. Schmidt (2011).

7. Historians, asserts Zinn (1990 [1970]: 13), need to "expose fallacious logic, spurious analogies, deceptive slogans, and those intoxicating symbols and concepts which drive people to murder.... We need to expose inconsistencies and double standards. In short, we need to become the critics of the culture rather than its apologists and perpetuators."

8. Zinn's dissertation on New York congressman Fiorello La Guardia was published in revised form as *LaGuardia in Congress 1917–1933: A Study of a Legislative Career That Bridged the Progressive and the New Deal Eras* (1959). Other early publications of scholarly note include *Albany, A Study in National Responsibility* (1962); *SNCC: The New Abolitionists* (2002 [1964]); "Abolitionists, Freedom-Riders, and the Tactics of Agitation" (1965a); *New Deal Thought* (1965b); and "Vacating the Premises in Vietnam" (1969).

9. Thanks to an anonymous reviewer for this important point.

10. The final chapter of *Vietnam: The Logic of Withdrawal* (Zinn 2002 [1967]) takes the form of an Oval Office speech that Zinn has written for the president to deliver to the public, announcing the withdrawal of American troops from Vietnam. Although the message is characteristically Zinn—its overarching tone might be referred to as *strength through peace*—the medium of fiction is new for Zinn. This stylistic choice represents an early effort to show how creative writing can be used to mobilize social change, and it may be seen as a harbinger of the theatrical plays that Zinn would write years later.

11. Zinn (2002 [1967]: 16).

12. Zinn (2002 [1967]: 26).
13. Zinn (2002 [1967]: 89–90).
14. Zinn (2002 [1967]: 107–108).
15. Powell (2010).
16. Also see Green (2003).
17. Noam Chomsky, "Manufacturing Consent." Presentationresentation at the University of Wisconsin (1989). See Herman and Chomsky (1988). Emphasis added.
18. Chomsky would likely agree with this distinction, but it is useful to demonstrate the emphasis of Zinn's approach. There are many ideological overlaps between the two scholars, who had many opportunities for interaction in their activist and personal lives. See Professor Chomsky's afterword in this volume for details on this relationship.
19. Zinn, for example, traveled to Japan in 1966 on a lecture tour and went to Hawaii in 1969 for discussions on his academic and activist work.
20. This story is recounted by two informants who posed as members of the Lawyers' Committee for Civil Rights Under Law and the Commission on Religion and Race of the National Council of Churches in New York City. The informants' names are redacted in the FBI files. *Howard Zinn FBI Files,* Section 2 (June 20, 1969 to August 22, 1974), 8. Released on July 30, 2010 as a result of a Freedom of Information Act (FOIA) request, http://www.fbi.gov/foia/electronic-reading-room/zinn-howard.
21. Zinn (1990 [1970]: 195).
22. Zinn (1990 [1970]: 207–208).
23. This change could simply be a natural result of one getting older and wanting to turn to family matters or "slowing down." He did, however, maintain a vigorous schedule of speaking engagements, interviews, and artistic pursuits. It also should be noted that Zinn gave speeches at many antiwar events leading up to the March 2003 invasion of Iraq and continued to voice his opposition to the contemporary wars (and war more generally) at roundtable discussions, community lectures, and university teach-ins until his passing.
24. In Zinn's formulation, "democracy must improve itself constantly or decay" (Zinn 2002 [1968]: 18).
25. Zinn (1968: 10–12).
26. *Justice* is defined as "the fair treatment of all human beings, the equal right of all people to freedom and prosperity" (Zinn 1991: 107–109).
27. Zinn (1968: 119).
28. Zinn (1968: 18).
29. Zinn (1991: 123). Emphasis in original.
30. The fifth of nine fallacies stipulated by Zinn in *Disobedience and Democracy* (1968).
31. Zinn (1968: 89–90). Although not cited, this echoes C. Wright Mills's *Power Elite,* in which politicians and the barons of industry game the system to ensure that capital flows to them and not to the general population.
32. Zinn (1991: 112–114).
33. "The ultimate test is not law, but justice.... Historically," Zinn asserts, "the most terrible things—war, genocide, and slavery—have resulted not from disobedience, but from obedience." He concludes that "actions outside the law or against the law, must be judged by their human consequences" (Zinn 1991: 128–129, 133).
34. Zinn (2002 [1964]: 219).
35. Zinn (2002 [1964]: 237).
36. John F. Kennedy Presidential Library and Museum, "Quotation from Dante's *Inferno,*" http://www.jfklibrary.org/Research/Ready-Reference/JFK-Miscellaneous-Information/Dante.aspx.

37. Zinn (1990 [1970]: 10).
38. Zinn (2001a: 123).
39. Zinn (1991).
40. In his exploration of America of the 1830s, Alexis de Tocqueville (2000 [1835, 1840]) noted the inherent contradictions among ideas endemic to American society and its democracy. Absolute liberty necessitates a restriction on equality, and vice versa. The French aristocrat also observed the antagonism between liberty and authority and between majority and minority rights. Zinnian political thought embodies the tensions that Tocqueville describes.
41. Cook and Cohen (2011).
42. Glavin and Morse (2003).
43. Vodovnik (2008). A variety of different ideas can be applied to Zinn's history and thinking; these concerns will be examined in much greater detail in later chapters. See, e.g., Richman (2011) on left libertarianism and Berkman (2003 [1928]) on communist anarchism.
44. We are indebted to Frances Fox Piven for this observation.
45. Zinn (2002 [1964]: 197).
46. Zinn (2002 [1964]: 200–201). Emphasis in original.
47. Zinn (1994: 201).
48. Zinn (2002 [1964]: 201). Emphasis in original.
49. Rousseau (1996 [1762]: 478).
50. Further expansion of this discussion can be found in Talisse (2009), Scott London's (2000) discussion of John Dewey's *Organic Democracy,* and in Dewey's own works, particularly *Democracy and Education* (1916). Deva Woodly's insightful comments at a Midwest Political Science Association panel encouraged us to think of Zinn in the context of "Deweyian tensions."
51. Zinn (2007a: 231).
52. In the introduction to his memoir, Zinn (1994: 11–12) indicates that this hopeful nature is largely due to his World War II military experience. Among his closest friends, Zinn was the only one who returned to the United States alive. Zinn attributes this to luck, and as a result he "owe[s] them something." "I have no right to despair," Zinn affirms. "I insist on hope."
53. Zinn (2005).
54. *Howard Zinn FBI Files,* Section 2 (June 20, 1969 to August 22, 1974), 92. The November 6, 1953 interview appears in *Howard Zinn FBI Files,* Section 1 (March 9, 1949 to April 2, 1968), 24–27, 285. At no place do the agents claim Zinn was uncooperative. The meeting was cordial, if not tense. The report does, however, say that Zinn refused to name names. Zinn denies membership in the Communist Party (CP), but acknowledges that members of organizations to which he belonged might also be CP members. Zinn was enrolled in the PhD program at Columbia at the time. The presumptive "concerns" of the FBI included his retrieval of prisoners of war from Vietnam with Daniel Berrigan (that included criticisms of particular actions taken by the military during the operation); previous discussions with FBI officers concerning freedom of speech and avowals of patriotism (in the sense of patriotism by dissent); and his highly public position as an effective, persuasive academic and public speaker.
55. *Howard Zinn FBI Files,* Section 2 (June 20, 1969 to August 22, 1974), 73–74; see also p. 57. He was incarcerated for one day, but was credited with two days and had to pay only $14. Zinn paid the fine so that he could make a previously scheduled trip to the west coast.

56. Zinn (1994: 185–186).

57. Joyce (2003: 85–91), Zinn (1994: 185–187). This exchange was only the first salvo in a fifteen-year battle in which Silber later countered by preventing Zinn from receiving salary increases or having teaching assistants assigned to his large lecture courses.

58. Zinn (2009a).

59. Zinn (1990 [1970]: Chapter 1).

60. Zinn (2002 [1964]: 250).

61. Aaron Henry and Ed King, the candidates for governor and lieutenant governor, respectively, of the Mississippi Freedom Democratic Party, received 80,000 votes outside the regular process (Zinn 2002 [1964]: 250).

62. For a more comprehensive discussion on this theme, see McAdam (1986).

63. Gladwell (2010) argues that online social networking creates more tenuous connections among activists in comparison to those forged among participants in direct action campaigns. These weaker online connections may bring more immediate success, such as a large turnout at a rally, but could possibly impede the growth of a long-term contentious political action. Increased political mobilization inspired by online activism may not transition to political organization. One might argue, however, that the initially "weak" bonds between online activists may strengthen over time as the participants engage in more contentious movement politics.

64. Worth (2011). The veracity of the Tunisia narrative has since been questioned. See, e.g., Day (2011).

65. On the use of social media by regimes in power, see Morozov (2011).

66. Steavenson (2011). In addition, Mo Ibrahim, the Sudanese billionaire, started one of the largest cell-phone networks in Africa and chairs a namesake foundation that awards money to African leaders, upon leaving office, who governed in a non-autocratic fashion. In speaking of the impact of cellular technology on the events in the Middle East and North Africa, Ibrahim says that "mobile phones are a fantastic way to break that [repressive government control over communications] monopoly.... [People] are swapping stories and sharing what's going on, who is corrupt, and that builds up a level of consciousness among the people. It helps them fight back" (Auletta 2011).

67. For a heartfelt report of this event, see Rothschild (2010).

CHAPTER 2

1. Indeed, this is one of the primary arguments of *The Politics of History* (1990 [1970]).

2. Zinn, interview with the author at Boston University (April 11, 2007).

3. Zinn, interview with the author at Boston University (April 11, 2007).

4. Joyce (2003: 172).

5. Eley (2010), Foner (1980), Handlin (1980), Joyce (2003: 168), Kazin (2004), Ndiaye (2004: 170), Novick (1988: 443–444), Wallace (1980: 27–38), and Zinn (2003 [1980]: 687–689).

6. Ndiaye (2004: 170), Wallace (1980: 27–38).

7. Zinn, interview with the author at Boston University (April 11, 2007).

8. Handlin (1980), Wallace (1980).

9. Zinn, interview with the author at Boston University (April 11, 2007).

10. Hunt (2003), Kazin (2004), and Novick (1988: 418–420).

11. Zinn, interview with the author at Boston University (April 11, 2007).

12. Zinn (1965b: xxvi). *New Deal Thought* is usefully studied as a radical critique of the shortcomings of the New Deal programs, especially for African Americans, small farmers, and other subsections of the working class. Published before Bernstein (1968) and Radosh and Rothbard (1972), *New Deal Thought* was characterized as an anticipation of the New Left critique. Also see Carson (1981: 58, 62) and Kidd (2005).

13. Joyce (2003: 46–50).

14. Joyce (2003: 46–50).

15. Zinn, interviews with the author (November 10, 2006; January 7, 2009, email correspondence); Zinn (2002 [1994]: 178); master's research paper for Professor Middlebruck, circa 1949, paper read and recorded by Ambre Ivol, Boston, MA; and (1972 [1964]: acknowledgments section). Zinn's first book on the South was dedicated to Fannie Lou Hamer.

16. Zinn (1972 [1964]: 99).

17. Zinn (1972 [1964]: 145–213).

18. "Joan Bowman to Howard Zinn, Aaron Henry Campaign," correspondence, *Zinn Research Papers,* Mississippi, October 15, 1963, Wisconsin State Historical Society.

19. The unusual thematic structure of Zinn's memoir indicates the prominence of his experiences in the 1960s and 1970s. See Zinn (2002 [1994]: Parts I and II).

20. Zinn (1990 [1970]: 5); Howe (1982: 162–195); Zinn (2002 [1994]: 110); Marcia Scott, "The Radical Historians' Caucus (NUC) and the A.H.A.: An Account." In *Radical Caucus in the AHA, Correspondence,* October 1970–c. 1973, 10–11; Howard Zinn, letter to Staughton Lynd, January 21, 1973; *Staughton Lynd Papers,* Folder 14, Box 5, Wisconsin State Historical Society.

21. Of course, Zinn continued to intervene as a public intellectual throughout the 1980s, 1990s, and 2000s, but he would largely do so by drawing on the richness of his earlier experiences in social movements.

22. Zinn, interview with the author at Boston University (April 11, 2007), Huberman (1947 [1932]: xi–xii, 328, 331–333, 342, 346).

23. Gornick (1977: 9–10, 31–33, 55, 74, 96–97).

24. "Every ex-President should have some place where he could go and hide his shame. A trip around the world would require a year, and by that time the voters would be so disgusted with the new president that the old one would come like a healing balm" (Nye 1894: 69–70).

25. Nye (1894: 70).

26. Nye (1894: 218).

27. Ameringer (1985 [1909]: x).

28. Ameringer (1985 [1909]: 5–6).

29. Ameringer (1985 [1909]: 50–51).

30. American communist historians had broached the subject, seeking "Black Vanguards," but did not make much progress until the later work of Du Bois protégé Herbert Aptheker.

31. Thompson (1963: 12–13).

32. Zinn (2003 [1980]: 10–11).

33. In an April 2007 interview with Ambre Ivol, Zinn could not remember precisely when he first read the book, but his copy is dated from the first edition in 1963.

34. See Ivol (2009) for a larger argument about the generational connections between the two historians.

35. Thompson (1963: 9). Zinn underlines the entire sentence in his copy.

36. Zinn (2003 [1980]: 635).

CHAPTER 3

1. Long (1969: 12), Carson (1981: 58, 62), and Zinn (2002 [1967]). The significance of that historical era can be noted throughout Zinn's work, e.g., Zinn (1994: 1–84; 2007a).

2. Novick (1988: 418), Hunt (2003: 142), Jacoby (2000 [1987]: 115), and Unger (1974: 140).

3. Jacoby (2000 [1987]: 164).

4. "Much of my information is gained firsthand, from being where SNCC people work, watching them in action, talking to them" (Zinn 2002 [1964]: acknowledgments). See also Ransby (2003: 259, 268, 283, 286).

5. Michael Harrington, quoted in Isserman (1993 [1987]: 123); Dorman (2002: 131–144).

6. Bell and Kristol (1968).

7. Is it about demographical development or intellectual maturation?

8. The narrowness of this schema is somewhat offset by the addition of "gentile cousins," including African American writers. Still, cultural homogeneity (Jewishness) is fundamental to the overall structure.

9. Bell (1960).

10. *Arguing the World* (1997).

11. Isserman (1993 [1987]: 37–75, 166–167, 174–176, 205, 212), Naison (1983), Kelley (1990), and Gilmore (2008: 6–11).

12. Zinn (1994: 171), Novick (1988: 419).

13. Dorman (2002: 79–86); Ivol (2009); Zinn (1994: 94); and Zinn, interview with the author at Boston University (September 24, 2003).

14. Joseph (2006: 3–6).

15. Mettler (2005).

16. *The Fog of War* (2003), McGovern (1997).

17. Novick (1988: 417–418) emphasizes the need to drop capital letters when dealing with the new left because it tends to "reify" a group that was actually quite heterogeneous— in political and generational terms.

18. "An entire generation of political activists had been jerked off the stage of history" (Schrecker 1998: 369).

19. Quoted in Zinn (1997b: 43).

20. Zinn, interview with the author at Boston University (April 11, 2007).

21. Such a definition is key to our remapping of the US Left, as depicted in Table 3-2.

22. Dorman (2002: 44), Fussell (1989: 4), and Novick (1988: 365). For Zinn's experience of the war, see Zinn (1994: 87–102).

23. Zinn (1994: 176–177, 179–180).

24. Schrecker (1998: 398).

25. Zinn, interview with the author at Boston University (April 11, 2007).

26. Ivol (2009, correspondence with Howard Zinn (November 27, 2007).

27. Zinn (1997b: 37–38). Most of the information gathered about those activist years came from regular personal interviews with Zinn between 2004 and 2009. Also see Schrecker (1998: 359–415).

28. Guthrie (1999).

29. Zinn (1997b: 46–47).

30. Joyce (2003: 45).

31. Zinn (1959: 230, 246–247, 259, 269); Zinn, correspondence with the author (November 27, 2007).

32. "Joseph Heller," *Columbia 250,* http://www.c250.columbia.edu/c250 _celebrates /remarkable_columbians/joseph_heller.html; "Remembering Norman Mailer," *On Point,* WBUR Radio (November 12, 2007), http://www.onpointradio.org/2007/11 /remembering-norman-mailer.

33. "Kurt Vonnegut Remembered," *Fresh Air,* National Public Radio (April 13, 2007), http://www.npr.org/templates/story/story.php?storyId=9567370.

34. Buhle, correspondence with the author (May 18, 2011). Also see Cheuse (1963), Heller (2003 [1951]), and Whitfield (2001).

35. Wallace (1983 [1976]: 127–129).

36. Buhle and Rice-Maximin (1995), Ivol (2007).

37. Quoted in Ransby (2003: 148).

38. Zinn, interview with the author at Boston University (April 11, 2007).

39. Cruse (1967: 162), Dittmer (1994), Joseph (2006), and Ransby (2003). As Cornel West (1993–1994) argues, the academic variable fails to bring out the whole range of black public figures.

40. Zinn (1972 [1964]: 50–51).

41. Zinn and Young, then head of the National Urban League, crossed paths again after the 1965 Montgomery, Alabama, march. See Williams (2002) and Zinn (1994: 66–68). The Double V campaign sought to achieve victory over the Axis powers abroad and against racial prejudice at home.

42. Polsgrove (2001: 177–180), Zinn (2002 [1964]: 86–88).

43. Zinn (1994: 74–75). Also see Ransby (2003: 310–311).

44. Zinn (1994: 74–75, 78, 81).

45. Zinn (1994: 126–138).

46. Zinn and Dellinger had both traveled to Japan in 1966, where peace initiatives were already under way (Zinn 1994: 126).

47. Zinn was among those who helped Daniel Berrigan go underground (Zinn 1994: 134–136).

48. Zinn (1994: 97).

49. Zinn, interviews with the author (February 28 and August 7, 2009), Zinn (1994: 116).

50. Chomsky, interview with the author (November 12, 2010); Barsky (1998: 103–104).

51. Newfield (1966: 37–38).

52. Barsky (1998: 41–56), Ivol (2009).

53. Terkel (2007: 110–115).

54. Zinn, interview with the author at Boston University (April 11, 2007).

55. Schrecker (2004).

56. Chomsky, interview with the author (November 11, 2010); Barsky (1998: 88, 106–107).

57. Lynd and Lynd (2009), Schrecker (2004).

58. Staughton Lynd opposed the party line at fourteen years old, while Eugene Genovese was rapidly expelled for "having zigged when [he] was supposed to zag." Both retained an interest in Marxism as a method but came to formulate their politics differently based on this early disillusionment with communism at the start of the Cold War era. See Novick (1988: 428, 432, 435–436). For a further discussion of these scholars' formative years, see Lynd and Lynd (2009) and Genovese (1995: 289–301).

59. The "good war" concept is taken from Studs Terkel's (1987) oral history of World War II, in which he uses quotation marks to emphasize the ambivalence of the association of the adjective "good" with the reality of warfare.

CHAPTER 4

1. Marx and Engels (1998: 571).

2. I should clarify that I neither knew Howard Zinn nor would regard myself as having special expertise in his life and work. I approach the subject from the point of view of an interest in what it is to be a radical intellectual and in doing so (hopefully) avoid the tendency to hagiography that might arise in an exploration of intellectual as exemplar.

3. Zinn (1997c: 500). This quotation comes from the essay "The Uses of Scholarship," to which we will return as a key text for this appraisal.

4. Numerous critics hold this view. See Callinicos (2006), Evans (2004), Fuller (2005), Furedi (2006), Jacoby (2000 [1987]), Johnson (2005), MacFarlane (2007), and Posner (2003).

5. Examples might include Nimtz (2000) or Reeves (2007).

6. For example, Collini (2006), Gramsci (2011), and Shils (1997). Of course, the division is conceptual and not always clear-cut. Collini (2006), for example, has a section of the text on individual thinkers, and Collini (1991) interweaves the two approaches.

7. See Hill (1991).

8. For a discussion of the concept, see Small (2002).

9. Richard Posner's book deserves more careful treatment than this passing reference and has been the subject of hostile reviews that belie its value, however flawed. A useful summary source is http://www.complete-review.com/quarterly/vol3/issue2/posner.htm (accessed August 15, 2011).

10. Zinn's is recorded in respect of media mentions, web hits, and scholarly citations between 1995 and 2000 as having 356 media mentions, 6,857 web hits, and eighty-four scholarly citations (Posner 2003: 206).

11. Actually, the historical truth of Socrates suggests a somewhat different representation than the classic one in sources such as Jaspers (1962), where Socrates is compared with Jesus Christ, the Buddha, and Confucius. Also see Waterfield (2009) and Wilson (2007).

12. See, for example, Frede (2011) and Raeff (1966).

13. These voices are most often associated with social commentary and political dissidence, with writings that could be located within the nascent social sciences. It is worth considering, however, that the history of intellectual thought has its own prejudices, and the philosophical and political enlightenment that inspired modernity were intertwined with a romantic enlightenment that can be traced from the Lakeland poets through to postmodern critics. See Beran (2001).

14. Zola (1997).

15. Nimtz (2000) is an exemplary study of Marx (and Engels) as a political activist and intellectual within working-class organizations, complementing the traditional focus on his writings.

16. Giddens (1998, 1999, 2000, 2002). For reference to Giddens's Libyan connections, see http://www.guardian.co.uk/education/2011/mar/04/lse-libya-anthony-giddens-gaddafi. An example of his outstanding and perceptive understanding of the Muammar al-Gaddafi regime includes the assessment: "Gaddafi's 'conversion' may have been driven

partly by the wish to escape sanctions, but I get the strong sense it is authentic and there is a lot of motive power behind it. Saif Gaddafi is a driving force behind the rehabilitation and potential modernisation of Libya. Gaddafi Sr., however, is authorising these processes."

17. Lenin's vanguardism and the role of the intellectual can be explored in Lenin (1968, 1989), Lih (2008), and Thatcher (2007).

18. The best presentation of Antonio Gramsci's writings on the intellectual can be found in Gramsci (2011). Volume 2 contains most of his observations on intellectuals.

19. He considers this in writings such as "Types of Periodicals" and his many musings on novels, writings, and the role of the intellectual in producing socialist journals in Gramsci (2011).

20. See Bensaid (2009a, 2009b), Birchall (2011), Cliff (1997, 2000), Mandel (1995), and Stutje (2009).

21. See Marcuse (1955, 1968, 1971), Katz (1982), Kellner (1984), and Abremeit and Cobb (2004).

22. See Hayden (2006), Horowitz (1967), and Mills (1959, 2000, 2008).

23. See Mills (1959: 196–214).

24. Spivak (1988: 24–28).

25. Foucault (2001).

26. For Zinn's thinking on this, see http://kasamaproject.org/2010/02/01/howard -zinn-je-ne-suis-pas-marxiste (accessed August 31, 2011).

27. Zinn (1997c: 420–426).

28. Zinn (1997d).

29. Much of what I cite is referenced from Zinn's shorter works from this collection.

30. Zinn (1997c: 16).

31. Zinn (1997c: 19).

32. Column reprinted in Zinn (1997c: 329).

33. Column reprinted in Zinn (1997c: 367–402).

34. Zinn (1997c: 499–508).

35. Zinn (1997c: 506).

36. Zinn eloquently outlines these points in a 2001 lecture on Social Disengagement, which can be heard at http://www. unwelcomeguests.net/070_-_Howard_Zinn_on _Social_ Disengagement_(The_Social_Role_of_The_Intellectual).

37. Said (1994: 84).

CHAPTER 5

1. Zinn (2002 [1964]).

2. Day (2005), Gelderloos (2007).

3. Zinn (1997c, 2007a).

4. Kornbluh (1964).

5. These two questions map onto what the editors call the "macro-concerns of direct democracy and disobedience and the micro-nature of dual convictions and dispositions." The question of how we participate deals with the macro-concerns, while why we participate is answered by the micro level.

6. Ward (1988 [1973]).

7. Leon Trotsky argued for the idea of permanent revolution, while many revolutionary anarchists see direct action as both a means to revolution and an end in itself. Richard Day (2005: 70) asserts that many social movements in the 1960s also argued that means

and ends should be in harmony. Colin Ward (1988 [1973]) argues that there are already existent institutions in society that enact these relations.

8. Writing during the nineteenth century, Michael Bakunin is probably the most famous advocate for anarchist revolution. Contemporary advocates of revolutionary anarchism include Peter Gelderloos (2007), Albert Meltzer (1996), and the Invisible Committee (2009 [2007]).

9. Graeber (2009: 203).

10. See Piven (2011) and Schneider (2011). Also see Graeber (2012) for his personal involvement in the Zuccotti Park Occupy camps.

11. Zinn (1997c) has collected a number of short pieces that tell these "in-a-nutshell"–type stories about American anarchists.

12. Zinn (1997c: 47).

13. Also see Zinn (2006a: 129).

14. Zinn (2001e: 41).

15. Zinn (2002: 67).

16. Zinn (2010b: 4).

17. Vodovnik (2008).

18. Unlike liberalism, where liberty and equality often contradict each other, anarchism argues for both liberty and equality to buttress and support the other.

19. It also seems strange to talk about Zinn's "political theory" as some set of ideas separate from his life, his activism, and his teaching. Certainly, Zinn made the personal political in a way rarely seen in academia.

20. Zinn (1997b: 62).

21. Zinn (2002 [1968]: 87).

22. Zinn (1991: 123).

23. Emphasis in the original. Zinn (2002: 7).

24. Zinn (2001e: 21).

25. My thanks to Joel Olson for the reminder on this point.

26. Jane Stembridge quoted in Zinn (2002 [1964]: 36).

27. The subtitle of Zinn's book on SNCC is *The New Abolitionists*. For an argument that the most radical of the antebellum abolitionists like William Lloyd Garrison and the Liberty Party were anarchist, see Perry (1973).

28. Dual power means living within capitalist and statist society while building alternate institutions that practice anarchism in everyday life.

29. In some states like Mississippi, Jim Crow was actually a tyranny of a numerical minority because blacks made up a majority of the population.

30. Zinn (2002 [1964]: 74) quotes Bob Moses from SNCC: "We believe the local F.B.I. are sometimes in collusion with the local sheriffs and chiefs of police, and that Negro witnesses aren't safe in telling inside information to local agents of the F.B.I."

31. Zinn (2002 [1964]: 200).

32. Zinn (2002 [1994]: 67).

33. For in-depth discussions of the IWW and their relationship to the growth of civil liberties and the selective incorporation doctrine for speech and association, see Dubofsky (1969), Foner (1965), Murphy (1979), and Preston (1963). More often than not, the speech and association rights of IWW leaders and members were not upheld by courts.

34. Zinn (2002 [1964]).

35. Zinn (2002 [1968]: 88). For Zinn (1991: 143), civil disobedience is "aimed directly at informing and arousing the public."

36. Zinn's book on SNCC is a masterful mix of reportage; normative political theory; nuts-and-bolts descriptions of meetings and organizing; and descriptions of the difficulties of consensus-building, decentralized organization, and spontaneity in protest movements.

37. Zinn (2002 [1968]: 87). Emphasis in original.

38. May (1994: 47).

39. Zinn (1991: 233).

40. Zinn (1991: 258) calls it "the puny act of voting."

41. Zinn (1991: 255).

42. Zinn (1991: 251).

43. Zinn (1991: 257).

44. Zinn (2006b: 12).

45. Zinn (2002 [1994]).

46. Zinn (2002 [1964]: 29).

47. Zinn (2003c: 49–50).

48. Zinn (2001e: 39).

49. Zinn (2001e: 22).

50. David Graeber (2009: 212) writes that anarchism is "an ethical discourse about revolutionary action. The basic principles of anarchism—self-organization, voluntary association, mutual aid, the opposition to all forms of coercive authority—are essentially moral and organizational."

51. Day (2005: 117).

52. Bakunin is most noted for his emphasis on complete revolution, but also see Meltzer (1996), Day (2005), and Graeber (2009).

53. Zinn (2001e: 21).

54. As Colin Ward writes in a 1958 column in the anarchist newspaper *Freedom*, revolution is impractical, utopian, and vague, and his anarchism "recognizes that the conflict between authority and liberty is a permanent aspect of the human condition and not something that can be resolved by a vaguely specified social revolution. It recognizes that the choices between libertarian and authoritarian solutions occur every day and in every way, and the extent to which we choose, or act, or are fobbed off with, or lack the imagination and inventiveness to discover alternatives to, the authoritarian solutions to the small problems is the extent to which we are their powerless victims in big affairs." Quoted in Goodway (2006: 316).

55. Sparrow, "Anarchist Politics and Direct Action." Quoted in Graeber (2009: 202).

56. Graeber (2009: 203).

57. Ward (1988 [1973]).

58. Goodway (2006: 316).

59. These are, of course, the final words of the famous preamble of the IWW's constitution. See Flank (2007:10).

60. To "fan the flames of discontent," as a number of later editions advertise on the front cover.

61. See Salerno (1989) and Rosemont (2003) for wide-ranging discussions of the culture and community of the IWW.

62. Zinn (2001e: 93). Emphasis in original.

63. Zinn (2001e: 87).

64. The editors refer to the importance of culture as Zinn's "disposition" toward making radical ideas accessible to a broader audience. Here, there is "an understanding and emphasis by Zinn toward the importance of influence and change through popular arts and culture."

65. Zinn (2006b: 10).
66. Zinn (2001e: 21).

CHAPTER 6

1. Alexander (1992: 100).
2. Released on July 30, 2010, as a result of a Freedom of Information Act request, http://www.fbi.gov/foia/electronic-reading-room/zinn-howard.
3. Zinn (2002 [1986]: viii).
4. Vodovnik (2008) and Zinn Papers, during interview with the author in Boston (March 13, 2008). In 2010 and 2011 the Howard Zinn Papers were relocated from Boston University to the Tamiment Library and Robert F. Wagner Labor Archives, New York University. More information about the Howard Zinn Papers, now fully indexed and processed, is available at http://dlib.nyu.edu/findingaids/html/tamwag/tam_542/.
5. Santos, Nunes, and Meneses (2008).
6. Zinn (2009 [1997]), Perlin (1979), and Falk (1978).
7. Zinn (1999: xii–xiii). See also Zinn (2003 [1990]: 275).
8. Bakunin in Dolgoff (1980: 255).
9. Howard Zinn, interview with the author in Wellfleet, MA (August 4, 2009).
10. Zinn (2002 [1964]: 7).
11. Zinn in Vodovnik (2012: ix).
12. Zinn in Vodovnik (2012: ix).
13. Zinn (2009 [1997]: 676–677).
14. Graeber (2004: 212).
15. Epstein (2001: 1).
16. Grubačić (2004: 35).
17. Zinn (2009 [1997]: 673).
18. Goldman (1969 [1910]: 63).
19. Zinn (2009 [1997]: 679).
20. Zinn (2002 [1968]: 25).
21. Scott (1990: 200).
22. Zinn, interview with the author in Boston (March 13, 2008).
23. Zinn (2002 [1994]: x).
24. Graeber (2007: 366).
25. Zinn (2002 [1973]: 237).
26. Zinn (2002 [1964]: 8).
27. Zinn (2009 [1997]: 438).
28. Zinn (2009 [1997]: 414).
29. Zinn (2009 [1997]: 709).
30. See also Novick (1988).
31. Zinn (1990 [1970]: 3).
32. Zinn (1990 [1970]: 14).
33. Lynd in Grubačić (2010: 120).
34. Zinn (2005 [1980]: 10).
35. Santos, Nunes, and Meneses (2008: xix).
36. Zinn (1990 [1970]: 6).
37. Zinn (2009 [1997]: 543).
38. Zinn (2002 [1964]: i).
39. Zinn (1990 [1970]: 33).

40. Zinn (1990 [1970]: 33).
41. Zinn quoted in Joyce (2003: 84).
42. Zinn (2002 [1974]).
43. Zinn (2009 [1997]: 608).
44. Zinn (2009 [1997]: 712).
45. Zinn (2009 [1997]: 684).
46. Zinn, interview with the author in Boston (March 13, 2008).
47. Zinn (2002 [1968]: 116).
48. Landauer (2010 [1910]: 249).
49. Landauer (2010 [1910]: 214).
50. Zinn (2002 [1964]: 275).
51. See also Bey (2003: 60).
52. Zinn (1999: 47).

CHAPTER 7

1. Quoted in Zinn (2003a: 204).
2. Various conservative commentators have challenged Zinn's scholarship as a contribution to leftist propaganda rather than to our knowledge of history. Implied or explicit in the criticism is a contention about the nature and possibility of objectivity. For Zinn, objectivity was neither possible nor desirable. He contended that scholarship in history needed to be provocative morally in order to challenge those quiet, unreflective pieties justified by the pervasive and tacit standard of "national interest." These pieties lead, in the long run, to passivity, pessimism, and despair. "If history is to be creative, to anticipate a possible future without denying the past, it should," wrote Zinn, "emphasize the new possibilities by disclosing those hidden episodes of the past when, even if in brief flashes, people showed their ability to resist, to join together, occasionally to win." To disclose such features of history is not to create fiction, but to disclose what is too easily forgotten. This type of effort is certainly worthy of the name "scholarship." Zinn (2003a: x).
3. An effect of Zinn's provocations can be observed in the smear campaign from the Right that continues even after his death. In August 2010, for example, Robert Stacy McCain, writing for the *American Spectator,* offered a studied account of Zinn's FBI file. This is a particularly large and interesting dossier. It begins in March 1949, and relies on informant testimony in an attempt to prove that Zinn was a member of the Communist Party and various front groups from 1947 until at least a decade later. For the record, Zinn was described as cordial but not forthcoming by FBI officials who questioned him, and he always maintained that he was never a member of the Communist Party. But for McCain, the testimony of unnamed informants about Zinn's Communist affiliations was part of a lifelong commitment against America and a clear indication of Zinn's hypocrisy in condemning violence in the name of the United States while turning a blind eye to the murderous acts of his "communist heroes."

The article was published after Zinn's death and made no mention of this. Rather, these baseless charges against Zinn were expanded to include his "liberal admirers," who apparently partake in his anti-Americanism by association. Zinn was a thorn in the side of many of the conservatives and conservative organizations that conceive of the university as a waste of public funds (at least for the courses they don't like) and the enemy of free speech by abusing (that is to say "using") this constitutional right. These include Lynne Cheney, David Horowitz, the National Alumni Forum (NAF), and the National Association of Scholars (NAS), and extend beyond charges of liberal bias in the humanities and sciences that animate the culture wars to anti-intellectual claims about the cost-ineffectiveness of higher education (particularly when education is extended to members of the public who have been traditionally disenfranchised).

4. According to the majority in *Garcetti v. Ceballos,* 547 U.S. 410 (2006), the professor's First Amendment rights, if she or he is a public employee, "do not insulate their communications from employer discipline." This case, so threatening to academic freedom, will be discussed in the next section. For a study of the constitutional underpinnings of academic freedom, and an argument for the coexistence of the constitutional and professional definitions of academic freedom, see Metzger (1988). Consider, too, the 2011 battle over the emails of University of Wisconsin professor William Cronon instigated by the state's Republican Party and its implications for free speech and academic freedom. See "Scholar as Citizen," at http://scholarcitizen.williamcronon.net.

5. This divide is captured by Richard Rorty (1996: 21), who observed, "As Americans use the term, 'academic freedom' names some complicated local folkways that have developed in the course of the past century, largely as a result of battles fought by the American Association of University Professors. These customs and traditions insulate colleges and universities from politics and from public opinion. In particular, they insulate teachers from pressure from the public bodies or private boards who pay their wages."

6. Finkin and Post (2009: 7).

7. Finkin and Post (2009: 7).

8. Zinn (2009b: 607).

9. For a discussion of the underlying epistemic rigidity of disciplinary boundaries in higher education, see Lamont (2009: Chapter 3).

10. Zinn (2009b: 609).

11. There were thoughtful critical responses to the book, too. Consider Michael Kazin's (2004) take on Zinn's "Manichean" view of history as it was presented in *A People's History of the United States,* as an example.

12. Indeed, this dynamic of uncovering the truth is a key to understanding Zinn's own take on academic freedom. He sees it from the student's side of the desk as a perilous wager that heightens the responsibility of the professor. "True, there is a tradition of academic freedom, but it is based on a peculiar unspoken contract. The student, in return for the economic security of a career and several years with some degree of free intellectual play, is expected upon graduation to become an obedient citizen, participating happily in the nation's limited pluralism (be a Republican or a Democrat, but please, nothing else)" (Zinn 2009b: 611).

13. Zinn (2009b: 610–611).

14. Zinn acknowledges that "without the lucky winning of tenure, John Silber's arrival as president of Boston University would have ended my job." Still, he was penalized for his various stances by being denied annual pay raises or even teaching assistants for his courses that attracted more than 400 students. See Zinn (2002 [1994]: 185). Zinn's example illuminates threats to academic freedom posed by the decline in the ratio of tenured faculty to pre-tenured and non-tenure-track, adjunct faculty in colleges and universities today, described by Cary Nelson (2010) as "the lumpen professoriate." See Bousquet (2008: 2). One effect of this shift is the reshaping of graduate education away from moving prospective professors through the degree process and toward academic careers, and toward a system that exploits the teaching labor of graduate students even as the number of students who complete their doctorates declines. Menand (2010: 153) examines the deleterious effect of this shift within higher education in terms of the intellectual conformism ("The academic profession in some areas is not reproducing itself as much as cloning itself") and disenchantment with academia. Zinn stands as an example

of what might be lost with the continued effacement of tenure. Already, the decline in tenured faculty leads to the exploitation documented by Marc Bousquet, Menand, and others, as well as the withdrawal of professors from campus governance, particularly where involvement entails resistance to corporate and military influences on curriculum and other vital areas of campus life.

15. Zinn (2002 [1994]: 186).

16. Zinn (2002 [1994]: 186).

17. Zinn (2002 [1994]: 186).

18. Zinn (2002 [1994]: 186–187).

19. The framers of the 1915 *Declaration* created a policy that was largely antithetical to various laws regarding the speech and intellectual rights of those employed by public institutions, as well as the conventions governing the relations of trustees and presidents of universities to their faculty. "As this was the legal landscape on which the 1915 *Declaration* was mapped, it is not surprising that the drafters drew no support from the law and made no claim to it." See the AAUP Report, "Protecting an Independent Faculty Voice: Academic Freedom after *Garcetti v. Ceballos*" (AAUP 2009: 68).

20. *Connick v. Myers,* 461 U.S. 138, 142 (1983), and *Pickering v. Board of Ed. of Township High School Dist. 205, Will Cty.,* 391 U.S. 563 (1968). For an overview of these cases and their implications for academic freedom, see Nelson (2010: 46–50).

21. "When public employees make statements pursuant to their official duties, they are not speaking as citizens for First Amendment purposes, and the Constitution does not insulate their communications from employer discipline" (Syllabus [court document], 1) This formulation, without making an exception for professors, is a direct contradiction of the terms of academic freedom and the role of professors on their campuses, set forth in the 1915 *Statement.* "The principle of academic freedom," wrote Arthur O. Lovejoy, "is ... from a purely economic point of view, a paradoxical one; it asserts that those who buy a service may not ... prescribe the nature of the service to be rendered." Quoted in Finkin and Post (2009: 33).

22. *Hong v. Grant,* 516 F. Supp. 2d 1158 (C.D. Cal. 2007); *Renken v. Gregory,* 541 F.3d 769 (7th Cir. 2008); and *Gorum v. Sessoms,* 2008 U.S. Dist. LEXIS 10366 (D. Del, February 12, 2008), 561 E3d 179 (3d Cir. 2009).

23. *Pickering v. Board of Education* (1968), *Connick v. Myers* (1983), and *Hong v. Grant* (2007).

24. See Butler (2006: 107–142). Inhibitions about raising controversial issues— i.e., Israel and Palestine—in academic forums are accentuated in the post-9/11 era and illuminate the sort of political quietism among faculty that Howard Zinn opposed as a renunciation of academic freedom. See also Carvalho and Downing (2010).

25. Cited in Nelson (2010: 48–49).

26. The AAUP did in fact file an *amicus* brief in *Garcetti v. Ceballos,* but there was no political extension to this expression of concern and dissent in the form of campus protests prior to the decision, or a unified response by colleges and universities to the decision.

27. Zinn (1990: 109).

28. When confronted by opponents of the state, Zinn was careful to express solidarity over shared goals while distinguishing his political strategies—his notion of democracy as a process that welcomed and empowered the voiceless—that were geared toward using state power to achieve desired ends. Zinn illustrated this thought while recounting a moment during the march in Selma in 1965. Demonstrations and marches had been met with mass arrests, and beatings so severe that the Johnson administration was embarrassed into sending the National Guard to protect the civil-rights workers. Zinn was walking with a pacifist named Eric Weinberger, who opposed the presence of the soldiers. He

asked Zinn what he thought; "'Yes, I'm glad they're here,' I said. I understood his point. He was holding steady to the pacifist-anarchist principle: do not use instruments of the state, even on your behalf; do not use coercion, even against violent racists. But I was not an absolutist on the use of the state if, under pressure, it becomes a force for good. We agreed to disagree" (Zinn 2002 [1994]: 201).

29. Zinn read Goldman for inspiration, not for political vision or strategy. I'm not sure how best to describe his orientation to anarchist politics. Was it a matter of revolutionary rhetoric employed for reformist ends, or was it a far simpler (and scholarly) matter of finding courage and imagination in the incendiary visions of those who struggled before you and with you? I lean toward the latter interpretation after reading Zinn's autobiography. His brand of anarchism (if I can call it that) was closer to the thinking and action he found in the pages of Thoreau. This was because he found in Thoreau an answer to the question that was probably the closest to Zinn's heart: *"How shall we live our lives in a society that makes being human more and more difficult?"* (Emphasis is Zinn's). (Zinn (2007b: 122). For other interpretations of Zinn's anarchism, see Chapters 5 and 6 of this volume. Boehme and Vodovnik both present Zinn's anarchist inclinations as being more pronounced than this reading suggests.

30. Zinn (1997c: 545).

31. By 1980, the Supreme Court presented a set of obstacles to faculty unionization by regarding the faculty of Yeshiva University as "managerial employees" and thus barred from the collective-bargaining rights guaranteed by the National Labor Relations Act. *NLRB v. Yeshiva University,* 444 U.S. 672 (1980). See the treatment of this case and the inclusion of Justice Brennan's dissent in Bousquet (2008: Chapter 3, Appendix A).

32. Benjamin (2010).

33. While Zinn expressed the values of individual freedom associated with liberalism, it should be noted that he resisted the label as a description of his politics. At around the age of seventeen, he participated in a protest in Times Square waged by young communists. Zinn was bludgeoned unconscious, and after awakening in a doorway he found that he could never again place his faith in free speech as guaranteed by the Constitution: "From that moment on, I was no longer a liberal, a believer in the self-correcting character of American democracy. I was a radical, believing that something fundamental was wrong in this country—not just the existence of poverty amidst great wealth, not just the horrible treatment of black people, but something rotten at the root. The situation required not just a new president or new laws, but an uprooting of the old order, the introduction of a new kind of society—cooperative, peaceful, egalitarian" (Zinn 2002 [1994]: 173).

34. Many thanks to my colleague Stephen Bird for raising this important point in his commentary on an earlier version of this essay.

35. National Public Radio (NPR) invited David Horowitz to comment on Howard Zinn's legacy on the occasion of his death in January 2010. Horowitz used the occasion to comment, "There is absolutely nothing in Howard Zinn's intellectual output that is worthy of any kind of respect. Zinn represents a fringe mentality which has unfortunately seduced millions of people at this point in time. So he did certainly alter the consciousness of millions of younger people for the worse." It should be noted that the inclusion of Horowitz in the tribute to the life and work of Zinn was met with significant criticism both of NPR's editorial policy that seemed designed to anticipate and preempt criticisms from the Right and of Horowitz's banal and shrill consideration of Zinn's life and work (not to mention Horowitz's mathematics). See the transcript and response at http://www .npr.org/blogs/ombudsman/2010/02/howard_zinns_obit.html. It also should be noted that the silliness of Horowitz's remarks was not an aberrant moment in his career as a critic of

the university as, so he characterizes it, a stronghold of liberal subversion. Zinn was also featured in Horowitz (2007).

36. "The 1940 *Statement* provides assurances for the protection of academic freedom, but defines 'academic freedom' only in the most general terms. Academic freedom requires 'full freedom in research,' 'freedom in the classroom,' and 'free[dom] from institutional censorship or discipline' for citizens and 'officers' of educational institutions" (Finkin and Post 2009: 48). These generalizations, it was understood, would be instantiated and substantiated by concrete challenges and the investigations that would ensue.

37. He was an academic who was not afraid to criticize the kind of scholarship he saw coming out of the academy that lacked political relevance, celebrated the trivial and the esoteric, and, worst of all distracted from the real suffering going on in the world in the name of "disinterestedness," "neutrality," and "objectivity." This is the sort of work where professors "publish while others perish." See Zinn (2009b: 533–542).

38. In this, Zinn seemed to tap into the transcendentalist antecedents on the intellectual life. "The intellect goes out of the individual, floats over its own personality, and regards it as a fact, and not as *I* or *mine*. He who is immersed in what concerns person and place cannot see the problem of existence. This the intellect always ponders" (Emerson 1926: 230).

Chapter 8

1. Zinn (2009b).
2. Strada (2005).
3. Arendt (1969).
4. "Howard Zinn: The Financial and War Crisis Have Created an Opportunity for Real Change, Pt5/5, Democracy and Militarism," *Real News* (October 26, 2008), http://therealnews.com/t2.
5. I had the great pleasure to study with Zinn, to learn great lessons from him, to remain inspired by his example, and to speak with him shortly before he died. It was altogether glorious to write parts of this essay as I participated in the Occupy Wall Street movement. I gathered some of my thoughts for this contribution while reading in the People's Library, which sat on the northeast corner of Liberty Square. As I marched through lower Manhattan with a friend in early October, I said, "I wish Zinn could be here now." My friend responded, "Howard is here." We looked out upon the vast crowd, people holding signs and chanting together for social justice. My friend was right. Howard was there. He was everywhere.
6. Zinn (1997 [1980]: 266–267). To see and hear Zinn make these and similar points, I recommend "On Human Nature and Aggression," which is from *You Can't Be Neutral on a Moving Train* (1994).
7. Zinn (1997 [1980]: 63).
8. Zinn (2007a: 177).
9. Zinn (1997 [1980]: 63).
10. Zinn shares these arguments in "On Human Nature and Aggression," in *You Can't Be Neutral on a Moving Train* (1994).
11. For those interested in a recent study that draws on science to contest that war is natural, see John Horgan (2012). Horgan maintains that war is a human invention and therefore can be overcome. He claims that science shows war is "far from being deeply rooted in our nature." While 80 percent of people he interviewed say war will never end, it is not science that backs up this perspective, but cultural perception. Horgan concludes

that while science proves neither a proclivity for war nor for peace, moral will is necessary to end war. See also the work of Steven Pinker (2011), an experimental psychologist, who argues that the human species is living with less violence now than in previous times. Both works, in different ways, can be read productively as one considers Zinn's position that it is possible to eradicate war.

12. Twain (1957: 664–665).

13. "Howard Zinn: The Financial and War Crisis Have Created an Opportunity for Real Change, Pt5/5, Democracy and Militarism," *Real News* (October 26, 2008), http://therealnews.com/t2.

14. Zinn (2002 [1967]: 51).

15. Arendt (1963: 287).

16. Arendt (1963: 287–288).

17. Beauvoir (1948: 49).

18. "On Human Nature and Aggression," in *You Can't Be Neutral on a Moving Train* (1994).

19. Zinn (2011a: 163).

20. For example, "I am a veteran of the Second World War. That was considered a 'good war,' but I have come to the conclusion that war solves no fundamental problems and only leads to more wars. War poisons the minds of soldiers, leads them to kill and torture, and poisons the soul of the nation" (Zinn 2005).

21. Zinn (2001b).

22. Zinn (2011a: 24).

23. Iraq Body Count, http://www.iraqbodycount.org/analysis/numbers/2011.

24. Zinn (2007a: 91).

25. Arendt (1969: 52).

26. Zinn (2007a: 60).

27. There is a debate among researchers over the proportion of civilian to military deaths in contemporary armed conflict. The Stockholm International Peace Research Institute, as well as a number of scholars such as Mary Kaldor and Dan Smith, estimates that the ratio for contemporary conflicts is as high as 9:1. However, a recent article by Adam Roberts (2010) challenges these figures, arguing that they are inaccurate and in some cases based on wild estimates. Roberts holds that the available evidence demonstrates a wider variety of civilian to military casualties from conflict to conflict. He concludes that the percentage of civilian casualties is closer to 40 percent, depending upon how casualties are defined. See Kaldor (1999: 100), Smith (1997: 24–25), and Stockholm International Peace Research Institute (SIPRI) (1990).

28. Zinn (2002 [1967]: 64).

29. Zinn (2002 [1967]: 64).

30. Zinn (2002 [1967]: 64).

31. Horwitz (2011: 1).

32. Hyde (2002: 259–280).

33. John Brown's last words are published in various books. For a recent study of Brown's legacy, see Horwitz (2011: 211–213, Chapter 10).

34. Zinn's *The People Speak* is both a book and a film. It had been performed many times before it was produced as a film.

35. Zinn (2002 [1967]: 65).

36. "Wars end in stalemates, as with the United States in Korea, or with Iran and Iraq, or in forced withdrawals, as the United States in Vietnam, the Soviet Union in Afghanistan. So called 'victories,' as Israel in the 1967 war, bring no peace, no security. Civil wars become endless, as in El Salvador, and after rivers of blood the participants must turn

to negotiated settlements. The contras in Nicaragua could not win militarily, and finally had to negotiate with a political solution" (Zinn 2003b: 296).

37. Tabeau and Bijak (2005).
38. Leitenberg (2006: 9).
39. Zinn (2005).

CHAPTER 9

1. Jamail (2007: 222–257).
2. Jubran (2004).
3. I'm speaking generally about the antiwar movement. There have been groups and individuals within the antiwar movement since the invasions of Afghanistan and Iraq who have fought against these trends, such as Dahlia Wasfi, Amer Jubran, and various socialist and anarchist groups. However, these groups and individuals have always been a minority.
4. Caputi (2011b).
5. Caputi (2012).
6. Taylor (2007: 342–343).
7. Smiley (2010).
8. Smiley (2010).
9. Gilbert (2006: 94–109).
10. Sosa (2009: 217).
11. I thank Professor David Lyons at Boston University Law School for helping me think through the complexities of collective responsibility.
12. Throughout this chapter, I use "group" and "collective" interchangeably.
13. Feinberg (1968: 681).
14. Feinberg (1968: 681–682).
15. Feinberg (1968: 681–682).
16. Feinberg (1968: 687).
17. This section is inspired by Joel Feinberg's (1968) taxonomy of different forms of collective responsibility.
18. Gilbert (2006: 109). Emphasis in original.
19. Gilbert (2006: 110).
20. Declaration of the Jury of Conscience at the World Tribunal on Iraq (2006: 168–178).
21. Räikkä (1997: 96).
22. Räikkä (1997: 104).
23. Räikkä (1997: 102–104).
24. Quinton (2011).
25. Reiff (2008: 235).
26. Reiff (2008: 210).
27. Reiff (2008: 210–213).
28. Reiff (2008: 224–228).
29. Reiff (2008: 226). Emphasis in original.
30. Jamail (2004).
31. Al-Darraji (2010a).
32. Mansour (2009: 275–339).
33. Jamail (2012).
34. Caputi (2011a).

35. Al-Darraji (2010b).
36. Graham (2006: 259–262).
37. Bandura (1999: 193).
38. McWilliams and Wheeler (2009: 92).
39. Caputi (2011a).
40. Caputi (2011c).
41. Lifton (2006: 340–341).
42. Zinn (1997d: 292).
43. Zinn (2002: 22–23).
44. Zinn (1994: 87).
45. Zinn (1994: 97).
46. Zinn (1994: 94).
47. Zinn (1994: 94).
48. Zinn (1997d: 283).
49. Zinn (1997d: 284–285).
50. Zinn (2006c).
51. Graham (2006: 258).
52. Tirman (2009).

CHAPTER 10

1. Zinn (2003c: 10).
2. Zinn (2002 [1994]: 143).
3. Zinn (2002 [1994]: 7).
4. "On the Spoken Word Movement of the 1990s," email correspondence between Bob Holman and Mark Miazga (December 22, 1998).
5. Zinn (2002 [1994]: 203).
6. Zinn (2002 [1994]: 207–208).
7. I borrow here from the counterpublic theory of Michael Warner (2002a, 2002b) and Nancy Fraser (1990).
8. Warner (2002b: 424–425).
9. Zinn (2001c).
10. Rich (2001).
11. Zinn (2010b).
12. Shulman (1996 [1972]).
13. Foucault (1989: 305–306).
14. Zinn (2003c: 31). Emphasis added.
15. Zinn (2002 [1994]: 152).
16. Zinn (2002 [1994]: 7).
17. The entire poem and further discussion of this controversy can be found at http://www.amiribaraka.com.
18. Importantly, during the same period as Baraka's dismissal, the National Library of Congress recruited Poet Laureate Billy Collins to project a pathos toward patriotism in an emotional poem called simply "The Names." The poem was read before a special joint session of Congress.
19. I use these interchangeably because I am not convinced it is useful, as I am arguing in this piece, to invoke these distinctions to classify political roles.
20. Zinn (2009 [1997]: 539–540).
21. Zinn (2009 [1997]: 694).

22. Burton (2003).
23. Zinn (2002 [1994]: 201).
24. Zinn (2002 [1994]: 208).
25. Zinn (2002 [1994]: 208).
26. Zinn (2002 [1994]: 201).
27. Goodman (1986).
28. Zinn (2004b: 84).
29. Zinn (2003c: 91).

CHAPTER 11

1. Hampton (2006).
2. Morgan (2010).
3. In addition, I should mention the correspondence I enjoyed with Zinn going back some twenty years. I am grateful for the many thoughts he shared with respect to my own writing projects, in particular for his generous willingness to write the foreword to my book *The Sixties Experience* (1991).
4. Although, of course, in his play *Marx in Soho,* Zinn used the actual language of Karl Marx in ways that helped shed light on contemporary ills.
5. Zinn (1994: 8).
6. Shulman (1996 [1972]).
7. A phrase I borrow from Lawrence Grossberg (1997), referring to ways in which consumerism and popular culture often revolve around providing a relatively powerless population "feelings of empowerment" that divert them from real political change.
8. Zinn (1994: 10).
9. As George Katsiaficas (1987: 10) puts it, "the massive awakening of the instinctual need for justice and for freedom."
10. Indeed, Paul Hawken (2007) has argued that the world is currently experiencing the "greatest social movement in history" in the "blessed unrest" of grassroots struggles for social justice and ecological sustainability.
11. See Morgan (2010) for a documented account of the role of the media in moving the United States from the hopeful democratic awakening of the 1960s to the neoliberal politics of today.
12. See Hallin (1989), Herman and Chomsky (2002), and Kellner (1990).
13. Hallin (1989: 116–117). Emphasis added.
14. See Morgan (2010).
15. As Gadi Wolfsfeld and William A. Gamson (1993: 119) have documented, many movement activists find that the mass media speak "mainstreamese," which means that either something of their message is "lost in translation" or they need to surrender "fundamental aspects of their raison d'être" by not challenging "what is normally taken for granted."
16. I acknowledge my debt to Todd Gitlin's (1980) seminal attention to this aspect of media coverage of the New Left.
17. See Morgan (2010: 16–17, 57–58).
18. See, notably, Dewey (1946, 1966 [1916]).
19. Zinn (1994: 5).
20. By democratic Left, I am thinking of a group far more extensive than those the mass media refer to as the "Left" (i.e., the liberal wing of the Democratic Party). I mean those on the Left who are committed to a vision of democracy as a process through which

the people are empowered in their personhood and their ability to shape their collective destiny. Much of this Left critiques rather than reinforces systemic forces that suppress this empowerment. It is democratic because it believes in bottom-up as opposed to top-down empowerment.

21. On the one hand, there is evidence from the global justice and the Occupy movements that the very same dynamics affect both media coverage and protest activity. See, for example, Ross (2002) on the former and media coverage of the violence and flag-burning in Oakland in late January 2012 for the latter. On the other hand, there is always the potential that the spread of "outsider" perspectives through the wider population via the Internet can shift the play of forces to which corporate media must respond.

22. See, for example, Cooper and Thee-Brenan (2011).

23. In this, I would suggest some interesting parallels between these protest actions and the Moratorium Against the War in Vietnam, of October 15, 1969. Occurring at a time when the majority of Americans (and much of the elite) wanted the United States out of Vietnam, and populated by "everyday Americans" all over the nation, the Moratorium was the only national antiwar protest that was able to get some of its messages through mass media that were, albeit briefly, fairly sympathetic in their coverage.

24. See, for example, Page and Jacobs (2009).

25. Pew Research Center (2012).

26. For more than twenty-five years, students taking my class on social movements and legacies of the 1960s have been greatly moved by the first-person accounts and video documentaries that have revealed the motives and objectives of sixties-era movements, as well as their problematic interactions with the wider culture. They have typically noted that their "values aren't that much different from" those they have studied, but they "don't see any place" where they can join in working for similar kinds of change.

27. Morgan (2010).

28. Field and Mulford (1994).

29. Morgan (2010: 330).

30. Quoted in Aufderheide (1992: 233).

CHAPTER 12

1. Zinn and Arnove (2004: 226).
2. Ferguson (2011).
3. Zinn (1995: 619).
4. Pear (2011).
5. Pear (2011).
6. Ferguson (2011).
7. Stiglitz (2011).
8. Stiglitz (2011).
9. Sherman and Stone (2010).
10. Zinn (1990 [1970]: 75).
11. Zinn (1990 [1970]: 75).
12. Zinn (1990 [1970]: 76).
13. Zinn (1990 [1970]: 75–76).
14. Zinn (1995: 619).
15. Zinn (1990 [1970]: 20).
16. Zinn (1995: 621).
17. Zinn (1993: 45).

18. Zinn (1993: 45).

19. Zinn and Arnove (2004: 25).

20. Zinn and Arnove (2004: 27).

21. See Paul Lauter's 2001 acceptance speech on the occasion of the Hubbell Award: http://als-mla.org/HMLauter.htm.

22. Zinn and Arnove (2004: 27).

23. Zinn and Arnove (2004: 25).

24. Zinn (1997c: 501).

25. Heslam (2011).

26. Zinn (1995: 25).

27. Zinn (1993: 33–34).

28. Zinn (1995: 284).

29. Zinn (1995: 280).

30. Zinn (1995: 286).

31. Zinn and Arnove (2004: 586).

32. Fanon (2004).

33. Part of the text comes from http://occupywallst.org/about/ and *The Declaration of the Occupation of New York City* (http://www.nycga.net/resources/documents/declaration/) and the *Principles of Solidarity* (http://www.nycga.net/resources/documents/principles -of-solidarity/). Occupy website continuity varies, so these references may no longer be accurate.

34. Howard Zinn's *The People Speak* (2004a).

35. http://zinnlectures.wordpress.com/2011/10/09/purpose-of-the-lectures.

36. Schechter (2011).

37. Zinn (2011a: 7).

38. Gresh (2011).

39. *The Guardian* (2010).

40. *The Guardian* (2010).

41. Solnit (2011).

42. Marzouki (2011).

43. Toensing (2011).

44. Haddad (2011).

45. Zinn (2011b: 145).

CHAPTER 13

1. In a 1966 essay on the "Historian as Citizen," published in the *New York Times Book Review*, Zinn "welcomes the emergence" of what he calls the *activist-scholar*. We discovered this source after conceptualizing our *scholar-activist*. We kept our original concept to maintain the focus of the project, rather than revise the term to comport with Zinn's language. This is not simply a matter of semantics. Since this volume is intended to assess Zinn's ideas and scholarship, as they pertain to past, contemporary, and future events, *scholar-activist* emphasizes the former and how it relates to the latter. See Zinn (2001d).

2. After the publication of *A People's History* and the popular response it engendered, Zinn was often described as the "people's historian." This flattering title, though, does not speak to the totality of his work and appeal.

3. There is often circumspection among academics and activists toward each other. If an academic is seen by colleagues as being *too involved* in the world, that academic may jeopardize her standing as a "serious scholar." If an activist attempts to situate her

own organization's efforts within broader explanatory frameworks, she may be perceived as inattentive to the immediate needs of the movement. There is no time for scholarly reflection when the struggle is upon us, activists might assert. Some notable instances notwithstanding, Zinn was often able to bridge these two worlds—in part through his personality and charm—without losing activist credibility and still maintaining a degree of academic legitimacy.

4. See Chapters 5 and 6 for a discussion of Zinn's inclusive, antidogmatic anarchism.

5. On the *Perestroika* movement, see Monroe (2005) and Schram (2003). On the merits of methodological pluralism, more generally, see Topper (2005). As Clyde Barrow (2008: 243) describes in language that would certainly resonate with Zinn, the founding of the Caucus for a New Political Science represented "*both* a methodological and an ideological dissent from the mainstream discipline." (Emphasis in original.)

6. Miller (2010). As we discuss later in this chapter, Eric Foner also supported aspects of Zinn's intellectual and historical method (although not all of them). "Professor Zinn writes with an enthusiasm rarely encountered in the leaden prose of academic history," Foner notes in his *New York Times* review of *A People's History* (Foner 1980). In a remembrance in the *The Nation*, Foner (2010) observes that he has "long been struck by how many excellent students of history first had their passion for the past sparked by reading Howard Zinn.... *A People's History* taught an inspiring and salutary lesson—that despite all too frequent repression, if America has a history to celebrate it lies in the social movements that have made this a better country."

7. These discussions have sometimes been internalized or embodied within the analysis, not necessarily explicitly acknowledged or discussed.

8. Zinn (1990 [1970]: 13).

9. Ambre Ivol and Paul Buhle, in Chapter 2, describe how the roots of this approach had been gradually developed over the preceding decades. Zinn was one of the first scholars, though, to explicitly write for an audience beyond academia, with the goal of reaching as many people as possible.

10. Zinn (1959; 1990 [1970]: 102–117). See Ambre Ivol's discussion in Chapter 3 of Zinn's research on Fiorello La Guardia.

11. See, e.g., Smolenski and Humphrey (2007). The pioneering work of the New Left historians has been appropriated by younger scholars. Their insights are no longer considered radical (or insurgent), but rather have achieved well-regarded disciplinary status.

12. Examples include Diana Butler Bass, *A People's History of Christianity: The Other Side of the Story* (HarperOne, 2009); Clifford D. Conner, *A People's History of Science: Miners, Midwives, and 'Low Mechanicks'* (Nation Books, 2005); Chris Harman, *A People's History of the World: From the Stone Age to the New Millennium* (Verso, 2008); Peter H. Irons, *A People's History of the Supreme Court: The Men and Women Whose Cases and Decisions Have Shaped Our Constitution* (Viking, 1999); Ray Raphael, *A People's History of the American Revolution: How Common People Shaped the Fight for Independence* (Harper-Perennial, 2002); and Dave Zirin, *A People's History of Sports in the United States: 250 Years of Politics, Protest, People, and Play* (New Press, 2008). Zinn apparently approved of this emulation, as he wrote the foreword for several of these books and served as editor of the New Press's *People's History* book series.

13. Tirman (2011). Furthermore, Eric Foner defends Zinn's normative reasoning by arguing against neutrality or objectivity in academic pursuits and in the classroom: "[T]he teachers you remember are the ones with a passion for history who made it clear what they thought. They were not polemicists. They respected the canons of historical scholarship, as Zinn did, but they cared deeply. That's why the whole subject of objectivity is a bit of a misnomer. If objectivity means you balance all of the evidence and weigh it, that's absolutely

correct. If objectivity means you have no opinions of your own, what kind of person is that? Who wants to hear from them?" Quoted in Miller (2010).

14. "The values may well be subjective (derived from human needs); but the instruments must be objective (accurate). Our values should determine the *questions* we ask in scholarly inquiry, but not the answers" (Zinn 1990 [1970]: 10). Emphasis in original.

15. Abend (2008: 2).

16. Abend (2008: 3).

17. Zinn (1991: 109).

18. Zinn (1991: 299).

19. Civil disobedience is the violation of the law for social justice (Zinn 1991: 107).

20. The achievement of peace, justice, or equality "requires a constant struggle, a continuous discussion among citizens, an endless series of organizations and movements, creating a pressure on whatever procedures there are" (Zinn 1991: 257).

21. "The means for achieving social change must match, morally, the ends" (Zinn 1991: 290).

22. Zinn focused primarily on issues of class, race, and war. Issues of identity do not figure prominently into his movement activities. This shortcoming, which he acknowledged in *A People's History of the United States, 1492–Present,* will be addressed more fully in the "Identity Politics" section below.

23. Zinn (1990 [1970]: 44).

24. As Ambre Ivol and Paul Buhle point out in Chapter 2 of this volume, Zinn is hardly alone in highlighting historical events that have not been previously discussed. What distinguishes him, however, is that he was one of the few scholars with the ability to address these issues in such breadth. His demeanor and witnessing of contemporary events enhanced his popularity.

25. Zinn (1991: 51).

26. Zinn (1990 [1970]: 80).

27. Zinn (1990 [1970]: 100).

28. Those of the nineteenth century were white New Englanders who bombarded "the South and the nation with words." These new abolitionists were mostly black, from the Deep South, "who make their pleas to the nation more by physical acts of sacrifice than by verbal declamation" (Zinn 2002 [1964]: 7).

29. They are similar to their predecessors in their "healthy disrespect for respectability; they are not ashamed of being agitators and trouble-makers; they see it as the essence of democracy" (Zinn 2002 [1964]: 8).

30. Zinn's experience in Albany, Georgia, in 1961–1962 (recounted in *The Politics of History*) provides a compelling justification for participant observation as a viable method for historical study: "Traditionally, historians avoid writing the history of contemporary events. But why? Yesterday is the past, as is the nineteenth century. A perspective one year after an event is no less valuable than a perspective a hundred years later, only different. And if historians must rely for data of the past on the reporting of others, which they then cherish as 'primary sources,' why should they not create their own primary sources for both present and future use?" (Zinn 1990 [1970]: 179).

31. Zinn (2002 [1964]: 26).

32. Zinn (2002 [1964]: 77).

33. Zinn (2002 [1964]: 186–189).

34. Zinn (2002 [1967]: 64–65).

35. We believe that Zinn might not have been as absolutist against violence as Boehme suggests in his chapter.

36. Zinn (2010b: vii).

37. Arguably, Zinn has not been treated as badly as Charles Beard. Richard Hofstadter argued in 1968 that "Beard's reputation stands like an imposing ruin in the landscape of American historiography. What was once the grandest house in the province is now a ravaged survival" (Hofstadter 1968: 344). Incidentally, Hofstadter's analysis was a mixture of both criticism and praise for Beard's work. Further, Beard has experienced a resurgence of late, in part through work informed by a unique combination of progressive rational choice and economic analyses throughout the 1990s and 2000s, as well as via a renewed appreciation of his skepticism toward armed American intervention. See, e.g., Bacevich (2002) for this latter critique.

38. "Michael Kazin on the Roots of the Occupy Movement," interview with the *Browser* (November 2011), http://thebrowser.com/interviews/michael-kazin-on-roots -occupy-movement. Mattson (2007) offers a similarly scathing review of *A People's History*. The tone of Mattson's critique is especially curious in hindsight, given his recent collaboration on a popular history of liberalism with Democratic partisan and pundit Eric Alterman, who is no one's definition of a dispassionate scholar. See Alterman and Mattson (2012).

39. Kazin's concern that the "little guy never wins" in Zinn's narrative is arguably also a simplification. That said, there is a real debate over the characterization of the progress of social justice and about the nature of Zinn's optimism. We return to this issue in the discussion of Zinn's optimism later in this chapter.

40. Kazin (2011: 270).

41. Fraser (1997, 2003).

42. Barsamian (1998: 5).

43. Zinn (2005 [1980]: 686–687).

44. See Noah (2012).

45. See, e.g., McKibben (2006) and Kolbert (2006).

46. ACLU (2010). The fine investigative journalism of Glenn Greenwald of *The Guardian* and Jeremy Scahill of *The Nation*—building upon the muckraking tradition that Zinn admired—calls attention to the use of unmanned military drones (and the resulting civilian deaths) and targeted assassinations as "acceptable" instruments of foreign policy.

47. "Michael Kazin on the Roots of the Occupy Movement," interview with the *Browser* (November 2011).

48. "The four Negro youngsters in Greensboro who in 1960 walked into Woolworth's acted *as if* they would be served; Garrison and Phillips, against all apparent common sense, acted *as if* they would arouse a cold nation against slavery; England in 1940 acted *as if* it could repel a German invasion; Castro and his tiny group in the hills behaved *as if* they could take over Cuba" (Zinn 2001d: 204–205). Emphasis in original.

49. Zinn clarified his thoughts on popular power and pessimism in *Failure to Quit* (Zinn 1993: 157), stating, "I can understand pessimism, but I don't believe in it. It's not simply a matter of faith, but of historical evidence. Not overwhelming evidence, just enough to give hope, because for hope we don't need certainty, only possibility."

50. Non-violence has been predominant except in the cases of Libya and Syria, and religious and military authoritarianism are still of concern in other nations (e.g., Tunisia, Egypt).

51. Davies, Steele, and Leigh (2010).

52. Norton (2011).

53. For an assessment of the possible demobilizing effects of public opinion polls, "clicktivism," and "checkbook activism" on participation and democracy, see Asher (2011), White (2010), and Putnam (1995), respectively.

54. For instance, Egypt 2012 compared to Egypt 2011, where the protestors were not organizationally prepared for success.

55. This is an important debate that is beyond the scope of this work. In 2010, Malcolm Gladwell's piece in *The New Yorker* created a large-scale debate over the impact of digital networks in the successes of activist movements and, later, of the Arab Spring. He later noted the potential for the power of dominant interests to use these collective tools to eavesdrop, infiltrate, or remove them from a social movement that has become too dependent upon them as a tool for communication and organization. For instance, the Egyptian government's ability to turn off cell-phone networks in Egypt required significant adjustment by activists and weakened the movement considerably, although it still succeeded. See Gladwell (2010), Howard (2011), Morozov (2011), Sander (2010), and Shirky (2011).

56. Both Morozov (2011) and Khiabany (2003) have critiqued the narrative of a globalized Internet world providing increased access and opportunity.

57. Organisation for Economic Co-operation and Development (OECD) (2008).

58. Smith et al. (2009), Syvertsen et al. (2011).

59. Earl et al. (2010: 439). See Figure 4 in particular.

60. Zinn (2010b: viii).

61. Zinn (2010b: ix).

62. Zinn also appreciated art as an end in itself, for beauty. Not all history, nor all art, needs to serve a utilitarian purpose. See Zinn (2003c: 7–37, esp. 7–8).

63. Certainly others exist. Marilyn Frankenstein (2010), for example, has written on the use of "culture jamming" as a way to integrate artistic expression and political concerns in the classroom.

64. Even his critics, including the aforementioned Kazin (2004), acknowledge that Zinn did not revel in his celebrity status because he "appears to lack the egomaniacal trappings of the breed."

65. "The People Speak" also includes performances by Bob Dylan, Lupe Fiasco, Josh Brolin, Viggo Mortensen, Danny Glover, Morgan Freeman, Benjamin Bratt, Darryl "DMC" McDaniels, Marisa Tomei, and John Legend. In fact, Bruce Springsteen's album *Nebraska* was directly inspired by Zinn (see Green 2003), and Jello Biafra of the political punk band The Dead Kennedys released audio of Zinn's speeches on his own record label, Alternative Tentacles.

66. Hofstadter (1968: 345).

67. In fact, his participation in the desegregation of the Atlanta Public Library system and other civil-rights activity led to his dismissal from Spelman College, and his well-documented battles with John Silber would have certainly resulted in another dismissal had he not already been awarded tenure. The significance of Zinn's job security during his most vocal years of activism during the Vietnam War era cannot be overstated.

68. Giroux (2011).

69. Carvalho and Downing (2010).

70. Nelson (2010).

71. Joyce (2003: 180–181).

72. For a fine summary of the generally gloomy view of the current state of American higher education, see Berrett (2011).

73. See, e.g., the case of Professor William Cronon at the University of Wisconsin–Madison (Sulzberger 2011).

74. Schuessler (2012).

75. Schrecker (2010).

76. Bousquet (2008).

77. We might add that (over)specialization in the social sciences has led to a decline of the generalist intellectual tradition to which Zinn belonged. As a result, campus-based

scholars are often *less useful* to the outside world than they once were because they produce research in a "culture … whose abstruse language guarantees public irrelevance and political impotence" (Gerami 2012).

78. Certainly, we hope we are wrong. Moreover, we disagree with this argument on normative grounds. Academics—regardless of their ideological orientations—should not be restrained in their academic and activist pursuits.

79. Barsamian (1998: 20).

AFTERWORD

1. Sections of this text are updated and revised versions of Chomsky (2003) and Chomsky (2010).

2. Arnove (2012).

References

Abend, Gabriel. 2008. "Two Main Problems in the Sociology of Morality." *Theory and Society* 37, 87–125.

Abremeit, John, and W. Mark Cobb, eds. 2004. *Herbert Marcuse: A Critical Reader.* London: Routledge.

Al-Darraji, Muhamad. 2010a. "Remember Fallujah." The Justice for Fallujah Project, http://thefallujahproject.org/home/node/77.

Al-Darraji, Muhamad. 2010b. "Testimonies of Crimes against Humanity in Fallujah: Towards a Fair International Crime Trial." Conservation Centre of Environmental & Reserves in Fallujah (CCERF) and Monitoring Net of Human Rights in Iraq, http://www.uruknet.info/?p=70261.

Alexander, Doris. 1992. *Eugene O'Neill's Creative Struggle: The Decisive Decade, 1924–1933.* University Park: The Pennsylvania State University Press.

Alterman, Eric, and Kevin Mattson. 2012. *The Cause: The Fight for American Liberalism from Franklin Roosevelt to Barack Obama.* New York: Viking.

Ambrose, Stephen. 1997. *Citizen Soldiers: The US Army from the Normandy Beaches to the Bulge to the Surrender of Germany (June 7, 1944–May 7, 1945).* New York: Simon & Schuster.

American Association of University Professors (AAUP). 2009. "Protecting an Independent Faculty Voice: Academic Freedom after *Garcetti v. Ceballos.* Report. November-December, http://www.aaup.org/NR/rdonlyres/B3991F98-98D5-4CC0-9102-ED26A7AA2892/0/Garcetti.pdf.

American Civil Liberties Union (ACLU). 2010. "Establishing a New Normal: National Security, Civil Liberties, and Human Rights Under the Obama Administration." July, http://www.aclu.org/files/assets/EstablishingNewNormal.pdf

Ameringer, Oscar. 1985 [1909]. *Life and Deeds of Uncle Sam.* Chicago: Charles H. Kerr Publishers.

Arendt, Hannah. 1963. *Eichmann in Jerusalem.* New York: Penguin.

Arendt, Hannah. 1969. *On Violence.* New York: Harcourt Brace & Company.

Arguing the World. 1997. First Run Features (109 minutes). Joseph Dorman, director.

Arnove, Anthony, ed. 2012. *Howard Zinn Speaks: Collected Speeches 1963 to 2009.* Chicago: Haymarket Books.

Arnove, Anthony. 2006. *Iraq: The Logic of Withdrawal.* New York: The New Press.

Asher, Herbert. 2011. *Polling and the Public: What Every Citizen Should Know.* 8th edition. Washington, DC: CQ Press.

Aufderheide, Patricia, ed. 1992. *Beyond PC: Towards a Politics of Understanding.* St. Paul, MN: Graywolf Press.

Auletta, Ken. 2011. "The Dictator Index: A Billionaire Battles a Continent's Legacy of Misrule." *The New Yorker* (March 7).

Bacevich, Andrew. 2002. *American Empire.* Cambridge, MA: Harvard University Press.

Bandura, Albert. 1999. "Moral Disengagement in the Perpetration of Inhumanities." *Personality and Social Psychology Review* 3:3 (August), 193–209.

Barrow, Clyde W. 2008. "The Intellectual Origins of New Political Science." *New Political Science* 30:2 (June), 215–244.

Barsamian, David. 1998. "Howard Zinn: The Future of History." Interview transcript (July 27–28), Cambridge, MA.

Barsky, Robert. 1998. *Noam Chomsky: Une Voix Discordante.* Paris: Odile Jacob.

Beard, Charles. 1986 [1913]. *An Economic Interpretation of the Constitution of the United States.* New York: Free Press.

Beard, Charles, and Mary Beard. 1927. *The Rise of American Civilization.* New York: Macmillan.

Beauvoir, Simone de. 1948. *The Ethics of Ambiguity.* New York: Citadel Press.

Bell, Daniel. 1960. *The End of Ideology: On the Exhaustion of Political Ideas in the Fifties.* Glencoe, IL: Free Press.

Bell, Daniel. 1980. *The Winding Passage: Essays and Sociological Journeys, 1960–1980.* Cambridge, MA: ABT Press.

Bell, Daniel, and Irving Kristol. 1968. *Confrontation: The Student Rebellion and the Universities.* New York: Basic Books.

Bellamy, Edward. 1887. *Looking Backward: 2000–1887.* Boston: Houghton Mifflin Company.

Bender, Thomas. 1997. "Recent Trends in the Historiography of Intellectuals in the United States." In *Histoire Comparée des Intellectuels,* Nicole Racine, Marie-Christine Granjon, and Michel Trébisch, eds. (Paris: CNRS: Institut d'Histoire du Temps Présent), 165–178.

Bender, Thomas, and Wilson Smith. 2008. *American Higher Education Transformed, 1949–2005: Documenting the National Discourse.* Baltimore: Johns Hopkins University Press.

Benjamin, Ernst. 2010. "The Eroding Foundations of Academic Freedom and Professional Integrity: Implications of the Diminishing Proportion of Tenured Faculty for Organizational Effectiveness in Higher Education." *AAUP Journal of Academic Freedom,* 1.

Bensaid, Daniel. 2009a. *Marx for Our Time: Adventures and Misadventures of a Critique.* London: Verso.

Bensaid, Daniel. 2009b. *Strategies of Resistance & "Who Are the Trotskyists?"* London: IMG Publications.

Beran, David. 2001. *In the Wake of Failed Revolution: Early British Romanticism, the Frankfurt School and French Post-Structuralism.* Oxford: Peter Lang.

Berkman, Alexander. 2003 [1928]. *What Is Communist Anarchism?* Oakland, CA: AK Press.

Bernstein, Barton, ed. 1968. *Towards a New Past: Dissenting Essays in American History.* New York: Pantheon Books.

Berrett, Dan. 2011. "In for Nasty Weather." *Inside Higher Ed* (May 16).

Bey, Hakim. 2003. *T.A.Z.: The Temporary Autonomous Zone, Ontological Anarchy, Poetic Terrorism.* Brooklyn, NY: Autonomedia.

Birchall, Ian. 2011. *Tony Cliff: A Marxist for His Time.* London: Bookmarks.

Bourdieu, Pierre. 2010. *Sociology Is a Martial Art.* New York: The New Press.

Bousquet, Marc. 2008. *How the University Works: Higher Education and the Low-Wage Nation.* New York: New York University Press.

Brokaw, Tom. 1998. *The Greatest Generation.* New York: Random House.

Buhle, Paul, and Edward Rice-Maximin. 1995. *The Tragedy of Empire.* New York: Routledge.

Burton, Sarah. 2003. "Duty of Expression: Thom Yorke and Howard Zinn Debate the Artist's Role in Saving the World." *Resonance Magazine,* http://www.resonancemag.com/feature_01.html.

Butler, Judith. 2006. "Academic Norms, Contemporary Challenges: A Reply to Robert Post on Academic Freedom." In *Academic Freedom after September 11,* Beshara Doumani, ed. New York: Zone Books.

Butler, Judith. 2010. *Frames of War: When Is Life Grievable?* London: Verso.

Callinicos, Alex. 2006. *Universities in a Neo-Liberal World.* London: Bookmarks.

Caputi, Ross. 2011a. "Seeing the Truth." The Justice for Fallujah Project. http://thefallujahproject.org/home/node/57.

Caputi, Ross. 2011b. "Fallujah Veteran: 'I Served The 1%.'" *Information Clearing House* (November 8), http://www.informationclearinghouse.info/article29663.htm.

Caputi, Ross. 2011c. "I'm Sorry for the Role I Played in Fallujah." *The Guardian* (December 22), http://www.guardian.co.uk/commentisfree/2011/dec/22/fallujah-us-marine-iraq.

Caputi, Ross. 2012. "After 9 Years in Iraq: Reflections on Peace, Nonviolence, and Reconciliation." *Common Dreams* (March 18), http://www.commondreams.org/view/2012/03/18-0.

Carlin, George. 2008. "God Bless America." *It's Bad for Ya.* Eardrum/Atlantic Records.

Carson, Clayborne. 1981. *In Struggle: SNCC and the Black Awakening of the 1960s.* Cambridge, MA: Harvard University Press.

Carvalho, Edward J., and David B. Downing, eds. 2010. In *Academic Freedom in the Post-9/11 Era.* New York: Palgrave Macmillan.

Cheuse, Alan. 1963. "Laughing on the Outside: Joseph Heller, *Catch-22.*" *Studies on the Left* 3:4, 81–87.

Chomsky, Noam. 2003. "Foreword." In *Howard Zinn: A Radical American Vision,* Davis Joyce, ed. Amherst, NY: Prometheus Books, 9–13.

Chomsky, Noam. 2010. "Remembering Howard Zinn." *Resist Newsletter* (March/April).

Cliff, Tony. 1997. *Party and Class.* 2nd revised edition. London: Bookmarks.

Cliff, Tony. 2000. *A World to Win: Life of a Revolutionary.* London: Bookmarks.

Collini, Stefan. 1991. *Public Moralists: Political Thought and Intellectual Life in Britain, 1850–1930.* Oxford: Oxford University Press.

Collini, Stefan. 2006. *Absent Minds: Intellectuals in Britain.* Oxford: Oxford University Press.

Comrades from Cairo. 2011. "To the Occupy Movement—The Occupiers of Tahrir Square Are with You." *The Guardian, London* (October 25).

Connolly, William E. 2002. *Neuropolitics: Thinking, Culture, Speed.* Minneapolis: University of Minnesota Press.

Cook, Steven A., and Jared Cohen. 2011. "Q&A with Steven A. Cook and Jared Cohen on Tunisia." *Foreign Affairs* (January), http://www.foreignaffairs.com/discussions/interviews/qa-with-steven-a-cook-and-jared-cohen-on-tunisia.

Cooper, Michael, and Megan Thee-Brenan. 2011. "Majority in Poll Back Employees in Public Sector Unions." *New York Times* (February).

Cronon, William. 2011. *Scholar as Citizen.* Blog. http://scholarcitizen.williamcronon.net.

Croteau, David. 2005. "Which Side Are You On? The Tension between Movement Scholarship and Activism." In *Rhyming Hope and History: Activists, Academics and*

Social Movement Scholarship, David Croteau, William Hoynes, and Charlotte Ryan, eds. Minneapolis: University of Minnesota Press, 20–40.

Cruse, Harold. 1967. *The Crisis of the Negro Intellectual*. New York: Morrow.

Curran, Giorel. 2006. *21st Century Dissent: Anarchism, Anti-Globalization and Environmentalism*. New York: Palgrave Macmillan.

Dalton, Roque. 1995 [1975]. "Like You (Como Tú)." In *Clandestine Poems/Poemas Clandestinos*, Jack Hirschman, trans. Seattle, WA: Curbstone Books, 39–40.

Davies, Nick, Jonathan Steele, and David Leigh. 2010. "Iraq War Logs: Secret Files Show How U.S. Ignored Torture." *The Guardian* (October 22).

Day, Elizabeth. 2011. "The Slap That Sparked a Revolution." The *Observer* (May 15), http://www.guardian.co.uk/world/2011/may/15/arab-spring-tunisia-the-slap.

Day, Richard J. F. 2005. *Gramsci Is Dead: Anarchist Currents in the Newest Social Movements*. London: Pluto Press.

Declaration of the Jury of Conscience at the World Tribunal on Iraq. 2006. In *Crimes of War: Iraq*, Richard Falk, Irene Gendzier, and Robert Jay Lifton, eds. New York: Nation Books, 168–178.

Deleuze, Gilles, and Felix Guattari. 1987. *A Thousand Plateaus: Capitalism and Schizophrenia*. Minneapolis: University of Minnesota Press.

Dewey, John. 1916. *Democracy and Education: An Introduction to the Philosophy of Education*. New York: The MacMillan Company.

Dewey, John. 1946. *The Public and Its Problems: An Essay in Political Inquiry*. Chicago: Gateway (reprint).

Dewey, John. 1966 [1916]. *Democracy and Education*. New York: Free Press (reprint).

DiFranco, Ani, and Utah Phillips. 1999. *Fellow Workers*. Righteous Babe Records. Ani DiFranco, producer.

Dittmer, John. 1994. *Local People: The Struggle for Civil Rights in Mississippi*. Chicago: University of Illinois Press.

Dolgoff, Sam, ed. 1980. *Bakunin on Anarchism*. Montréal: Black Rose Books.

Donnelly, Ignatius. 1960 [1890]. *Caesar's Column: A Story of the Twentieth Century*. Cambridge, MA: Belknap Press of Harvard University Press.

Dorman, Joseph. 2002. *Arguing the World: The New York Intellectuals in Their Own Words*. New York: The Free Press.

Duberman, Martin. 2012. *Howard Zinn: A Life on the Left*. New York: The New Press.

Dubofsky, Melvyn. 1969. *We Shall Be All: A History of the Industrial Workers of the World*. Chicago: Quadrangle Books.

Du Bois, W. E. B. 1935. *Black Reconstruction in America, 1860–1880*. New York: Free Press.

Dyson, Michael Eric. 2011. "Malcolm X Revisited." *The Brian Lehrer Show*. WNYC, New York Public Radio (April 5).

Earl, Jennifer, Katrina Kimport, Greg Prieto, Carly Rush, and Kimberly Reynoso. 2010. "Changing the World One Webpage at a Time: Conceptualizing and Explaining 'Internet Activism.'" *Mobilization* 15:4, 425–446.

Eley, Tom. 2010. "Howard Zinn (1922–2010)." *World Socialist*. http://www.wsws.org/articles/2010/feb2010/zinn-f15.shtml.

Emerson, Ralph Waldo. 1926. "Intellect." In *Emerson's Essays*, Irwin Edman, ed. (New York: Harper Colophon Books).

England, George Allen. 1974 [1912]. *Darkness and Dawn*. Westport, CT: Hyperion Press.

Epstein, Barbara. 2001. "Anarchism and the Anti-Globalization Movement." *Monthly Review* 53:4, 1–14.

Etzioni, Amitai. 2006. "Are Public Intellectuals an Endangered Species?" In *Public Intellectuals: An Endangered Species?* Amitai Etzioni and Alyssa Bowditch, eds. London: Rowman and Littlefield, 1–27.

Evans, Mary. 2004. *Killing Thinking: The Death of the Universities*. London: Continuum.

Evans, Sara, and Harry Boyte. 1992. *Free Spaces: The Sources of Democratic Change in America*. Chicago: University of Chicago Press.

Falk, Richard A. 1978. "Anarchism and World Order." In *NOMOS—Yearbook of the American Society for Political and Legal Philosophy*, J. Roland Pennock and John W. Chapman, eds. New York: New York University Press.

Fall, Bernard. 1967. *Last Reflections on a War*. New York: Doubleday.

Fanon, Frantz. 2004. *The Wretched of the Earth*. New York: Grove Press.

Feinberg, Joel. 1968. "Collective Responsibility." *Journal of Philosophy* 65:21, 674–688.

Ferguson, Thomas. 1995. *Golden Rule, The Investment Theory of Party Competition and the Logic of Money Driven Political Systems*. Chicago: University of Chicago Press.

Ferguson, Thomas. 2011. "Why They Just Say No: Posted Prices and the Capitol Hill Stalemate Machine." *Washington Spectator* (October 15).

Field, Connie, and Marilyn Mulford. 1994. *Freedom on My Mind*. San Francisco: California Newsreel.

Finkin, Matthew W., and Robert C. Post. 2009. *For the Common Good: Principles of American Academic Freedom*. New Haven, CT: Yale University Press.

Flank, Lenny, ed. 2007. *I.W.W.: A Documentary History*. St. Petersburg, FL: Red and Black Publishers.

Foner, Eric. 1980. "Majority Report: *A People's History of the United States*." *New York Times Book Review* (March 2).

Foner, Eric. 2010. "Zinn's Critical History." *The Nation* (February 22).

Foner, Philip S. 1965. *History of the Labor Movement in the United States: Volume IV, The Industrial Workers of the World 1905–1917*. New York: International Publishers.

Fortas, Abe. 1968. *Concerning Dissent and Civil Disobedience*. New York: New American Library.

Foucault, Michel. 1989. *Foucault Live: Interviews, 1966–1984*. Sylvere Lotringer, ed. New York: Semiotexte.

Foucault, Michel. 2001. *Fearless Speech*. Los Angeles: Semiotexte.

Frankenstein, Marilyn. 2010. "Studying Culture Jamming to Inspire Student Activism." *Radical Teacher* 89 (Winter), 30–46.

Fraser, Nancy. 1990. "Rethinking the Public Sphere: A Contribution to the Critique of Actually Existing Democracy." *Social Text* 25/26, 56–80.

Fraser, Nancy. 1997. *Justice Interruptus: Critical Reflections on the "Postsocialist" Condition*. New York: Routledge Press.

Fraser, Nancy. 2003. "Social Justice in the Age of Identity Politics: Redistribution, Recognition, and Participation." In *Redistribution or Recognition? A Political-Philosophical Exchange*, Nancy Fraser and Axel Honneth, eds. London: Verso, 7–109.

Frede, Victoria. 2011. *Doubt, Atheism, and the Nineteenth-century Russian Intelligentsia*. Madison: University of Wisconsin Press.

Freire, Paulo. 1995. *Pedagogy of Hope: Reliving Pedagogy of the Oppressed*. New York: Continuum Publishing Company.

Fuller, Steve. 2005. *The Intellectual*. Cambridge, UK: Icon Books.

Furedi, Frank. 2006. *Where Have All the Intellectuals Gone? Confronting 21st Century Philistinism*. London: Continuum.

Furlong, Paul, and David Marsh. 2002. "A Skin Not a Sweater: Ontology and Epistemology in Political Science." In *Theory and Methods in Political Science*, David Marsh and Gerry Stoker, eds. New York: Palgrave Macmillan, 17–41.

Fussell, Paul. 1989. *Wartime: Understanding and Behavior in the Second World War*. New York: Oxford University Press.

Galeano, Eduardo. 1995. "Window on Utopia." In *Walking Words*, Mark Fried, trans. New York: W. W. Norton & Company. Reprinted in *The Nation* (June 12, 1995).

Gelderloos, Peter. 2007. *How Nonviolence Protects the State*. Cambridge, MA: South End Press.

Genovese, Eugene. 1995. *The Southern Front: History and Politics in the Cultural War*. Columbia: University of Missouri Press.

Gerami, Puya. 2012. "Generalists, Specialists, and Others: An Interview with George Scialabba." May 15, http://www.georgescialabba.net/mtgs/2012/05/generalists -specialists-and-ot/print.

Giddens, Anthony, ed. 2001. *The Global Third Way Debate*. Cambridge, UK: Polity.

Giddens, Anthony. 1998. *The Third Way: The Renewal of Social Democracy*. Cambridge, UK: Polity.

Giddens, Anthony. 1999. *Runaway World: How Globalization Is Reshaping Our Lives*. London: Profile.

Giddens, Anthony. 2000. *The Third Way and Its Critics*. Cambridge, UK: Polity.

Giddens, Anthony. 2002. *Where Now for New Labour?* Cambridge, UK: Polity.

Gilbert, Margaret. 2006. "Who's to Blame? Collective Moral Responsibility and Its Implications for Group Members." *Midwest Studies in Philosophy* 30:1 (September), 94–114.

Gilmore, Glenda Elizabeth. 2008. *Defying Dixie: The Radical Roots of the Civil Rights Movement: 1919–1950*. New York: W. W. Norton & Company.

Giroux, Henry A. 2011. "Neoliberal Politics as Failed Sociality: Youth and the Crisis of Higher Education." *Logos: A Journal of Modern Society & Culture* 10:2, http:// logosjournal.com/2011/neoliberal-politics-as-failed-sociality-youth-and-the-crisis -of-higher-education.

Gitlin, Todd. 1980. *The Whole World Is Watching: Mass Media in the Making and Unmaking of the New Left*. Berkeley: University of California Press.

Gladwell, Malcolm. 2010. "Small Change: Why the Revolution Will Not Be Tweeted." *The New Yorker* (October 4).

Glavin, Paul, and Chuck Morse. 2003. "War Is the Health of the State: An Interview with Howard Zinn." *Perspectives on Anarchist Theory* 7:1 (Spring), 1, 8–10.

Goldman, Emma. 1969 [1910]. *Anarchism and Other Essays*. Mineola, NY: Dover Publications.

Goodman, Walter. 1986. "Stage: 'Emma,' Howard Zinn's Tale of Radicals." *New York Times* (February 17).

Goodway, David. 2006. *Anarchist Seeds beneath the Snow: Left-Libertarian Thought and British Writers from William Morris to Colin Ward*. Liverpool: Liverpool University Press.

Gornick, Vivian. 1977. *The Romance of American Communism*. New York: Basic Books.

Graeber, David. 2004. "The New Anarchists." In *A Movement of Movements, Is Another World Really Possible?* Tom Mertes, ed. New York: Verso, 202–217.

Graeber, David. 2007. *Possibilities: Essays on Hierarchy, Rebellion, and Desire*. Oakland, CA: AK Press.

Graeber, David. 2009. *Direct Action: An Ethnography*. Edinburgh: AK Press.

Graeber, David. 2012. "Concerning the Violent Peace Police: An Open Letter to Chris Hedges." *n+1*, http://nplusonemag.com/concerning-the-violent-peace-police.

Graham, Keith. 2006. "Imposing and Embracing Collective Responsibility: Why the Moral Difference?" *Midwest Studies in Philosophy* 30:1 (September), 256–268.

Gramsci, Antonio. 2011. *Prison Notebooks Volume II*. Joseph A Buttigieg, ed. New York: Columbia University Press.

Green, James. 2003. "Howard Zinn's History." *Chronicle of Higher Education* (May 23), B13–14.

Gresh, Alain. 2011. "Neither with the West, Nor against It." *Le Monde Diplomatique*, English edition; http://mondediplo.com/2011/03/02arabworld.

Grossberg, Lawrence. 1997. *Dancing in Spite of Myself*. Durham, NC: Duke University Press.

Grubačić, Andrej, ed. 2010. *From Here to There: The Staughton Lynd Reader*. Oakland, CA: PM Press.

Grubačić, Andrej. 2004. "Towards Another Anarchism." In *World Social Forum: Challenging Empires*, Jai Sen et al., eds. New Delhi: The Viveka Foundation, 35–43.

Guthrie, Woody. 1999. "Ludlow Massacre." *Hard Travelin'*. New York: Asch Records.

Haddad, Bassam. 2011. "Interview with Hossam El-Hamalawy on the Role of Labor Unions in the Egyptian Revolution." *Jadaliyya* (April 30), http://www.jadaliyya.com/pages/index/1187/english-translation-of-interview-withhossam-el-ha.

Hahnel, Robin. 2010. "Election Redux: Learning from the 2010 Midterm Elections, Part 1: Lessons for Others." *ZSpace Commentary* (November 4), http://www.zcommunications.org/election-redux-learning-from-the-2010-midterm-elections-part-1-lessons-for-others-by-robin-hahnel.

Hallin, Daniel. 1989. *The "Uncensored War": The Media and Vietnam*. Berkeley: University of California Press.

Hampton, Henry, producer. 2006. *Eyes on the Prize: The Time Has Come, 1964–1966*. Alexandria, VA: PBS Video.

Handlin, Oscar. 1980. "Arawaks." *American Scholar* 49 (Autumn), 546–550.

Hartz, Louis. 1955. *The Liberal Tradition in America*. New York: Harcourt, Brace & World.

Hawken, Paul. 2007. *Blessed Unrest: How the Largest Movement in the World Came into Being and Why No One Saw It Coming*. New York: Viking.

Hayden, Tom. 2006. *Radical Nomad: C. Wright Mills and His Times*. London: Paradigm Publishers.

Hedges, Chris. 2011. "A Decade after 9/11: We Are What We Loathe." *Truthdig .com* (September 10), http://www.truthdig.com/report/item/nationalism_in_the_aftermath_of_9_11_20110910/.

Heller, Joseph. 2003 [1951]. *Catch-22*. New York: Simon & Shuster.

Herbert, Bob. 2010. "A Radical Treasure." *New York Times* (January 29).

Herman, Edward S., and Noam Chomsky. 1988. *Manufacturing Consent*. New York: Pantheon Books.

Herman, Edwardf S., and Noam Chomsky. 2002. *Manufacturing Consent: The Political Economy of Mass Media*. 2nd edition. New York: Pantheon.

Heslam, Jessica. 2011. "Fun Takes a Holiday in Somerville." *Boston Herald* (October 14).

Hill, Christopher. 1991. *The World Turned Upside Down: Radical Ideas during the English Revolution*. Harmondsworth: Penguin Books.

Hirschman, Albert O. 1970. *Exit, Voice, and Loyalty: Responses to Decline in Firms, Organizations, and States*. Cambridge, MA: Harvard University Press.

Hofstadter, Richard. 1968. *The Progressive Historians: Turner, Beard, Parrington*. New York: Alfred A. Knopf.

Honig, Bonnie. 2001. *Democracy and the Foreigner*. Ithaca, NY: Cornell University Press.

Horgan, John. 2012. *The End of War*. San Francisco: McSweeney's.

Horowitz, David. 2007. *The Professors: The 101 Most Dangerous Academics in America*. New York: Regnery Press.

Horowitz, Irving. 1967. *Power, Politics and People: The Collected Essays of C. Wright Mills*. Oxford: Oxford University Press.

Horwitz, Tony. 2011. *Midnight Rising: John Brown and the Raid that Sparked the Civil War*. New York: Henry Holt & Company.

Howard, Philip N. 2011. "Review of *The Net Delusion: The Dark Side of Internet Freedom*." *Perspectives on Politics* 9:4 (December), 897.

Howe, Irving. 1982. *Margin of Hope: An Intellectual Biography*. New York: Harcourt Brace Jovanovich.

Huberman, Leo. 1947 [1932]. *We, the People: The Drama of America*. New York: Harper and Brothers Publishers.

Hunt, Andrew. 2003. "How New Was the New Left? Re-Thinking New Left Exceptionalism." In *The New Left Revisited*, John McMillian and Paul Buhle, eds. Philadelphia: Temple University Press, 139–155.

Hyde, Lewis, ed. 2002. "A Plea for Captain John Brown." In *The Essays of Henry D. Thoreau*. New York: North Point Press, 259–280.

Isserman, Maurice. 1993 [1987]. *If I Had a Hammer: The Death of the Old Left and the Birth of the New Left*. Chicago: University of Illinois Press.

Ivol, Ambre. 2007. "Retour sur les Évolutions Intellectuelles Des Historiens De La 'Nouvelle Gauche': Étude Comparative de William A. Williams et Howard Zinn (1950–1980)." In *La Politique Éxtérieure des Etats-Unis au XXe Siècle: le Poids des Déterminants Éxtérieurs*, Pierre Melandri et Serge Ricard, eds. Paris: L'Harmattan, 55–75.

Ivol, Ambre. 2009. "US Intellectual Generations: The Life and Work of Howard Zinn (1922–)." La Sorbonne Nouvelle.

Jacoby, Russell. 2000 [1987]. *The Last Intellectuals: American Culture in the Age of Academe*. New York: Basic Books.

Jamail, Dahr. 2004. "Fallujah Rebels, Residents, Police Celebrate Victory over U.S. Marines." *New Standard* (May 10), http://newstandardnews.net/content/index.cfm /items/323.

Jamail, Dahr. 2007. *Beyond the Green Zone: Dispatches from an Unembedded Journalist in Occupied Iraq*. Chicago: Haymarket Books.

Jamail, Dahr. 2012. "Seven Years after Sieges, Fallujah Struggles." *Al Jazeera* (January 4), http://www.aljazeera.com/indepth/features/2012/01/201212102823143370.html.

James, C. L. R. 2001 [1937]. *The Black Jacobins: Toussaint L'Ouverture and the San Domingo Revolution*. New York: Penguin Books.

Jasper, James M. 1997. *The Art of Moral Protest: Culture, Biography, and Creativity in Social Movements*. Chicago: University of Chicago Press.

Jaspers, Karl. 1962. *The Great Philosophers: The Foundations, the Paradigmatic Individuals: Socrates, Buddha, Confucius, Jesus; The Seminal Founders of Philosophical Thought: Plato, Augustine, Kant* (The Great Philosophers Volume 1). London: Harcourt, Brace and World.

Johnson, Paul. 2005. *Intellectuals*. London: Phoenix Books.

Joseph, Peniel E. 2006. *Waitin' til the Midnight Hour: A Narrative History of Black Power in America*. New York: Henry Holt & Company.

Joseph, Peniel E. 2011. "Still Reinventing Malcolm: Manning Marable Rescues the Man from the Mythology." *Chronicle of Higher Education Review* (May 1), B6.

Joyce, Davis D. 2003. *Howard Zinn: A Radical American Vision*. Amherst, NY: Prometheus Books.

Jubran, Amer. 2004. "Is the US Anti-War Movement Pro-Resistance?" New England Committee to Defend Palestine (February 4), http://www.onepalestine.org/resources /articles/Antiwar.html.

Kaldor, Mary. 1999. *New and Old Wars: Organized Violence in a Global Era.* Stanford, CA: Stanford University Press.

Katsiaficas, George. 1987. *The Imagination of the New Left: A Global Analysis of 1968.* Boston: South End Press.

Katz, Barry. 1982. *Herbert Marcuse and the Art of Liberation.* London: Verso.

Kazin, Michael. 2004. "Howard Zinn's History Lessons." *Dissent* (Spring).

Kazin, Michael. 2011. *American Dreamers: How the Left Changed a Nation.* New York: Knopf.

Kelley, Robin. 1990. *Hammer and Hoe: Alabama Communists during the Great Depression.* Chapel Hill: University of North Carolina Press.

Kellner, Douglas. 1984. *Herbert Marcuse and the Crisis of Marxism.* London: Macmillan.

Kellner, Douglas. 1990. *Television and the Crisis of Democracy.* Boulder, CO: Westview Press.

Khiabany, Gholam. 2003. "Globalization and the Internet: Myths and Realities." *Trends in Communication* 11:2, 137–153.

Kidd, Stuart. 2005. "Review of *New Deal Thought.*" *Journal of American Studies* 39:2, 352–353.

Kocieniewski, David. 2011. "Tax Benefits from Options as Windfall for Businesses." *New York Times* (December 29).

Kolbert, Elizabeth. 2006. *Field Notes from a Catastrophe: Man, Nature, and Climate Change.* New York: Bloomsbury Press.

Kornbluh, Joyce L. 1964. *Rebel Voices: An IWW Anthology.* Chicago: Charles H. Kerr Co.

Lamont, Michèle. 2009. *How Professors Think: Inside the Curious World of Academic Judgment.* Cambridge, MA: Harvard University Press.

Landauer, Gustav. 2010 [1910]. *Revolution and Other Writings: A Political Reader.* Oakland, CA: PM Press.

Leitenberg, Milton. 2006. "Deaths in Wars and Conflicts in the 20th Century." Cornell University Peace Studies Program, Occasional Paper #29 (August).

Lenin, Vladimir I. 1968. *Selected Works.* London: Progress Publishers.

Lenin, Vladimir I. 1989. *What Is to Be Done? Burning Questions of Our Movement.* Harmondsworth: Penguin.

Lifton, Robert Jay. 2006. "Conditions of Atrocity." In *Crimes of War: Iraq*, Richard Falk, Irene Gendzier, and Robert Jay Lifton, eds. New York: Nation Books, 340–341.

Lih, Lars T. 2008. *Lenin Rediscovered: What Is to Be Done in Context.* New York: Haymarket Books.

Lipsitz, George. 2001. *Time Passages: Collective Memory and American Popular Culture.* Minneapolis: University of Minnesota Press.

London, Jack. 1991 [1908]. *Iron Heel.* London: Pluto Press.

London, Scott. 2000. "Organic Democracy: The Political Philosophy of John Dewey." http://www.scottlondon.com/reports/dewey.html.

Long, Priscilla. 1969. *The New Left: A Collection of Essays.* Boston: Porter Sargent.

Lorde, Audre. 1984. "The Master's Tools Will Never Dismantle the Master's House." In *Sister Outsider: Essays and Speeches by Audre Lorde.* Freedom: CA: Crossing Press, 110–113.

Löwy, Michael. 1998. "Les Intellectuels Juifs." In *Pour une Histoire Comparée des Intellectuels*, Michel Trébisch and Marie-Christine Granjon, eds. Paris: IHTP: CNRS, Bruxelles, éditions Complexe.

Lynd, Staughton, and Alice Lynd. 2009. *Stepping Stones: A Memoir of a Life Together.* Lexington: Lexington Books.

MacFarlane, Bruce. 2007. *The Academic Citizen: The Virtue of Service in University Life*. London: Routledge.

Mandel, Ernest. 1995. *Trotsky as an Alternative*. London: Verso Books.

Mannheim, Karl. 1952. "The Problems of Generations." In *Essays on the Sociology of Knowledge*, Paul Kecskemeti, ed. New York: Oxford University Press, 276–322.

Mansour, Ahmed. 2009. *Inside Fallujah*. Northhampton: Olive Branch Books, 275–339.

Marable, Manning. 2011. *Malcolm X: A Life of Reinvention*. New York: Viking.

Marcuse, Herbert. 1955. *Reason and Revolution*. London: Routledge and Kegan Paul.

Marcuse, Herbert. 1968. *Negations: Essays in Critical Theory*. Boston: Beacon Press.

Marcuse, Herbert. 1971. *Studies in Critical Philosophy*. Boston: Beacon Press.

Marcuse, Herbert. 1991 [1965]. *One Dimensional Man: Studies in the Ideology of Advanced Industrial Society*. Boston: Beacon Press.

Marx, Karl, and Friedrich Engels. 1998. *The German Ideology*. New York: Prometheus Books.

Marzouki, Nadia. 2011. "Tunisia's Wall Has Fallen." *Middle East Report Online* (January 19), http://www.merip.org/mero/meroO11911.html.

Mattson, Kevin. 2007. "History Lesson." *Democracy: A Journal of Ideas* 3 (Winter), 79–87.

May, Todd. 1994. *The Political Philosophy of Poststructuralist Anarchism*. University Park: The Pennsylvania State University Press.

McAdam, Doug. 1986. "Recruitment to High-Risk Activism: The Case of Freedom Summer." *American Journal of Sociology* 92:1 (July), 64–90.

McCain, Robert S. 2010. "The Case against Howard Zinn." *American Spectator* (August 2). http://spectator.org/archives/2010/08/02/the-case-against-howard-zinn.

McChesney, Robert W. 2010. "Foreword." In *Wisconsin Uprising: Labor Fights Back*, Michael D. Yates, ed. New York: Monthly Review Press, 11–18.

McGovern, George. 1997. *Grassroots: The Autobiography of George McGovern*. New York: Random House.

McKibben, Bill. 2006. *The End of Nature*, 2nd edition. New York: Random House.

McWilliams, Timothy, and Curtis Wheeler. 2009. "Al-Anbar Awakening, Volume 1, American Perspectives." Marine Corps University Press, http://marines.mil/unit/hqmc/Documents/historical/Al-AnbarAwakeningVolI.pdf.

Meltzer, Albert. 1996. *Anarchism: Arguments For and Against*. Edinburgh: AK Press.

Menand, Louis. 2010. *The Marketplace of Ideas: Reform and Resistance in the American University System*. New York: W. W. Norton & Company.

Mettler, Suzanne. 2005. *The G.I. Bill and the Making of the Greatest Generation*. New York: Oxford University Press.

Metzger, Walter P. 1988. "Profession and Constitution: Two Definitions of Academic Freedom in America." *Texas Law Review* 66, 1265–1322.

Miller, Marjorie. 2010. "An Experts' History of Howard Zinn." *Los Angeles Times* (February 1).

Mills, C. Wright. 1959. *The Sociological Imagination*. Harmondsworth: Penguin.

Mills, C. Wright. 2000. *Letters and Autobiographical Writings*. Berkeley: University of California Press.

Mills, C. Wright. 2008. *The Politics of Truth*. Oxford: Oxford University Press.

Monroe, Kristen Renwick, ed. 2005. *Perestroika! The Raucous Rebellion in Political Science*. New Haven, CT: Yale University Press.

Moore, Barrington. 1966. *Social Origins of Dictatorship and Democracy: Lord and Peasant in the Making of the Modern World*. Boston: Beacon Press.

Morgan, Edward P. 1991. *The Sixties Experience: Hard Lessons about Modern America.* Philadelphia: Temple University Press.

Morgan, Edward P. 2010. *What Really Happened to the 1960s: How Mass Media Culture Failed American Democracy.* Lawrence: University Press of Kansas.

Morozov, Evgeny. 2011. *The Net Delusion: The Dark Side of Internet Freedom.* New York: Public Affairs.

Murphy, Paul L. 1979. *World War I and the Origin of Civil Liberties in the United States,* New York: W. W. Norton & Company.

Myers, Gustavus. 1910. *The History of Great American Fortunes.* Chicago: Charles H. Kerr.

Naison, Mark. 1983. *Communists in Harlem during the Great Depression.* New York: Grove Press.

Ndiaye, Pap. 2004. "Une Histoire Populaire des États-Unis de 1492 à Nos Jours." *Genèse* 55 (June).

Neal, Dave. 1997. "Anarchism: Ideology or Methodology?" http://www.infoshop.org/library/Dave_Neal:Anarchism:_ideology_or_methodology.

Nelson, Cary. 2010. *No University Is an Island: Saving Academic Freedom.* New York: New York University Press.

Newfield, Jack. 1966. *The Prophetic Minority.* New York: The New American Library.

Nimtz, August, Jr. 2000. *Marx and Engels: Their Contribution to the Democratic Breakthrough.* New York: State University of New York Press.

Noah, Timothy. 2012. *The Great Divergence: America's Growing Inequality Crisis and What We Can Do About It.* New York: Bloomsbury Press.

Norton, Quinn. 2011. "Anonymous 101: Introduction to the Lulz." *Wired Magazine* (November 8), http://www.wired.com/threatlevel/2011/11/anonymous-101.

Novick, Peter. 1988. *That Noble Dream: The "Objectivity Question" and the American Historical Profession.* New York: Cambridge University Press.

Nye, Bill. 1894. *Bill Nye's Comic History of the United States.* Chicago: Thompson and Thomas.

Oppenheim, James. 1911. "Bread and Roses." *American Magazine* 73:2 (December), 214.

O'Reilly, Kenneth. 1982. "A New Deal for the FBI: The Roosevelt Administration, Crime Control, and National Security." *The Journal of American History* 69:3 (December), 638–658.

Organisation for Economic Co-operation and Development (OECD). 2008. *Growing Unequal? Income Distribution and Poverty in OECD Countries.* October, http://www.oecd.org/document/4/0,3343,en_2649_33933_41460917_1_1_1_1,00.html.

Page, Benjamin I., and Lawrence R. Jacobs. 2009. *Class War? What Americans Really Think about Economic Inequality.* Chicago: University of Chicago Press.

Panikkar, Raimon. 1999. *The Intrareligious Dialogue.* Mahwah, NJ: Paulist Press.

Patton, Paul. 2005. "Deleuze and Democracy." *Contemporary Political Theory* 4:4 (November), 400–413.

Pear, Robert. 2011. "It's Official: The Rich Get Richer." *New York Times* (October 26), A20.

Perlin, Terry M. 1979. *Contemporary Anarchism.* New Brunswick, NJ: Transaction Books.

Perry, Lewis. 1973. *Radical Abolitionism: Anarchy and the Government of God in Antislavery Thought.* Ithaca, NY: Cornell University Press.

Petrović, Gajo. 1978. *Mišljenje revolucije: Od ontologije do "filozofije politike."* Zagreb: Naprijed.

Pew Research Center. 2012. "Rising Share of Americans See Conflict between Rich and Poor." (January 11), http://www.pewsocialtrends.org/2012/01/11/rising-share-of-americans-see-conflict-between-rich-and-poor.

Phelps, Christopher. 2010. "Howard Zinn, Philosopher." *Chronicle of Higher Education* (February).

Pinker, Steven. 2011. *The Better Angels of Our Nature: Why Violence Has Declined.* New York: Viking.

Piven, Frances Fox. 2011. "A Proud, Angry Poor." *The Nation* (December 14), http://www.thenation.com/article/165158/proud-angry-poor.

Polsgrove, Carol. 2001. *Divided Minds: Intellectuals and the Civil Rights Movement.* New York: W. W. Norton & Company.

Posner, Richard. 2003. *Public Intellectuals: A Study in Decline.* Cambridge, MA: Harvard University Press.

Potter, David M. 1954. *People of Plenty: Economic Abundance and the American Character.* Chicago: University of Chicago Press.

Powell, Howard. 2010. "Howard Zinn, Historian, Dies at 87." *New York Times* (January 27).

Preston, William, Jr. 1963. *Aliens and Dissenters: Federal Suppression of Radicals, 1903–1933.* New York: Harper & Row.

Prysner, Michael. 2008. "Winter Soldier Testimony." (March), transcript and video available at http://www.globalresearch.ca/index.php?aid=22054&context=va.

Putnam, Robert. 1995. "Bowling Alone: America's Declining Social Capital." *Journal of Democracy* 6:1 (January), 65–78.

Quinton, Pennie R. 2011. "'Unsung Hero' Brian Haw, 1949–2011." *Al Jazeera* (June 20), http://english.aljazeera.net/indepth/features/2011/06/201162081348694801.html.

Radosh, Ronald, and Murray Rothbard, eds. 1972. *A New History of Leviathan: Essays on the Rise of the American Corporate State.* Boston: E. P. Dutton & Co.

Raeff, Mark. 1966. *Origins of the Russian Intelligentsia: The Eighteenth-Century Nobility.* London: Mariner Books.

Räikkä, Juha. 1997. "On Disassociating Oneself from Collective Responsibility." *Social Theory and Practice* 23:1 (Spring), 93–109.

Ransby, Barbara. 2003. *Ella Baker and the Black Freedom Movement: A Radical Democratic Vision.* Chapel Hill: University of North Carolina Press.

Reeves, Richard. 2007. *John Stuart Mill: Victorian Firebrand.* London: Atlantic Books.

Reiff, Mark. 2008. "Terrorism, Retribution, and Collective Responsibility." *Social Theory and Practice* 34:2 (April), 209–242.

"Remembering Norman Mailer." 2007. *On Point*, WBUR Radio (November 12), http://www.onpointradio.org/2007/11/remembering-norman-mailer.

Restrepo, Eduardo, and Arturo Escobar. 2005. "Other Anthropologies and Anthropology Otherwise: Steps to a World Anthropologies Framework." *Critique of Anthropology* 25:2, 99–129.

Rich, Adrienne. 2001. *Arts of the Possible: Essays and Conversations.* New York: W. W. Norton & Company.

Richman, Sheldon. 2011. "Libertarian Left: Free-Market Anti-Capitalism, The Unknown Ideal." *American Conservative* (March).

Roberts, Adam. 2010. "Lives and Statistics: Are 90% of War Victims Civilians?" *Survival* 52:3 (June–July).

Rorty, Richard. 1996. "Does Academic Freedom Have Philosophical Presuppositions?" In *The Future of Academic Freedom*, Louis Menand, ed. Chicago: University of Chicago Press, 21–42.

Rosemont, Franklin. 2003. *Joe Hill: The IWW & the Making of a Revolutionary Workingclass Counterculture.* Chicago: Charles H. Kerr Publishing Company.

Ross, Stephanie. 2002. "Is This What Democracy Looks Like? The Politics of the Anti-Globalization Movement in North America." *Socialist Register 2003: Fighting Identities: Race, Religion, and Ethno-Nationalism*, Halifax, Nova Scotia: Fernwood Publications, 281–304.

Rothschild, Matthew. 2010. "At Howard Zinn's Memorial Service." *The Progressive* (April 7), http://progressive.org/wx040710.html.

Rousseau, Jean-Jacques. 1996 [1762]. "On the Social Contract." In *Modern Political Thought: Readings from Machiavelli to Nietzsche*, David Wootton, ed. Indianapolis: Hackett Publishing.

Said, Edward. 1994. *Representations of the Intellectual: The 1993 Reith Lectures*. London: Vintage.

Said, Edward. 2004. *Humanism and Democratic Criticism*. New York: Columbia University Press.

Salerno, Salvatore. 1989. *Red November, Black November: Culture and Community in the Industrial Workers of the World*. Albany: The State University of New York Press.

Sanbonmatsu, John. 2004. *The Post-Modern Prince: Critical Theory, Left Strategy, and the Making of the New Political Subject*. New York: Monthly Review Press.

Sander, Thomas. 2010. "Why the Revolution Won't Be Tweeted." http://socialcapital.wordpress.com/2010/09/29/why-the-revolution-wont-be-tweeted.

Santos, Boaventura de Sousa. 2004. "The World Social Forum: Toward a Counter-Hegemonic Globalisation (Part I)." In *World Social Forum: Challenging Empires*, Jai Sen et al., eds. New Delhi: The Viveka Foundation.

Santos, Boaventura de Sousa, João Arriscado Nunes, and Maria Paula Meneses. 2008. "Opening Up the Canon of Knowledge and Recognition of Difference." In *Another Knowledge Is Possible: Beyond Northern Epistemologies*, Boaventura de Sousa Santos, ed. New York: Verso, ix–lxii.

Schechter, Danny. 2011. "Dispatch: Unions Pledge Support As #Occupy Wall Street Enters Third Week." *Huffington Post* (October 1), http://www.huffingtonpost.com/danny-schechter/dispatch-unions-pledge-su_b_990074.html.

Schmidt, Peter. 2011. "Historians Criticized as Often AWOL from Public Debate over 'War on Terror.'" *Chronicle of Higher Education* (January 12).

Schneider, Nathan. 2011. "Thank You, Anarchists." *The Nation* (December 19). http://www.thenation.com/article/165240/thank-you-anarchists.

Schram, Sanford F. 2003. "Return to Politics: Perestroika and Post-Paradigmatic Political Science." *Political Theory* 31 (December), 831–851.

Schrecker, Ellen, ed. 2004. *Cold War Triumphalism*. New York: The New Press.

Schrecker, Ellen. 1998. *Many Are the Crimes: McCarthyism in America*. New York: Little, Brown.

Schrecker, Ellen. 2010. *The Lost Soul of Higher Education: Corporatization, the Assault on Academic Freedom and the End of the American University*. New York: The New Press.

Schuessler, Jennifer. 2012. "Academia Occupied by Occupy." *New York Times* (May 1).

Scott, James C. 1990. *Domination and the Arts of Resistance: Hidden Transcript*. New Haven, CT: Yale University Press.

Scott, Marcia. October 1970–c. 1973. "The Radical Historians' Caucus (NUC) and the A.H.A.: An Account." In *Radical Caucus in the AHA, Correspondence*.

Sherman, Arloc, and Chad Stone. 2010. "Income Gaps between Very Rich and Everyone Else More Than Tripled in Last Three Decades, New Data Show." Center on Budget and Policy Priorities (June 25), http://www.cbpp.org/cms/?fa=view&id=3220.

Shils, Edward. 1997. *Portraits: A Gallery of Intellectuals*. Chicago: University of Chicago Press.

Shirky, Clay. 2011. "The Political Power of Social Media." *Foreign Affairs* (January/February).

Shulman, Alix Kates. 1996 [1972]. *Red Emma Speaks: An Emma Goldman Reader.* Amherst, NY: Prometheus Books.

Simons, A. M. 1911. *Social Forces in American History.* New York: Macmillan Co.

Singh, Nikhil Pal. 2004. *Black Is a Country: The Unfinished Struggle for Democracy.* Cambridge, MA: Harvard University Press.

Sirinelli, Jean-François. 1989. "Générations et histoire politique." *Vingtième siècle* 22:22 (April–June), 67–80.

Sitrin, Marina. 2011. "Horizontalism: From Argentina to Wall Street." *North American Congress on Latin America (NACLA) Report on the Americas* 44:6 (November/December).

Small, Helen. 2002. *The Public Intellectual.* Oxford: Wiley-Blackwell.

Smiley, Marion. 2010. "Collective Responsibility." *Stanford Encyclopedia of Philosophy,* http://plato.stanford.edu/archives/fall2010/entries/collective-responsibility.

Smith, Aaron, Kay Lehman Schlozman, Sidney Verba, and Henry Brady. 2009. *Pew Internet & American Life Project,* http://www.pewinternet.org/Reports/2009/15—The-Internet-and-Civic-Engagement.aspx.

Smith, Dan. 1997. *The State of War and Peace Atlas.* London: Penguin Books.

Smolenski, John, and Thomas J. Humphrey, eds. 2007. *New World Orders: Violence, Sanction, and Authority in the Colonial Americas.* Philadelphia: University of Pennsylvania Press.

Solnit, Rebecca. 2011. "Letter to a Dead Man about the Occupation of Hope." *The Nation* (October 18), http://www.thenation.com/print/article/164039/letter-dead-man-aboutoccupation-hope.

Sosa, David. 2009. "What Is it Like to Be a Group?" *Social Philosophy and Policy* 26:1, 212–226.

Spivak, G. C. 1988. "Can the Subaltern Speak?" In *Marxism and the Interpretation of Culture,* Cary Nelson and Lawrence Grossberg, eds. London: Macmillan, 271–313.

Steavenson, Wendell. 2011. "On the Square: Were the Egyptian Protestors Right to Trust the Military?" *The New Yorker* (February 28).

Stiglitz, Joseph E. 2011. "Inequality of the 1%, by the 1%, for the 1%." *Vanity Fair* (May).

Stockholm International Peace Research Institute (SIPRI). 1990. "Major Armed Conflicts in 1989." *SIPRI Yearbook 1990.* Oxford: Oxford University Press.

Strada, Gino. 2005. *Green Parrots: A War Surgeon's Diary.* New York: Charta Books.

Stutie, Jan Willem. 2009. *Ernest Mandel: A Rebel's Dream Deferred: A Biography.* London: Verso Books.

Sulzberger, A. G. 2011. "Wisconsin Professor's E-Mails Are Target of G.O.P. Records Request." *New York Times* (March 26).

Syvertsen, Amy K., Laura Wray-Lake, Constance A. Flanagan, D. Wayne Osgood, and Laine Briddell. 2011. "Thirty-Year Trends in U.S. Adolescents' Civic Engagement: A Story of Changing Participation and Educational Differences." *Journal of Research on Adolescence* 21:3 (September), 586–594.

Tabeau, Ewa, and Jakub Bijak. 2005. "War-Related Deaths in the 1992–1995 Armed Conflicts in Bosnia and Herzegovina: A Critique of Previous Estimates and the Latest Results." *European Journal of Population* 21, 187–215.

Talisse, Robert B. 2005. "Deliberative Democracy Defended: A Response to Posner's Political Realism." *Res Publica* 11, 185–199.

Talisse, Robert B. 2009. "Precis of *A Pragmatist Philosophy of Democracy.*" *Transactions of the Charles S. Pierce Society* 45:1, 45–49.

Taylor, Richard. 2007. "Determinism and the Theory of Agency." In *Ethical Theory: An Anthology*, Russ Shafer-Landau, ed. Oxford: Blackwell Publishing, 340–343.

Terkel, Studs. 1987. *"The Good War": An Oral History of World War Two*. New York: Pantheon Books.

Terkel, Studs. 2007. *Touch and Go*. New York: The New Press.

Thatcher, Ian. 2007. "Lenin, Trotsky and the Role of the Socialist Intellectual in Politics." In *Marxism, Intellectuals and Politics*, David Bates, ed. London: Palgrave, 43–67.

The Fog of War, Eleven Lessons in the Life of Robert McNamara. 2003. Sony Pictures (95 minutes). Errol Morris, director/producer.

The Guardian. 2010. "U.S. Embassy Cables: Terrorists Damage Bouteflika's Credibility." (December 6) http://www.guardian.co.uk/world/us-embassy-cables-documents /142554.

The Invisible Committee. 2009 [2007]. *The Coming Insurrection*. Cambridge, MA: Semiotexte.

The Most Dangerous Man in America: Daniel Ellsberg and the Pentagon Papers. 2009. First Run Features (92 minutes). Judith Ehrlich and Rick Goldsmith, directors.

The People Speak. 2009. A&E Home Video (150 minutes). Matt Damon, Josh Brolin, Chris Moore, Anthony Arnove, and Howard Zinn, producers.

Thompson, Edward Palmer. 1963. *The Making of the English Working Class*. London: Gollanz.

Tirman, John. 2009. "Iraq's Shocking Human Toll: About 1 Million Killed, 4.5 Million Displaced, 1–2 Million Widows, 5 Million Orphans." *Alternet* (February 2), http:// www.alternet.org/world/123818.

Tirman, John. 2011. "Citizen Zinn." *The Nation* (May 6).

Tlemçani, Rachid. 2011. "La Culture de l'Emeute est la Seule Expression Politique Audible." *el Watan* (February 8), http://www.elwatan.com/entretien/la-culture-de -l-emeute-est-la-seule-expression-politique-audible-08-02-2011-110774_121.php.

Tocqueville, Alexis de. 2000 [1835, 1840]. *Democracy in America*. Harvey C. Mansfield and Delba Winthrop, eds. Chicago: University of Chicago Press.

Toensing, Chris. 2011. "Tunisian Labor Leaders Reflect Upon Revolt." *Middle East Research and Information Project* 41 (Spring), http://www.merip.org/mer/mer258 /tunisian-labor-leaders-reflect-upon-revolt-.

Topper, Keith. 2005. *The Disorder of Political Inquiry*. Cambridge, MA: Harvard University Press.

Twain, Mark. 1957. "The Mysterious Stranger." In *The Complete Short Stories of Mark Twain*, Charles Neider, ed. New York: Doubleday & Company.

Tyler, Robert L. 1966. "The American Veterans Committee: Out of a Hot War and Into the Cold." *American Quarterly* 18:3 (Autumn), 419–436.

Unger, Irwin. 1974. *The Movement: A History of the American New Left, 1959–1972*. New York: Dodd, Mead, and Company.

Vodovnik, Žiga. 2008. "An Interview with Howard Zinn on Anarchism: Rebels against Tyranny." *Revolution by the Book*: AK Press Blog, http://www.revolutionbythebook .akpress.org/an-interview-with-howard-zinn-on-anarchism-rebels-against-tyranny.

Vodovnik, Žiga. 2012. *A Living Spirit of Revolt: The Infrapolitics of Anarchism*. Oakland, CA: PM Press.

Walker, Alice. 2000. "Beyond the Peacock: The Reconstruction of Flannery O'Connor." In *In Search of Our Mother's Gardens: Womanist Prose*. Orlando, FL: Mariner Press, 42–59.

Walker, Alice. 2010. "Saying Goodbye to My Friend Howard Zinn." *Boston Globe* (January 31).

Wallace, Mike. 1980. "A History of Class, Race and Sex Struggles." *Monthly Review* (December), 27–38.

Wallace, Mike. 1983 [1976]. "Interview with William Appleman Williams." In *Visions of History*, MARHO: Radical Historians Organization, eds. New York: Pantheon Books, 125–146.

Ward, Colin. 1988 [1973]. *Anarchy in Action*. London: Freedom Press.

Warner, Michael. 2002a. *Publics and Counterpublics*. New York: Zone Books.

Warner, Michael. 2002b. "Public and Counter Publics (Abbreviated Version)." *Quarterly Journal of Speech* 88:4, 413–425.

Waterfield, Robin. 2009. *Why Socrates Died: Dispelling the Myth*. London: Faber and Faber.

West, Cornel. 1993–1994. "The Dilemma of the Black Intellectual." *Journal of Blacks in Higher Education* 2 (Winter), 59–67.

White, Micah. 2010. "Clicktivism is Ruining Leftist Activism." *The Guardian* (August 12), http://www.guardian.co.uk/commentisfree/2010/aug/12/clicktivism-ruining-leftist-activism.

Whitfield, Stephen J. 2001. "Joseph Heller's *Catch-22*: Still the Best Catch There Is." In *Rethinking Cold War Culture*, Peter J. Kuznick and James Gilbert, eds. Washington, DC: Smithsonian Institution Press, 175–200.

Williams, Rudi. 2002. "Whitney M. Young, Jr.: Little-Known Civil Rights Pioneer." *American Forces Press Services* (February 1).

Williams, William Appleman. 1961. *The Contours of American History*. Chicago: Quadrangle Books.

Williams, William Appleman. 1998 [1959]. *Tragedy of American Diplomacy*. New York: W. W. Norton & Company.

Wilson, Emily. 2007. *The Death of Socrates: Hero, Villain, Chatterbox, Saint*. London: Profile Books.

Winock, Michel. 1989. "Les Générations Intellectuelles." *Vingtième siècle, Revue d'histoire* 22:22 (April–June), 17–38.

Wolfsfeld, Gadi, and William A. Gamson. 1993. "Movements and Media as Interacting Systems." *Annals of the American Academy of Political and Social Science* 528:1 (July), 114–125.

Wolin, Sheldon. 2008. *Democracy Incorporated: Managed Democracy and the Specter of Inverted Totalitarianism*. Princeton, NJ: Princeton University Press.

Worth, Robert F. 2011. "How a Single Match Can Ignite a Revolution." *New York Times* (January 21).

Wray, Stefan. 1999. "On Electronic Civil Disobedience." *Peace Review* 11:1 (March), 107–111.

You Can't Be Neutral on a Moving Train. 2004. First Run Features (78 minutes). Deb Ellis and Denis Mueller, directors.

Zinn, Howard, ed. 1974. *Justice in Everyday Life: The Way It Really Works*. Boston: Beacon Press.

Zinn, Howard. 1959. *LaGuardia in Congress 1917–1933: A Study of a Legislative Career That Bridged the Progressive and the New Deal Eras*. New York: W. W. Norton & Company.

Zinn, Howard. 1962. *Albany, A Study in National Responsibility*. Atlanta: Southern Regional Council.

Zinn, Howard. 1965a. "Abolitionists, Freedom-Riders, and the Tactics of Agitation." In *The Antislavery Vanguard: New Essays on the Abolitionists*, Martin B. Duberman, ed. Princeton, NJ: Princeton University Press, 417–451.

Zinn, Howard. 1965b. *New Deal Thought*. Indianapolis: The Bobbs-Merrill Company.

Zinn, Howard. 1968. *Disobedience and Democracy: Nine Fallacies on Law and Order*. New York: Random House.

Zinn, Howard. 1969. "Vacating the Premises in Vietnam." *Asian Survey* 9:9 (November), 862–867.

Zinn, Howard. 1972 [1964]. *The Southern Mystique*. 2nd edition. New York: Simon & Schuster.

Zinn, Howard. 1980. *A People's History of the United States*. New York: Harper-Perennial.

Zinn, Howard. 1990 [1970]. *The Politics of History*. Chicago: University of Illinois Press.

Zinn, Howard. 1990. *Declarations of Independence: Cross-Examining American Ideology*. New York: HarperCollins Publishers.

Zinn, Howard. 1991. *Declarations of Independence: Cross-Examining American Ideology*. New York: Harper-Perennial.

Zinn, Howard. 1993. *Failure to Quit: Reflections of an Optimistic Historian*. Monroe, ME: Common Courage Press.

Zinn, Howard. 1994. *You Can't Be Neutral on a Moving Train: A Personal History of Our Times*. Boston: Beacon Press.

Zinn, Howard. 1995. *A People's History of the United States, 1492–Present*. Revised and updated edition. New York: Harper-Perennial.

Zinn, Howard. 1997 [1980]. *A People's History of the United States*. Teaching edition. New York: The New Press.

Zinn, Howard. 1997a. "The Problem Is Civil Obedience." In *The Zinn Reader: Writings on Disobedience and Democracy*. New York: Seven Stories Press, 436–444.

Zinn, Howard. 1997b. "The Politics of History in the Era of the Cold War: Repression and Resistance." In *The Cold War and the University: Toward an Intellectual History of the Postwar Years*, André Schiffrin, ed. New York: The New Press, 35–72.

Zinn, Howard. 1997c. *The Zinn Reader: Writings on Disobedience and Democracy*. New York: Seven Stories Press.

Zinn, Howard. 1997d. "The Bombing of Royan." In *The Zinn Reader: Writings on Disobedience and Democracy*. New York: Seven Stories Press, 280–292.

Zinn, Howard. 1999. *Marx in Soho*. Cambridge, MA: South End Press.

Zinn, Howard. 2001a. "How Free is Higher Education?" in *Howard Zinn on History*. New York: Seven Stories Press, 121–129.

Zinn, Howard. 2001b. "A Just Cause, Not a Just War." *The Progressive* (December).

Zinn, Howard. 2001c. "Artists of Resistance." *The Progressive* (July).

Zinn, Howard. 2001d. "Historian as Citizen." *Howard Zinn on History*. New York: Seven Stories Press, 202–210.

Zinn, Howard. 2001e. *Howard Zinn on History*. New York: Seven Stories Press.

Zinn, Howard. 2002 [1964]. *SNCC: The New Abolitionists*. Cambridge, MA: South End Press.

Zinn, Howard. 2002 [1967]. *Vietnam: The Logic of Withdrawal*. Cambridge, MA: South End Press.

Zinn, Howard. 2002 [1968]. *Disobedience and Democracy: Nine Fallacies on Law and Order*. Cambridge, MA: South End Press.

Zinn, Howard. 2002 [1973]. *Postwar America: 1945–1971*. Indianapolis and New York: The Bobbs-Merrill Company.

Zinn, Howard. 2002 [1974]. *Justice in Everyday Life: The Way It Really Works*. Cambridge, MA: South End Press.

Zinn, Howard. 2002 [1986]. *Emma: A Play in Two Acts about Emma Goldman, American Anarchist*. Cambridge, MA: South End Press.

Zinn, Howard. 2002 [1994]. *You Can't Be Neutral on a Moving Train: A Personal History of Our Times*. Boston: Beacon Press.

Zinn, Howard. 2002. *Terrorism and War*. New York: Seven Stories Press.

Zinn, Howard. 2003 [1980]. *A People's History of the United States: 1492–Present*. New York: Harper-Perennial Classics.

Zinn, Howard. 2003 [1990]. *Passionate Declarations: Essays on War and Justice*. New York: Harper-Perennial.

Zinn, Howard. 2003a. *The Twentieth Century*. New York: Harper-Perennial.

Zinn, Howard. 2003b. *Passionate Declarations: Essays on War and Justice*. New York: HarperCollins Publishers.

Zinn, Howard. 2003c. *Artists in Times of War*. New York: Seven Stories Press.

Zinn, Howard. 2004a. *The People Speak: American Voices, Some Famous, Some Little Known*. New York: Harper Perennial.

Zinn, Howard. 2004b. *Failure to Quit: Reflections of an Optimistic Historian*. Cambridge, MA: South End Press.

Zinn, Howard. 2005 [1980]. *A People's History of the United States: 1492–Present*. New York: Harper-Perennial.

Zinn, Howard. 2005. "Against Discouragement." Spelman College Commencement Address (May 15).

Zinn, Howard. 2006a. *Original Zinn: Conversations on History and Politics*. New York: Harper-Perennial.

Zinn, Howard. 2006b. "The Common Cradle of Concern." Interviewed by Mark Nepo. In *Essays on Deepening the American Dream*. Kalamazoo, MI: Fetzer Institute.

Zinn, Howard. 2006c. "After the War." *The Progressive* (January), http://www.progressive.org/mag_zinn0106.

Zinn, Howard. 2007a. *A Power Governments Cannot Suppress*. San Francisco: City Lights.

Zinn, Howard. 2007b. "Henry David Thoreau." In *A Power Governments Cannot Suppress*. San Francisco: City Lights.

Zinn, Howard. 2009 [1997]. *The Zinn Reader: Writings on Disobedience and Democracy*. New York: Seven Stories Press.

Zinn, Howard. 2009a. "Against Discouragement." Transcript of interview with David Barsamian, Alternative Radio (February 6).

Zinn, Howard. 2009b. *The Zinn Reader: Writings on Disobedience and Democracy*. 2nd edition. New York: Seven Stories Press.

Zinn, Howard. 2010a. "Obama at One." *The Nation* (February 1).

Zinn, Howard. 2010b. *Three Plays: The Political Theater of Howard Zinn. Emma, Marx in Soho, Daughter of Venus*. Boston: Beacon Press.

Zinn, Howard. 2011a. *On War*. 2nd edition. New York: Seven Stories Press.

Zinn, Howard. 2011b. *On History*. 2nd edition. New York: Seven Stories Press.

Zinn, Howard. 2012. "An Occupied Country." In *The Historic Unfulfilled Promise*. San Francisco: City Lights Publishers, 121–128.

Zinn, Howard. 2012 [2010]. "A Fresh Look at Anarchism." In *Anarchy of Everyday Life: Notes on Anarchism and Its Forgotten Confluences*, Žiga Vodovnik, ed. Oakland, CA: PM Press [Ljubljana: Zalozba Sophia].

Zinn, Howard, and Anthony Arnove. 2004. *Voices of a People's History of the United States*. New York: Seven Stories Press.

Zola, Émile. 1997. *The Dreyfus Affair: "J'Accuse" and Other Writings*. London: Yale University Press.

Index

About the Contributors

Stephen Bird is Assistant Professor of Political Science at Clarkson University. He specializes in energy and environmental politics, energy poverty, social and policy networks, and US politics, particularly democratic participation and social justice. His publications cover a range of material on policy networks, electricity liberalization and governance, energy burden, and environmental risk. He holds an MA in government from Harvard University and a PhD from Boston University.

Adam Silver is Assistant Professor of Political Science at Emmanuel College. He specializes in American political institutions, political parties and organizations, campaign strategies and electoral politics, social movements, and state and local politics. He has served as a policy analyst and legislative director in the New York State Senate. He received his MA in history from SUNY Albany and his PhD in political science from Boston University.

Joshua C. Yesnowitz is a lecturer and doctoral candidate in political science at Boston University. He teaches courses in American government, including race in American political thought, media and politics, political parties, and social-movement theory and practice. His writing has appeared in the *Journal of Political Science Education, Le Monde Diplomatique, New Political Science, Polity,* and *Social Movement Studies.* Joshua is currently completing a dissertation on the history of higher education and student political participation, and is coeditor of *African Americans in American Foreign Policy: From the Era of Frederick Douglass to the Age of Obama* (University of Illinois Press, forthcoming). He holds an MA from Boston College and a BA from Skidmore College.

CONTRIBUTORS

Eric Boehme is Assistant Professor of Political Science at Denison University in Granville, Ohio. He writes on issues of race and class in the United States using the tools of critical theory, postmodernism, and postcolonialism. Dr. Boehme's work also looks at practical examples of how various progressive movements have pursued radical democracy.

Paul Buhle is Emeritus Senior Lecturer in History and American Civilization at Brown University, and is author or editor of thirty-five books and collections. These include histories of radicalism in the United States and the Caribbean, studies of popular culture, and a series of nonfiction comic art volumes. He is coauthor, with Howard Zinn and Mike Konopacki, of *A People's History of American Empire* (2008).

Ross Caputi is an antiwar veteran and a graduate of Boston University. His research interests are in ethical theory, linguistics, and moral psychology. Ross spent three years in the Marine Corps and did one deployment to Iraq from June 2004 to January 2005. During that time Ross participated in the second siege of Fallujah, one of the bloodiest operations of the Iraq War. Ross's experiences led him into the antiwar movement, and at Boston University he acted as president of the Boston University Anti-War Coalition (September 2010 to May 2011) and founded the Justice for Fallujah Project, which he still runs today. Ross is originally from Fitchburg, Massachusetts, and plans to pursue postgraduate work in philosophy and linguistics.

Noam Chomsky is Professor Emeritus at the Massachusetts Institute of Technology. He is an American linguist, philosopher, cognitive scientist, and activist. Chomsky is well known in the academic and scientific community as one of the fathers of modern linguistics, and a major figure in analytic philosophy. Since the 1960s, he has also become known more widely as a political dissident, referring to himself as a libertarian socialist. He is the author of more than 150 books and has received worldwide attention for his activism.

Martín Espada has published seventeen books in all as a poet, editor, essayist, and translator. *The Republic of Poetry*, a collection of poems published by Norton in 2006, received the Paterson Award for Sustained Literary Achievement and was a finalist for the Pulitzer Prize; his collection *The Trouble Ball* was published by Norton in 2012. A collection of essays, *The Lover of a Subversive Is Also a Subversive,* was released in 2010 by the University of Michigan. An earlier book of poems, *Imagine the Angels of Bread* (Norton, 1996), won an American Book Award and was a finalist for the National Book Critics Circle Award. Other books of poetry include *A Mayan Astronomer in Hell's Kitchen* (Norton, 2000), *City of Coughing and Dead Radiators* (Norton, 1993), and *Rebellion Is the Circle of a Lover's Hands* (Curbstone, 1990). He has received numerous awards and fellowships, including the American Book Award, the Robert Creeley Award, the Charity Randall Citation, the National Hispanic Cultural Center Literary Award, the PEN/Revson Fellowship, and a Guggenheim Foundation Fellowship. His poems have appeared in *The New Yorker,* the *New York Times Book Review, Harper's, The Nation,* and *The Best American Poetry.* His work has been translated into ten languages; collections of poems have recently been published in Spain, Puerto Rico, and Chile. A former tenant lawyer, Espada is a professor in the Department of English at the University of Massachusetts–Amherst.

Irene Gendzier is Professor in the Department of Political Science at Boston University. She writes on subjects of US foreign policy in the Middle East and problems of development. Professor Gendzier is the author of *Notes from the Minefield: United States Intervention in Lebanon and the Middle East, 1945–1958* (Columbia University Press, 1997, 2006) and coeditor with Richard Falk and Robert J. Lifton of *Crimes of War: Iraq* (Nation Books, 2006), to which she contributed the essay "Democracy, Deception, and the Arms Trade: The U.S., Iraq, and Weapons of Mass Destruction." She is currently completing a study of the foundations of US foreign policy in the Middle East in the period 1945–1949, entitled *Dying to Forget.*

Ambre Ivol is Assistant Professor of American Civilization at the University of Nantes (France). She has worked for a number of years on Howard Zinn's intellectual trajectory in the context of her PhD research at the University of the Sorbonne. She defended her dissertation in 2009 on the subject of US intellectual generations, with a special focus of the forgotten so-called "good-war generation." During her time in Boston (2005–2009), she worked with Howard Zinn and had access to his personal files at Boston University. She is currently codirecting a documentary film for French public television with filmmaker Nicolas Djian, on the topic of the forgotten legacy of the black liberation movement. Her research interests include US public intellectuals, generational history, and the legacy of social movements in the United States.

Edward P. (Ted) Morgan is University Distinguished Professor of Political Science at Lehigh University, where he teaches courses such as "Social Movements and Legacies of the 1960s," "Propaganda, Media, and American Politics," and "Organizing for Democracy." He is the author of the recently published *What Really Happened to the 1960s: How Mass Media Culture Failed American Democracy* (University Press of Kansas, 2010), as well as *The Sixties Experience: Hard Lessons about Modern America* (Temple University Press, 1991).

Patricia Moynagh is Assistant Professor of Government and Politics at Wagner College. Dr. Moynagh specializes in political theory, with a focus on modern European political and social thought and feminist theory. She is coeditor and contributor to *Simone de Beauvoir's Political Thinking* (University of Illinois Press, 2006). She has also written articles on citizenship responsibility and Hannah

Arendt in scholarly journals. Patricia is currently writing a book on freedom and the challenges of coexistence.

Alix Olson is pursuing a PhD in political theory at the University of Massachusetts–Amherst. Her research interests include modern and contemporary social and political theory, artistic subculture movements, and the politics of sex and sexuality. Alix also is a writer, performer, and internationally touring spoken-word artist-activist. She is the author of numerous articles, including a *Ms. Magazine* cover story, "Road Poet on a Mission." Alix has published several volumes of poetry and is the editor of *Word Warriors: 35 Women Leaders in the Spoken Word Revolution* (Seal Press, 2007). She has received a New York Foundation for the Arts Award, a Barbara Deming Grant, and was OUTMUSIC's Out-Activist of the Year.

Frances Fox Piven is Distinguished Professor of Political Science and Sociology at the CUNY Graduate Center. Before coming to the Graduate Center, she taught at Boston University, Columbia University, New York University Law School, the Institute of Advanced Studies in Vienna, the University of Amsterdam, and the University of Bologna. Her books deal with the development of the welfare state, political movements, urban politics, and electoral politics. Among them are *Regulating the Poor* (1972, updated in 1993); *Poor People's Movements* (1977); *The New Class War* (1982; updated 1985); *Why Americans Don't Vote* (1988); *The Mean Season* (1987); *Labor Parties in Post-Industrial Societies* (1992); *The Breaking of the American Social Compact* (1997); *Why Americans Still Don't Vote* (2000); *The War at Home* (2004); and *Challenging Authority: How Ordinary People Change America* (2006). Dr. Piven is the recipient of numerous honors and awards, including the C. Wright Mills Award and the Award for Public Understanding of Sociology from the American Sociology Association.

Paul Reynolds is Reader in Sociology and Social Philosophy at Edge Hill University in the UK. His research interests are in radical theory, philosophy, and ethics, with special reference to the politics and ethics of sexuality and difference; Marxist and post-Marxist theory and politics; and the role of the intellectual in public life. He is a member of the editorial board of *Historical Materialism: Research in Critical Marxist Theory*, coconvener of the International Network for Sexual Ethics and Politics (http://www.insep.ugent.be/), and coconvener of the Cultural Difference and Social Solidarity network (http://www.difference-andsolidarity.org/).

Christopher C. Robinson teaches political theory and public law at Clarkson University in Potsdam, New York. He is the author of *Wittgenstein and Political Theory: The View from Somewhere* (Edinburgh University Press, 2009), and a forthcoming book on the radical democratic path to sustainability, *Democracy and Ecological Economics: The Politics of Sustainability.*

Žiga Vodovnik is Assistant Professor of Political Science at the Faculty of Social Sciences, University of Ljubljana, and a research fellow at Harvard University– FAS, History of American Civilization. His teaching and research focus on social movements in the Americas, contemporary political theories and praxes, and the history of political ideas. He is the author of *Anarchy of Everyday Life—Notes on Anarchism and Its Forgotten Confluences* (foreword by Howard Zinn; Zalozba Sophia 2010, PM Press 2012).